A Poem dedicated to all the Yost Ancestors who have gone before you and I...Tim C. Stadler

Dear Ancestor

Your tombstone stands among the rest
Neglected and alone
The name and date are chiseled out
On polished marble stone
It reaches out to all who care
It is too late to mourn

You did not know that I exist
You died and I was born
Yet each of us are cells of you
In flesh and blood and bone
Our blood contracts and beats a pulse
Entirely not our own

Dear Ancestor..the place you filled
One hundred years ago
Spreads out among the ones you left
Who would have loved you so
I wonder how you lived and loved
I wonder if you knew
That someday I would find this spot
And come to visit you.

Author Unknown

Introduction by the author

My name is Tim C. Stadler, I was born August 30, 1963 in Tulsa Oklahoma. My father is Edward Purdy Stadler. He married Janice Clara Yost. I am a Great Great Great Great Great Grandson of Hans Casper Yost born 1712 in Meinz Germany.

I want to welcome you to the latest and most detailed compilation of the Yost family. This book was over 4 years in the writing and collecting. There are other Yost's along the way such as my Uncle Leon Ralph Yost and his wife Marjorie Anne Powell Nelson Yost who did research. But with the advent of the Internet and Ancestry.com web site, me and my cousin Larrie Kaye Yost-Ciano and distant cousin Michael Holodinski who I stumbled on while on the Internet have been able to make great strides in researching the family. We are both police officers who used the Internet to find our family ancestry. The history of the Yost Family should be examined from the beginning. This first section may appear to be long, but if you truly want to learn about and respect our ancestors, you really should read this section before going to all the neat pictures and documents I have discovered and recovered in this book.

One common trait I have found within all the male Yost's is, we all believe in Jesus Christ, the Lord our Savior. We have all been religious men and women. The Yost men have one other thing in common. We were and all are, willing to fight. They may not have all served in the military, but if the time came, they are willing to fight for their family, their country, and their God. Throughout history the Yost men were willing to serve in time of war. Some even served both in the military, and in civilian life as Sheriff's and police officers. Although my research finds the Law Enforcement is few in number.

Most were farmer's when our country started. Three made muskets for the Revolutionary War. A large number fought for the Revolutionary Cause. A large number also fought in the Civil War, on both sides. I have yet to find any Yost's that died in battle.

Never forget from where you came. Never forget the principles the early Yost's provided.

Family   **Country**   **God**

Famous People our Yost line is related to

Signed the Declaration of Independence

Button Gwinnett (1735 – 1777) – Georgia Representative has one of the most famous signatures in American History. This signer of the Declaration of Independence has a Georgia County named for him. He is Henry Marshall Yost's 13th cousin 1 time removed.

Caesar Rodney (1728 – 1784) – Delaware Representative was active in the political beginnings of the United States of America. Caesar signed the Declaration of Independence as a representative of Delaware. He was also a member of the Continental Congress and President of Delaware during the Revolutionary War. He is Henry Marshall Yost's 9th cousin 2 times removed.

William Williams (1731 – 1811) – A merchant and a politician of Connecticut, signed the Declaration of Independence. He was a Harvard graduate who studied theology. He is Henry Marshall Yost's 6th cousin 2 times removed.

Presidents of the United States of America

Elizabeth Kortright Monroe (1768 – 1830) – Elizabeth was the First Lady and wife of President James Monroe. She spent many of her years as First Lady frail and sickly. She is Henry Marshall Yost's 7th cousin 1 time removed.

Julia Gardiner Tyler (1820 – 1889) – Julia was the 2nd wife and 3rd First Lady of President John Tyler. She was the First Lady for the last 8 months of her husband's term. She is Henry Marshall Yost's 8th cousin 1 time removed.

Rutherford Birchard Hayes (1822 – 1893) – 19th President of the United States of America. He was known for his honesty and military involvement in the American Civil War. After the scandal ridden years of the Grant administration, Hayes restored trust to the presidency and ended the Reconstruction during his term. He is Henry Marshall Yost's 6th cousin 2 times removed.

Grace Anna Goodhue Coolidge (1879 – 1957) – Grace Goodhue Coolidge was a strong support for her husband, Calvin Coolidge, during his rise in politics. Her extroverted friendliness brought balance to his shyness. She is Henry Marshall Yost's 6th cousin 5 times removed.

Scientists and Explorers

Sir Isaac Newton (1643 – 1727) – Sir Isaac Newton was a Scientist and Mathematician. He is regarded as one of the greatest scientists and mathematicians in history. He described 3 laws of motion that also govern the entire earth and celestial bodies surrounding it. He is Henry Marshall Yost's 5th cousin 6 times removed.

John C. Fremont (1813 – 1890) – John led several surveying expedition through the United States including the Oregon Trail and the Sierra Nevadas. He is Henry Marshall Yost's 8th cousin 1 time removed.

Humphrey Davy (1778 – 1829) – Humphrey was an English Chemist, invented the first electric light. He is also credited with the isolation of many elements through a process we now call electrolysis. He is Henry Marshall Yost's 9th cousin 3 times removed.

William Charles Wentworth (1790 – 1872) – William was an Australian explorer, journalist, and politician. He was a leading figure in early New South Wales. He helped explore the Blue Mountains, founded a newspaper, and helped draft the New South Wales constitution. He is Henry Marshall Yost's 13th cousin 1 time removed.

Actors, Actresses, and Writers

Vina Fay Wray (1907 – 2004) – Vina is best remembered for her roll as Ann Darrow, the blonde seductress of the gigantic, prehistoric gorilla in the classic horror/adventure film King Kong (1933). She is Henry Marshall Yost's 4th cousin 4 times removed.

Agatha Christie (1890 – 1976) – Agatha was an English who is the world's best known crime-fiction writer. She wrote famous mysteries "Death on the Nile" and "The Mousetrap". She is Henry Marshall Yost's 6th cousin 4 times removed.

Emily Dickenson (1830 – 1886) – Emily is considered one of the most influential poets in American History. During her lifetime she published only a few poems, though her writing career produced over 1700 poems (all published posthumously). She is Henry Marshall Yost's 8th cousin 1 time removed.

Laura Ingalls Wilder (1867 – 1967) – Laura's experiences growing up in the unsettled West inspired her famous children's series Little House on the Prairie. She is Henry Marshall Yost's 8th cousin 2 times removed.

Jonathan Swift (16667 – 1745) – Jonathan is well known for his satirical prose such as Gulliver's Travels and A Modest Proposal. Jonathan was also an ordained minister in the Church of Ireland. He is Henry Marshall Yost's 7th cousin 4 times removed.

Richard Lovelace (1618 – 1657) – Richard was an English Nobleman and poet. His "Lucasta" poems brought him fame. He is Henry Marshall Yost's 7th cousin 4 times removed.

John Steinbeck (1902 – 1968) – John's writing is characterized by portrayals of working class families in California. He won the Nobel Price for Literature as well as the Pulitzer

Price. Two of his most famous works are The Grapes of Wrath and Of Mice and Men. He is Henry Marshall Yost's 8th cousin 3 times removed.

Alfred Tennyson – (1809 – 1892) – Alfred, Lord Tennyson is remembered for his classical poetry. "Idylls of the King", written in 1885 is a work derived from the legend of King Arthur and is one of Tennyson's most famous pieces of writing. He is Henry Marshall Yost's 9th cousin 3 times removed.

Winslow Homer (1836 – 1910) – Winslow is famous for painting landscapes and his engravings. He was an artist during the Civil War Era. Winslow's subject matter was often pastoral and depicted the farms and landscapes of the United States. He is Henry Marshall Yost's 10th cousin 1 time removed.

George Orwell (1903 – 1950) – Eric Arthur Blair is most commonly recognized by his pen name, George Orwell. His political commentary is a major theme in his most famous works: "1984", "Animal Farm", and "Down and Out in Paris and London". He is Henry Marshall Yost's 10th cousin 2 times removed.

Mae West (1893 – 1980) – May was born Mary Jane West, is considered one of the most controversial stars of the 1930's. Her scripts often endured huge amounts of censorship, but also huge success with audiences. She wrote and starred in She Done Him Wrong and I'm No Angel." She is Henry Marshall Yost's 9th cousin 4 times removed.

Audrey Hepburn (1929 – 1993) – Audrey Kathleen Ruston, born in Belgium, continues to be a figure of iconic beauty and classic film. Her award-winning role in "Roman Holiday" marked the beginning of her long and successful movie career. She is Henry Marshall Yost's 9th cousin 5 times removed.

Laurence Olivier (1907 – 1989) – Laurence was an academy Award-winning actor, director, and producer. He acted in such films as Wuthering Heights, Pride and Prejudice, and Spartacus. Olivier also appeared in many plays throughout his career. He is Henry Marshall Yost's 10th cousin 3 times removed.

Outlaws

Butch Cassidy (1866 – 1908) – Robert Leroy Parker was part of an imfamous group of train and bank robbers, called the Wild Bunch. He is Henry Marshall Yost's 3rd cousin 3 times removed.

James "Wild Bill" Hickock (1837 – 1876) – James Butler "Wild Bill" Hickock was a legendary gunfighter and law man in the American West. Many characters in Western novels are fashioned after Hickock. He is Henry Marshall Yost's 8th cousin 1 time removed.

The History of the Yost (Joust) Family

Prior to inventions of the surname, our ancient ancestors were called "Jodocus the Just" meaning "Strivers of the Just". Jodocus the Just, is the earliest record of the famiy, and it is written that he was living in the mountainous regions of the Black Forest during the 19th century, "a peace-maker of the tribe". It is not until the 12th Century that the name appears as a surname Jost, Joust, Jobst in Southern Germany. Bavaria, and Ober Valley. In the 4th Century, a Jost is in the royal family of the Hesse-Cassels, as a Count, and the Count Jost's grandson of direct inheritance "became the Baron Von Rosenburg."

Germany Early History

The Germanic tribes, which probably originated from a mixture of peoples along the Baltic Sea coast, inhabited the northern part of the European continent by about 500 B.C. By 100 B.C., they had advanced into the central and southern areas of present-day Germany. At that time, there were three major tribal groups: the eastern Germanic peoples lived along the Oder and Vistula rivers; the northern Germanic peoples inhabited the southern part of present-day Scandinavia; and the western Germanic peoples inhabited the extreme south of Jutland and the area between the North Sea and the Elbe, Rhine, and Main rivers. The Rhine provided a temporary boundary between Germanic and Roman territory after the defeat of the Suevian tribe by Julius Caesar about 70 B.C. The threatening presence of warlike tribes beyond the Rhine prompted the Romans to pursue a campaign of expansion into Germanic territory. However, the defeat of the provincial governor Varus by Arminius at the Battle of the Teutoburg Forest in A.D. 9 halted Roman expansion; Arminius had learned the enemy's strategies during his military training in the Roman armies. This battle brought about the liberation of the greater part of Germany from Roman domination. The Rhine River was once again the boundary line until the Romans reoccupied territory on its eastern bank and built the Limes, a fortification 300 kilometers long, in the first century A.D.

The second through the sixth centuries was a period of change and destruction in which eastern and western Germanic tribes left their native lands and settled in newly acquired territories. This period of Germanic history, which later supplied material for heroic epics, included the downfall of the Roman Empire and resulted in a considerable expansion of habitable area for the Germanic peoples. However, with the exception of those kingdoms established by Franks and Anglo-Saxons, Germanic kingdoms founded in such other parts of Europe as Italy and Spain were of relatively short duration because they were assimilated by the native populations. The conquest of Roman Gaul by

Frankish tribes in the late fifth century became a milestone of European history; it was the Franks who were to become the founders of a civilized German state.

Germany The Protestant Reformation

On the eve of the Protestant Reformation, the institutions of the Holy Roman Empire were widely thought to be in need of improvement. The Habsburg emperors Frederick III (r. 1440-93) and his son Maximilian I (r. 1493-1519) both cooperated with individual local rulers to enact changes. However, the imperial and local parties had different aims, the former wishing to strengthen the empire, the latter aiming to secure greater independence by formalizing their rights and ensuring regular procedures for the conduct of public business. In 1489 the procedures of the imperial diet, the Reichstag, in which representatives of all states within the empire met, were reorganized. One of the reforms allowed participation in the diet by representatives of the towns. In 1495 Maximilian declared an empire wide peace and made arrangements to reduce the lawlessness and violence that often marked relations among local rulers.

Maximilian's reforms were not enough to cure the ills of the empire, and relations between it and the princes and ecclesiastical states often were tense. Disputes frequently involved complicated constellations of powers with occasional interference from abroad, most notably France. Charles V (r. 1519-56) was elected emperor in 1519 only after he paid large bribes to the seven electors and agreed to many restrictions on his powers, restrictions he often later ignored (see fig. 3).

A changing economy also made for discontent among those unable to profit from new conditions. Some of the empire's inhabitants had become quite rich, most notably the Fugger family of Augsburg, whose members had replaced the bankers of northern Italy as Europe's leading financiers. The Fuggers had come to manage the financial affairs of the Habsburg Dynasty, which, in combination with increased trade between south and north, made Germany Europe's financial center for a few decades. However, other groups in Germany were experiencing hardship. A burgeoning rural population found it difficult to get enough to eat, and many peasants went to the towns to seek a living. Municipal officials responded by seeking to bar rural newcomers. Within towns that were not prospering, relations between the classes became more tense as social mobility was reduced by a declining economy.

Martin Luther

On the eve of All Saints' Day in 1517, Martin Luther, a professor of theology at Wittenberg University in Saxony, posted ninety-five theses on a church door. Luther's primary concern was the sale of indulgences--papal grants of reduced punishment in the afterlife, including releases from purgatory. First written in Latin, the theses were soon translated into German and widely distributed. Summoned by church authorities to explain his writings, Luther became embroiled in further controversy and in 1520 wrote his three most famous tracts, in which he attacked the papacy and exposed church corruption, acknowledged the validity of only two of the seven sacraments, and argued for the supremacy of faith over good works. In 1521 Luther was summoned to appear before Emperor Charles V at the Diet of Worms. Refusing to recant his writings, he was banned under the Edict of Worms. Secreted away by the ruler of Saxony, Frederick the Wise, Luther retreated to the castle of Wartburg, where he worked on a translation of the New Testament and wrote numerous religious tracts.

Luther's disagreements with the doctrines of the Roman Catholic Church set off a chain of events that within a few decades destroyed Germany's religious unity. Although one of the most influential figures in German history, Luther was only one of many who were critical of the Roman Catholic Church. However, because of the power of his ideas and the enormous influence of his writings, it is he who is regarded as the initiator of the Protestant Reformation. Luther quickly acquired a large following among those disgusted by rampant church corruption and unfulfilled by mechanistic religious services. Many warmed to his contention that religion must be simplified into a close relationship of human beings with God without the extensive mediation of the Roman Catholic Church and its accretion of tradition.

Luther magnified the inherent potency of his ideas by articulating them in a language that was without rival in clarity and force. He strove to make the Scriptures accessible to ordinary worshipers by translating them into vernacular German. This he did with such genius that the German dialect he used became the written language of all of Germany. Without Luther's translation of the Bible, Germany might have come to use a number of mutually incomprehensible languages, as was the case in the northwestern part of the Holy Roman Empire, where local dialects evolved into what is now modern Dutch. Luther also wrote hymns that are still sung in Christian religious services all over the world.

A less exalted reason for the wide distribution of Luther's doctrines was the development of printing with movable type. The Reformation created a demand for all kinds of religious writings. The readership was so great that the number of books printed in Germany increased from about 150 in 1518 to nearly 1,000 six years later.

Luther's ideas soon coalesced into a body of doctrines called Lutheranism. Powerful supporters such as princes and free cities accepted Lutheranism for many reasons, some because they sincerely supported reform, others out of narrow self-interest. In some areas, a jurisdiction would adopt Lutheranism because a large neighboring state had done so. In other areas, rulers accepted it because they sought to retain control over their subjects who had embraced it earlier. Nearly all the imperial cities became Lutheran, despite the fact that the emperor, to whom they were subordinate, was hostile to the movement. Historians have found no single convincing explanation of why one area became Lutheran and another did not, because so many social, economic, and religious factors were involved.

Given the revolutionary nature of Lutheranism and the economic and political tensions of the period, it is not surprising that the Reformation soon became marked by violence and extremism. The Knights' War of 1522-23, in which members of the lower nobility rebelled against the authorities in southwestern Germany, was quickly crushed. Some of the rampaging knights were ardent supporters of Luther. The Peasants' War of 1524-25 was more serious, involving as many as 300,000 peasants in southwestern and central Germany. Influenced somewhat by the new religious ideas but responding mostly to changing economic conditions, the peasants' rebellion spread quickly, but without coordination. It also received support from some dissatisfied city dwellers and from some noblemen of arms who led its ragged armies. Although the peasants' rebellion was the largest uprising in German history, it was quickly suppressed, with about 100,000 casualties. In the 1530s, the Anabaptists, a radical Christian sect, seized several towns, their objective being to construct a just society. They were likewise brutally suppressed by the authorities.

Luther opposed the peasants' cause and wrote an impassioned tract demanding their quick suppression. However radical his religious views, Luther was a social and political conservative. He believed that the end of the world was imminent and regarded practical affairs as having little importance compared with the effort to win eternal salvation. Therefore, he counseled obedience to worldly authorities if they allowed freedom of worship. Lutheranism thus became a means of upholding the worldly status quo and the leaders who adopted the new faith. In contrast to England, where Protestantism retained a significant radical social element, German Protestantism became an integral part of the state. Some historians maintain that this integration of state and church has deprived Germany of a deeply rooted tradition of political dissent as found in Britain and the United States.

Germany - The Thirty Years' War, 1618-48

Germany enjoyed a time of relative quiet between the Peace of Augsburg, signed in 1555, and the outbreak of the Thirty Years' War in 1618. The empire functioned in a more regular way than previously, and its federal nature was more evident than in the past. The Reichstag met frequently to deal with public matters, and the emperors Ferdinand I (r. 1556-64) and Maximilian II (r. 1564-76) were cautious rulers concerned mostly with strengthening their family's hold on Austria and adjacent areas. Rudolf II (r. 1576-1612) was an indolent and capricious ruler who generally followed his advisers' counsel. As a result, some German states were able to expand their territories by annexing smaller neighbors in the absence of an engaged and attentive emperor. Local rivalries engendered tensions that often were based on religious affiliation.

The Counter-Reformation and Religious Tensions

The Peace of Augsburg brought peace but did not settle the religious disagreements in Germany. For one thing, its signatories did not recognize Calvinism, a relatively stringent form of Protestantism that was gaining prominence around the time the Augsburg treaty was signed, in what has been called the Second Reformation. Adherents to both Calvinism and Lutheranism worked to spread their influence and gain converts in the face of the Counter-Reformation, the attempt of the Roman Catholic Church to regroup and reverse the spread of Protestantism. Followers of all three religions were at times successful, but only at the expense of the others.

Fear of religious subversion caused rulers to monitor the conduct of their subjects more closely. Attempting to help the modern reader understand the intensity and pervasiveness of this fear, Mary Fulbrook, a noted British historian of Germany, has likened it to the anxiety prevailing in the first years of the Cold War. An example of the social paranoia engendered by the religious tensions of the period is Protestant Germany's refusal until 1700 to accept the Gregorian calendar introduced by the papacy in 1582 because the reform entailed a one-time loss of the days between October 5 and 14. Many Protestants suspected that Roman Catholics were attempting somehow to steal this time for themselves.

By the first decades of the seventeenth century, religious controversy had become so obstructive that at times the Reichstag could not conduct business. In 1608, for example, Calvinists walked out of the body, preventing the levying of a tax to fight a war against the Turks. In the same year, the Evangelical Union was established by a few states and cities of the empire to defend the Protestant cause. In 1609 a number of Roman Catholic states countered by forming the Catholic League. Although both bodies were less concerned with a sectarian war than with the specific aims of their member states, their formation was an indication of how easily disputes could acquire a religious aspect.

Germany - The Age of Enlightened Absolutism, 1648-1789

Although the Holy Roman Empire no longer had a significant role in European politics after the Thirty Years' War, it remained important in Germany, providing a framework for the many German states' and cities' conduct of their public affairs. The Reichstag, which remained in session at Regensburg from 1663 until the empire's dissolution in 1806, provided a forum for the settlement of disputes. On occasion, votes were taken to remove incompetent or tyrannical rulers of member states. The empire's most important service was that it provided a measure of security to Germany's many small states and free cities, without which some would have been swallowed up by larger neighbors. Because of its weakened condition, the empire could no longer dominate Germany, even when headed by ambitious and capable men such as Charles VI (r. 1711-40). During the 1720s, he attempted unsuccessfully to breathe new life into the empire. Later emperors returned to the traditional Habsburg practice of using the imperial throne to benefit their own dynastic holdings.

For nearly a century after the Peace of Westphalia, the main danger to German states came from abroad. France was the chief threat, seizing parts of southwestern Germany in the late 1600s, among them the city of Strasbourg in 1681. French troops also fought on German soil during the War of the Spanish Succession (1701-14). In addition to these military actions, France formed alliances with some German states, most significantly with Bavaria, which sought support against neighboring Austria. The Ottoman Empire also posed a threat. In 1683 its forces besieged Vienna. The Germans ultimately were successful against the Ottoman Empire, and after the Treaty of Passarowitz of 1718, the Turks were no longer a danger.

Austria and Prussia

The most important German power after the Peace of Westphalia was Austria, followed by a few other states with much smaller populations, most notably Brandenburg, Saxony, and Bavaria. Austria retained its preeminence until the second half of the nineteenth century, but in the eighteenth century Brandenburg had become a serious rival, annexing valuable Austrian territory. The rivalry came to form the so-called dualism of the empire, that is, the presence in it of two powerful states, neither of which was strong enough to dominate the empire and for that reason sought the support of smaller states. The smaller states worked to derive their own advantages from German dualism, none being willing to cede sovereignty to either Austria or Prussia.

In 1648 Brandenburg was a small state in northern Germany. It had been ruled by the Hohenzollern Dynasty since the late fifteenth century and consisted of the core region and its capital, Berlin; eastern Pomerania; an area around Magdeburg; the former holdings of the Knights of the Teutonic Order in eastern Prussia; and some smaller holdings in western Germany. Brandenburg became known as Prussia in 1701 when its ruler crowned himself King Frederick I of Prussia. Prussia acquired the rest of Pomerania after defeating Sweden in the Great Northern War (1700-21). Prussia's increase in size and influence may be attributed to a succession of capable leaders, all of whom enjoyed long reigns. The first was Frederick William (r. 1640-88), known as the Great Elector. He increased his family's power by granting favors to the nobility, weakening the independence of the towns, and maintaining a professional standing army. His son Frederick I (r. 1688-1713) established Prussia as a kingdom. Frederick further strengthened the army, but not nearly as much as his son Frederick William I (r. 1713-40), who also modernized the kingdom's bureaucracy. Frederick II (r. 1740-86), known to posterity as Frederick the Great, continued along the same lines as his father but showed much greater imagination and ruthlessness, transforming his small kingdom into one of the great powers of Europe.

In 1740 Frederick seized Silesia, a wealthy province that belonged to the Habsburgs and had a population of about 1 million inhabitants. Maria Theresa (r. 1740-80), the new Habsburg empress, was unable to regain possession of Silesia, which remained under Prussian control at the end of the War of the Austrian Succession (1740-48). Frederick retained Silesia even after facing a coalition of France, Austria, and Russia during the Seven Years' War (1756-63). Frederick expanded Prussian territory still further in 1772, when, with his erstwhile enemies Russia and Austria, he took part in the First Partition of Poland. This last seizure was highly beneficial to Frederick because it linked eastern Prussia with much of his kingdom's western holdings.

Although Prussia and Austria were rivals, they had some important characteristics in common. Neither state was populated by a single people, but by numerous peoples speaking different languages and belonging to different religions. Neither state was located entirely within the empire. Both had sizable territories to the east of the empire, and it was there that they hoped mainly to expand. Both states were governed by enlightened monarchs, who, having only to cajole the nobility with occasional concessions, saw government as for the people but not by the people. Hence, both states were governed by the most efficient methods known to the eighteenth century, and both were fairly tolerant according to the standards of the time. Prussia accepted many Protestants expelled from other states, most notably the Huguenots who fled France after the Edict of Nantes in 1685. Austria became one of the first states to allow Jews to settle where they liked within its boundaries and to practice the professions of their choice.

Our Yost Descendants

The earliest record we have of the Yost family is that of Jacob Joust who was born before 1634 in probably, the Duchy of Franconia, Germany., and died before 1707 in probably, the Duchy of Franconia, Germany. He married RACHEL ____?____. Jacob Joust was a "Burgesse" in the District of Meintz, in the Duchy of Franconia. Children of JACOB JOUST and RACHEL ____?____ were, Jacob Joust and Peter Joust.

Jacob Joust married CHARTHARINE ____?____. Jacob appears in a record dated 1710, as a member of a Protestant Colony in Franconia. Jacob and Chartharine had the following children. Christian Joust (JOST) and Klaus (Nicklaus) Joust (JOST).

In 1714, Christian and Klaus are recorded in a religious migration to the Kingdom of Wurtemberg and in 1727-28, they are named in a "war on the Protestants" in Emmen Valley of Switzerland "near Langnau". In this record it mentions that Christian was killed and his wife, Barbara was imprisoned at Berne where shortly after she died, and the land and property of Christian was confiscated, leaving his children destitute.

At a meeting early in 1728, held at Berne, Switzerland, a resolution was passed to "transport these provident and destitute religious agitators to a Dutch port for transport to England". Queen Anne of England had issued a proclamation offering religious freedom to all the persecuted religious refugees along the Rhine, in her American Colonies. In the list of the impoverished religious agitators of the Emmen Valley were given the sons and daughters of Christian with their ages: Jacob, age 18; Gasper (Casper), age 16; Chartharine, age 14; Heinrich, age 11, Barbara, age 8; and John, age 4.

The Dutch and English histories describing the immigration of the German and Swiss immigrants to America, relate that thousands upon thousands of these harassed and distressed people flocked to the Dutch Ports for passage to England. Their history consumes volumes of records that according to the historian, Eshelmann "are the darkest pages in the annals of Christian people". Even after every available ship was pressed into service to relieve the stress of ever increasing horde of these "Palatines", hundreds died from exposure and starvation in Holland and England awaiting transportation to America. In the effort to relieve the situation many were bound out as servants in England and as the early American immigration records do not list a female Yost, it can be construed that they remained in England, for a record says "these German and Swiss females are industrious housekeepers". Another record states that the Palatine females on marrying were freed of their bondage

The settlement of Pennsylvania by the Germans is an epic tale of faith and zeal, of sacrifice and achievement in the development of America. The story has been told and the Pennsylvania German Pioneers have come into their rightful place as builders of our nation.

The land that came to be known as Pennsylvania was granted by King Charles II of England to William Penn in 1681 in exchange of a debt of 16,000 pounds which the British Crown owed to his father. It was the largest tract ever granted in America to a single individual, he had simple title to more than 40,000 square miles of territory. Under his Charter, Penn was governor of the Province, which he and his sons held as proprietaries, with the exception of about two years under William III, until the Revolution of 1776. Pennsylvania was not a colony of any foreign power; as a British subject Penn owed his allegiance to the crown. While the government of Pennsylvania was proprietary in form, it was English in substance and all non-British subjects were known as foreigners.

In order to obtain settlers for his land, Penn visited the Rhine Provinces, whose once peaceful valley's, thriving fields and vine clad hills had become the hunting ground of political and religious fanatics. Penn and his agents told the news of his acquisition and invited the Rhinelanders, the suffering Palatines, to help him found a State in which religious and civil liberty would prevail. From the Germantown settlement in 1683, to the revolution, a large scale immigration followed,

When the pioneers arrived, Pennsylvania vas in the hands of British subjects. Penn's agents were Englishmen; the English language was used; English Common Law was in force. It soon became a matter of concern to these Englishmen that such a large body of Continentals, speaking another language and accustomed to another form of government should be admitted to the land, even though they came at the invitation of Penn, himself.

In 1727, the Provincial Council, passed a law requiring all Continentals who arrived at Philadelphia to take oaths of allegiance to the British Crown. Two years later they were required to take oaths of abjuration and fidelity to the proprietor and laws of the province. The oaths were administered and subscribed to before public officials,

These immigrant ancestors of ours came not to a ready-made republic of opportunity but to a virgin land inhabited by savages. Many were men of eminence in the fatherland others came up from the penury and virtual slavery of the redemption system. Together they worked, fought and won America's battles and led in public service, industry, science, education invention and in the art of agriculture which is the foundation of our national wealth and of human progress.

The journey to Pennsylvania was not an easy journey. This journey began in May and ended in October, fully half a year later amid much hardship. The Rhine boats had to pass 26 custom houses, where the ships were examined as it suited the convenience of the custom-house officials. The ships were detained and the passengers had to spend much money. The trip down the Rhine took from four to six weeks before arriving at Holland where they were detained from five to six weeks, while the ships were waiting to be passed through the custom-house or waiting for favorable winds. Unless they had the right winds the ships sailed from eight to twelve weeks before reaching Philadelphia. Even with the best wind the voyage lasted seven weeks.

The passengers being packed densely, without proper food and water were soon subject to all sorts of disease, such as dysentery, scurvy, typhoid and small-pox. The children were the first to be attacked and died in large numbers. The terrors of disease, were much aggravated by frequent storms through which ships and passengers had to pass.

One ship after another arrived in the port of Philadelphia, just when the rough and severe winter was before the door. One or more merchants received a list of the freights and the agreement which the emigrants signed in their own hand in Holland, as well as the bills for their travel down the Rhine and the advances of the new-landers for provisions they received on the ships "on account". Formerly the freight for a single person was six to ten Louis d'ors, but later it amounted to fourteen to seventeen Louis d'ors (the equivalent of the Louis d'or is about $4.50, though its purchasing power at that time was much greater).

According to the law, before the ship was allowed to cast anchor at the harbor, the passengers are all examined by a physician, as to whether any contagious disease existed among them. Then they were led in procession to the City Hall to render the oath of allegiance to the King of Great Britain. After that they were brought back to the ship. Then announcements are printed in the newspapers, stating how many of the new arrivals are to be sold. Those who still had money were released. The ships became the market place. The buyers made their choice among the arrivals and bargained with them for a certain number of years and days. They were taken to the merchant, where their passage and other debts were paid and received from the government authorities a written document that made the newcomers their property for a definite period. In a few years of service, in spite of all difficulties and hardships, they emerged as successful farmers. It only shows of what sturdy stock these pioneers were made.

Nearly 50,000 embarked for the land of Penn, nearly 20,000 who sailed died at sea, the remainder reached their goal. Southeastern Pennsylvania was settled almost exclusively of Swiss and German settlers. They filled the valleys of the Susquehanna and Schuylkill and their tributaries. Before the Revolution, some moved down the Shenandoah, crossed the Alleghenies and into the Cumberland. They multiplied and drifted into the Ohio valley and at the beginning of the 19th century they settled in Lower Canada. They also went into Indiana, Illinois region, Kansas and the Dakota section and the northwest. Their descendents moved into all the vast area of Middle West and far-western America as well as eastern America.

The Swiss and German labored under many problems and difficulties which people of today would find it hard to believe. They were foreigners and as such were held in disfavor by the English government of this providence even though Penn gave them a special invitation to come and settle here. The Swiss and Germans were hard workers and by being thrifty they began to make progress and money and were looked upon with jealousy by other settlers among them. It is believed that the noble life and struggles of the Swiss and Germans of eastern Pennsylvania, and especially of Lancaster County, were the very backbone of Industrial Lancaster County.

They were persecuted for their religious faith for many years in their homeland and in this new land. They were known by their plain dress, moral life, their temperate living and their refusal to take part in government and oaths. They did not believe in infant baptism, transubstantiation, force, war or political affairs. As far back as the Year 1000, they were called Anabaptists or Waldenseans and many suffered martyrdom for their faith. In 1203, these Anabaptists or Waldenseans had the Holy Scriptures translated into their own language and they did not practice any other doctrine. They carefully followed the Ten Commandments and the Sermon on the Mount.

Ernest Muller, a preacher in Langnau, wrote that among the Mennonite families living in and around Langnau, Switzerland in 1621, was a family headed by Christian Yost, and a daughter of Stinnis Gibbel was living with them. Also a Klaus Yost and his wife. Others with the surnames of Baumgardner, Probst or Brobst, Moritz, Bichsel or Bixler, Ruch or Reich, Studder (a powerful youth), Utzenberger, Dellenbach, Raeber or Reber, Kreyenbuel or Graybill, Greber or Garber and Rothlisperger. Among the families of eastern Pennsylvania we find the familiar names of Baumgardner, Probst or Brobst, Ruch, Yost, Raeber or Reber, Kreyenbuel or Graybill, Bixler, Gibbel or Garber. This shows that some members of most of the families in Switzerland helped to establish the land of Penn. The community of Langnau had a population of 7,000, about 18 miles directly east of Berne in the Emmen Valley, which extends from the northeast to southeast of Berne.

Christian Joust (JOST) Married BARBARA ___?___. They had the following children.

 Jacob Joust (JOST), born 1710, Europe; died 1755, America.

Arrived at Philadelphia on 23 August 1728. The list of Palatine Passengers imported in the Ship Mortonhouse, John Coultas, commander, from Rotterdam, but last of Deal, arrived the 23rd day of August 1728, listed as Jacob Joost. Qualified 24th august 1728. (*From minutes of Provincial Council, printed in Colonial Records, Vol 111, page 327.) He settled in Limerick Township, Philadelphia County. He died of a "Bone Fever". The first Yost of record to be buried in America. He left two sons: Nicholas and Henry.

(*The Allegiance lists were incorporated in the Provincial Council minutes from 1727 until 1736 and were published by the State of Pennsylvania in 1852 under the title of 'Colonial Records".)

Hans Casper Yost, born 1712, near Meintz, Duchy of Franonia; d. 1777, George Towne, Maryland (now Georgetown, Washington, D.C.).

Chartharine Yost (JOST), born 1714.

Heinrich Yost JOST, born 1717; died before 1792, probably, Luzerne County, Pennsylvania. Heinrich Jost (later called Henry), landed at Philadelphia in 1738, and was bound out on a farm in Luzerne County, Pennsylvania, where he died prior to 1792.

Barbara Yost JOST, born 1720.

Johan Yost JOST, born 1724, Wurtemberg, Germany; died 1781, Northumberland County, Pennsylvania. Johan Jost, (later called John), arrived in America about 1741, settled in Lancaster County, Pennsylvania, removed ato York County and died in Northumberland County about 1780-1781. John's family migrated north out of Pennsylvania, instead of south as his nephew's, John.

Mainz or Mayence, 20 miles Southwest of Frankfort, originally a Celtic Settlement on whose site the Romans under Drusus erected a fortified camp called Magontiaasumusin in 13 B.C.

My Aunt Sally Powell married my Uncle Leon Ralph Yost. They spent years traveling the World researching both the Yost family and the Powell family. Aunt Sally and Uncle Leon Yost did a lot of research back in the 1960 – 1980's by letter, and by actually visiting the town's where the Yost's lived. They even corresponded and visited Germany in their research. As of the year 2008, I have all the research, all the letters, documents, pictures, etc, from Aunt Sally Yost. .

"Mainz(Maintz) or Mayence, 20 miles S.W. of Frankfort, originally a Celtic Settlement on those site the Romans under Drusus erected a fortified camp called Magontiasumusin in 13 B.C.

Bishop Sidonius was the founder of modern Mainz, and with Charlemagne's encouragement this town developed into the first ecclesiastical city of the Roman Empire in the 10th Century. The Archbishop of Mainz became the primate of Germany. By the 14th Century Mainz led the 100 member league of Rhenish towns and was one of the most powerful Medieval German cities.

However, in 1562 it was conquered by Archbishop Nassu, and it lost many of its privileges. The city became the cradle of Printing through the activities of Johann Gutenburg, a native of Mainz, and allegedly the first printer of the Bible in about 1450. A University was founded in 1477 and was suppressed by the French in 1798 and re-established in 1946.

The Thirty Year War broke the power of the Archbishop and the French Revolution finished it. The citizens of Mainz favored the Revolution and welcomed the French Tropps in 1792."

Ships Lists - Yost Passengers
1727 – 1775

1. Jacob Jost 2 persons	Ship William and Sarah	18 Sept. 1727
2. Jacob Joost	Ship Mortonhouse	23 Aug, 1728
3. Gasper Joust age 21 Clearance qualified 17 Aug, 1733 as Hans Casper Joost	Ship Samuel	17 Aug, 1733
4. Peter Yost age 18	Ship Samuel	30 Aug. 1737
5. Conrad Jost Clearance qualified as Johan Conrad Yost	Ship Andrew Gally	26 Sept. 1737
6. Peter Joost Age 55 When qualified taken the last name of Jost	Ship Glasgow	9 Sept 1738

7. Joanis Joost age 17 When qualified and oath taken the name was written Johannes Jost	Ship Glasgow	9 Sept. 1738
8. Leopald Jost age 36	Ship Friendship	20 Sept. 1738
9. Nicholas Joost	Ship Davy	25 Oct. 1738
10. France Jhost age 22 Qualified and subscribed to oath as Frantz Jost	Ship Loyal Judith	25 Nov. 1740
11. Philip Jost Qualified as Philip Jost; subscribed to oath as Philip Just	Ship St. Mark	26 Sept. 1741
12. Michel Jost	Ship Elliot	24 Aug. 1749
13. Conrath Yost	Ship Phoenix	15 Sept. 1749
14. Johan Nickle Jost	Ship Gally	13 Aug. 1750
15. Martin Jost	Ship Phoenix	28 Aug. 1750
16. Nicklaus Jost	Ship Phoenix	28 Aug. 1750
17. Johan Conrad Jost	Ship Edinburg	16 Sept. 1751
18. John Gerg Jost	Ship Edinburg	14 Sept. 1753
19. Simeon Jost Qualified as Simmom Jost; subscribed to oath as Simon Jost	Ship Neptune	24 Sept. 1753
20. Casper Joost Qualified as Casper Jost	Ship Phoenix	1 Oct. 1754
21. Nicholas Jost	Ship Tyger	19 Nov. 1771
22 John August Jost	Ship Sally	23 Aug. 1773
23. Jacob Jost	Ship King of Prussia	9 Oct. 1775

Hans Casper Yost's birth name was Gasper Jost (or Joust), later known as Casper.

Hans Gasper Yost (Jost) arrived at the Port of Philadelphia on August 17, 1733 at the age of 21 years. He was a Redemptioner passenger on the Ship Samuel of London, mastered by Huqh Percy. The ship's original clearance on this passage, was out of Rotterdam, Holland, with one stop at Deal, London. It took eleven weeks to cross the Atlantic and en-route forty-one died of a fever said to have been caused by the fouling of drinking water stored in old wine casks.

Pennsylvania German Pioneers

Jacob Koger	Matthias (O) Rubichon
Jacob Mattheus Manser	Johannes Vögle
Sebastian (O) Trockenmiller	Jacob Henrich
Gideon (O) Hoffer	Philip Melchior Meyer
Hans Rihl	Philip Jörg Wahnsidel
Johan Martin Schöpfele	Johann Peter Apfel
Johann Paul Derst	Georg (O) Wypert
Henrich Geck	Jan Jacob Scherr

October 17th 1732.
At the Courthouse before the Governor and several Magistrates the foregoing Qualifications were taken & subscribed by the several foreigners whose Names are contained on this Leaf.
Robt Charles, Cl. Con.

[List 29 A] [Passengers imported in the Ship Samuel, Hugh Percy, Master, from Rotterdam. Qualified August 17, 1733.]

	AGES		AGES
Hans Peter Fry	44	Matthew Ley	28
Listen Walter	33	Peter Pysell	44
Hans Jerick Strohaver	33	Michal Stersebagh	42
Casper Elias Tayler	37	Meliker Freys	32
Abraham Koon	50	Hans Wervell	54
Frederick Koon	22	Hans Jerick Wervell	18
Hans Jacob Symmer	24	Martin Jibe	47
Jacob Rusher	52	Bernard Wolf	29
Christian Krapts	33	Gasper Joust	21
Hendrick Bishop	20	Salomon Miller	22
Jerick Rouk, Senr.	48	Hans Wolf Iseman	22
Jerick Rouk, Junr.	24	Hans Jacob Hoff	33
Hans Jacob Rouk	17	Jacob Matthews	29
Peter Coonts	47	Leonard Wise	29
Hans Jacob Reed	45	Johannes Cresiner	23
Leonard Lightner	36	Philip Hettser	18
Hans Jerick Peck	30	Gillian Smith	40
Hans Jacob Tamooroon, sick	36	Christian Lafell	22
Andrews Fry	35	Gasper Iseman	53
Frederick Leyday	38	Meliker Wagner	48
Frederick Alterfer	18	Augustus Wagner	19
Michall Smith	34	Jacob Kimmerling	24

On arrival at the Delaware River anchorage off Philadelphia, over one hundred immigrants were too sick to land at once, but Hans Gasper Yost was named with one hundred and seventy others, who disembarked on the day of the ship's arrival and signed the Oath of Allegiance to the King of England. The first legal document in our American Ancestral Records,

The Ship Samuel of London was or eighty ton register, about sixty feet long and thirty feet at its widest, in the class of sailing ships of those days, called Brigantines. The passenger list in its original clearance, records "eighty-six females and eighty-nine males above the age of sixteen, and sixty-two females and fifty-four males under sixteen - in all, two hundred and ninety-one passengers from the Provinces of Franconia, chiefly and from other districts contingent to the Rhine.

Hans Gasper Yost was born in the year 1712, near Meintz, Duchy of Franconia (close to what is now Frankfort-on- the-Main, Germany). Hans Gasper Yost was bound out to William Moerschel (Marshall) of Lancaster County, Pennsylvania, and served him two years to redeem his foreign transportation debt. William Moerschel (Marshall) was the son of Toby Moerschel (Marshall) who emigrated from Holland prior to 1700. William Marshall had a daughter, Eleanor, who married Casper Yost shortly after his freedom from his redemption. Casper Yost received his Naturalization Septermber 21, 1760 in Lancaster Pennsylvania.

IN PENNSYLVANIA. 53

The foregoing is a true and perfect List, taken from the original Certificate under the Hand of William Allen, Esqr., remaining in my office.

[And in like manner, in September Term following, to wit: On the twenty-fourth day of September, 1760, at the said Supream Court, before the said Judges in pursuance of the aforesaid Act of Parliament, the, following Persons, viz:]

Jurors' names.	County.	Sacrament, when taken.
Jacob Ekert,	Berks County,	18th September, 1760
Jacob Focks,	Philadelphia,	7 September, 1760
Martin Alstat,	Berks,	do.
Nicholas Alstat,	do.	do.
Michael Feithorn,	do.	14 September, 1760
Adam Epler,	do.	10 August, 1760
John Cunnus,	Berks,	7 September, 1760
Philip Faass,	Philad'a,	21 September, 1760
Peter Buker,	Lancaster,	do.
Philip Runk,	do.	do.
Casper Yost,	do.	do.

The first property tax record of Casper is dated 1742, in which year he paid "$1.6.0 on a farm of forty acres, 1 horse and 1 cattle." In 1756, he and his family abandoned their clearing on account of numerous murdering, burning raids of the Indians. In 1765, he again flees with his family from "the wholesale slaughtering by the Indians in Lebanon Towne (Township) where all around Yost's Mill were massacred" - and evidently gives up pioneering on farms. It is stated in this last Indian raid, that Casper "rode the valley warning the approach of the Indians". No record could be found giving the owner of this "Yost Mill" and what Yost family was "wiped out". Whether or not Casper and his family suffered any physical harm is not of record.

From Aunt Sally and Uncle Leon Yost Ancestry Research is the following hand written entry:

Pennsylvania Archives
Series Third Volume 17 Page 144 Lancaster County 1771

Lebanon Township	Amount Tax	Year
Casper Yost	2.0	1771
Lebanon Township Page 421		
Casper Yost	2.0	1773

In 1765, Casper Yost paid a provincial business tax in Lancasterboro, Lancaster County, Pennsylvania of $4.10.0 as a tanner. Sometime prior to 1769 or the spring of that year, Casper and family removed to the Antietam Valley of Maryland, no doubt answering the solicitation of Rev. Funk who recently established a church near Elizabeth Towne (now Hagerstown).

On August 16, 1771, Casper purchased from Beatty and Hawkins of Prince George County, Maryland, a lot in the addition to George Towne, Frederick County, subdivided in a tract known as "Knave's Disappointment" – being lot no. 88, having a frontage on high street of 90 feet with a variable depth of 150 feet extending toward the Potomac River. (About 1333 this lot is now being used as an oil station and fronts on Pennsylvania Avenue, about 50 feet east of the Rock Creek Park Bridge, in the business section of Georgetown which is in the western part of Washington, D.C.).

On June 23, 1772, Casper's son, Henry, purchased lot No. 142 in the same tract, adjoining Casper's lot in the rear and bordering on Rock Creek. This lot was later purchased from Henry by his brother, John, who built on it a furnace and forge for making guns. The price of both lots was the same, f6 sterling and assuming "an alienation rent of ½ penny per annum".

In the George Towne Hundred census of 1776, the house of Casper is listed as follows: Casper, age 64; Eleanor, age 58; Tobias, age 21; Susannah, age 17; Philip, age 14. In the same list, by the same census taker and but one family removed, proving them close neighbors, was Casper's son, John 33; his wife, Rebecca, age 27; and children, Katherine, age 7; Mary, age 4; Elizabeth, age 2 and John Jr., age 5.

On August 4, 1777, an inventory of the estate of Casper Yost was filed at George Towne, amounting to f216.10.4. As such inventories were filed, with few exceptions, within thirty days after death, it can be reasonably presumed that he died in the early part of July. As the record of his immigration gave him as 21 on arrival in 1733, he was about 65 years old when he died.

Of his wife, Eleanor, a descendent through her son, John, says that Eleanor died in 1780 at the home of John, in Fairfax Court House, Va., which is a short distance south of the Potomac River from George Towne of that time. Eleanor's pet name was Patsy.

Hans Casper Yost's Last Will and Testament Page 1

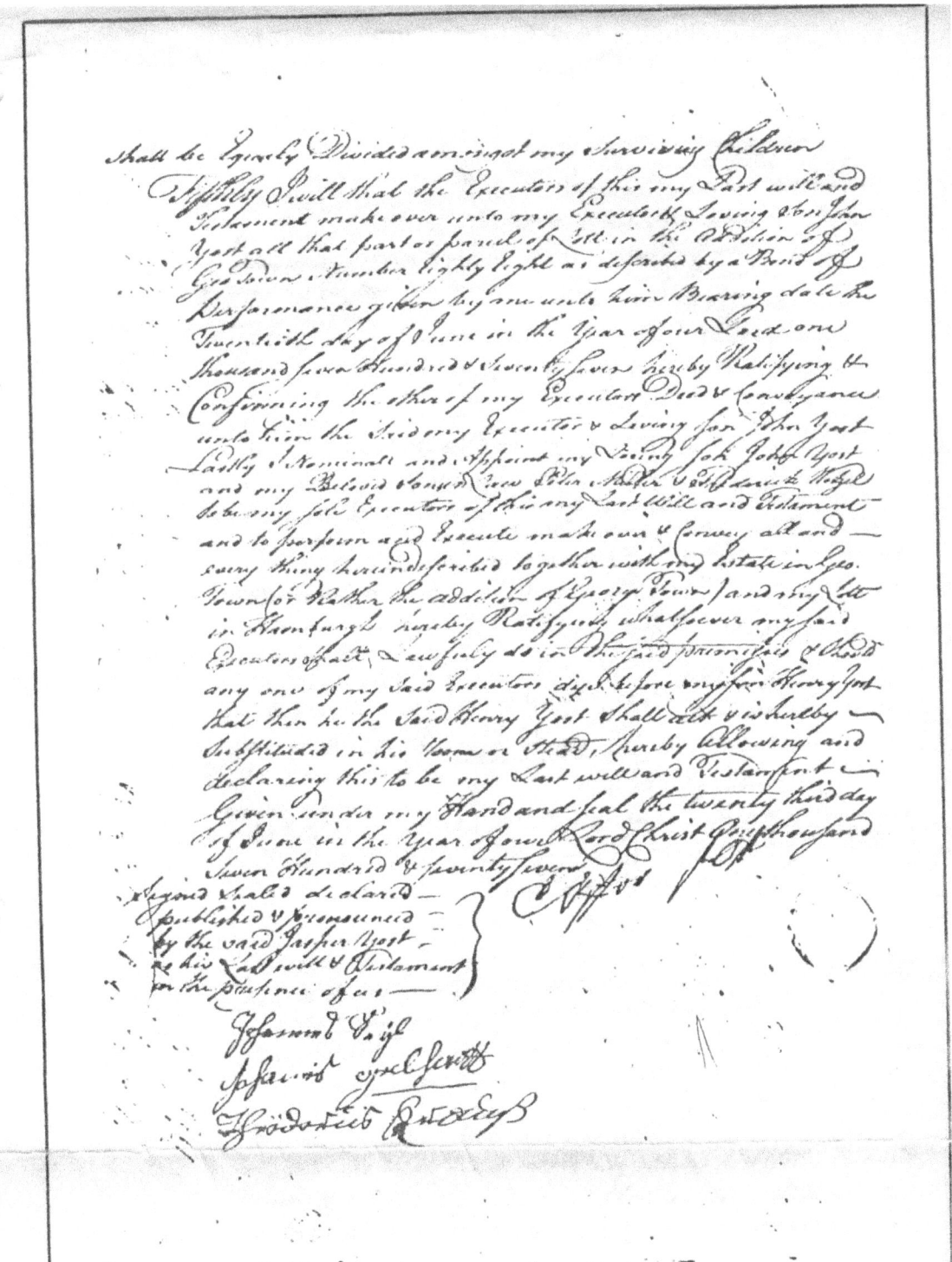

Hans Casper Yost's Last Will and Testament Page 2

Last will and Testament of Casper Yost deciphered

In the name of God Amen I Casper Yost
of George Town in Montgomery County and Province of
Maryland in being at present weak in body but of perfect
Mind and memory, Thanks be to the Almighty therefore,
Have thought proper to make this my last will and testa
ment inform and Moreover following, to wit, I give
unto God my Soul who gave it, to be by him received,
through the Merit and Salvation of Jesus Christ our Lord
and my Body to the Earth from which it was taken to be
Buried in a Christian Decent Manner. And as touching,
then my Worldly Affairs I give and bequeath in manner
and form following
Imprimis after my Funeral Expenses and Just Debts shall
be paid I give and bequeath unto my beloved wife Helena
Chathrina Fifty Pounds Fifty Pounds Common Cur and together with a
complete Bed with all its furniture, six pewter plates and one pewter
Dish and one pewter Basson and all five pound per Annum
During the minority of my son Philip out of the Rent of
My house in Georgetown, but should she enter again into
Matrimony or my son Philip should die before he
Comes of age then Said Annuity is to cease and de….
Paid by my executors no longer
Secondly it is my will that all the residue of my Estate
Both real and Personal. Shall be Equally Divided Amongst
My Eight Loving Children my sons Casper, John,
Henry, Philip and my daughters, Anna Elizabeth, Margaret
Anna, Susannah.
Thirdly I will that my Personal Estate be sold at Public
Sale within Six Months after my decease and equally
Divided amongst my children, and my real estate in
Georgetown and my lots In Harrisburgh be sold in like
Manner. When my son Philip shall come to full age of
Twenty and one year, but should my son Philip die before
He arrives to said age, then it is to be sold accordingly within
Six months after his decease, and divided as before, mentioned
Fourthly, should any of my children die without heirs.
Of their body then it is my will that his or her portion shall

Be equally divided amongst my surviving children
Fifthly I will that the execution of this my last will and
Testament makeover unto my executor and loving son John
Yost all that part or parcel of both in the addition of
Georgetown number Eighty Eight as described by a bond of
Performance given by me unto him bearing date the
Twentieth day of June in the year of our lord one
Thousand Seven Hundred and Seventy Seven hereby ratifying and
Confirming the other of my executor Deed and Conveyance
Unto him the said my Executor and Loving son John Yost
Lastly I nominate and appoint my loving son John Yost
And my beloved sons in law Peter Miller and Fredrick Wetzel
To be my sole executor of this my last will and testament
And to perform and execute make over and convey All and
everything here in described together with my estate in the
town of Georgetown the addition of Georgetown and my lots
in Hamburgh hereby ratifying whatforever my land
Executors of all Lawfully do in the said promises and should
Any one of my said executors die before any my son Henry Yost
That then he the said Henry Yost shall act and is hereby
substituted in his Room or stead, thereby allowing and
Declaring this to be my last will and testament
Given under my hand and seal the Twenty Third day
Of June in the year of our Lord One Thousand
Seven Hundred and Seventy Seven

Signed Sealed and Declared ----   Casper Yost
Published and Pronounced
By the said Casper Yost
As his Last Will and Testament
In the Presence of Us
         ....
         ....
         ....

Children of HANS CASPER AND ELEANOR Marshall (MOERSCHEL) YOST were

Henry Yost, born 1749, near Lebanon, Pennsylvania; died 1803, Staunton, Augusta County, Virginia. (See in-depth story on Henry Yost later in book)

Christian Yost, born 1737; m. _____ KREBS, Pennsylvania. Christian was the oldest son of Hans Casper Yost. According to the administration of his estate in Washington County, Maryland, 1784, Christian provided ten pounds for the maintenance of his father's, Casper, grave in Georgetown. In the land warrants of Maryland, Christian received title 36 acres in Frederick County, being re-survey call "old Plott". He added to it in 1765 a tract called "Yost's Narrow Chance" of 20 acres and "Yost's Claim" of 50 acres. In a title to Albert Flourey 1786, the farm was called "Yost's Claim Enlarged", comprising of 281 acres.

George Yost, born 1739; m. _____ RITCHIE, Pennsylvania. George Yost was the second child of Hans Casper Yost. George rented 200 acres of land in Freder (Frederick?) County, Maryland from 1762 to 1765. (The property under lease to Robert Swan, by Lord Baltimore). George purchased a plot of ground he named "Yost's Disappointment" in 1766 and added to it a tract called "Yost's Ridge" in 1767.

In Aunt Sally and Uncle Leon Yost's research that I was given by Sally's son Butch I found the following hand written entry of research:

Book by Mr. Brumbaugh, Washington, D.C.

Page 55

"No. 51 Leased September 28, 1762 to Robert Swan for 21, 180 acres George Yost tenant in possession: on rent 01-16-0; Aliena fine, 3-1-0; fine due, 3-12-0"

Page 59

"51. (A) September 28, 1762 (B) Robert Swan (C) 177 ¼ (D) George Yost (E) 1-16-0 (F) 3-12-0 (L) 21 years
Has Lordships Manor of Monocosy in Fredrick County 1768"

Volume 1 Penn. Church Records
Page 286 Maryland Fredrick County
    Va??? Name Nov. 9-12, 1769
       George Yost (D-R) Demcrat Republican
          (F) Federalist

George and his wife had five children, Phillip, Harmon, George, and two daughters, names unknown.

George Jr. married and had a son Permenus Wesley Yost. Permenus married Elzena Jane Ammon. They had a son **Fielding Harris Yost** born April 30, 1871 in Fairview West Virginia, died August 20, 1946 in Ann Harbor Michigan.

Fielding Harris Yost after taking a law degree in 1897 at the University of West Virginia, he became the Head Football Coach at the University of Michigan. He was known as "Hurry Up Yost", he coached Michigan's famous "Points a minute" football team (1901- 1905) and devised outstanding blocking and signaling systems, as the Athletic Director at Michigan from 1921 – 1946 he developed the Universities Facilities and Intramural sports program to meet his ideal of sports for all. His 1901 team won the 1st Rose Bowl. He wrote the book, "Football for Players and Spectators" in 1905.

He was educated at La Fayette College and University of West Virginia where he played on the tackle football teams. Shortly after his graduation in 1897, he was hired to be the coach of Ohio Wesleyan University. In his first season his team had 7 victories, 1 tie and 1 defeat. In the next two years he coached successfully at the Universities of Nebraska and Kansas, winning 17 games and loosing just 2. After another victorious season at Stanford University in 1900 he was hired at the University of Michigan. He remained there for the next 25 years becoming the Athletic Director in 1921. The first 5 teams he coached were developed and known as the "point a minute eleven". Playing 57 games with 55 wins, 1 tie, and 1 loss. The teams scored a total of 2,821 points to their opponents 40. 4 of his teams went undefeated and united. Twice his teams tied for the National Championship. Twice his teams won the Western Conference Championship, and 6 others shared the conference championship. Fielding Yost originated the "Key Halfback", now known as the Tailback position. He was the first to use the 9 man line and devised several highly successful blocking methods and signaling systems. He died in Ann Harbor Michigan August 20, 1946 while still serving as the Athletic Director.

Fielding Harris "Hurry Up" Yost

College Football Hall of Fame
Inducted: 1951 as a coach

Always in a hurry, thus the nickname "Hurry Up," Fielding Harris Yost gained national acclaim as a college football coach at Michigan at the turn of the century. Yost's travels included a stop at West Virginia, where he earned a law degree and played football in 1895-96. After his two years at WVU, the Fairview, W.Va., native took the Michigan coaching job at age 30 in 1900. Four years later, he showed his appreciation for his alma mater at West Virginia by beating the Mountaineers 130-0, a score that didn't endear him to the West Virginia faithful. That 1904 Michigan squad was called the "Point-A-Minute" team. Later the athletic director at Michigan, he was singularly instrumental in building the nation's largest football stadium at Michigan. He was inducted into the College Football Hall of Fame in 1951. He died August 20, 1946, in Ann Arbor, Mich.

Fielding Harris Yost

Fielding Harris Yost (Center) with 1904 Michigan Football Team

Fielding Harris Yost

Eleanor Yost, born 1741; died 1755, age 14 years. Eleanor Yost was the twin sister of Elizabeth Yost.

Elizabeth Yost, born 1741. Elizabeth Yost was the twin sister of Eleanor Yost. There is no Marriage record found for Elizabeth.

John Yost, born 1743, Lancaster County, Pennsylvania; d. 1826, Tazewell County, Virginia. He married REBECCA BONHAM Bet. 1767 - 1768 in Maryland.

Established at Georgetown, Maryland. In 1775 he contracted with the Committee of Safety for muskets at 4 pounds, 5 shillings each, and rifles at 4 pounds, 15 shillings each. This contract remained in effect until 1782.

According to reliable tradition in the Yost family, John served in the Revolutionary War under General George Washington and was in the battle of Lexington. It is said that he made guns for Washington's Army.

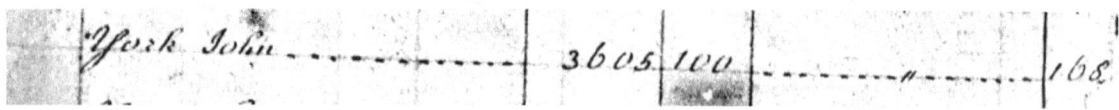

1788 Land Survey for Revolutionary War, John Yost given 100 acres

The Yost Rifle Sold to President George Washington

Portrait of George Washington by Charles Willson Peale

George Washington, never exactly a cheerful or chipper soul, was today even more glum than usual. It was May 21, 1772, and all day he had been posing for his portrait motionless, awkwardly dressed in an antique uniform originally tailored for a younger, slimmer man. The painter—an up-and-coming artist by the name of Charles Willson Peale—was certainly taking his time about it.

And then, at last, Washington was allowed to see the result. There he was, looking suspiciously more youthful (Peale knew how to flatter his subjects) than his forty years might suggest, but otherwise the likeness was most accurate. There he stood, Colonel George Washington of the defunct Virginia Regiment, officer, gentleman, loyal servant of His Majesty, and veteran of the French and Indian War.

Peale's portrait of Washington—the earliest authentic likeness of the man that is known to exist—is distinguished from hundreds of other pictures of eighteenth-century soldiers hanging in the world's museums in one remarkable respect. It's easy to overlook, but, subtly protruding from behind Washington's left shoulder, is the muzzle of an American rifle.

This particular arm had probably been commissioned two years before, in early 1770. In March of that year Washington was staying with his friend Robert Alexander, and according to his diary, they often "went out a hunting" foxes; but he one day rode to "George Town" (then a small place eight miles upstream from Alexandria, Virginia) to pick up "my rifle" from the gunsmith John Jost (or Yost) for £6 and 10 shillings. (An exact conversion to today's dollars is extremely difficult to determine, but $1,400 is a very rough approximation.) Gratifyingly, the cost of the firearm was partly offset by Washington's winning of £1 and 5 shillings from his host at cards, while its fineness can be gauged by the fact that during the Revolution Jost would make rifles for American troops invoiced at £4 and 15 shillings each—and this after prices had already soared owing to inflation. Washington may well have paid more than a 100 percent premium for the privilege of owning a custom-made Jost.

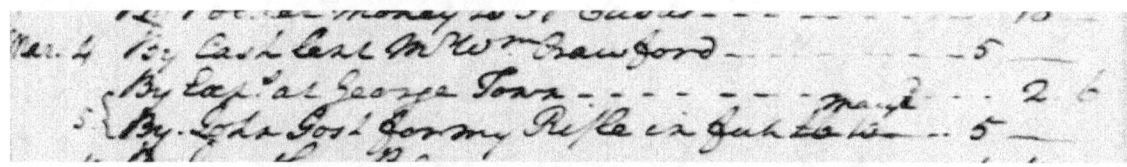

Diary Image of George Washington's Diary. Last line By John Yost for my Rifle

March 1770

5.   Mr. Magowan went to Dumfries and I to Mr. Rt. Alexanders on a hunting Party where I met Mr. B. Fairfax but first I went over to George Town returng. to Mr. Alexanders at Night.

Established in 1751, Georgetown, Md. (now part of Washington, D.C.), was at this time a small but active trading community at the mouth of Rock Creek, eight miles up the Potomac River from Alexandria. At Georgetown today GW paid John Jost £6 10s. Maryland currency for a rifle and apparently dined at one of the town's two taverns. He also played cards either at Georgetown or at Robert Alexander's house, winning £1 5s. (LEDGER A, 302; RICE, 2:87–88).

John and his brother Henry were the only two sons of Hans Casper and Eleanor (Marshall) Yost who removed from Maryland into the southwestern part of Virginia. Henry migrated down the Wilderness Trail (Shenandoah Valley), but John traveled down "east of the blue ridge" by way of Culpeper and Charlotte.

John and Henry's history in Virginia is associated in the histories of the Virginia Valley from Augusta County to the "spring gardens" west of New River, in what is now Tazewell and Wythe County. Both were prominent gunsmiths of Maryland during the Revolution and both served in the German Regiments of Maryland. After the war, they went back to the soil and farmed for a while but in later years, both moved into town and opened up tanning shops and conducted the business of saddle and harness makers. It is said of the early Yost's that they were poor farmers but excellent tradesmen, excelling in the making of "wagons, saddles, harness, and transportation smithing".

Source:

Annals of John Yost Sr. (Proceedings of the Council of Safety of Maryland, seated at Annapolis; copied from original records in the Archives of Maryland and Baltimore.)

"At a meeting of the Council of Safety for the Province of Maryland at the City of Annapolis on Sunday 7 July 1776: Council met, were present: The Hon'ble Daniel of St Thomas Jenifer Esqr.: Charles Carroll, Barrister, Bejamin Rumsoy & James Tilghman, Esquires.

Ordered: The Council contract with John Yost for the making of 300 Muskets at four pounds, fifteen shillings each to be delivered at the terms and in the proportion expressed in his bond.

Ordered: That the Treasurer of the Western Shore pay the said John Yost, one Hundred Fifty Pounds common money to enable him to comply with his Contract."

Following records are orders of the same Committee:

Tuesday, 23 July 1776

Copy of letter No. 70 was sent to John Yost of George Towne: (Council to Yost) We are very desirous of knowing exactly what Arms you have ready for the public, that we may send for them as soon as you get a wagon load, or such number as will be worth while sending fore; let us know by first good opportunity, and if none offers, and your arms be ready, hire an Express and we will pay him. 23 July 1776.

Tuesday, 30 July 1776

Ordered, that John Yost deliver to Capt. Edward burgess all the Muskets he has made for the public.

(Council to C. Beatty and others) Commissioners of Gun Lock Manufactory,

Gent'n.,

As a considerable time has elapsed since your erecting your Gun Lock factory, we are in great hopes you have made a number for the use of this Province.

The Province is in great distress for Arms; few of the Troops raised for the Flying Camp are supply'd with them and the Militia will not lend theirs. There is an absolute necessity therefore that you immediately send them down what Locks you have. We expect

Firelocks from John Yost, they have come from thence if you contrive them there. We desire also to know how many Locks you made per week. We have barrels enough here and in Kent for the Locks you can make. 30th July 1776

Thursday, 1 August 1776 (Yost to Council) George Towne, Aug 1, 1776

Gentlemen of the Council:

I have received your letter dated the 23 July and finding you desirous to know what Compliment of Arms I had ready for the Public. I have them all ready of the First Contract including the Bayonets, which I expect this day with and Express that I have sent for them. I have also been much detained in the last Contract by repairing old Arms for the Militia, che Con'l finding it very necessary. If I am now not deceived in receiving of the Bayonets I hope I can dispatch all by the latter end of this week. I am Gen't. in duty bound, John Yost.

Saturday, 10th August 1776:

Ordered: That the Treasurer of the Western Shore pay to John Yost fifty pounds common money being the Balance due him on his Contract with the Council of Safety in November last.

Wednesday 25 Sept 1776 (John Yost to Council) George Town, Sept 13, 1776

Gentlemen,

In consequence of your Favor of the 6th Instant, I have to inform you that I have erected a Horse Mill for boring Gun Barrels, that I am now employed with all the workmen I have in making Locks, Screws, Mounting and gorging Barrels ready for boring, but cannot proceed to that part of the work before I receive the Materials (Steel in particular) which I purchased at Philadelphia some time ago; having been disappointed by Mr. Jesse Hollingsworth of Baltimore, who I am informed, had neglected to bring them from the Head of El in his packet; probably a missive from you to him on this occasion, might be of Service to hasten their Conveyance.

I was told by the Manager of the Gun Lock Manufactory at Frederick Towne, that they forge Gun Locks much faster than they can finish them off: as that is the case, I should be glad to furnish myself from thence with 300 ready forged Locks, provided the terms are admissible.

If this proposal is agreeable, I hope I may shortly be furnished with proper Authority through you, or some other Department, to receive that Quantity, as it will greatly further my work.

I have nine hands employed at present, and have engaged two more; whom I expect will be at work for me in less than a Fortnight.

With great Respect, I am Gentlemen

Your most Ob't Servant,

John Yost

Wednesday, 25 Sept 1776

Ordered: That Mr. John Yost of George Towne deliver to Lieutenant Frederick Skinner all the Muskets he has ready made for the public service.

Friday, 1 November 1776

Ordered: That Western Shores Treasurer pay Robert Peters for use of John Yost six Pounds, thirteen shilling and six pence. Adjourned 'till next day 10 o'clock.

Mar 27, 1777

Said Treasurer pay John Yost two hundred Pounds in advance on his contract for arms."

Casper Yost, JR., born 1745; m. Magdalen Shaefer, Pennsylvania.

Pennsylvania Council of Safety Revolutionary War

Present: Thomas Wharton, Jun., David Rittenhouse, Samuel Morris, Sen., John Bayard, Joseph Blewer, Given Biddle, Henry Keppele, Jun., Francis Gurney, Samuel C. Morris, Fred. Kuhl, John Bull.
Commissions were this day granted for Officers of the Fourth Battalion of Associators in Northumberland County, viz:
Philip Cole, Colonel; Thomas Sutherland, Lieutenant-Colonel; Thomas Foster, First Major; **Casper Yost, Second Major**; Devalt Miller, Standard Bearer; James McCoy, Adjutant.
First Company: John Clark, Captain; Henry Pongius, First Lieutenant; James Moor, Second Lieutenant; Patrick Watson, Ensign

William S. Yost, born 1747; married first Elizabeth Clover in 1766. He then married Agnes Zimmerman, Pennsylvania November 27, 1768.

Quoting Aunt Sally Powell Yost's research, "William removed from Lancaster County, PA. Prior to 1782, taking up a farm in Fairfax, County, Virginia. In the 1782 census of Virginia, William had 8 in family, three sons under 16 and 5 females, including his wife.

William Yost's Will

In the name of god Amen, I William Yost of the County of Morgan and State of Virginia, being in a perfect state of health and of perfect mind and memory, thanks be to god for the same, I do make and ordain this my last Will and Testament. I will that all my just debts and funeral charges shall be paid and satisfied. I give and bequeath to my beloved wife Elizabeth Yost one bed and bedding, the young sorrel horse, and a cow and the chest which she brought to the place, and the big brass kettle and the little brass kettle and the little iron pot and a side saddle. And also one hundred & twenty dollars that her brother borrowed, she is to take toward her third. All goods and chattels and plantation shall be sold. The plantation shall be sold in yearly payments. The goods and chattels shall be sold at public sale. My wife Elizabeth Yost shall draw the third of all my estate. The money shall be equally divided among all my children. My daughter Mary, my son John, my daughter Catherine, my son Peter, my daughter Elizabeth, my son William. My daughter Catherine I will sixteen dollars besides the equal divide. I also will to my son William thirty five dollars in cash besides the equal divide. My herein named Executors of my personal estate of goods and chattels after my decease and any money of the sale and plantation shall be equally divided whatever cash and notes is after my decease shall be divided equally. And lastly I do ordain and appoint my trusty friends Matthias Ambrose and Peter Michael and hereby give them full power and absolute authority to execute this and legally to convey my lands, to do in all cases as is herein therein my last will and testament mentioned. In witness whereof I have hereunto set my hand and seal this 8th day of November in the year 1822. Signed sealed acknowledged by the said William Yost as his last Will and Testament in the presence of us

James A Brown
Adam Arnold
Sarah Miller
Morgan County, Va.

At a court held for said County on Monday the 5 day of January 1824. This last Will and Testament of William Yost was presented in Court, proved by the oaths of James A Brown, Adam Arnold & Sarah Miller and ordered to be recorded. Teste O. Ornick, Clerk

Catherine Yost, born 1752.

Jacob Yost, born 1754. Died 1754. The record said, died infant. Member of the family believe this is a mistake and Jacob lived to leave descendants. (But not authentic trace has been found to date.)

JOURNAL OF THE COMMITTEE OF OBSERVATION OF THE MIDDLE DISTRICT OF FREDERICK COUNTY, MARYLAND

November 29, 1775 The Committee met according to Adjournment. Rolls of the following Companies of Militia in this district were returned to the Committee.

The Game Cock Company received its name from the jaunty cap that they wore and the waving plume or cockade that distinguished the frontiersmen of Tom's Creek. Their uniforms were not flashy compared to those in the regular army. In a correspondence of the Maryland Council of Safety in the latter part of 1776, stated that money would be given out in advance, however, hunting shirts will be a convenient and good uniform if they can be had.
The Game Cock Company comprised of many men of German decent which rendered a valuable service during the Revolutionary War. Among the German settlers were the Hockersmiths, the Cregers, and the Williamses to name a few. Jacob Sheets who built Sheet's Mill on Piney Creek was a Private in Captain Baltzell's Company. His descendants resided in the Tom's Creek hundred during the time of the War for Independence. **The Game Cock Company participated in most of the important engagements of the Revolutionary War, and assisted at the siege of Yorktown and in the capture of British General Cornwallis.**

Captain Peter Mantz's Company
Peter Mantz, Capt.; Adam Grosh, 1st Lt.; Peter Adams, 2d Lt.; Nicholas White, Ensn.; Christopher Collenberger, John Waggoner, Leonard Lartz, Baltzer Martz, **Sergeants**; Jacob Snider, Peter Tertesebaugh, Godfrey Hollar, Casper Missell, Corporals; John Row, Drummer; **Jacob Yost**, Filer, and 68 Privates

ARMS MAKERS
of MARYLAND

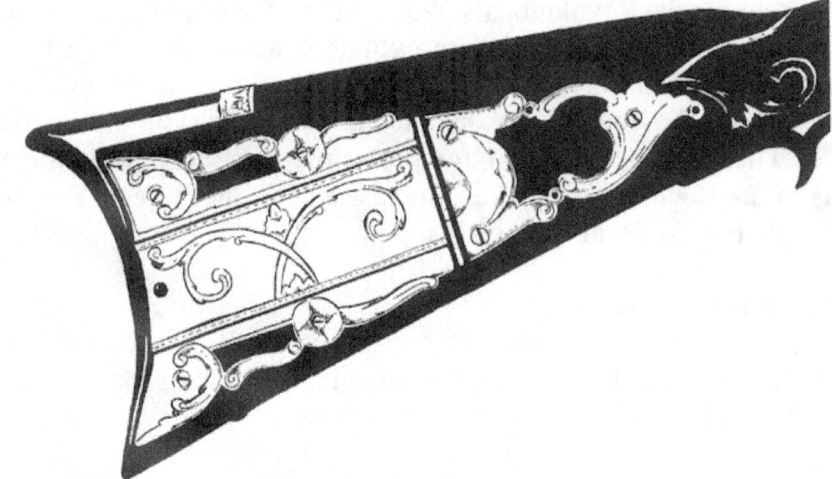

by DANIEL D. HARTZLER

HISTORICAL SOCIETY OF
CARROLL COUNTY, MD.
EAST MAIN STREET
WESTMINSTER, MD. 21157

Longrifle Series

Y

YANTIS, JOHN   Washington, D. C.

Yantis, John
    1862   bds 707 7th st   gunsmith
[Boyd's Washington and Georgetown Directory]

YOST, HENRY   Frederick

On 14 December 1775 Henry Yost and John Unsell agreed to produce muskets together for the Council of Safety. In June of 1776 29 rough muskets with pickers, wipers and one bullet mould were returned to them, classed unfit for service.

Ordered That Mr Henry Yost and Mr John Unseld deliver to Capt. George Stricker all the Musquets and Bullet Moulds which are now finished by them for the use of this Province.

April 4, 1776 Council of Safety
Ordered That Mr Henry Yost and Mr John Unseld deliver to Capt. George Stricker all the Musquets and Bullet Moulds which are now finished by them for the use of this Province.
[AM, p. 308]

YOST, JOHN   Georgetown

January 17, 1776 Youst to Council, Georgetown
Having applied to The Committee of observation for a sufficient quantity of Powder for proving the guns, which I have engaged to furnish The Council of Safety, which I have refused without your approbation should be glad you would please to nominate a man in town to see the Guns proved as it is inconvenient to me, at present to leave the Business. Mr Deakins has left town, which prevent his writing, to you according to agreement, I hope gentleman youl Please to let me know what I am to expect as the guns cannot be delivered or finished otherwise than by your granting a Licence for Powder.
[AM, p. 100]

January 20, 1776 Council of Safety
Ordered That Mr Stephen West deliver to John Youst or Ordered the Quantity of ten Pounds weight of Gunpower (out of that purchased by the Convention from him) to prove the Musquets made by the said Youst for the use of this Province.
[AM, p. 99]

March 8, 1776 Council of Safety
Ordered, That the Treasure of the Western Shore to John Youst two Pounds eleven Shillings, and seven Pence Currency for repairing Guns.
[AM, p. 214]

March 27, 1776 Council to Youst
The Council of Safety desire you will be as expeditious as you possibly can in supplying the Muskets &c you engaged to make for the Province, and inform us whether you have any now completed as we are in very great Want of them and will send for them as soon as you have a Number ready.
[AM, p. 293]

July 7, 1776 Council of Safety
The Council contracted with John Yost for the making of 300 Muskets at 4 pounds 5 shillings each and 100 Rifles at 4 pound pounds 15 shillings each.
[American Archives, 5th Series, Vol. I, p. 1331]

August 1, 1776 Yost to Council
I have received your letter dated the 23 of July and finding you desirous to know what Compliment of Arms I had ready for the Publick. I have them all ready of the first contract including the Banyonets which I expect this day with an Express that I have sent for them. I have also been much detained in the last contract by repairing old arms for the militia the Cort. finding it very necessary . . .
[AM, p. 159] [American Archives, 5th Series, Vol. I, p. 707]

September 13, 1776 Yost to Council, George Town
In Consequence of your Favour of the 6th. Instant, I have to inform you that I have erected a Horse Mill for boring Gun Barrels; that I am now employed with all my Workman I have in making Locks, screws, Mounting and forging Barrels ready for boring, but cannot proceed to that part of the Work before I receive the Materials (Steel in particular) which I purchased at Philadelphia sometime ago; . . . I was told by the manager of the Gun Lock Manufactory at Frederick Town, that they forge Gun Locks much faster then they can finish them off; as that is the Case, I should be glad to furnish myself from thence with 300 ready forged Locks, provided the Terms are admissible. If this Proposal is agreeable, I hope I may shortly be furnished with proper Authority through you, or some other Department, to receive that Quantity, as it will greatly further my work. I have nine Hands employed at present and have engaged two more, who I expect will be at work for me in less than a fortnight.
[AM, p. 271]

March 27, 1777 Council of Safety
That the said Treasure pay to John Yost two hundred pounds in advance on his Contract for arms.
[AM, p. 191]

July 16, 1781 Murdoct to Council
. . . John Yost, who has already repaired several public Arms, and is now employed about repairing those you last sent to this County, has made frequent Applications to me for money and now he tells me that he cannot go on with the work, nor longer Maintain his Family without regular Payments, so that he must stop unless he can be paid for it . . .
[AM, p. 351]

Yost, John   Frederick County
    3 males of more than 16 years
    3 males under 16 years
    5 females
[1790 Federal Census]

YOUNG, C. E.   Cumberland

Young, C. E.
    1887   Cumberland   gun & locksmith
[Maryland Directory & State Gazetteer, 1887, The Baltimore Publishing Co.]

Mary Yost, born 1755; married John Keller April 25, 1778 in Frederick County, Maryland.

> **Early Marriages.**—The first law directing the issuing of marriage licenses in Maryland was passed in 1777, the second year of the State constitution. The following is an official list of the licenses issued for the first three years after the passage of the law:
>
> 1778.
> March 19. William Logan to Margaret Shelar.
> " 24. Archibald Morrow to Margaret Hitton.
> " 25. Benjamin Padgett to Ann Green.
> " 28. Samuel Archibald to Catherine Cock.
> April 6. Richard Boseman to Susanna Holtz.
> " 7. John Silver to Ann Springer.
> " 17. Joseph McDonald to Anna Shell.
> " 18. George Scuteball to Catherine Cline.
> " 21. Richard Wells to Edith Coe.
> " 23. David Miller to Catherine Heffner.
> " 23. Maj. Peter Mantz to Catherine Howard.
> " 23. Peter Humbert to Rebecca Bunn.
> " 24. John Kemp to Barbara Huff.
> " 25. John Keller to Mary Yost.

Frederick County Maryland first Marriages

Tobias Yost, born 1757. Died 1784. Tobias Yost never married.

APPENDIX A - COMMISSIONED OFFICERS

Name	Rank	Date	Cty	Bn	Company
Woolrich, Philip	Ensign	04-02-77	BA		Capt.W.Wilkinson
Woolsey, George	Ensign	----04-76	BA	Town	Capt.Wm.Buchanan
Woolsey, George	2nd Lt	06-06-76	BA	Town	Capt.Smith
Woolsey, George		07-11-76	BA		
Wootton, Richard	1st Lt	03-01-76	PG	25th	Capt.H.Magruder
Wootton, Richard		25-09-76			
Wootton, Singleton	2nd Lt	03-01-76	PG	25th	
Wootton, Singleton	1st Lt	01-05-78	PG	25th	Capt.H.Magruder
Wootton, Wm.Turner	QM	13-01-76	PG	25th	
Worley, Thomas	1st Lt	- -	WA		
Worth, Jonathan	1st Maj	08-05-77	KE	27th	
Worthington, John	1st Lt	22-02-76	AA	Svrn	Capt.Hall
Worthington, Nicholas Jr.	2nd Lt	22-02-76	AA	Svrn	Capt.Hall
Worthington, Nicholas Jr.	Capt	19-06-77	AA	7th	
Worthington, Nicholas	1st Maj	12-01-76	AA	Svrn	
Worthington, Nicholas	Colonel	26-01-77	AA	Svrn	
Worthington, Nicholas	Capt	02-03-78	AA	Svrn	
Worthington, Thos.of Nich	2nd Lt	19-09-77	AA	ElkR	Capt.Burgess
Worthington, William	1st Lt	18-10-82	AA	Svrn	Capt.V.Conoway
Wright, Benjamin	Ensign	11-04-76	AA	7th	Capt.Watts
Wright, Gavin	Ensign	22-09-77	SO	PrAn	Capt.T.Irving
Wright, Isaac	Ensign	17-12-81	CA	14th	Capt.T.Eaton
Wright, Jacob	Capt	20-05-78	DO	3rd	
Wright, Jacob	Capt	23-08-81	DO	Up	
Wright, James	1st Lt	06-07-76	DO		Capt.Waters
Wright, James	Capt	20-05-78	DO	3rd	
Wright, James	Capt	23-06-79	DO	Up	
Wright, Jonathan	Lt	06-06-76	PG	25th	
Wright, Nathaniel	Capt	16-03-76	QA		
Wright, Robert	2nd Lt	03-01-76	QA	5th	Capt.G.Baynard
Wright, Thomas	Colonel	12-01-76	QA	20th	
Wright, Thomas	Colonel	18-03-76	QA	20th	
Wroth, James	Ensign	22-06-78	CE	Bohe	Capt.J.W.Veazey
Wylie, Luke	Capt	31-10-80	BA	GPUp	
Wyly, Greenbury	Ensign	23-10-81	BA	GPUp	Capt.Wm.Lane
Yates, Jonathan	Capt	07-03-76	CH		
Yates, Jonathan	Maj	19-01-81	CH	12th	
Yates, Thomas	Capt	25-09-80	BA	Town	
Yates, Thomas	Capt	18-10-80	BA	Town	
Yates,---	Capt	28-01-77	BA		
Yieldhall, Gilbert	Ensign	22-02-76	AA	Svrn	Capt.Hall
Yieldhall, Gilbert	Ensign	14-06-76	AA	Svrn	Capt.Hall
Yost, Henry	1st Lt	22-06-78	WA	2ndW	Capt.J.Funk
Yost, Herman	Capt	29-11-75	FR	1st	
Yost, John Hd.	Capt	03-03-77	FR	33rd	
Yost, Tobias	Capt	04-08-80	MO	Lwr	Capt.D.Rhintzell
Young, Abraham	2nd Lt	12-09-77	MO	29th	Capt.W.Johnson
Young, Abraham	2nd Lt	07-12-76	MO		Capt.J.Johnson
Young, George	Ensign	17-11-80	WA		
Young, Hugh	2nd Lt	-04-76	BA	Town	Capt.J.Sterrett
Young, Jacob	Capt	16-02-76	FR		Minuteman
Young, James	Capt	25-09-80	BA	Town	

From Book "The Maryland Militia in the Revolutionary War" By S.Eugene Clements and F. Edward Wright Copyright 1987

Susanna Yost, born 1759; married Frederick Kokendoffer in 1779

In research from Aunt Sally and Uncle Leon Yost's was found the following hand written entry:

Book by Mr. Brumbaugh, Washington D.C.
Maryland Colonial Church, Fredrick County, 1767 – 1768
Page 514
Montgomery County Mass
Kukendoffer, Fredrick and Susanna Yost December 29, 1779

Philip Yost, born 1762; married Melander Morris in 1785. They had two known children, Charity, born 1797 and Mary born 1801, and others.

In going through Aunt Sally and Uncle Leon Yost's research that Sally's son Butch sent me, I found the following hand written research:

By Mr. Brumbaugh, Washington, D.C., Maryland Colonial Church, Fredrick County, 1767-1768 Volume II.

Page 545
"April 15, 1798
      Yost, Charity of Philip and Melander
           Born August 17, 1797
           Prince George Parish Baptism

Pennsylvania Archives

Franklin County Land Warrants 1784-1895
A(3) XXV 3-5, County Philadelphia 1779
Page 25   John Yost, Fredrick Township 4.0.0
Page 31   PhilipYost 5.5.0 Frankford and New Hanones Township

World War II Liberty ship
SS Casper S. Yost

| 2112 | SS *Casper S. Yost* | Casper S. Yost | standard | 23 September 1943 | 15 October 1943 | Sold private 1947, scrapped 1972 |

The **Liberty ships** were cargo ships built in the United States during World War II. They were cheap and quick to build, and came to symbolize U.S. wartime industrial output. Based on vessels ordered by Britain to replace ships torpedoed by German U-boats, they were purchased for the U.S. fleet and for lend-lease provision to Britain. Sixteen American shipyards built 2,751 Liberties between 1941 and 1945, easily the largest number of ships produced to a single design.

Displacement:	7,000 tons deadweight
Length:	441 ft 6 in (135 m)
Beam:	56 ft 10.75 in (17.3 m)
Draft:	27 ft 9.25 in (8.5 m)
Propulsion:	Two oil fired boilers, triple expansion steam engine, single screw, 2500 horsepower (1.9 MW)
Speed:	11 to 11.5 knots (20 to 21 km/h)
Range:	
Complement:	41
Armament:	Stern-mounted 4 in (102 mm) deck gun for use against surfaced submarines, variety of anti-aircraft guns.
Capacity:	9,140 tons cargo

Henry Yost's life

Henry was born 1749 in near Lebanon, Pennsylvania, and died 1803 in Stauton, Augusta County, Virginia. He married POLLY MARIE WAGGONER in Harper Ferry, West Virginia, daughter of CHRISTIAN WAGGONER. She was born 1752, and died 1819.

Henry Yost was the eighth child of Hans Casper and Eleanor (Moerschel) Yost.

He removed with his father's family from Lancaster Boro in 1768 or 1769 to near Elizabeth Towne, Frederick County, Maryland (now Hagerstown, Washington County).

In 1772 he purchased a lot in George Towne, Frederick County, Maryland, but shortly after sold it to his brother John, and returned to his former home at Elizabeth Towne.

On 23 June 1772, Henry purchased lot No. 142 in the same tract adjoining Casper's lot in the rear and bordering on Rock Creek. This lot was later purchased from Henry by his brother John and was established as a forge for making guns (muskets).

There is no tax record in Lancaster County, Pennsylvania nor in Frederick County, Maryland showing Henry as a farmer and it was not until 1775 that he appears in the History of Maryland as a gunsmith, 1775-1781, according to records he owned and operated a factory for the making of rifles, muskets, ball molds and other gun accessories of the times and also did gun repairing as well. Preceding the actual Declaration of Independence in 1776, the furnishing of arms to the hurriedly mustered troops "was a sore trial and tribulation for foreign guns were few and foreign orders unreasonably delayed" and every patriot so talented was called upon to make guns and other arms. Henry and his brother John, were no doubt gunsmiths before the necessity of their services were called upon, for they received orders as soon as district committees were appointed to authorize the purchase and payments.

There were two committees of war preparation appointed in Maryland; The Committee of Safety, seated at Annapolis -- the Committee of Observation, seated at Elizabeth Towne. It was the latter that directed orders to Henry Yost, who lived in or near Elizabeth Towne. The following record was copied exactly as it appeared in the Archives of Maryland:

"Proceedings of the Committee of Observation for Elizabeth Towne District, July 28th, 1775. A list of rifles appraised for Capt. Cresap's Company", (32 gunsmiths were listed with appraisals of their manufactured weapons, of which 18 were ordered delivered. Of the eighteen, three were selected from the supply of Henry Yost. The highest appraisal was to Peter Wirtz at 5.15.0, and the lowest to John Boozer at 2.10.0 Henry's guns were second highest at 4.15.0 and with him in his class was Francis Waggoner, Henry's brother-in-law.)

The following description is the only Maryland record showing the muskets made by Henry Yost and John Yost. There is no original gun in known existence, made by the American gunsmiths for the Militia and Continental Line during the revolution, neither the Smithsonian Institute nor War Department at Washington, haven't even a Copy. The make of all guns had his name engraved in brass on the lock or barrel.

"For the Maryland Militia and Continental Line: Musquets must be 42" long - 3/4" at bore - 1 1/2" at breach and 7/8" at muzzle - with good bouble bridal locks - black walnut or maple stocks - plain strong brass mountings - bayonets with steel blade 17" long - steel ramrods, double screws - priming wires and brushes fitted thereto: with a pair of brass molds with every 80 muskets, to cast 12 bullets on one side and on the other side to cast shot of such size as that the muskets will chamber three of them".

"Proceedings of the Committee of Observation for Elizabeth Towne District, Feb 5th, 1776."

"Henry Yost having been charged with making use or selling the powder allowed him by this Committee to Prove his Muskets, is Honorably Acquitted, and he has fully satisfied the Committee he is clear of the Charge."

"Journal of the Committee of Observation for the District of Elizabeth Towne. Proceeding of the Committee - Met July 25, 1776, John Stull, Esq., in the chair: Received of Henry Yost, 2 rifles and 1 musquet at L13, to be delivered to Coln'l Henry Shriock."

"Thursday, Jan 16, 1777. Ordered that the Western Shore Treasurer pay to Henry Yost, one hundred pounds of the new emission for repairing muskets on Account."

"Tuesday 30 Jan, 1781. Ordered that the Western Shore Treasurer pay to to Henry Yost, one hundred Pounds of new emission for repairing muskets on Account."

According to employees at the National Firearms Museum, "Henry Yost as a Frederick County gun maker had some problems. He was awarded two contracts - one independent contract of 75 muskets and one contract of 80 muskets in concert with neighbor John Unseld for the Maryland Commissary of Stores. Neither contract was fulfilled and the few pieces that were completed were actually returned to Yost and Unsold as unfit for service. Collectors have generally considered that these muskets were broken up into parts and their markings "scrubbed" (removed) and offered for sale elsewhere in the former colonies. Finding a military Henry Yost-marked musket may not be possible.

John Yost of Fredericktown seemed to have better success. Producing both lock plates and completing two contracts of 300 muskets, one of these Yost's muskets was observed in a display at a Maryland Arms Collectors show in 1976. Any other surviving examples of John Yost arms may well be concentrated in the Pennsylvania/Maryland/Virginia border area, but we know no examples in museum collections."

Record Pertaining to Henry Yost's service record

Upper District of Frederick County, Maryland; Enrolled as able bodies, over 16 and under 53; February 1775* Henry Yost.

March, 1776 - Signed as an Associator, Henry Yost

February, 1778 - Patriots Oath of Fidelity to Maryland and the Cause; List No. 17, signer No. 161, Henry Yost. List sworn to by John Stull. (There were 1598 men in 11 return in the Province of Maryland and these signers were called "The Patriots of Maryland").

March 1778 - Henry Yost was Commissioned First Lieutenant for the Upper District of Frederick County (this district is now Washington County, Maryland). This was a German Regiment as the 4th and 5th regiments of Maryland. He was in charge of an armory near Harper's Ferry on the Maryland side of the Potomac.

Henry Yost was a soldier in the 4th Regiment of Maryland, a German Regiment, as was the 5th also. When the British occupied Washington, D.C. in the war of 1812 - 1814, the Revolutionary records of Maryland and Virginia 'with a lot of other irreplaceable documents were destroyed by them."

WAR OF 1812-1814

A MUSTER ROLL OF CAPT. JACOB FRYER'S COMPANY OF MONTGOMERY COUNTY, OCTOBER THE 11TH 1814.

Captain.
Jacob Fryer.

1st Lieut.
Henry Houck.

2d Lieut.
Jacob Yost +

Ensign.
John Smith.

Sergeants.
1st. Jonah Markley.
2nd. Jacob Bartman.
3rd. Jacob Wanemaker.
4th. Jacob Fryer.

Corporals.
1st. Peter Burger.
2nd. Peter Yost. +
3rd. John Yost. +
4th. George Houck.

Trumpeter.
Henry Yost. +

Privates.

George Kulp.
Samuel Detwiler.
Lewis Jones.
Abraham Neas.
Samuel Esterline.
Anthony Botting.
George Fryer.
Henry Specht.
Frederick Shafer.
John Sweesboitz.
Abraham Zern.
John Smith.

William Burger.
Samuel Wisman.
Jonas Fetzer.
Henry Bickel.
Daniel Houck.
Daniel Yost. +
Lemuel Shuler.
William Brooks.
Jacob Jough.
Richard Peters.
Frederick Smith.
Henry Royer.

Pennsylvania Archives - 6th Series V 8

A record of Henry, handed down through the generations, is that Henry Yost was in charge of an Armory near Harper's Ferry, but on the Maryland side of the Potomac. There was such an Armory located about where New Brunswick, Maryland is today. Two other Armories at Harper's Ferry were built for the 1812 war and used during the Civil War but since torn down and obliterated.

Shortly after the Revolutionary War, Henry moved with his family down the Valley of Virginia, over the Wilderness Trail, and settled in Augusta County, Virginia, in that section then that became the Southeast district of Pendleton County, West Virginia of today. From approximately 1781-82 to 1790, there is no printed or family record to show any permanent removal of Henry. In 1790 he paid a tithable in the South Fork District of Augusta County. In 1793, 96, and 1800, he appeared at Tinkling Springs (now Staunton) Virginia, as consent to marriages of his three daughters, Elizabeth, Rebecca and Polly Eleanor, was given there. In 1809, he purchased 250 acres on the New River, in the then Wythe County, Virginia and sold it to his son, Rev. Casper Yost of Wytheville in 1819. In 1812 he purchased two lots in Fincastle, Botetourt County, Virginia, one a residence site and one a business location "adjoining the dam". In 1796 he was delinquent, having moved from his Augusta County district to Millton (now Rockingham County). In 1820 he paid a tithable in Bland County, Virginia. That Henry followed the gun making business during the Revolution proves that he was capable at it and no doubt it was the most profitable business at that time, but he was a tanner, saddler and harness maker when he died. Henry's father, Casper, was a tanner by trade and a farmer by necessity. When he abandoned farming and moved to Lancaster Boro, Pennsylvania, he went in the business of a tanner and no doubt his sons learned that trade from him.

Name:	**Elizabeth Yost**
Date:	23 May 1793
Notes:	This marriage record was originally published in "Chronicles of the Scotch-Irish Settlement in Virginia, 1745-1800. Extracted from the Original Court Records of Augusta County" by Lyman Chalkley.
Remarks:	Bride is the daughter of Henry Yost, who consents. Consent also given by A. Mustoe.
Description:	Spouse
Bond_Date:	23 May 1793

Name:	**Rebecca Yost**
Date:	22 Jun 1796
Notes:	This marriage record was originally published in "Chronicles of the Scotch-Irish Settlement in Virginia, 1745-1800. Extracted from the Original Court Records of Augusta County" by Lyman Chalkley.
Remarks:	Bride is the daughter of Henry Yost, who put up bond.
Description:	Spouse
Bond_Date:	1 Jun 1796

Name:	**Henry Yost**
Date:	22 Jun 1796
Notes:	This marriage record was originally published in "Chronicles of the Scotch-Irish Settlement in Virginia, 1745-1800. Extracted from the Original Court Records of Augusta County" by Lyman Chalkley.
Remarks:	Bride is the daughter of Henry Yost, who put up bond.
Description:	Bondsman
Bond_Date:	1 Jun 1796

40   Washington Co. Liber C
                       Md.

of four Shillings & Sixpence Sterling & the aforesaid Henry Yost for himself his heirs
Executors & Administrators doth Covenant Promise Grant & agree to and with the
said Abraham Leightoe his heirs and Assigns that he the said Henry Yost & his heirs
Executors & Administrators the aforesaid Lott & premisses with all the appourtenances
unto him the said Abraham Leightor his heirs & Assigns shall and will Warrant and fore
Defend against all persons Claiming the same from by or under him the said
Henry Yost his heirs Executors or Administrators In Witness whereof the said Henry
Yost hath hereunto set his hand & Seal the day above Written

Signed Sealed & Delivered   Henry Shryock
In the presents of ——   Henry Schnebely   Henry Yost (Seal)

Recd the date above written of Abraham Leighton One hundred & Ninety Pounds Specie
the Consideration above Written

Witness H Shryock   Henry Yost
         H Schnebely

Maryland Washington County Set on the fourth day of April 1782 Came Henry Yost
Before us the Subscribers two Justices for Washington County & Acknowledged the above
Deed to be his Act & Deed & the Lott & premisses therein Mentioned to be the right &
Estate of Abraham Leightor his heirs & Assigns fforever

              Acknowledged Before   H Shryock
                                        Henry Schnebely

At the Request of George Stikelather was the following Deed record April 6th 1782; to wit,

This Indenture made the sixth day of April in the year of our Lord one Thousand Seven
Hundred & Eighty two Between Frederick Kishel of Washington County and state of Maryland
Merchant of the one part and George Stikelother of the County and State aforesaid wheelright
of the other part Witnesseth that the said Frederick Kishel for and in Consideration of the
Sum of One Thousand and fifty pounds Current Money to him in hand paid by the said George
Stikelother the Receipt whereof he doth hereby Acknowledge hath granted Bargained and Sold
by these presents Doth Grant Bargain and sell unto him the Said George Stikelother his
heirs and Assigns forever one half a Lott of ____ lying ____ in Elizabeth Town
in Washington County and State of Maryland

Henry Yost Document, April 4, 1782

Henry and Polly Marie (Waggoner) Yost had 10 known children.

The children are listed as: Elizabeth Yost, Jacob Yost, John Yost, Rebecca Yost, Henry Marshall Yost, Polly Eleanor Yost, James Casper Yost, William Yost, Fletcher Harris Yost, and David Greiner Yost.

Of Henry and Polly Yost's children, it has been proved that the first five were born in what is now Washington County, Maryland, the last five in what was Augusta County, Virginia prior to 1793.

(This list of children's names conflicts with other historical data. For instance, in the "Children of Henry Yost" Jacob Yost's biography mentions, twice, a brother George, who was a minister and moved to Clareborne, Tennessee. However, that is the only information given and there is no George listed as a child of Henry Yost. George is not the same person as David Greiner Yost. Polly Eleanor Yost is also not mentioned in the "Children of Henry Yost". There are nine children listed there, they are: Elizabeth, Jacob, John, Rebecca, Henry Marshall, James Casper, William, Fletcher Harris and David Greiner.

Polly Waggoner's name also given as "Wagner". She was the eldest daughter of Christian Waggoner, a Swiss.

Children of HENRY and POLLY MARIE (WAGGONER) YOST are:

James Casper Yost, born 11 March 1785, Stauton, (Harpers Ferry), Augusta County, Virginia; died 05 January 1850, buried in West End Cemetery, Wytheville, Wythe County, Virginia. James Casper Yost was a Minister in the Methodist Church. James Casper Yost married Euphemia Hughes Bickle born September 22, 1787 in Augusta County Virginia, died April 18, 1862. They were married February 16, 1806. They had the following children, Lewis Marshall Yost born April 26, 1826, Mary Yost born February 02, 1807, John Cooper Yost born January 23, 1809, James Lockhart Yost born March 07, 1811, Margaret Bickle Yost born June 05, 1813, Adeline Cooper Yost born September 05, 1815, William Owen Yost born March 01, 1818, Fletcher Harris Yost born January 05, 1821, Henry Adams Yost born September 23, 1823, Jane Yost born May 15, 1830, Ellen Yost born 1835,

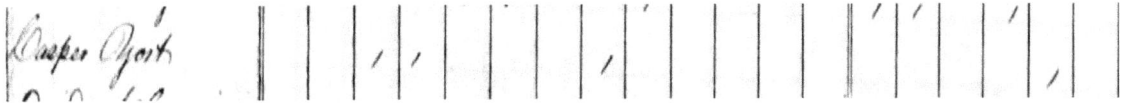

1840 James Casper Yost Virginia Wythe County

About James Casper Yost

On February 9, 1832, Francis Pearman married Asher Pickett. They were ministered by Casper Yost (Methodist Episcopal). Wythe County Marriages page 189

Birth: Mar. 11, 1785, USA
Death: Jan. 5, 1850, USA

Rev. Casper Yost was buried in the old M.E. graveyard on the west side of town of Wytheville, Virginia. The church has since been removed to the east side of town on Church Street. The grave marker, a white sand stone head-piece stands about three feet high is located at the foot of a chestnut tree planted at his burial. Inscription reads: "In memory of Rev. Casper Yost, born March 11, 1785, died Jan 5 1850 - Eighteen Years a Pastor of the Methodist Church and Forty-Eight Years a Member". James Casper and Euphemia Hughes (Bickle) Yost had 10 children.

Burial:
West End Cemetery
Wytheville
Wythe County
Virginia, USA

James Casper Yost was a Methodist Minister and was known as Reverend Casper Yost.

He was the seventh child of Henry Yost and Polly Waggoner.

Casper Yost was a Justice in Wythe County, Virginia in 1807. He was a wagon maker, farmer, and minister. In the Astor Library in New York City, New York, there is a history of Missionary or Itinerant Methodist Ministers in South West Virginia showing a wood cut of Casper Yost sitting in a pulpit chair.

Casper Yost came to Wythe County, Virginia in the early part of 1800, he was a Methodist Pastor for 18 years and a member for 48 years. He served as trustee on several church boards, and figured in more church organizations in Wythe County than any single individual of his day. On October 10, 1828, Casper and his wife deeded to the Methodist Episcopal Church 1 1/2 acres of land for the building of the Mount Ephraim Church which was a place of worship for over 100 years.

Virginia Land History
From the Library of Virginia
Richmond, VA
Early Years

Helm sold a total of 350 acres to John Leedy on December 4, 1813; the land lying south of where John Leedy lived…"that of which bought of John Crockett it ran a course with Leedy's land…and was corner to Allford's land".

In 1844, "John Leedy of the County of Wythe and State of Virginia of the one part and Casper Yost high Sheriff of Wythe County and State aforesaid of the other part Witnesseth that whereas the said John Leedy has been taken and is now in the custody of the high Sheriff of Wythe County on a Writ of Capias and [illegible] suit out of the Clerks Office of the County Court of Wythe in the name of John A. Simmerman for the sum of $3.75 with interest from the 4th day of April 1824 till paid and $1.34 costs and whereas the said John Leedy being unable to discharge the debt aforesaid; and wishing to avail himself of the benefit of an insolvent Debtor. Beginning at or upon the partition line between the said Leedy land and the land of Samuel Crockett Decd… a corner of Alford's and Leedy's land and with his line to the beginning. Twenty-five acres as above named to be laid off on the north side bot. of John Crockett and after the special direction of said Leedy but neverless to include the house and part of a field in which the said Leedy lived at the time he purchased said land of one George Helm…".1[60]

Casper Yost late high Sheriff of the County of Wythe and State of Virginia to Samuel Cassell the 16th day of June 1849. "…which said tracts of land was advertised and the said Samuel Cassell became the purchaser thereof…".2[61]

Rev. Casper Yost was buried in the old M.E. graveyard on the west side of town of Wytheville, Virginia. The church has since been removed to the east side of town on Church Street. The grave marker, a white sand store head-piece stands about three feet high is located at the foot of a chestnut tree planted at his burial. Inscription reads: "In memory of Rev. Casper Yost, born March 11, 1785, died Jan 5 1850 - Eighteen Years a Pastor of the Methodist Church and Forty-Eight Years a Member".

The Olive Branch Methodist Church and Cemetery, Wythe County, Virginia
by Edgar M. "Russ" Bralley
Bristol, Virginia
with some notes by Luther Armbrister

On Christmas Eve of 1784, the Methodist Episcopal Church in America was formally established by action of the "Christmas Conference" at Lovely Lane Protestant Episcopal Chapel in Baltimore, Maryland. The Methodist movement was an offshoot of the Protestant Episcopal Church, also called the Established Church, Anglican Church or the Church of England. Rev. Thomas Cooke, who had been sent to America by John Wesley for this purpose, convened the conference. At that time (Bishop) Francis Asbury was elected as "general superintendent" by the sixty preachers in attendance. At another conference in Baltimore in 1828, a group of church members, known as the "Associated Methodist Churches," began to move to form a completely separate denomination, which would come to be known as the Methodist Protestant Church or the Methodist Episcopal Church in America. It was around this time that the Bralley family were attending camp meetings in Wythe County, which was founded circa 1819. It is likely the Bralleys were impressed by visits of Bishop Francis Asbury, for they are mentioned as adherents attending the Asbury Campground meetings in the mid-1820's. The Olive Branch Methodist Church was founded in 1833 on land donated to the Methodist Church by James Bralley and his wife, Hannah Smyth Bralley. It is not known why they chose to name the church Olive Branch, but there is speculation that it was upon the brigantine Olive Branch that John Bralley traveled from Ireland to the American colonial port of Philadelphia in the mid 1700's. The Rev. James Fisher (10 December 1810 - 27

December 1888) served the church and help raise funds for the second church building, was "two years an exhorter and forty-seven years a faithful preacher." A memorial to Rev. Fisher is located in the present church. There are numerous unmarked graves in the cemetery, including many of the older Bralley graves. Family tradition holds that James Bralley (1765 - 1854) is actually buried under the church, but the author believes that is not true. His oldest son, Samuel Guy Bralley died in the year preceeding James' death (1795 - 1853) and his grave is well away from the church and in fairly good condition, althought the stone is broken. John Bralley's (1797 - 1866) stone is new and replaces an older one, now missing. It was placed there by the descendants of Cabble Bralley in the late 1990's. It is unknown if immigrant ancestor John Bralley of Ireland is buried in the cemetery. The Olive Branch Methodist Church cemetery is adjacent to the Olive Branch Methodist Church, located on two acres on Virginia State Route 604 just north of the intersection with Virginia State Route 619, between Porter's Crossroads and Austinville. The cemetery is both marked and named on the U.S.G.S. topographic map for Austinville. A great deal of this cemetery data was probably collected in 1983 and supplemented in 2002. In the card file in the Kegley Library the cemetery is identified as Olive Branch.

The Olive Branch Methodist Episcopal Church Deed, 1833

This Indenture made this 9 day of March in the year of our lord one thousand and thirty three Between James Brawley and Hannah Brawley his wife of the first part, and Joshua Percival, Wendell Swecker, Burgess Williams, Burrell Wall, John Nuckol and Jacob Fisher, Trustees in trust for the uses and purposes herein after mentioned of the other part, all of the County of Wythe and State of Virginia.

Witnessed that the said Jas. Brawley and Hannah Brawley, his wife, for and in consideration of the sum of ----- dollar to them in hand paid and upon the sealing and delivery of these presents the receipt whereof is herby acknowledged hath given, granted, bargained, sold, released, confirmed and conveyed, and by these presents doth give, grant, bargain, sell, release, confirm and convey unto them the said Joshua Percival, Wendell Swecker, Burgess Williams, Burrell Wall, John Nuckol and Jacob Fisher, and their successors (trustees in trust for the uses and purposes herein after mentioned and declared) all the estate, right, title, interest, property, claim and demand whatsoever, either in law or equity, which he the said James Brawley & wife hath in or upon all and singular a certain lot or piece of land, situate, lying and being in the County and State aforesaid, on the waters of New River, bounded and butted as follows, viz; Beginning on a small ash in a hollow near a spring, thence S. 5° E. 30 ¼ poles, crossing the road to a black oak near the same, thence S. 81 ½ W. 25 poles to a large chestnut, thence N. 33° E. 40 ¼ poles to the Beginning containing and laid out for two acres one rood & twenty nine poles, together with all and singular the houses, woods, water, ways, privileges, and appurtenances thereto belonging or in any wise appertaining: To have and to hold all the singular the above mentioned and described lot or piece of land, situate, lying & being as aforesaid, together with all and singular the houses, woods, waters, ways and privileges thereto belonging, or in any wise appertaining unto them the said Joshua Percival, Wendell Swecker, Burgess Williams, Burwell Wall, John Nuckoll & Jacob Fisher and

their successors in office forever, in trust, that they shall erect and build, or cause to be erected & built, thereon, a house or place of worship for the use of the members of the Methodist Episcopal Church in the United States of America, according to the rules and discipline which from time to time may be agreed upon and adopted by the Ministers and preachers of the said Church, at their general conferences in the United States of America, and in further trust and confidence that they shall at all times, forever hereafter, permit such ministers and preachers, belonging to said Church, as shall from time to time be duly authorized by the general conferences of the Ministers and preachers of the said Methodist Episcopal Church, or by the annual conferences, authorized by the said general conferences, to preach and expound God's holy word therein; and in further trust and confidence that as often as any one or more of the trustees herein before mentioned shall die, or cease to be a member or members of the said Church, according to the rules and discipline as aforesaid, then & in such case it shall be the duty of the stationed minister or preacher (authorized as aforesaid) who shall have the pastoral charge of the members of the said Church, to call a meeting of the remaining trustees, as soon as conveniently may be: and when so met, the said minister or preacher shall proceed to nominate one or more persons to fill the place or places of him or them whose office or offices has (or have) been vacated as aforesaid. Provided the person or persons also nominated shall have been one year a member or members of the said Church immediately preceding such nomination, and be at least twenty one years of age; and the said trustees, so assembled, shall proceed to elect and be a majority of votes, appoint the person or persons so nominated to fill the vacancy or vacancies, in order to keep up the number of six trustees forever. And the said James Brawley and Hannah Brawley his wife doth by these presents warrant and forever defend, all and singular the before mentioned and described lot or piece of land with the appurtenances thereto belonging unto them the said Joshua Percival, Wendell Swecker, Burgess Williams, Burrell Wall, John Nuckoll and Jacob Fisher and their successors, chosen and appointed as aforesaid, from the claim or claims of them the said James Bralley and Hannah Brawley his wife, their heirs and assigns and from the claim or claims of all persons whatever.
In testimony whereof the said James Brawley and Hannah Brawley his wife hath hereunto set their hands and seals the day and year aforesaid.

Sealed in presence of: James Bralley (Seal)
Hannsh S. Bralley (Seal)

Virginia: Wythe County, to wit:
We, Casper Yost and William Crawford, Justices of the Peace in the County and State aforesaid, do hereby certify that James Brawley, party to a certain deed bearing date the 9: day of March 1833 and hereunto annexed, personally appeared before us in our county aforesaid, and acknowledged the same to be his act and deed, and desired us to certify the said acknowledgment to the Clerk of the County Court of Wythe in order that the said deed may be recorded.
Given under our hands & seals this 9 day of March 1833.

Casper Yost (Seal)
William Crawford (Seal)

Virginia: Wythe County, to wit:
We, Casper Yost and William Crawford, Justices of the peace in the County and State aforesaid do hereby certify that Hannah Brawley, wife of James Brawley, parties to a certain deed bearing date on the 9 day of March 1833 and hereunto annexed, personally appeared before us in our County aforesaid, and being examined by us privily and apart from her husband and having the deed aforesaid fully explained to her the said Hannah Brawley, she acknowledged the same to be her act and deed and declared that she had willingly signed, sealed, and delivered the same, and that she wished not to retract it. Given under our hands and seals this 9 day of March 1833.

Casper Yost (Seal)
William Crawford (Seal)

Virginia: At a Court held for Wythe County, at the Courthouse on Monday the 14: day of October 1833. This Deed of bargain & sale was returned to Court, and with the certificate of acknowledgement & privy examination annexed, ordered to be recorded.
Teste: J. P. Mathess, Cl

Children of James Casper Yost and Euphemia Hughes Bickle:

Lewis Marshall Yost born April 26, 1826

Mary Yost born February 02, 1807

John Cooper Yost born January 23, 1809 in Wythe County, Virginia, died October 29, 1891 Equality, Illinois, and is buried in the Old Cemetery there. John married Julia Ann Sibley born March 14, 1814 in Kentucky, died October 19, 1863. They were married March 31, 1835. Their children were Enos Sybly Yost born 1852, Casper C. Yost born 1837, John Yost born 1840, Euphemia Yost born 1841, William Fletcher Yost born 1848, Elizabeth Yost born unknown.

John Cooper and Julia Ann Sibley Yost Marriage License

1860 Census Gallatin County Illinois, Town of Equality

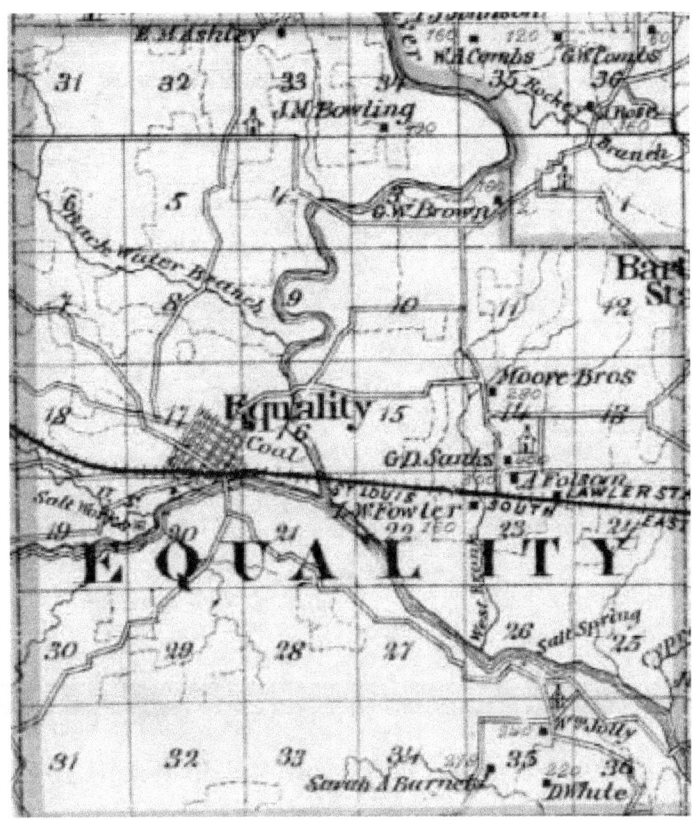

1867 Equality Illinois Map

John Cooper Yost's son John Yost married Mary E. Gregg born in Illinois. John fought in the Civil War and received a pension.

John Yost born 1835 in Illinois, married Mary Elizabeth Gregg born 1845 in Illinois. They were married 1880 in Gallatin, Illinois. They had the following children: William Cooper Yost born August 1863, Casper Turner Yost born January 1866, Joel Francis Yost born 1869, Elizabeth "Lizzie" Ann Yost born October 1872,

Hugh Lewis Yost, Casper Turner Yost's son, World War II Draft Registration

John Yost's Civil War Pension

John is noted in the following book

HISTORY

OF

Gallatin, Saline, Hamilton, Franklin and Williamson Counties,

ILLINOIS.

From the Earliest Time to the Present; together with Sundry and Interesting Biographical Sketches, Notes, Reminiscences, Etc., Etc.

ILLUSTRATED.

Chicago:
THE GOODSPEED PUBLISHING CO.,
1887.

Front Cover

LIST OF COUNTY OFFICERS.

The county officers of Gallatin County have been as follows: *Sheriffs.*—Marmaduke S. Davenport, George Robinson, Ephraim Hubbard, Dr. Henry Boyers, John Lane, 1833; Thomas Tong, 1842; John T. Walters, 1848; Joseph B. Barger, 1850; Richard Richeson, 1853; Thomas Wilson, 1854; James Davenport, 1855; James H. McMintry, 1857; John T. Walters, 1858; Parker B. Pillow, 1862; John M. Eddy, 1863; George B. Hick, 1865; W. L. Blackard, 1867; George B. Hick, 1869; Joel Cook, 1871; John Yost, 1875-80, inclusive; Robert J. Bruce, 1885-86, and J. F. Nolen, 1886 to the present time.

Page 43

GALLATIN COUNTY.

House, and J. M. Wasson in 1875. For governor in 1880 Gallatin County cast for S. M. Cullom 1,052 votes, Lyman Trumbull 1,567, and for A. J. Streeter (Greenbacker) 18. In 1882 the vote for the various officers was—Congress: Townshend, 1,555; Ross, 986; State senator: Blanchard (Democrat) 1,448; Morris (Republican) 1,043; representatives: Bowman (Democrat) 2,358; Gregg (Democrat) 2,198; Boyer (Republican) 1,429; McCartney (Republican) 1,469; county judge: E. D. Youngblood (Democrat) 1,302; Milton Bartley (Independent Democrat) 700; Rhoades (Republican) 460; sheriff: Bruce (Democrat) 1,425; Yost (Republican) 1,077; clerk of the county court: Silas Cook, 2,247, no opposition; treasurer: Mayhew (Democrat) 1,182; Smyth (Republican) 1,292. In 1886 the vote was as follows— State Treasurer: Ricker (Democrat) 1,579; Farmer (Republican) 1,240; congressman: townshend (Democrat) 1,722; Martin (Republican) 1,015; State senator: Richeson (Democrat) 1,454; Yost (Republican) 1,273; county judge: Youngblood (Democrat)

Page 65

HISTORY OF ILLINOIS. 167

The vote on State senator was, for John Yost, Republican, 1,870; J. D. Richeson, Democrat, 1,708. County Clerk, J. H. Pearce, Republican, 1,857; W. E. Burnett, Democrat, 1,713. Sheriff, W. W. Largent, Republican, 1,890; W. C. Baker, Democrat, 1,682; County Treasurer, P. Taylor, Republican, 1,808; Alsey Harris, Democrat, 1,737. County superintendent of schools, James E. Jobe, Republican, 1,847; G. B. Parsons, Democrat, 1,708. County commissioner, J. L. Cain, Republican, 1,906; Lewis Baker, Democrat, 1,665. The only Democrat officer now in the county is John J. Parish, for State's attorney, elected in 1884. In the Forty-ninth Representative District the Republicans elected two representatives to the General Assembly, William G. Sloan and Simon S. Barger, and the Democrats one, J. F. Taylor.

Page 167

men, and raised quite large families." Other early settlers of Cave Township were John McCreery with his family, and his son Alexander with his young wife, who came from Kentucky in 1817. The former settled in the place now known as the Fancy farm. Alexander McCreery brought his household and kitchen furniture along with him in a pair of saddle bags. He settled the farm now occupied by Judge Wm. Elstun. Aaron Neal and his brother Moses, settled near the present site of Parrish, in 1812. Isaac Moberly, John Hall, Nathan Clampet, John W. Swafford, Nathaniel Jones, John Plasters, Wm. Jackson, David Williams, James Isaacs, Thomas Lampley, J. L. Cantrell, John Harlow and Henry Yost, were all early settlers in the southeastern part of the county. John Jones and his son John, and his son Wiley, the father of W. R. Jones, the ex-sheriff of Franklin County, came from Tennessee in 1830, and settled in Cave Township.

Page 340

SOCIETIES.

Benton Lodge, No. 64, F. & A. M., was organized in 1848 and received its charter from the Grand Lodge of Illinois, bearing date of October 5 of that year. Its charter members were Samuel K. Casey, W. M.; George W. Akin, S. W.; Walter S. Akin, J. W.; Tilman B. Cantrell, Wm. A. Denning, W. S. Crawford, Robert Yost and Isaac Mulkey. All of these brothers have passed on to that "undiscovered country, from whose bourne no traveler returns." This lodge has now about seventy-five members, and is in a flourishing condition.

Unknown Robert Yost Page 411

James Casper Yost and Euphemia Hughes Bickle children cont'd:

James Lockhart Yost born March 07, 1811, Wythe County, Virginia, died February 23, 1868. James married Nancy Ellen Wygal born 1813.

Margaret Bickle Yost born June 05, 1813, Wythe County, Virginia. Margaret married Abraham Hamilton Goodpasture on October 11, 1842 in Marion County, Virginia. Abraham was born July 10, 1810, died September 8, 1854

Adeline Cooper Yost born September 05, 1815, Wythe County, Virginia, died June 13, 1885. Adeline married William Grossclose on April 23, 1836 in Wythe County, Virginia.

Adaline Cooper Yost (Grossclose) Grave Marker Bland, Bland, Virginia, United States

William Owen Yost born March 01, 1818, Wytheville, Wythe County, Virginia, died May 24, 1890, Buried at Jeffersonville Cemetery, Tazewell, Virginia. William married Elizabeth Jane Whitman on November 3, 1845. Elizabeth was born October 21, 1827, Virginia, died August 18, 1898.

Fletcher Harris Yost born January 05, 1821, Wythe County, Virginia. Died 1874, Buried at Equality, Gallatin County, Illinois. Fletcher married Susan Daughtery on June 03, 1858 in Gallatin Illinois.

Fletcher Harris Yost 1864 IRS Tax Assessment, Illinois.

Henry Adams Yost born September 23, 1823, Wythe County, Virginia, died July 14, 1871, buried in Virginia died of Potts disease of the spine. He was married, his wife is uknown.

Jane Yost born May 15, 1830, Virginia, died August 17, 1831.

Ellen Yost born 1835, Tazewell County, Virginia. Ellen married Francis M. Mitchem. Francis on March 15, 1869 in McDowell County, W.V.. Francis was born 1835, Tazewell County, Virginia.

Elizabeth Yost, born 1771, Washington County, Maryland; died 1798, near Middlebrook, Virginia of Smallpox. She married John David Greiner May 23, 1793 at Tinkling Springs Church, Augusta County, Virginia presided over by Reverend John McCue (marriage record Vol 2, page 310 of Augusta, Virginia). They had one child Jacob born 1795 before the whole family died of Smallpox in 1798.

Jacob Yost, born Bet. 1773 - 1774, Virginia; died 1874, the home of his son Dr. William Yost, Greeneville, Kentucky, and is buried in the Old Cemetery there. He married Matilda Johnson born born March 31, 1793. She died July 04, 1852. They had the children, William Henry, Eliza, Elvira Elizabeth, Sarah Catherine, and Chatman. He then married Sarah McDonald.

J. W. Diederich stands beside the gravestone of Eliza Yost.
The inscription reads:
Eliza Yost
DIED NOV 20, 1887
AGED 65 YRS, 5 MO.
18 DAYS
"A precious one from us has gone
A voice welcomed is stilled
_____ is vacant in our home
_____ above can be filled"

The Yost brothers, Henry Marshall, Jacob, and George left Virginia early in 1819 via Clareborne, Tennessee, where George settled. Henry and Jacob moved to Gallatin, Tennessee, then to Logan County, Kentucky where Jacob settled. Henry moved on to Benton, Illinois.

Jacob was a Presbyterian - his father was German Reform which is Presbyterian.

Jacob owned and operated a "Tavern", located about 2 miles east of Auburn. It was a log house and was razed not many years ago, and a fairly new brick house stands there today. Some of the old trees stand on the yard yet. The tavern of that day served a multiple purpose, it provided food, bedding and drinks, also food and care for horses of the overnight guests, and sometimes even a fresh team (of horses) in case of an emergency. These places were sometimes called "Stagecoach Inns" and were located about every 10 miles apart in the early days.

John Yost, born 1776; married Christina Woland, 06 June 1799, Augusta County, Virginia. John Yost died in June of 1870 in Clearfork Tazewell Virginia. John Yost was the third child of Henry Yost and Polly Waggoner. Christina Woland was mentioned in her father's will. Record also show John Yost married Adeline Cooper in 1805. Adeline Cooper Yost died 1860 in Clearfork Tazewell Virginia. The records also show they had the following children, William Henry Yost born 1800, Lozenzo Dow Yost born 1803, Henry B Yost born 1808, Mary Polly Yost born 1809, Adeline Yost born 1820, John Yost born 1821, David Genesis Yost born 1822, Euphemia Yost 1825, Julia Yost 1828.

Children of John Yost, Christina Woland, and Adeline Cooper were:

Adeline Yost born 1805

William Henry Yost born February 5, 1800 married Temperance "Tempy" Bonham on April 08, 1830 in Tazewell County, Virginia. They had the following children, Henry Yost born 1830, William Bonham Yost born 1832, David Yost born 1840.

Census 1860 Tazewell Virginia

Census 1880 Clear Fork Tazewell Virginia

William Henry Yost and Temperance had the following children:

Henry Yost born January 1830 Tazewell Virginia, died August 21, 1865 in Croftsville, Tazewell, Virginia.

David Yost born 1850 in Tazewell County Virginia, died 1850.

William Bonham Yost born December 14, 1832 in Clear Fork Tazewell County, Virginia. William married Gilliam Louvenia "Gillie Ann" Shrader on November 25, 1858. Gillie Ann was born July 1837 in Virginia.

Census 1860 Tazewell Virginia

Gilliam Louvenia "Gillie Ann" Shrader Grave Marker

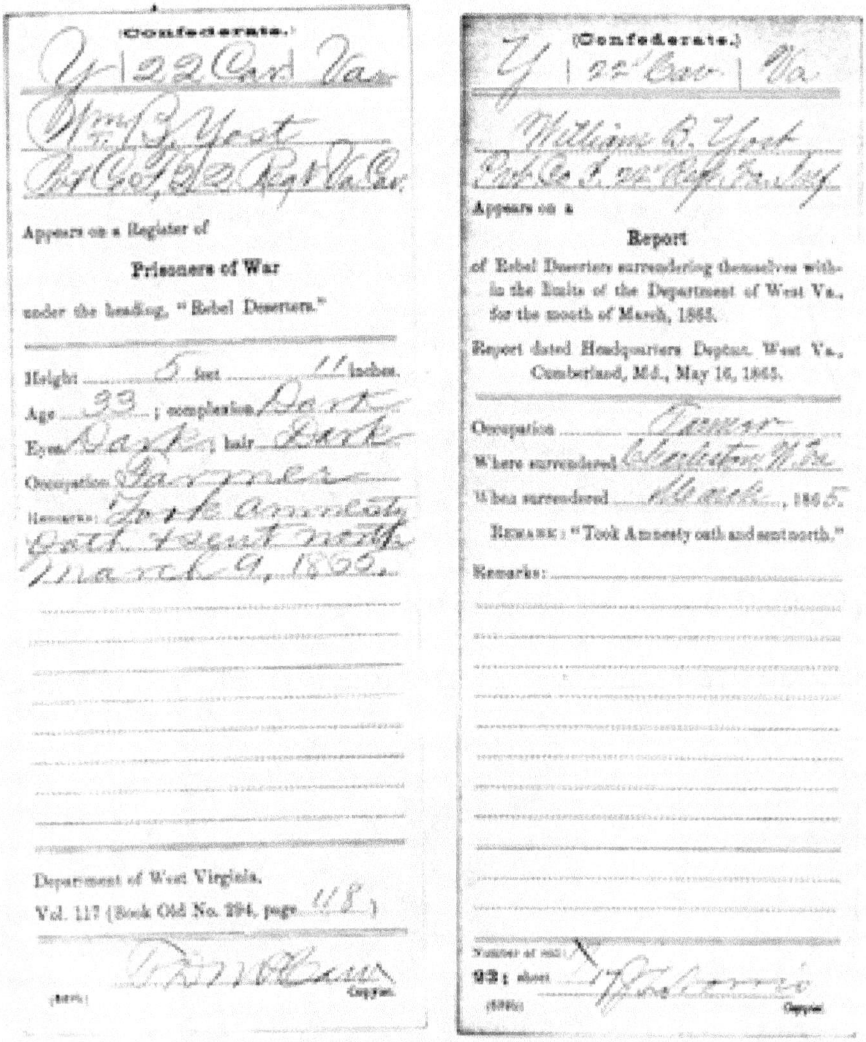

(Confederate.)

Y | 22 Cav. Va.

Wm. B. Yost
Pvt Co. F, 22 Reg't Va. Cav.

Appears on a Register of

Prisoners of War

under the heading, "Rebel Deserters."

Height 5 feet 11 inches.
Age 33; complexion Dark
Eyes Dark; hair Dark
Occupation Farmer
Remarks: Took amnesty oath & sent north March 9, 1865.

Department of West Virginia.
Vol. 117 (Book Old No. 294, page 118)

[illegible] Copyist.

(Confederate.)

Y | 22 Cav. | Va.

William B. Yost
Pvt. Co. F, 22 Reg't Va. Inf.

Appears on a

Report

of Rebel Deserters surrendering themselves within the limits of the Department of West Va., for the month of March, 1865.

Report dated Headquarters Deptmt. West Va., Cumberland, Md., May 16, 1865.

Occupation Farmer
Where surrendered Charleston W. Va.
When surrendered March, 1865.
Remark: "Took Amnesty oath and sent north."
Remarks:

Number of roll:
23; sheet

[illegible] Copyist.

William Bonham Yost Confederate Civil War Papers

William Bonham Yost and Gillie had the following children

Christina Martha. Yost born 1860
George Washington Yost born 1861 - 1919
David Sylvester Yost born 1862 - 1947
Sarah Annabelle Yost born 1864 - 1954
William Henry Yost born Oct. 8, 1866 died May 8, 1938 in Maple Hill Cemetary Bluefield Tazewell County Virginia, USA married Rachel Louthan

Maple Hill Cemetary Bluefield Tazewell County Virginia

Robert Sheffield "Sheffey" Yost born 1869 - 1936

Joseph Eldridge Yost born August 28, 1869 died 1945 Falls Mills, Tazewell, Virginia

Joseph Eldridge Yost

Joseph Eldridge Yost Grave Marker

Joseph also married Elizabeth Clementine Franklin in 1891. Elizabeth was born March 4, 1864 in Sumner Tennessee. She died October 30, 1934 in Falls Mills, Virginia.

Elizabeth Clementine Franklin Yost

Elizabeth Clementine Franklin Yost Grave Marker

Joseph and Elizabeth had the following children:

Virgie May Yost born 1892 died 1945
William Kyte Yost born July 20, 1894 in Tazewell Virginia, died October 4, 1949 in Baker Florida

William Kyte Yost

William Kyte Yost Grave Marker

Bryan Jospeph Yost born April 30, 1900 in Virginia. Died December 21, 1972 in Durham North Carolina.

Bryan Joseph Yost

William Bonham Yost and Gillia Anne Luvena Schrader Yost had the following children cont'd:

Mary Alice Yost born 1872, died 1954
Ulysses Sidney Yost born February 3, 1873 in Pinhook, Tazewell, Virginia, died April 22, 1953 in Washington, Oregon

Sally, Sid, Eva Yost

Sid Yost

Ulysses Sidney Yost Grave Marker Tazewell Virginia

James Charles Yost born May 22, 1876 in Pinhook, Tazewell, Virginia, died August 8, 1954 in Malheur, Oregon.

Frances "Frank" Marion Yost born February 21, 1878 in Pinhook, Tazewell, Virginia

Lula T. Yost born February 25, 1880 in Pinhook, Tazewell, Virginia. Married Samuel Preston McBride.

Bishop Price Yost born September 3, 1884 in Pinhook, Tazewell, Virginia. Died Rocky Gap, Bland, Virginia.

Ulysis Sidney Yost list of Children

Polly "Mary" Yost born 1812
Lorenzo Dow Yost born 1803 in Tazewell County Virginia, died 1879. Lorenzo married Polly Stump born 1808 in Tazewell County Virginia, died after 1880. Married 1825 in Tazewell County Virginia.

Children of Lorenzo Dow Yost and Polly Stump were:
John M. Yost born December 05, 1825 married Martha Carnes born November 28, 1830 in Virginia
William M. Yost born 1828
Lorenzo Dow Yost born 1836
George Washington Yost born November 27, 1832 in Tazewell County Virginia, died April 25, 1863 in Missouri. George married Ellie "Aily" Ann Poe born November 15, 1837 in Tennessee, died November 20, 1900 in Placer Oregon.

Children of George Washington Yost and Ellie "Aily" Ann Poe were:
George Lorenzo Yost born December 14, 1862

George Washington Yost

Ellie "Aily" Ann Poe and son George Lorenzo Yost

Emily Yost 1842
Harris Erastus "Harrison" Yost born March 18, 1845 died April 29, 1905
Married Elizabeth Bourne born October 11, 1849 died May 13, 1945

Burial: Maple Hill Cemetery Bluefield Tazewell County Virginia, USA

Harris E. Yost and Elizabeth had the following children:

Walter Vertegan Yost married Ida M. Shawver born Jul. 24, 1871 died Apr. 3, 1964

Burial: Maple Hill Cemetery Bluefield Tazewell County Virginia, USA

    James Bourne Yost
    Martha "Mattie" Belle Yost
    Lorenzo Dow Yost
    Fannie Parris Yost
    Charles George Yost
    Bertie Alice Yost
    Margaret Armenta Yost
    Harry Erastus Yost
    Maria Louise Yost
    Ott Gillett Yost
    Arly Gypsy Yost

Charles Alexander Yost born August 28, 1849 died July 10, 1913 married May 12, 1874 to Elizabeth Nuckles.

Burial: Maple Hill Cemetery Bluefield Tazewell County Virginia, USA

Elizabeth J. Yost born 1836
Sarah A. Yost born 1841
Paris Yost born 1844

Children of John Yost, Christina Woland, and Adeline Cooper continued:

John Yost
David George Yost
Euphemia Yost
Julia Yost

Rebecca Yost, born 1778; died 1850, Stauton, Augusta County, Virginia; married Sampson Eagon, born February 06, 1769 in Hagerstown, Maryland. They were married 22 June 1796, Augusta County, Virginia. Rebecca Yost was the fourth child of Henry Yost and Polly Waggoner. Sampson Eagon was one of the founders of the First Methodist Church established in Augusta County, Virginia. For several years prior to the erection of the church the services were held in his wagon shop "on the rear of his home lot" and to this day his place is known as Gospel Hill. They had the following children, David, Rebecca, John, Sally, Catherine, William, James born March 1, 1818, and Elizabeth.

Henry Marshall Yost, born 23 May 1780, Elizabeth Towne, Washington County, Maryland; died 22 March 1846, buried on his farm known as Fancy Farm in Franklin County, Illinois. (See Henry Marshall's Life later in book)

William Yost, born. 1788 in Augusta, Staunton, Virginia. William Yost was the eighth child of Henry and Polly (Waggoner) Yost. William joined the Army and was still in service in 1828.

Fletcher Harris Yost, born 1791 in Augusta, Staunton, Virginia.

David Greiner Yost, born 1798; died 1843, of suicide. David married Maria L. Carter, but had the following children, R.D. Yost, Olive Carter Yost, George T. Yost, Mary Elizabeth Yost, Melissa Olive Yost, Eunice Alma Yost, Alice E. Yost, Ida M. Yost,

David was admitted to the Maryland Bar from Fort Cumberland in 1818, age 25.

On June 17, 1823 he purchased a Pew in the Episcopal Church of Hagerstown, Maryland for $151.00 plus annual rent of $30.00. In 1840, David G. Yost was a church Trustee.

He was a prominent member of the Hagerstown Bar and became wealthy in business real estate, but through a venture in a promotion scheme, lost his fortune and in 1843 committed suicide. A column press notice said "Hagerstown had lost, in the death of David G. Yost, one of it's most prominent citizens."

David and Maria's son George T. Yost married Hattie Fletcher. George T. Yost fought in the Civil War and received a pension

George T. Yost Civil War Pension

George Washington Yost (REV.). George is not mentioned in the list of the children of Henry Yost and Polly Waggoner. However, he is mentioned twice in the biography of his brother, Jacob Yost. First, it is mentioned that George and his brother Casper (James Casper Yost) were Methodist Ministers. Their father was German Reform, which is

Presbyterian. Second, it is mentioned that George left Virginia early in 1819 with his brothers Henry Marshall and Jacob via Clareborne, Tennessee, where George settled.

Note: The Yost brothers, Henry Marshall, Jacob, and George left Virginia early in 1819 via Clareborne, Tennessee, where George settled. Henry and Jacob moved to Gallatine, Tennessee, then to Logan County, Kentucky where Jacob settled. Henry moved on to Benton, Illinois.

Jacob was a Presbyterian - his father was German Reform which is Presbyterian.

Jacob owned and operated a "Tavern", located about 2 miles east of Auburn. It was a log house and was razed not many years ago, and a fairly new brick house stands there today. Some of the old trees stand on the yard yet. The tavern of that day served a multiple purpose, it provided food, bedding and drinks, also food and care for horses of the overnight guests, and sometimes even a fresh team (of horses) in case of an emergency. These places were sometimes called "Stagecoach Inns" and were located about every 10 miles apart in the early days.

Henry Marshall Yost's Life

Henry was born May 23, 1780 in Elizabeth Town, Washington Co. Maryland. He married first Mary "Polly" Early born May 30, 1781 in Virginia. The had the following children, Nancy Mitchell born June 26, 1806, John Wesley born September 24, 1807, Jane born July 16, 1809, Henry Marshall born June 24, 1811, Mary Wagner born January 10, 1813, Betsy Greiner born November 11, 1814, David Greiner born March 06, 1817, Samuel Eagon born December 07, 1818, and Roberts Early born September 30, 1820.

Henry Marshall Yost was born 23 May 1780 in Elizabeth Towne, Washington County, Maryland, and died 22 March 1846. He is buried on his farm in Franklin County, Illinois. He married (1) MARY POLLY EARLY 18 August 1805 in Botetourt Co, IL. She was born 30 May 1781 in VA and died 10 July 1822 in Franklin Co, IL. He married (2) LYDIA ELEANOR ROBERTS in at or near Roberts Settlement, near the other Jordon

Fort on 12 November 1822. She was born 17 December 1795 in Maryland and died 15 September 1875 in Metropolis, IL at the age of 80 years.

KNOW ALL MEN BY THESE PRESENTS, That we, David G Yost & John W Yost & Wesley Yost of the County of Franklin and state of Illinois, are held and firmly bound unto the people of the State of Illinois in the penal sum of Four Thousand Dollars, current money of the United States, which payment, well and truly to be made and performed, we and each of us, bind ourselves, our heirs, executors, administrators, jointly, severally, and firmly by these presents. Witness our hands and seals, this 27th day of April A.D. 1846. The Condition of the above Obligation is such, that if the said David G Yost & John W Yost Administrators of all and singular the goods and chattels, rights and credits of Henry Yost Sr. deceased, do make, or cause to be made, a true and perfect inventory of all and singular the goods and chattels, rights and credits of the said deceased, which shall come to the hands, possession, or acknowledge of the said David G Yost & John W Yost as such administrators or to the hands of any person or persons for them; and the same so made do exhibit, or cause to be exhibited, in the court of the Probate for the said County of Franklin agreeably to law, and such goods and chattels, rights and credits, do well and truly administer according to law, and all the rest of the said goods chattels, rights and credits, which shall be found remaining upon the account of the said administrators, the same being first examined and allowed by the Court of Probate shall deliver and pay unto such person or persons, respectively, as may be legally entitled thereto; and further, do make a just and true account of all their actings and doings therein, when thereunto required by the said Court; and if it shall hereafter appear that any last will and testament was made by the deceased, and the same be proved in Court, and letters testamentary or of administration be obtained thereon, and the said David G Yost & John W Yost do, in such case, on being required thereto, render and deliver up the letters of administration, granted to them as aforesaid, and shall in general do and perform all other acts which may at any time be required of them by law, then this obligation to be void, otherwise to remain in full force and virtue.

Signed, sealed and delivered in the presence of

C. Palmer

David G Yost   SEAL
John W Yost   SEAL
Wesley Yost   SEAL

We John W Yost & David G Yost do solemnly swear, that we will well and truly administer on all and singular the goods and chattels, rights and credits of Henry Yost Senr deceased; and pay all such claims and charges against his estate, so far as his goods and chattels and effects shall extend, and the law charge us and that we will do and perform all other acts required of us by law, to the best of our knowledge and abilities.

Sworn to and subscribed before me, this 27th day of April 1846

Saml N Casey Clk
Co Com Court

David G Yost
John W Yost

Henry Marshall Yost's Will being Probated

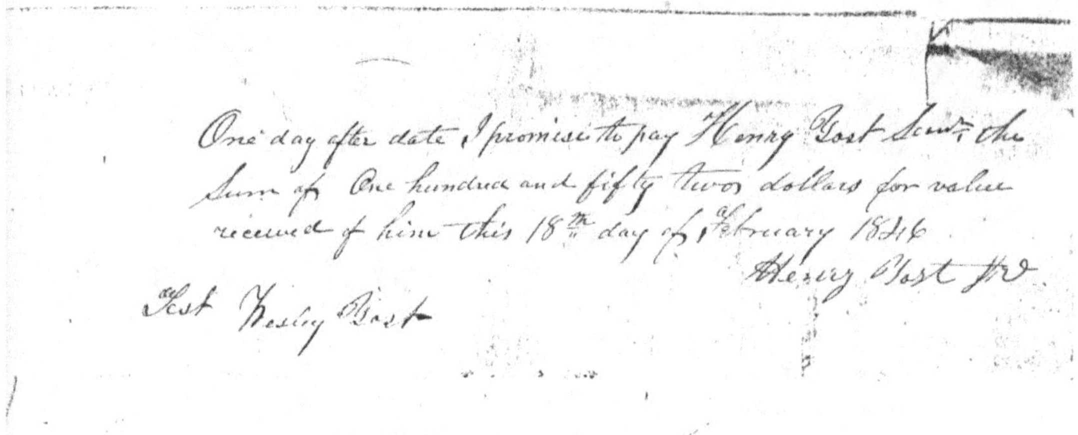

One day after date I promise to pay Henry Yost Senr the Sum of One hundred and fifty two dollars for value received of him this 18th day of February 1846

Henry Yost Jr.

Test Wesley Yost

Henry Marshall Yost's Will being Probated

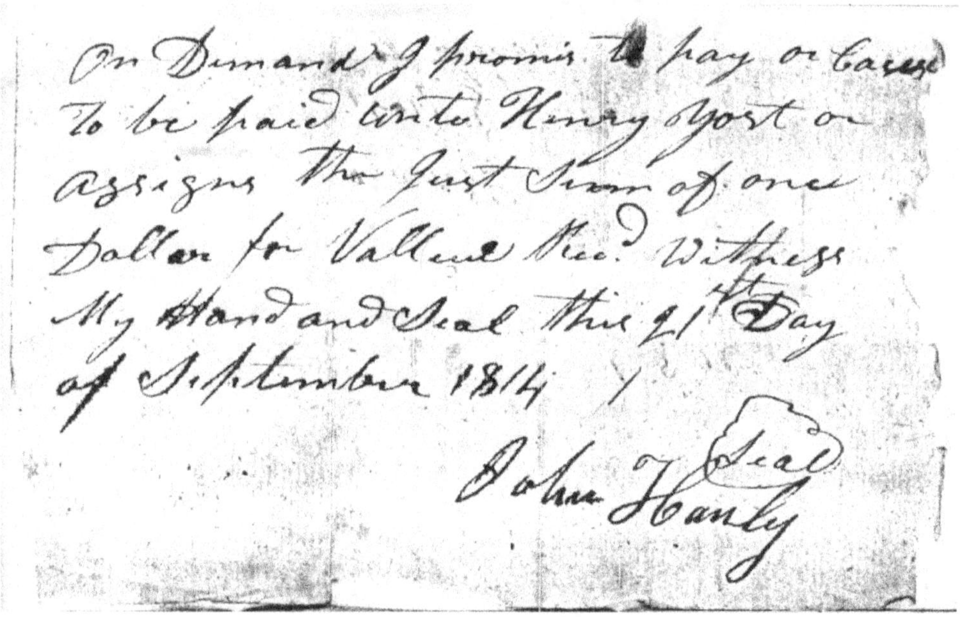

On Demand I promise to pay or Cause To be paid unto Henry Yost or assigns the Just Sum of one Dollar for Vallue Recd Witness My Hand and Seal this 21st Day of September 1814

John Hanly (Seal)

Henry Marshall Yost's Will being Probated

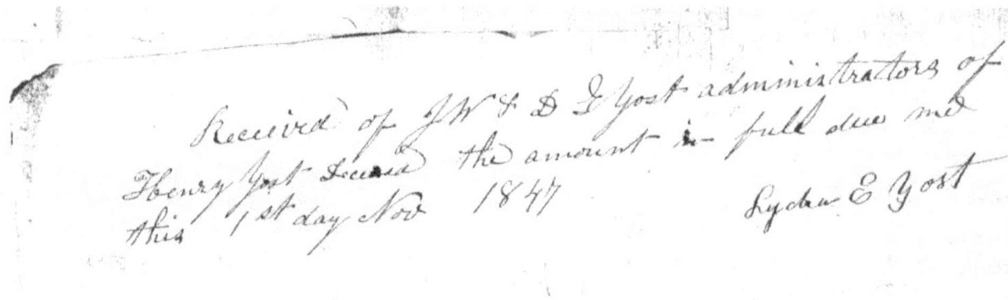

Received of J W & D I Yost administrators of Henry Yost deceased the amount in full due me this 1st day Nov 1847

Lydia E Yost

Henry Marshall Yost's Will being Probated

Estate of Mr Henry Yost Dec'd to J. Smith Dr.
by D. Yos[t]

March 23d 1846	to visit & medicine for W.J.Yos[t]	
do 24th	to visit &c.	
do 28th	to one vial of Drops	
do do	to Pills &c	
do 30th	to visit &c	
do do	to one vial of Drops	
do do	to Purgative Pill	
do do	to Tonic do	
do 31st	to visit &c	
do do	to Antimony & Nitre	
do do	to Blue & Cathartic Pills	
April 2nd	to visit & medicine &c. &c.	
	Whole Amt.	

Henry Marshall Yost's Will being probated

1845	Henry Yost to John M[?] Dr		
	" making Razor hand[le]		25
	" 2 bench pins [?] band & welding		50
	Repairing plow		18
	Laying do		50
	Sharping 2 plows		25
	mending bolt		12
	making [clep?]		13
	" Iron & making Ring for [?]		18
	Repairing chains		25
	Laying colter		25
	mending Ox ring		13
	mending crank for [?] mill		43
	hook on distepe [?] for do		13
	Sharping 2 plows & cutting screw		37
	making rod cutting do		25
	Sharping plow		12
	turning do & welding on bar		75
	Laying do		50
	do colter		13
	Sharping plow		12
	do do		13
	making latch & catch		13
	Turning plow & welding on bar		75
	welding wing on do		25
	Sharping 2 plows		25
	mending pitchfork		12
	Strapping sythe		25
	Repairing Buggy		50
	Repairing [?] mill [?]		25
1846	Repairing harness	25	7 80
	Repairing Buggy	25	1 00
	do plow	13	8 82
	do do	37	
	Credit by cash		6 00
			2 82

Henry Marshall Yost's Will being Probated

Henry Marshall Yost's Will being Probated

Henry Marshall Yost married first, Mary Polly Early. They had nine children.

In a copy of a letter I have from Kathryn Yost Boyd (that I, Tim Stadler, possess) dated April 10, 1937, Alhambra, California she writes, "He married first, Mary (called Polly) Early, of the Early family of Virginia; an Aunt of General Jubal Early of Confederate fame, Aug 18, 1805, Fincastle, Botetourt Co. Va. She was the daughter of Jame Matten Early and Jane (Gatewood) Early. Mary was born May 30th 1781 Virginia and died July 10, 1822 Franklin Co., Ills., age forty one yrs. The mother of 9 children."

He and Mary "Polly" and eight of their nine children left Virginia around 1819 and moved to Illinois and settled near Fort Jordon, Franklin County, Illinois.

During the trip they were crossing a stream in the wrong place and in deep water and Henry's wife Polly fell out of the wagon. She was saved from drowning but contracted cold fever from which she never fully recovered.

Their youngest son, Roberts Early Yost, was born in their new home "Fancy Farm," just purchased from Mr. John McCreery. Fine breed of stock and poultry were raised here. His rail fences were laid with the precision of a surveyor. Henry was neat and orderly, both at to his person, family, and property. What he did, he did well or not at all. His home, inside and out were scrupulously clean. During the years of his ownership, the farm was the show place of the county and was shown with pride to all new settlers. Polly brought several Silver Leaf Poplar saplings from Virginia which made the farm beautiful. In 1933, four of these trees were still standing by the house. The name "Fancy Farm" was given to the place by Green Mitchell, who ran the store a quarter mile away in 1825. The first Post Office in Corinth Township was at "Fancy Farm" and Henry M. Yost was appointed Postmaster February 19, 1835. Henry was a man of religious honesty and integrity, was a charter member of the Zion Church at Cornith in 1823, and Liberty Church near his home in 1826. As success was measured in his day, he was wealthy and too generous for his own good. When baby Roberts was about two years old, his mother died, leaving seven children, all under fifteen years of age. Two children preceded her in death.

LIBERTY CHURCH AND MARKER NEAR FIRST SETTLEMENT IN FRANKLIN COUNTY

Franklin County Illinois 1867 Map

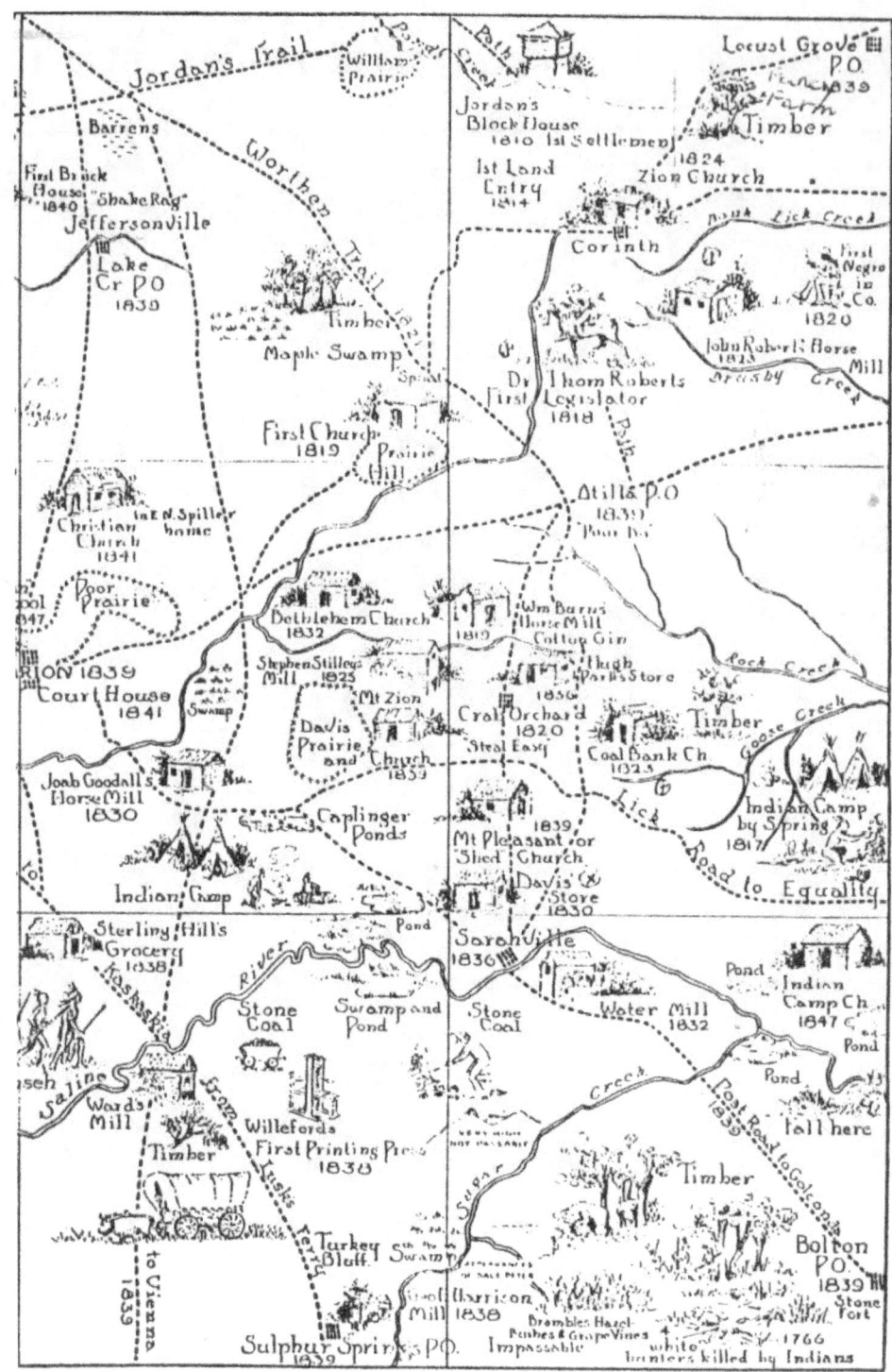

Williamson County Illinois Centennial Pictorial Map

Henry Marshall Yost land Purchase in Franklin County Illinois July 8th, 1838

220

THE UNITED STATES OF AMERICA.

CERTIFICATE No. 4323

To all to whom these Presents shall come, Greeting:

WHEREAS Henry Yost of Franklin County Illinois has deposited in the **GENERAL LAND OFFICE** of the United States, a Certificate of the REGISTER OF THE LAND OFFICE at Shawneetown whereby it appears that full payment has been made by the said Henry Yost according to the provisions of the Act of Congress of the 24th of April, 1820, entitled "An Act making further provision for the sale of the Public Lands," for

the West half of the South West quarter of Section thirty six, in Township seven South, of Range four East, in the District of lands subject to sale at Shawneetown, Illinois, containing eighty acres

according to the official plat of the survey of the said Lands, returned to the General Land Office by the **SURVEYOR GENERAL**, which said tract has been purchased by the said Henry Yost

NOW KNOW YE, That the United States of America, in consideration of the Premises, and in conformity with the several acts of Congress, in such case made and provided, HAVE GIVEN AND GRANTED, and by these presents DO GIVE AND GRANT, unto the said Henry Yost and to his heirs, the said tract above described: **TO HAVE AND TO HOLD** the same, together with all the rights, privileges, immunities, and appurtenances of whatsoever nature, thereunto belonging, unto the said Henry Yost and to his heirs and assigns forever.

In Testimony Whereof, I, Martin Van Buren PRESIDENT OF THE UNITED STATES OF AMERICA, have caused these Letters to be made PATENT, and the SEAL of the GENERAL LAND OFFICE to be hereunto affixed.

GIVEN under my hand, at the CITY OF WASHINGTON, the twenty eighth day of July in the Year of our Lord one thousand eight hundred and thirty eight and of the INDEPENDENCE OF THE UNITED STATES the Sixty third.

BY THE PRESIDENT: Martin Van Buren

By A. Van Buren Jr Sec'y.

Jos S Wilson Acting Recorder of the General Land Office.
ad interim

136

THE UNITED STATES OF AMERICA

CERTIFICATE No. 5259

To all to whom these Presents shall come, Greeting:

WHEREAS Henry Gost, of Franklin County, Illinois,

has deposited in the GENERAL LAND OFFICE of the United States, a Certificate of the REGISTER OF THE LAND OFFICE at Shawneetown whereby it appears that full payment has been made by the said Henry Gost, according to the provisions of the Act of Congress of the 24th of April, 1820, entitled "An Act making further provision for the sale of the Public Lands," for the South East quarter of Section two, in Township eight South, of Range four East, in the District of lands subject to sale at Shawneetown, Illinois, containing one hundred and sixty acres,

according to the official plat of the survey of the said Lands, returned to the General Land Office by the SURVEYOR GENERAL, which said tract has been purchased by the said Henry Gost.

NOW KNOW YE, That the United States of America, in consideration of the Premises, and in conformity with the several acts of Congress, in such case made and provided, HAVE GIVEN AND GRANTED, and by these presents DO GIVE AND GRANT, unto the said Henry Gost,

and to his heirs, the said tract above described: TO HAVE AND TO HOLD the same, together with all the rights, privileges, immunities, and appurtenances of whatsoever nature, thereunto belonging, unto the said

Henry Gost, and to his heirs and assigns forever.

In Testimony Whereof, I, Martin Van Buren PRESIDENT OF THE UNITED STATES OF AMERICA, have caused these Letters to be made PATENT, and the SEAL of the GENERAL LAND OFFICE to be hereunto affixed.

GIVEN under my hand, at the CITY OF WASHINGTON, the twenty eighth day of July in the Year of our Lord one thousand eight hundred and thirty eight and of the INDEPENDENCE OF THE UNITED STATES the Sixty third.

BY THE PRESIDENT: Martin Van Buren

By M. Van Buren Jr. Sec'y.

Jo. S. Wilson, Acting Ad interim
Recorder of the General Land Office.

With the exception of Ewing College, of which mention will herafter be made, the county has never been distinguished for high schools. "In the year 1841 the Legislature incorporated the Benton Academy with Walter S. Akin, John Ewing, John P. Maddox, Zachariah Sullens, Thomas Thompson, John Edgerly, Benjamin Smith, Daniel D. Thomas, Abraham Rea, Wm. Browning, Abel Ward, Silas M. Williams, John R. Williams, Elijah Taylor, Moses Neal, John Dillon, Robert Towns, and Lemuel R. Harrison as trustees. They bought the lot upon which the Benton District School building now stands, and erected a two story frame upon it. But the academy did not prove a success, perhaps for the reason that the Legislature permitted everything taught in it but theology. The building was sold by the trustees, and became the property of the Benton School District. It in time gave way to a more stately edifice, which was erected in 1868. In 1841 an act was passed, by the Legislature of the State, incorporating a college at or within two miles of the residence of Alexander McCreery in this county, to be known as the 'Fancy Farm College' with Alexander McCreery, Henry Yost, Sion H. Mitchell, Richard Cantrell, Wm. Jones, Wm. Mitchell and John Roberts as trustees. The object of that incorporation, as stated in the act, was to promote science and literature. The school did not flourish, however, and nothing now remains of it but the name of 'Fancy Farm.'"

Page 420 - History of Franklin County Illinois

424   FRANKLIN COUNTY.

the most noted of the pioneer Methodist Churches in the county. It grew out of the efforts of Rev. Braxton Parrish and other pioneer settlers, and among the early members thereof were S. H. Mitchell and wife (parents of Rev. J. G. Mitchell, now of Benton), Henry Yost and wife, John Waller and wife, and Alexander McCreery and wife. Although Mr. McCreery killed and skinned the deer on Sunday morning, it seems that through the efforts of the preacher who caught him in that violation of one of God's commands, and perhaps of other Christian settlers, he was soon brought within the fold. This church has always labored with zeal. Henry Yost, David Yost and J. G. Mitchell were local preachers produced by this society, and Rev. R. M. Carter, who has become an eminent minister, was converted in this church, and afterward licensed to preach therein. Among the prominent members of Liberty Church at present are Z. C. Mitchell, W. A. Stewart, Cyrus McCreery, Cyrus and Samuel Tate, Dr. R. Poigndexter, Col. Marvel and Judge Wm. Elstun and their families. It is the strongest church of that denomination within the county, having a membership of about 150. From the *nuclei* of these two pioneer churches others of the same denomination were subsequently established throughout the county. A Methodist Episcopal society was organized at Benton very soon after the town was established, and the church edifice was erected about the year 1851. The present membership is about 132.

Page 424 - History of Franklin County Illinois

Henry married second, Lydia Eleanor Roberts. Lydia lived in the Roberts Settlement near the other Jordon Fort when Henry and Lydia were married. After the death of Henry, Lydia remained at "Fancy Farm" until about 1852, when she moved to Benton, Illinois. Henry and Lydia had six children.

Children of HENRY and MARY POLLY (EARLY) YOST are:

Nancy Mitchell Yost born June 26, 1806

John Wesley Yost was born September 24, 1807 in Fincastle, Botetort, Virginia and died January 14, 1890 in Mount Vernon, Jefferson, Illinois. He married Mary Jane Roberts February 1, 1831. She was born 1811 and died 1851. After Mary Jane's death, he married Sabrina Hobbs.

Jane Yost born July 16, 1809

Notes on Mary Jane Roberts and Wesley Yost

Written by Mrs. Katherine Yost Boyd, Alhambra, California.

Mary Jane, daughter of John Sutton and Margaret Caughey Roberts, was born in Wilson County, Tennessee. She was seven years old when the family made their momentous journey into the new Illinois Country, old enough to have memories of the dangers along the wilderness road - wild animals, Indians, rocky roads, turbulent streams to cross in the covered wagons, the ride on the ferry boat over the Ohio River--also the joy at having arrived at home of Grandfather John Roberts. She sadly recalled in later years the death of her dear mother, a happy, singing Irish girl. But she received kind treatment from her new mother, Sarah Johnson.

With only the advantage of schooling in the little log schoolhouse near their church, and what she got from reading and listening to conversations of her elders, she reached womanhood, and at the age of 20 years married one of the "Yost boys" from the neighboring church (Liberty Community). He was also a stepson of her Aunt Lydia.

Wesley Yost was born to Henry and Mary Early Yost in Botetourt County, Virginia and was about nine when they came to Illinois and bought "Fancy Farm". Wesley filed on land adjoining that of his father-in-law. He was a good farmer and progressive, for before long he set up a carding machine. This relieved the women of the neighborhood of much tedious labor. His partner was William Rufus, who had come home after working for a year at the Galena, Illinois Lead Mines, with his savings to invest in something other than farming. (After his marriage, however, he decided to farm.) He and his wife Mary Jane had nine children, all born in the present Corinth Township, before March 1850, when they sold the farm "Cedar Crest" to Dr. S. M. Mitchel from Indiana. After the home was sold they moved to Mt. Vernon, Illinois.

MARY JANE ROBERTS AND WESLEY YOST

Mary Jane, Dau. of John Sutton and Margaret(Caughey)Roberts, was born in Wilson Co., Tenn., was 7 when the family made their momentous journey into the new Ill., Country, old enough to have memories of the dangers along the wilderness road-wild animals, Indians, rocky roads, turboulent streams to cross in the covered wagons, the ride on the Ferry Boat over the Ohio River--also the joy at having arrived at home of Grandfather John Roberts. She sadly recalled in later years the death of her dear Moyher, a happy, singing Irish girl. But she received kind treatment from her new mother, Sarah Johnson.

With only the advantage of schooling in the little log school house near their churvh, and what she got from reading and listening to conversations of her elders, she reached womanhood, and at the age of 20 years married one of the "Yost Boys" from the neighboring church (Libery" Community. He was also a stepson of her Aunt Lydia.

Wesley Yost was born to Henry and Mary Early Yost in Botetourt Co. Vir. and was about 9 when they came to Ill., and bought "Fancy Farm". Wesley filed on land adjoining that of his father-in-law. He was a good farmer and progressive, for before long he set up a carding machine. This relieved the women of the neighborhood of much tedious labor. His partner was Wm. Rufus, brother of his wife, who had come home after working for a year at the Galena Ill., Lead Mines, with his savings to invest in something other than farming, (After his marriage however he decided to farm)He and his wife Mary Jane had 9 children all born in the present Corinth Township, before Mar. 1850, when they sold the farm "Cedar Crest" to Dr. S.M. Mitchel from Ind. After the home was sold they moved to Mt. Vernon, Ill.

Mt.Vernon,Ill.,Pearl YostB.2,Nov.1885,died 22,Jan. 1922,married 11,1,1904 John P. Wolfe of Terre Haute,Ind.son of Levi and Martha (Gillan) Wolfe Ray yost ,b.18,June,1887,John Thomas Yost b. 17 Aug.1889,Robert Francis Yost,b.9,July,1892,died 17,Occt. 1931,married 4,Sept.1917 Lucille Kelling,dau.of Josrph and Margaret (Davenport) Kelling,Aurell Lora Yost b.26,Aug.1901,married 2,Apr.1922,Tony Gockel of Mo.son of Antone and--- (Ernetz) Gockel,2 children Tony Eugene Gockelb. 29,Oct.1903,John Robert Gockelb.11,Nov.1926.

5.Robert Early Yost,b.28,Nov.1859,Mt.Vernon,Ill.died 27,Feb.1923 Manchester,New Hampshire,married 22,Jan.1885,Elizabeth H.Beaty,2 children Wm.Yost and Aurall Yost,St.Louis,Mo.Elizabeth died,Robert then married 7,Sept.1927,Ella Janseendied 22,Aug.1884,Stillman Valley,Ill.

Mrs.Katherine Yost Boyd

Alhambra,Calif.

William Henry Yost born January 08, 1832 in Franklin County, Illinois. Died January 12, 1887 in Bosque County, Texas. William married Sarina Holiday Jonson on November 4, 1854. Sarina was born February 18, 1833 in Illinois, died February 12, 1899 in Bosque County, Texas.

William Henry and Sarina Holiday Yost had the following children:

George Albert Yost born 1856 in Illinois. George married Fanny P. Saint.

George and Fanny had the following children:

Ollie Morris Yost born January 15, 1884 in Texas and died December 23, 1969 in Greenville, Hunt County, Texas. He married Ruth Kate Nance. She was born 1890 and died 1966.

Fannie Saint Yost

William R. Yost was born January 31, 1863 in Hunt County, Texas and died December 14, in San Angelo, Texas. He married Mamie Lancaster November 12, 1896. He was buried in Johnson Memorial Cemetery, Knox County, Texas.

Obituary
Written by J. B. French, San Angelo, Texas

W. R. Yost, son of W. H. and Serena, was born in Hunt County, Texas, January 31, 1863. He was married to Miss Mamie Lancaster November 12, 1896, and died in San Angelo, Texas December 14, 1913.

Mr. Yost was reared to manhood in Bosque County, where he lived until 1901, when he moved to Altus, Oklahoma. With his wife, he settled near Desmoines, N.M. in March 1912. He was converted and joined the Methodist church some years ago and lived a consistent life until his death.

Besides a loving wife, he leaves two brothers, G. A. Yost of Greenville, Texas, and C. G. Yost of Munday, Texas, and one sister, Mrs. J. B. French of this city. He was laid to rest in Johnson cemetery, Munday, Texas, to await the resurrection.

Charles Gano Yost born December 25, 1865 in Greenville, Hunt, Texas, died February 02, 1961 in Munday, Knox County, Texas. Married Thomas Ida Jones born August 13, 1867 in Meridian, Bosque, Texas, died April 27, 1912 in Munday, Knox County, Texas. Charles is bured in the Johnson Memorial Cemetery in Munday, Texas.

Charles Gano Yost in 1930

Birth: Dec. 25, 1865
         Hunt County
         Texas, USA

Death: Feb. 2, 1961
         Knox City
         Knox County
         Texas, USA

He died at the Knox County Hospital of a heart attack after a previous stroke. He was also a retired farmer and widower who lived 4 miles northwest of Munday, Texas.

Charles Gano Yost

Article from the "Wichita Falls Times", Wichita Fall, Texas, Saturday, March 1, 1958
Title: "C. G. Yost Was Munday's First Customer in 1901"
By Keith Shelton, Staff Writer
Monday, March 1

First customer in the first store built in Munday was probably C. G. Yost, a retired farmer who lives on the homestead he came to in 1899 three and a half miles northwest of Munday.
Yost, now 92, says he and Mrs. Yost, who died in 1912, bought the first bill of dry goods from the Alexander Mercantile Co., which was the first store in what is now Munday.
There were a grocery store, post office, a blacksmith shop, and a wagon yard on the hill known later as West Munday, but in 1901, Alexander of Haskell built the mercantile company nearer where the railroad was supposed to pass through.
Gradually the town shifted to the new site, and in 1906 the railroad came to that part of Knox County.
Yost, who had worked on his father's farm in Bosque County, came to Knox County in 1899 and leased a quarter section from the Wichita Valley Railroad.
He came to Munday in the summer, went back to Bosque County and got married September 22, 1899. That same fall he brought his new wife to Munday.
He has raised mostly cotton and wheat on the land since that time and has reared four sons and a daughter who died in 1952.
Yost had never been in a hospital when he spent 10 days there two years ago for an upset stomach. But he still eats whatever he wants with no restrictions on his diet. He has a hearty appetite, according to his son, Virgil, who now farms the homestead. His hearing is failing, but he still reads avidly by use of glasses.

Long-Time Subscriber:
Yost has been a subscriber to the Wichita Falls newspapers since about 1914 and reads the paper thoroughly every day.
But Yost never mastered the art of driving a car. His son says, "It wouldn't stop when he hollered 'Whoa' ."
Yost was born on Christmas Day in 1865, the year the Civil War ended. His father was a Civil War veteran.
When he came to Knox County in 1899 at the age of 34, Yost brought his modern equipment including one-row, riding cultivators and plows. Just prior to that time, every other section of land was farmland and every other section . . . (unreadable).
By the time he arrived, the state land had been sold and he leased land from the railroad. When it was put up for sale in 1900, he bought the 160 acres near Munday.
In the early days, Yost ran a freight wagon in his spare time to the railroad terminals at Stamford and Seymour.

Never Voted Republican:
First time he ever voted for a president was for Grover Cleveland in 1888 when he lost to Benjamin Harrison. Yost didn't remember who it was, but said, "it was a Democrat and it was 1888. I never voted Republican in my life."
Yost, who retired in 1930, has three sons actively engaged in agriculture. Clyde Yost

farms two miles northwest of Munday, Seth Yost five and a half miles northwest and Virgil Yost farms the homestead.

Another son, Dewitt, lives in Fort Worth.

The land had only been under cultivation about eight years when Yost came to Munday. Then, the sandy soil would support fine wheat and some corn. But as the soil was worn down, corn ceased to grow and now it is mostly cotton land.

But in 1956, two oil wells were drilled on his land. One is almost a 100-barrel well but the short allowable and few producing days have drastically cut income from the wells.

My Memories of Papa Yost

By Carolyn Yost McConnell

We always called my grandfather Yost "Papa" and referred to him as Papa Yost. My earliest memories of him are when I was quite a young girl, Papa usually spent a week or so with us during the summer, and he would take my brother and me on walks. We lived near the Masonic Home and School in Fort Worth at that time, and we would walk over to the playground there, which was open to the public, and play on the swings, slide, and merry-go-round. Those were special times for us.

When we would visit him and our aunts, uncles, and cousins at the farm near Munday, Texas, I remember that every day Papa would go out to the cotton field and chop weeds. He continued to do that into his nineties. I loved him very much and was quite sad when he passed away at the age of 95. I always felt lucky to have had him with us for as long as we did.

Charles and Thomas Ida "Tommie" had the following children:

Willie Seth Yost born July 7, 1900, Munday, Knox, Texas, died July 28, 1974, Munday, Knox, Texas. Seth married Dora Virginia Rister July 17, 1951 in Knox County, Texas. She was born 1905 in Goree, Knox, Texas and died June 14, 1984 in Blanco, Blanco, Texas.

Willie Seth Yost

Birth: Jul. 7, 1900
Knox County
Texas, USA

Death: Jul. 28, 1974
Munday
Knox County
Texas, USA

He was a retired farmer who died of a stroke at the Leisure Lodge Nursing Home. Willie was the son of Charles Gano Yost and Thomas "Tommie" Ida Jones. He was survived by his widow Dora and was a veteran of WWII.

Name:	Willie S Yost
Birth Year:	1900
Race:	White, Citizen *(White)*
Nativity State or Country:	Texas
State of Residence:	Texas
County or City:	Knox
Enlistment Date:	23 Sep 1942
Enlistment State:	Texas
Enlistment City:	Abilene
Branch:	Branch Immaterial - Warrant Officers, USA
Branch Code:	Branch Immaterial - Warrant Officers, USA
Grade:	Private
Grade Code:	Private
Term of Enlistment:	Enlistment for the duration of the War or other emergency, plus six months, subject to the discretion of the President or otherwise according to law
Component:	Selectees (Enlisted Men)
Source:	Enlisted Man, Regular Army, after 3 months of Discharge
Education:	2 years of high school
Civil Occupation:	Farm hands, general farms
Marital Status:	Single, without dependents
Height:	71
Weight:	158

Willie Seth Yost

Charles Dewitt Yost born April 2, 1902, Munday, Knox, Texas, died May 16, 1980, Fort Worth, Tarrant, Texas. Dewitt married Thelma Pearl Chitwood on May 22, 1931 in Wichita Falls, Texas. Thelma Pearl Chitwood born December 23, 1904, Haskell County, Texas, died October 29, 1992, Burleson, Tarrant, Texas.

**Papa Yost & Dewitt and Thelma Pearl
about 1931**

**Dewitt & Thelma Pearl
about 1970**

Charles Dewitt Yost Grave Stone Fort Worth Texas

Charles Dewitt, who was always called Dewitt, was the second of five children of Charles Gano Yost and "Tommie" Ida Jones. He grew up on his family's farm near Munday, Wise County, Texas. When he was ten years old (and his youngest sibling, Clyde, was just a toddler), their mother died of breast cancer. A few years later, Charles (Papa Yost) was remarried to a widow who had several children from her first marriage. She gave preferential treatment to her own children, mistreated her step children, and lied to Papa about their behavior. She also died of breast cancer after the children were all grown. I do not know whether Papa Yost ever became aware of her treatment of them, but Papa was a good, kind man and, to my knowledge, he had little, if any, idea of what was going on at the time. However, I've been told that the three youngest children got the brunt of the mistreatment from their stepmother, after Daddy and his older brother, Seth, had left home. My father never held the way he was treated by his stepmother against his father, and never even told my brother and I about it. We didn't know anything about it until Mother told us a little of it after Daddy's death.

Dewitt always wanted to get an education, but because he was needed on the farm he was about 21 years old when he graduated from high school. The closest high school at the time was in the town of Goree, about five miles from Munday. He got a job as dishwasher in an eating place there and rented a room in a boarding house. He graduated as valedictorian of his class, and was awarded a college scholarship. After attending The University of Texas for one semester, he decided to go to Brantley-Draughon Business School in Fort Worth, instead, so that he could finish sooner, get a job, and help his sister, May Bell (the only girl in the family), to leave the farm and go to nursing school. She graduated from St. Joseph's School of Nursing in Fort Worth and joined the WACS in

World War I as an Army Nurse. Meanwhile, Dewitt graduated from business school and went to work in the office of the Fort Worth and Denver Railroad in Wichita Falls, Texas on June 7, 1927. There, he met my mother, Thelma Pearl Chitwood, who was teaching school in Wichita Falls at the time. They met at the Methodist Church there and dated until their marriage on May 22, 1931. In 1934, shortly before I was born, he was transferred to the Fort Worth accounting office, where they spent the rest of their lives. In June of 1967, after a forty year career, he retired from his position of General Accountant at the Fort Worth and Denver Railroad (owned by Burlington Lines by that time). When he died of melanoma cancer on May 16th, 1980, Mother and Daddy were only one year and a few days short of what would have been their golden wedding anniversary. Thelma Pearl had survived him by twelve years and five months when she died on October 29, 1992. He was a devoted husband, father, and grandfather, and is still sorely missed by his children and grandchildren.

When Daddy died, his funeral was held in the First United Methodist Church of Fort Worth, after which he was buried in the Chitwood plot of the cemetery at Decatur, Texas. The family was driven to the burial service in the funeral home limousine, and when we got to the railroad crossing located near the cemetery, a long Burlington Northern train was passing by. To me, that was a "21-car salute" to my father.

Information courtesy of Carolyn Yost McConnell (Thelma Carolyn Yost)

Charles "Dewitt" Yost and Thelma Pearl Chitwood had the following children:

Thelma Carolyn Yost born September 23, 1934, Fort Worth, Texas. Carolyn married Richard Craig McConnell on September 1, 1953 in Fort Worth Texas.

Richard & Carolyn's Wedding - Going Away Picture September 1, 1953

Richard & Carolyn 1980

Carolyn Yost and Richard Craig McConnell had the following children:

Cathy Lynn McConnell, born May 29, 1956, Austin, Texas. She married Mark Shipman January 7, 1978 in Mineral Wells, Palo Pinto, Texas. They were divorced in 1992.

Cathy McConnell and Mark Shipman had the following children:

Kelsey Erin Shipman, born October 22, 1985 in Austin, Travis, Texas.

Alison Paige Shipman, born December 7, 1988 in Portland, Multnomah, Oregon.

Cathy-June 1977   **Kelsey December 2007**   **Allison 2006**

Cindy Lou McConnell born August 26, 1960, Fort Worth, Texas. Cindy Lou later changed her name to Cinda Laine. Cinda married Mark Cheney September 20, 1986 in Fort Worth, Tarrant, Texas. They were divorced March 1998.

Cinda McConnell and Mark Cheney had the following children:

Claire Elaine Cheney, born December 11, 1991 in Fort Worth, Tarrant, Texas.
Eric Arthur Cheney, born August 7, 1995 in Fort Worth, Tarrant, Texas.

Cinda about 1980   **Claire Fall 2008**   **Eric, Spring 2009**

Connie Lee McConnell born December 29, 1962, Fort Worth, Texas. Connie married Dan Giles Townsend September 17, 2002 in Iceland.

Dan and Connie with Jasper 2006   **Connie and Jasper 2008**

Charles Dewitt Yost, Jr. born March 7, 1937. Charles married Donna Marie Woodward September 12, 1964 in Portland, Oregon. Donna Marie Woodward born August 19, 1941, Portland, Oregon.

Charles & Donna Yost Wedding Picture September 12, 1964   **Charles & Donna Yost Valentine Banquet, February 14, 2008**

Charles and Donna Yost had the following children:

Jay Charles Yost
Jon Craig Yost
Jim Carl Yost

Jay Charles Yost, born August 20, 1970 in Eugene, Oregon. Jay married Eileen JoAnnValenzuela June 3, 2006 in Chico, California. She was born October 15, 1982 in Arizona.

Jay and Eileen Yost had the following child:

Gracie Paloma Yost born July 20, 2008, in Chico, Butte, California.

Jay & Eileen's wedding picture

Jay, Eileen, and Gracie Yost, December 2008

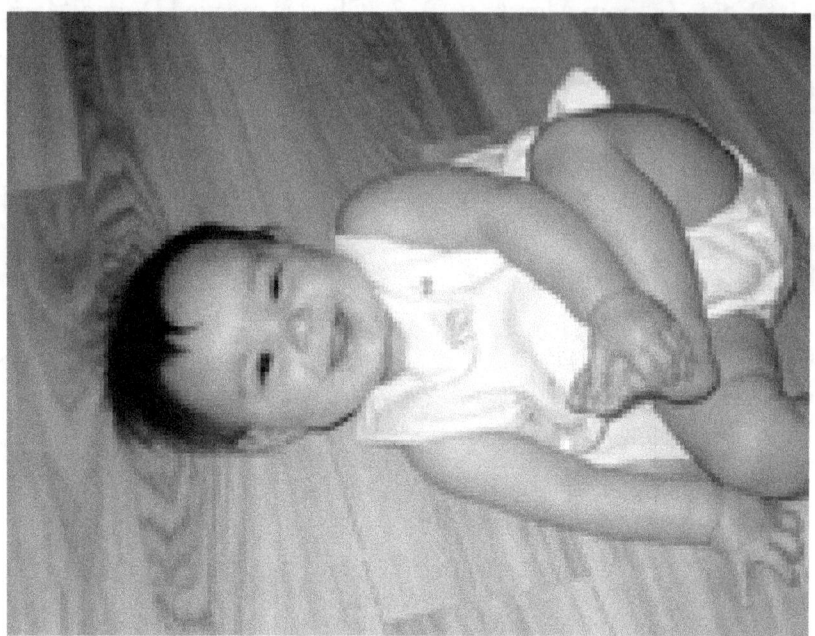
Gracie, Spring 2009

Jon Craig Yost born April 16, 1972 in Bandon, Coos, Oregon. Jon married Barbara Carlsen on December 18, 2004. She was born May 28, 1974 in Coos Bay, Coos, Oregon.

Jon and Barb

LOCAL BOY RETURNS WITH MEDICAL DEGREE

With the rapid advances in medicine, Jon Yost, M.D., said that when he looks back in 20 years to how he practices pediatrics today, it will probably look "caveman like". He sees the role of genetics and the understanding of the DNA process opening up treatments and cures that today look space age.

For this young doctor in his first year of pediatric practice, returning to a small town in Oregon allows him to be a "full-fledged doctor, and use his medical training to the fullest."

When he graduated from Bandon High School, he was like every other young person who wants to experience life, get out of the small town, and go to a big city.

From Bandon, it was on to OSU in Corvallis, then OHSU in Portland, and finally to residency at Children's National Medical Center in Washington, D.C. Every move to a larger and more urban area ultimately led him right back to the South Coast and everything he missed.

Mostly, he missed the sense of community and knowing his neighbors. He certainly doesn't miss the traffic and safety issues of a big city. When he called Doernbecher Children's Hospital in Portland from D.C. and asked about openings for pediatrics in Oregon, Bay Clinic was on that list. "It seemed like fate," he said, "and when we met, we clicked." It was full circle for this new doctor as he had once been a patient of Dr. Terrell Clarke's. Today, Dr. Clarke and Dr. Joe Morgan are his mentors.

The best of part of pediatrics is that you get to see your patients again and again, so you get to know them and their issues. "In medical school, there was the allure of other specialties with their technologies and sciences, but it's the relationships with families and children that's rewarding for me. I had my first inkling that I would go with pediatrics at my first well baby check," he remembered.

"We have good medical services for children, and the hospital's nurses and staff are well trained," Dr. Yost said. We always have the safety net of OHSU, but we have a good medical situation with good physicians and children that are well cared for. Parents really want to do what's best for their kids, and the community really supports its pediatricians."

Jon and Barbara Yost have the following children:

Mitchell Schall-Yost, Barbara's son from her first marriage, was born July 6, 1999 in Coos Bay, Coos, Oregon.

Mitchell Schall-Yost, Spring 2008

Mitch playing soccer, Spring 2009

Maggie Marie Yost, born September 8, 2006 in Coos Bay, Coos, Oregon.

Maggie, Fall 2008, age 2

Maggie, April 2009, age 2 ½

Natalie Kate Yost born March 19, 2009 in Coos Bay, Coos, Oregon.

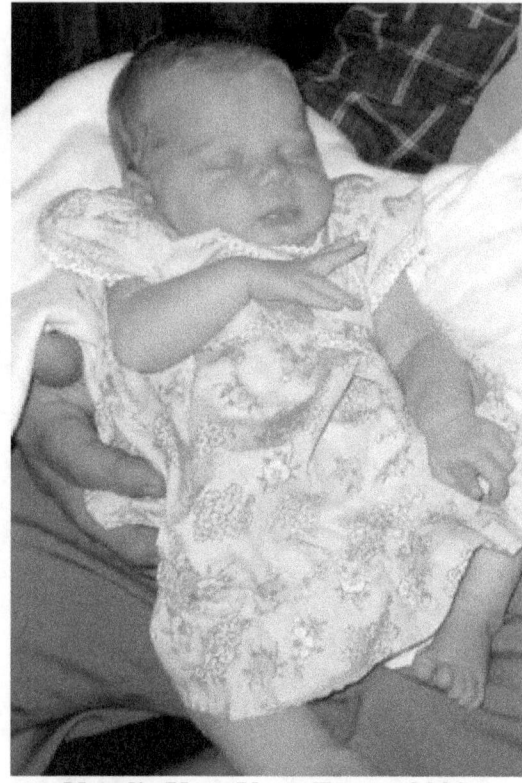
Natalie Kate Yost, Easter 2009

Jim Carl Yost born August 5, 1975 in Bandon, Coos, Oregon. He married Benita Lee Lewis September 20, 2008 in Ketchikan, Alaska. She was born July 27, 1975, in Alaska.

Jim and Benita Yost Wedding Pictures

Thomas Virgil Yost was born December 19, 1905, Munday, Knox, Texas and died June 28, 1967, Munday, Knox, Texas. He married Frankie D. Beecher on May 3, 1929 in Texas. She was born Thomas Virgil Yost, born December 19, 1905, Munday, Knox, Texas, died June 28, 1967, Munday, Knox, Texas. Virgil married Frankie D. Beecher on May 3, 1929 in Texas. She was born March 21, 1909 in Dublin, Texas and died February 25, 1996.

Thomas Virgil Yost

Thomas Virgil Yost

**Thomas Virgil Yost Johnson Memorial Cemetery Munday
Knox County
Texas, USA**

Virgil Yost and Frankie Beecher had the following children:

Tommie Francis Yost
Charles Everett Yost

Phyllis LeAnn Yost

Tommie Francis Yost, born November 25 1932, Munday, Knox, Texas. She married Felton Raynes June, 1947, Munday, Knox, Texas. He was born April 21, 1929 in Knox County, Texas, died December 11, 1998.

Tommie Yost & Felton Raynes Wedding Picture   Tommie Yost Raynes 1972

Tommie Yost and Felton Raynes had the following children:

Larry Alan Raynes was born April 2, 1951. He married Barbara Chavez, in 1972. They later divorced. He married Linda Edgman, born February 9, 1953, on November 9, 1983.

Larry and Linda Edgman Raynes

Larry Raynes and Barbara Chavez had the following children:

Heather Eve Raynes
Kristopher Raynes, born December 21, 1974

Heather Eve Raynes, born October 4, 1973. She married Rodney Hack. They have two children: Hayden Dean, born June 7, 2004, and Halle Eve, born January 13, 2008.

Heather, Halle & Hayden   **Top row: Hayden & Heather**   **Larry Raynes and**
                              Lower row: Rodney & Halle   **Halle Hack 2009**
                              Christmas 2008

Shelley Ann Raynes, born November 27, 1955. She married John Moseley September 9, 1956.

Shelley Raynes and John Moseley had the following child:

Megan Kristine Moseley, born November 9, 1985.

Megan Moseley, with Uncle Larry Raynes, and Mother Shelley Raynes Moseley

Charles Everett Yost born June 2, 1936, Munday, Knox, Texas, died May 21, 2001 in Wichita Falls, Wichita, Texas. Charles married Gerrie Boggs in 1954 in Munday, Knox County, Texas. They were divorced. Charles married Gaylia June Mobley.

Charles Everett and Gaye Mobley Yost

Charles Yost and Gerrie Boggs had the following child:

Tracee Lin Yost, born October 8, 1958, in Munday, Knox, Texas. She married Ray Anthony Herring.

Tracee Yost and Ray Herring have the following children:

Kristin Paige Herring, born June 22, 1983. She married Matt James in 2008.
Jessimy Kippin Herring, born November 11, 1988.

Tracee Yost Herring with daughters Kristin and Jessimy

Charles Yost and Gaye Mobley had the following children:

Leanna Camille Yost, born March 11, 1974 in Munday, Knox, Texas. She died March 5, 1979 in a horseback riding accident in Munday, Knox, Texas.

Charles "Chad" Everett Yost, Jr., was born May 22, 1970. He married Gayle Owens.

Chad Yost and Gayle Owens had the following child:

Trevor Thomas Yost, born April 8, 2008.

Trevor, Gayle, and Chad Yost

Trevor, May 2009

Phyllis LeAnn Yost, born February 13, 1945 in Knox County Hospital, Knox City, Texas. She married James Douglas McGrady on October 26, 1963. They later divorced. She married Elmo Dunn on February 6, 1973.

Elmo & Phyllis Dunn

Phyllis Yost as flower girl at Carolyn's wedding

May Bell Yost was born April 28, 1907, Munday, Knox, Texas, and died April 10, 1952, Dallas, Texas. She became a Registered Nurse and served in the Women's Army Corps as a Nurse in World War II.

Maybelle Yost age 2   **Maybelle Yost holding niece, 1934**

May Bell Yost Johnson Memorial Cemetery Munday
Knox County
Texas, USA

Barney Clyde Yost born September 7, 1908, Munday, Knox, Texas, died September 20, 1994, Munday, Knox, Texas. Clyde married Elva Loren Cluck February 9, 1931 in Munday, Knox, Texas. Elva Loren Cluck born January 24, 1914, Knox County, Texas, died May 27, 1986, Munday, Knox, Texas.

Tommie Yost with Clyde about 1909

Clyde and Elva Cluck Yost had the following children:

Shirley Ann Yost was born November 10, 1934, in Munday, Knox County, TX and died June 14, 2003 in Valencia, Los Angeles County, California. She married Jerry Anderson. He was born November 26, 1930 in McAllen, Hildalgo County, TX and died March 25, 2006 in Valencia, Los Angeles County, California.

Shirley Yost, September 1, 1953, bridesmaid in Carolyn's wedding

Shirley Yost and Jerry Anderson had the following child:

Mark Anderson born October 25, 1958 in Hildago County, Texas. He married Leslie Anderson.

Mark and Leslie Anderson had the following children:

Travis Anderson
Luke Anderson

Ronald Clyde Yost born November 19, 1943, Knox County, Texas. He married Mary Jon Emils. She was born November 19, 1945 in Oklahoma City, Oklahoma.

Ronald Clyde Yost

Ronald Clyde and Mary Jon Yost had the following children:

Amy Susan Yost was born October 9, 1973 in at Presbyterian Hospital, Dallas, Dallas, Texas, died July 16, 1982 in Dallas, Dallas, Texas.

Timothy Ronald Yost, born April 14, 1978, at Presbyterian Hospital in Dallas, Dallas, Texas.

Tim Yost

John Clyde Yost, born October 3, 1986 at Swedish Hospital in Denver, Colorado.

Robert L. Yost was born August 8, 1867 in Texas and died July 9, 1907, in Knox County, Texas. He married Sallie Edna Alexander about 1902. She was born 1881 and died 1965.

Robert L. and Sallie Alexander Yost had the following children:

Gracie Yost, born about 1902

Jesse L. Yost was born September 28, 1903 in Texas and died August 17, in Munday, Knox County, Texas. He married Ola Iris Rowell. She was born September 4, 1906 and died January 21, 2004 in Munday, Knox, Texas. Jesse and Ola are buried in Johnson Memorial Cemetery, Munday, Knox County, Texas.

Obituary of Ola Iris Yost, The Wichita Falls, Texas <u>Times Record News</u>

MUNDAY - Ola Iris Yost, 97, of Munday died Wednesday, January 21, 2004 in Munday.

   Services will be at 2:00 p.m. Friday at Munday First Baptist Church with the Rev. Don Hendrix officiating and the Rev. Randy Gressett assisting. Burial will be in Johnson Memorial Cemetery under the direction of McCauley-Smith Funeral Home.
   Mrs. Yost was a homemaker.
   Survivors include a son, Foy Lee Yost of Niland Calif.; nine grandchildren; 15 great-grandchildren; and seven great-great-grandchildren.

Jesse and Ola Yost had the following children

Foy Yost, born about 1924

Mildred Yost was born about 1928. She married Clyde R. "Junior" Hendrix, Jr..

Mildred Yost and Junior Hendrix had the following children:

Donald Wayne Hendrix
Melissa Sue Hendrix. She married Kyle Wayne Josselet. He was born January 4, 1957 in Haskell, Texas.

Joe Lynn Yost was born April 26, 1930 in Munday, Knox County, Texas and died June 1, 1996 in Fort Worth, Tarrant County, Texas. He is buried in Laurel Land Cemetery, Fort Worth, Tarrant, Texas. He married Elnora Frances Dahl.

Joe Lynn and Elnora Frances Dahl Yost had the following children:

Rebecca Lynn Yost, born June 20, 1958
Sheila Ruth Yost, born May 26, 1959

Betty Sue Yost was born March 8, 1932 in Munday, Knox, Texas, and died October 1, 1968 in Sherman, Texas. She married Joe Layne Womble Joe Layne Womble about 1950.

Betty Sue Yost and Joe Womble had the following children:

Joe Layne Womble, Jr.
Jimmy Lynn Womble

Joe Layne Womble, Jr., was born December 30, 1952, in Munday, Knox, Texas. He married Suzanne McCormick July 10, 1976 in Lubbock, Texas.

Joe Layne, Jr. and Suzanne McCormick Womble had the following child:

Joe Russell Womble, born December 30, 1979 and died September 27, 1980.

Jimmy Lynn Womble, born June 22, 1956 in Midland, Texas. He Married Brenda G. Warren about 1963.

Mary Yost was born in December 27, 1870 and died December 5, 1935. She married James Buchanan "J.B." French August 25, 1892 in Texas.

Mary Yost and J. B. French had the following children:

Alma Holiday French was born November 13, 1893 in Greenville, Hunt, Texas and died in Sacramento, California. She married William Osmond Monroe. He was born in Wills Point, Texas and died in 1941 in San Angelo, Tom Green, Texas.

Alma French and William O. Monroe had the following child:

Wilda Joy Monroe, born September 20, 1925 in Tom Green County, Texas.

Charlotte Nanette "Nettie" Yost was born about 1873 in Texas and died in 1901 in Mangum Greer, Oklahoma. She married Lemuel C. Jones in 1895.

Nettie Yost and Lemuel Jones had the following children:

Clarence Cecil Jones

Dena Jones, born 1897, died May 5, 1905 in Snyder, Oklahoma.

Edith Jones, born and died in 1901, in Munday, Knox, Texas.

Clarence Cecil Jones was born October 10, 1896 in Eulogy, Bosque County, Texas and died September 1, 1969 in Munday, Knox, Texas. He is buried in Johnson Memorial Cemetery, Knox County, Texas. Clarence married Mary Frances "Fannie" McGregor. She was born May 15, 1898 in Mansfield, Johnson County, Texas, and died in August 1975 in Amarillo, Randall County, Texas, and is also buried in Johnson Memorial Cemetery.

**Notes on Clarence Jones
(Courtesy of Carolyn Yost McConnell)**

By the time he was nine years old, Clarence was the only surviving member of his immediate family. His mother, Nanette "Nettie" Yost, and youngest sister, Edith Jones (born in 1901), both died in 1901. At first, I thought that his mother and Edith probably died at the same time (at childbirth), but records show that his mother died in Mangum, Oklahoma, while Edith died in Munday, Texas. His father, Lemuel Cornelius Jones, and sister, Dena, both died in 1905 in Snyder, Oklahoma. I wonder if they were in some kind of accident together. I believe Nettie's parents, were William H. Yost and Sarina H. Johnson. The 1910 census shows Clarence as a nephew, living with William R. Yost, a son of William and Sarina Yost, and his wife Mamie Lancaster Yost in Jackson, Oklahoma. William had a sister, Charlotte Yost. She was referred to as Charlotte Janette in some 1933 family correspondence, and I believe her name was actually Charlotte Nanette. Therefore, I think Nettie was William's sister, Charlotte.

When I was a young girl, and would visit my father's relatives in Munday, Texas, we always visited with Clarence and Fannie. I never would have guessed that he had experienced such a traumatic early childhood. My father told me that Clarence was his double cousin - related on both the Jones and Yost sides of his family. Unfortunately, I didn't think to ask (or don't remember) how he was related to the Yosts. However, thanks to ancestry.com, I've been able to confirm my above suppositions.

Clarence and Fannie McGregor Jones had the following children:

Evelyn **Juanice** Jones was born in 1923. She married Victor A. Zagarola.

Juanice Jones and Victor Zagarola had the following children:

Patricia Ann Zagarola
Stephen Wayne Zagarola
Victor Lewis Zagarola

Jack **Doyle** Jones was born in 1924. Jack married Martha Jane Burns.

Doyle and Martha Burns Jones had the following children:

Bruce Wayne Jones
David Shelton Jones
Priscilla Katherine Jones

George Albert Yost

William R. Yost

Robert L. Yost

Mary Yost

Charlotte Janette Yost

William Henry Yost and Sarina Holiday Yost children cont'd

Robert Lee Yost
Mary Margaret Yost
Charlotte Janette Yost
John Augustus Yost
Rufus Stewart Yost
Thomas Roberts Yost

George David Yost
Sidney E. Yost
Marion C. Yost
Walter Scott Yost
John T. Yost
Oscar Yost
Robert E. Yost

John Augustus Yost born January 22, 1834,

Rufus Steward Yost born December 02, 1835,

Thomas Roberts Yost born October 22, 1838,

George David Yost born November 23, 1839, Corinth Williamson County Illinois, USA, died Jun. 7, 1922 Chippewa County Minnesota, USA buried Louriston Township Cemetery, Chippewa County Minnesota, USA

Mary Margaret Yost born September 16, 1842,

Sidney Eleanor Yost born October 13, 1844,

Marion C. Yost born September 28, 1846,

Walter Scott Yost born February 24, 1850, died October 26, 1873 buried in the Corinth Zion Methodist Cemetery in Williamson County Illinois, USA

Walter Scott Yost, Williamson County Illinois

After Mary Janes death Wesley Yost married **Sabrina Hobbs** of Mt. Vernon, Illinois. She was born in Sumner County Tennessee, but her parents came to Jefferson County, Illinois before she was grown. They had the following children:

Sarah Jane Yost born August 21, 1854, died September 11, 1859 in Mt.Vernon, Illinois.

John Thomas Yost born August 21, 1855, died September 6, 1929 in Mt. Vernon, Illinois, leaving his wife Lorena Smith, daughter of Harris Smith, and a son Morris Yost born May 10, 1898, married May 8, 1918 to Hazel Talor, born November 16, 1897 in Princeton, Indian. She was the daughter of George H. and Alice (Van Winkle) Taylor.

They had the following children:

Betty Lou Yost born March 28, 1921
Mary Loraine Yost born October 27, 1922

Charles Wesley Yost born March 9, 1856 in Washington County, Illinois, died May 17, 1883 in Mt. Vernon, Illinois. He married Lena Messman of Central City, Illinois in 1897.

They had the following children:

Walter Scott Yost born December 4, 1878
Allen W. Yost born March 10, 1880, died 1920 in Mt. Vernon, Illinois.

Oscar Yost born October 16, 1857, died December 22, 1916 in Mt. Vernon, Illinois. He married Loula Francis born January 20, 1860 on April 23, 1881. Loula was the daughter of James and Lucinda Francis.

Oscar and Loula Yost had the following children:

Jessie M. Yost born October 1, 1883, died November 24, 1907, married May 11, 1903 to Roscoe Stratton of East St. Louis, Illinois. He was one of Charles Augustus Stratton's sons.

Frank Yost born April 28, 1882

442   WILLIAMSON COUNTY.

Pulley, Thomas Culbreath, William T. Davis, Nicholas B. Chenoweth and Alfred Ferrell.

Town 10 south, Range 3 east: 1816, Thomas Griffith; 1833, Gabrial Sanders, James Hill and Cutworth Harrison; 1836, Sterling Hill, Thomas Loudon and Henry H. Hudgens; 1838, Elias McDonald. Only a few tracts of land in this township were entered prior to 1850.

Town 8 south, Range 4 east: 1814, Francis Jordan; 1819, Richard Ratcliff and Thomas Roberts; 1833, Isaiah Harlow; 1836, David M. Logan, Matthew G. Martin, Enoch Newman and Wesley Yost; 1837, Levi Summers, George Whitley, William Francis, James Milligan, William A. Roberts, John S. Roberts and James R. Stewart.

Page 442 - History of Franklin County

Hearne History - Page 498 – 499

Purnell Hearne, of Corinth, Ill., says:

My grandfather, Purnell Hearne, was born in Maryland; married his cousin, Nancy Rachel Hearne, and moved to North Carolina in early life, and then moved to Tenn., Wilson Co., about the year 1800. Children: Nancy, Brunetta (given on the family tree as Nector), Thomas, James W., Milbra, Purnell, Stephen L., William H. Ebenezer, Sarah and Alafar. William H. Hearne is my father, and he married Susan H. Turner. I, Purnell N. Hearne, was born Mar. 3, 1829, married Nancy A. Gill, Nov. 15, 1849. Children: Ebenezer W., born Aug. 18, 1851; Martha Lee, born Apr. 14, 1859, and Sept. 10, 1884, married Geo. W. Willard, who was born in Williamson Co., Ill., Nov. 11, 1854, and they have one child, Sophia, born Sept. 19, 1890; Perlemon H., born Dec. 10, 1861; Rufus A., born June 29, 1864, died Jan. 6, 1890; Lavinia A., born Nov. 11, 1866.
Nancy A. my wife died Feb. 22 1870, and I married Mary M. Yost Mar. 26, 1871.. Children: Mirta E., born July 18, 1873; Charles N., born Sept. 17, 1875; Alva M., born Feb. 13, 1878. As to my religious pursuasion, I am a local preacher in the Methodist Episcopal Church; in politics I am a Prohibitionist, and am a farmer

THE UNITED STATES OF AMERICA.

CERTIFICATE No. _____

To all to whom these Presents shall come, Greeting:

WHEREAS Wesley Yost of Franklin County Illinois has deposited in the GENERAL LAND OFFICE of the United States, a Certificate of the REGISTER OF THE LAND OFFICE at Shawneetown whereby it appears that full payment has been made by the said Wesley Yost according to the provisions of the Act of Congress of the 24th of April, 1820, entitled "An Act making further provision for the sale of the Public Lands," for the North half of the South West quarter of Section twenty two in Township eight South of Range four East in the District of Lands subject to sale at Shawneetown Illinois containing eighty acres

according to the official plat of the survey of the said Lands, returned to the General Land Office by the SURVEYOR GENERAL, which said tract has been purchased by the said Wesley Yost.

NOW KNOW YE, That the United States of America, in consideration of the Premises, and in conformity with the several acts of Congress, in such case made and provided, HAVE GIVEN AND GRANTED, and by these presents DO GIVE AND GRANT, unto the said Wesley Yost and to his heirs, the said tract above described: **TO HAVE AND TO HOLD** the same, together with all the rights, privileges, immunities, and appurtenances of whatsoever nature, thereunto belonging, unto the said Wesley Yost and to his heirs and assigns forever.

In Testimony Whereof, I, Martin Van Buren PRESIDENT OF THE UNITED STATES OF AMERICA, have caused these Letters to be made PATENT, and the SEAL of the GENERAL LAND OFFICE to be hereunto affixed.

GIVEN under my hand at the CITY OF WASHINGTON, the twenty eighth day of July in the Year of our Lord one thousand eight hundred and thirty eight and of the INDEPENDENCE OF THE UNITED STATES the Sixty third

BY THE PRESIDENT: Martin Van Buren

By A. Van Buren, Sec'y.

Jos. S. Wilson acting Recorder of the General Land Office.
ad interim

THE UNITED STATES OF AMERICA

CERTIFICATE No. 5041

To all to whom these Presents shall come, Greeting:

WHEREAS Wesley Yost, of Franklin County, Illinois

has deposited in the GENERAL LAND OFFICE of the United States, a Certificate of the REGISTER OF THE LAND OFFICE at Shawneetown whereby it appears that full payment has been made by the said Wesley Yost according to the provisions of the Act of Congress of the 24th of April, 1820, entitled "An Act making further provision for the sale of the Public Lands," for the West half of the North West quarter of Section twenty two, in Township eight South, of Range four East, in the District of Lands subject to sale at Shawneetown, Illinois, containing eighty acres.

according to the official plat of the survey of the said Lands, returned to the General Land Office by the SURVEYOR GENERAL, which said tract has been purchased by the said Wesley Yost

NOW KNOW YE, That the United States of America, in consideration of the Premises, and in conformity with the several acts of Congress, in such case made and provided, HAVE GIVEN AND GRANTED, and by these presents DO GIVE AND GRANT, unto the said Wesley Yost

and to his heirs, the said tract above described: TO HAVE AND TO HOLD the same, together with all the rights, privileges, immunities, and appurtenances of whatsoever nature, thereunto belonging, unto the said Wesley Yost

and to his heirs and assigns forever.

In Testimony Whereof, I, Martin Van Buren PRESIDENT OF THE UNITED STATES OF AMERICA, have caused these Letters to be made PATENT, and the SEAL of the GENERAL LAND OFFICE to be hereunto affixed.

GIVEN under my hand at the CITY OF WASHINGTON, the twenty eighth day of July in the Year of our Lord one thousand eight hundred and thirty eight and of the INDEPENDENCE OF THE UNITED STATES the Sixty third

BY THE PRESIDENT: Martin Van Buren

By M. Van Buren Jr Sec'y.

Jos. S. Wilson, Acting RECORDER of the General Land Office. ad interim

Henry Marshall Yost born June 24, 1811 in Wythe County Virginia, died January 7, 1876 in Missouri. He married Jane Catherine Stewart born October 6, 1816 in Sumner Tennessee, died April 12, 1857. They were married December 12, 1833.

1850 Census Franklin County Illinois

They had the following children:

George Roberts Yost born March 14, 1847 in Williamson, Fancy Farm, Illinois, died July 28, 1917 in Chicago, Illinois. He married Bertha Balmer

1880 Census St Louis Missouri

George Roberts Yost in the Civil War

George Yost was only 14 years old when he joined the crew of the U.S.S. CAIRO, yet he had the foresight to keep a journal of daily activities while on board the Union Gunboat. Since all of the U.S.S. CAIRO's official papers went down with her when she sank over 130 years ago, the Yost Journal is the only primary source of information that remains about this unique Civil War Gunboat.
Although several books have been written about the U.S.S. CAIRO, these books were not written by eyewitnesses, and are thus considered secondary sources. Researchers often consult primary or original sources, like the Yost Journal To make an original document more readable, it is often necessary to transcribe, or write out, the document. By transcribing the journal of George Yost, we have learned much about the career of the U.S.S. CAIRO and her crew.

Journal Underway for Memphis

Friday Oct 24th

At 12 am we rec'd mail on board. I rec'd one letter from Father he says that Dempsey who is on board the "Louisville" at this place has been sick for some time. and I who am within 1/4 of a mile of him did not know that he was sick until the news had travelled 350 miles up the river. and gave me time to receive a letter which travelled the same distance. and gave me the first intimation that anything was out of the way. well. and with the same boat which brought the mail, orders came for the "Cairo" to get underway. and go up the river as soon as possible. I stated the case to the Executive officer and asked his permission to go out in one of the boats that were going ashore. to set me off on the "Louisville" and call for me as they came back (which would have been no trouble at all as the "Louisville" is lying between me and the shore.) but no I could not go. I then wrote my brother a letter and enclosed Father's. and asked the officer of the deck if the boat which was going to take the mail ashore could throw the letter aboard the "Louisville" but no it could not be done would take too much time. very well perhaps I shall be even with some of them yet

Translation

1862 Journal Underweigh for Memphis 51

Friday Oct 24th
At 12 m. [midday] we reced mail on board. I recd one letter from Father he says that Dempsey who is on board the "Louisville" at this place has been sick for some time, and I who am within 1/4 of a mile of him did not know that he was sick until the news had traveled 350 miles up the river and gave me time to receive a letter which traveled the same distance and gave me the first intimation that anything was out of the way, well, and with the same boat which brought the mail orders came for the "Cairo" to get under way and to go up the river as soon as possible. I stated the case to the Executive Officer and asked his permission to go out in one of the boats that were going ashore to set me off on the "Louisville" and call for me as they came back (which would have been no trouble at all as the "Louisville" is lying between us and the shore) but no I could not go. I then wrote my brother a letter and enclosed Fathers and asked the officer of the deck if the boat which was going to take the mail ashore could throw the letter aboard the "Louisville" but no it could not be done would take too much time. Very well perhaps I shall be even with some of the yet.

The U.S.S. Cairo was one of seven ironclad gunboats named in honor of towns along the upper Mississippi and Ohio rivers. These powerful ironclads were formidable vessels, each mounting thirteen big guns (cannon). On them rested in large part, Northern hopes to regain control of the lower Mississippi River and split the Confederacy in two.

The "city class" gunboats were designed by Samuel M. Pook and built by river engineer James B. Eads. Cairo was constructed at Mound City, Illinois, and commissioned in January 1862. The Cairo was destined to see only limited action in the engagement at Plum Point in May and in the battle of Memphis in June. Her most significant action came six months later when she kept a rendezvous with destiny.

The Cairo's skipper, Lt. Commander Thomas O. Selfridge, Jr., was rash and ambitious, a stern disciplinarian, but an aggressive and promising young officer. On the cold morning of December 12, 1862, Selfridge led a small flotilla up the Yazoo River, north of Vicksburg, to destroy Confederate batteries and clear the channel of torpedoes (underwater mines). As the Cairo reached a point seven miles north of Vicksburg the flotilla came under fire and Selfridge ordered the guns to ready. As the gunboat turned towards shore disaster struck. Cairo was rocked by two explosions in quick succession which tore gaping holes in the ship's hull. Within twelve minutes the ironclad sank into six (6) fathoms (36 feet) of water without any loss of life. Cairo became the first ship in history to be sunk by an electrically detonated torpedo.

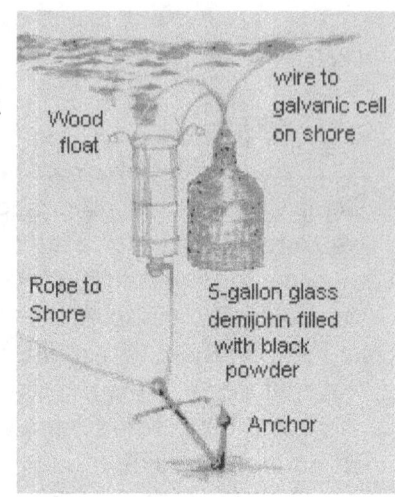

Over the years the gunboat was soon forgotten and her watery grave was slowly covered by a shroud of silt and sand. Impacted in mud, Cairo became a time capsule in which her priceless artifacts were preserved. Her whereabouts became a matter of speculation as members of the crew had died and local residents were unsure of the location.
By studying contemporary documents and maps, Edwin C. Bearss, Historian at Vicksburg National Military Park, was able to plot the approximate site of the wreck. With the help of a pocket compass and iron bar probes, Bearss and two companions, Don Jacks and Warren Grabau, set out to discover the grave of the Cairo in 1956. The three searchers were reasonably convinced they had found the Cairo, but three years lapsed before divers brought up armored port covers to positively confirm the find. A heavy accumulation of silt, swift current, and the ever-muddy river deterred the divers as they explored the gunboat. Local enthusiasm and interest began to grow in 1960 with the recovery of the pilothouse, an 8-inch smoothbore cannon, its white oak carriage and other artifacts well preserved by the Yazoo mud. With financial support from the State of Mississippi, the Warren County Board of Supervisors and funds raised locally, efforts to salvage the gunboat began in earnest. Hopes of lifting the ironclad and her cargo of artifacts intact were crushed in October of 1964 when the three inch cables being used to lift the Cairo cut deeply into its wooden hull. It then became a question of saving as much of the vessel as possible. A decision was made to cut the Cairo into three sections. By the end of December the battered remains were put on barges and towed to Vicksburg. In the summer of 1965 the barges carrying the Cairo were towed to Ingalls Shipyard on the Gulf Coast in Pascagula, Mississippi. There the armor was removed, cleaned and stored. The two engines were taken apart, cleaned and reassembled. Sections of the hull were braced internally and a sprinkler system was operated continually to keep the white oak structural timbers from warping and checking.

In 1972, the U.S. Congress enacted legislation authorizing the National Park Service to accept title to the Cairo and restore the gunboat for display in Vicksburg National Military Park. Delays in funding the project halted progress until June of 1977, when the vessel was transported to the park and partially reconstructed on a concrete foundation near the Vicksburg National Cemetery.

The recovery of artifacts from the Cairo revealed a treasure trove of weapons, munitions, naval stores and personal gear of the sailors who served on board. The gunboat and its artifacts can now be seen along the tour road at the U.S.S. Cairo Museum.

On December 12, 1862, the Cairo was busy clearing Confederate torpedoes (today called an underwater mine) from the muddy Yazoo River. Upon hearing small arms fire, Commander Selfridge thought his vessel was under attack and ordered Cairo into position. Two Confederate sailors, Acting Masters Zedekiah McDaniel and Francis M. Ewing, whose names are lost to history, hid behind a river bank and waited as the Cairo maneuvered.

At the right moment, they detontated the torpedoes with an electric charge. Two explosions ripped a large hole in the port bow causing the Cairo to quickly fill with water. It sank to the bottom, in six fathoms (36 feet) of water, within twelve minutes with no loss of life. The Cairo became the first armored warship in history to be sunk by an electronically detonated mine.

After one hundred years on the bottom of the Yazoo River, efforts were made to raise the Cairo. But over the years silt and river sediment had accumulated inside the vessel. As the Cairo was lifted from the bottom it began to bend and buckle from the added weight. Without warning, the lifting cables sliced deep into its wooden hull cutting the boat into three sections.

The remains of the Cairo were lifted from the river, placed on barges and towed to Ingalls Shipyard on the gulf coast in Pascagoula, Mississippi. It remained in storage until 1977, when the Cairo was donated to the National Park Service for preservation. The gunboat restoration project was completed in 1984.

Armor: Iron Plating on the USS Cairo

The starboard (right) side of the gunboat shows gun ports number 3 and 4. The iron plating was mounted as part of the sloping casemate that enclosed the gun deck. The 2 1/2 inch thick charcoal plate iron was originally backed by a two foot thickness of white oak timbers. Without the wood to absorb the shock of shot and shell hitting the iron, the metal would have shattered like glass.

Thirteen BIG Guns

The Cairo carried thirteen big guns. This 32 pounder Navy smoothbore, mounted on its original carriage, could fire a solid 32 pound cannon ball about a mile. It required an eleven man crew to load, maneuver and fire.

Capstan

The gunboat's capstan was capable of moving weights of several tons. It was a steam-driven or hand driven winch used for pulling in the anchor, moving guns on the gun deck and hauling lines.

Fire Tube Boilers

Cairo's five fire-tube boilers are among the oldest and best surviving examples of the type designed for boats plying the western waters. The boilers operated at 140 pounds per square inch steam pressure and consumed almost a ton of coal per hour.

Paddlewheel

Cairo's recessed paddle wheel is similar to the well-known stern wheel. It was placed within the raceway between the casemates to protect the wheel from enemy cannon fire. This paddle wheel propelled the gunboat at a speed of 6 knots (about 7 m.p.h.). The buckets or paddles were probably made of uniform-width wood and could easily be replaced when damaged.

Cairo Museum Exhibits: Personal Effects

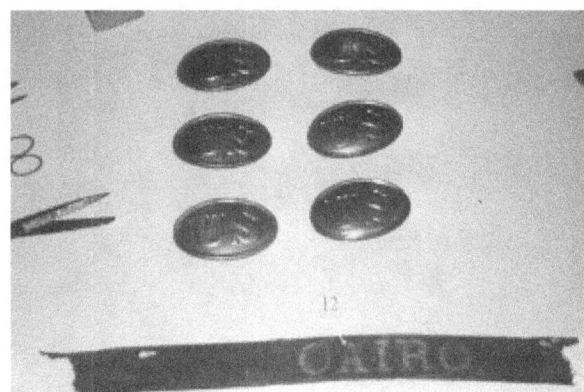

"we fired one Gun at the Fort just as she was sinking I saved 2 Revolvers and most of us saved something-some of us saved our bags some hammocks some all and several saved nothing except theirselves"
    George Roberts Yost 15 year old Crewman

As there was very little time for saving personal belongings, the crew had to abandon things such as these U.S. brass belt buckles and this silk "Cairo" hat band.

Close-up of soap dishes (upper center) and different glass ink wells used by the sailors.

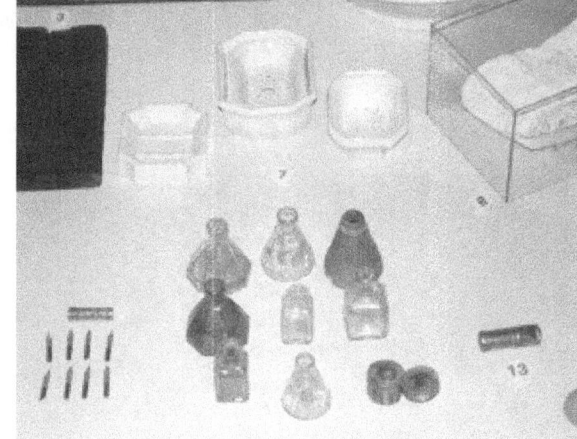

Thousands of personal items were abandoned to the river as the gunboat went swiftly to the bottom of the muddy Yazoo.

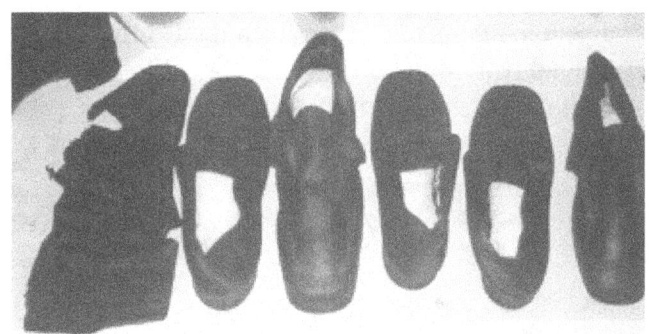

Most government-issue shoes of the Civil War period had a common last, but Cairo's leather shoes were lefts and rights. One of the boat's officers had bunions, as was evidenced by the heavy work boots which had been cut and patched (far left).

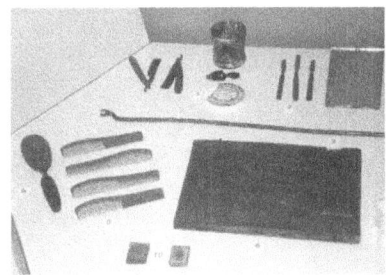

The men's shaving gear included razors, shaving cups and brush. Other personal accessories found included toothbrush handles, mirrors and hard rubber combs. All but two of the combs were found in the Quarter Master's storeroom and were evidently not issued. The combs are stamped U.S. Navy on one side and I.R. COMB CO. GOODYEAR'S PATENT MAY 6, 1851.

The personal items recovered reflect the diverse training and backgrounds of the sailors. A U.S. Marine Corps hat insignia (upper left) was found on the gunboat along with a tin canteen, wooden carvings known as scrimshaw (lower right) and several ambrotypes (early type of photograph). One of the ambrotypes is of a woman and young girl, perhaps the wife and daughter of one of Cairo's crew.

Cairo Museum Exhibits: Weapons

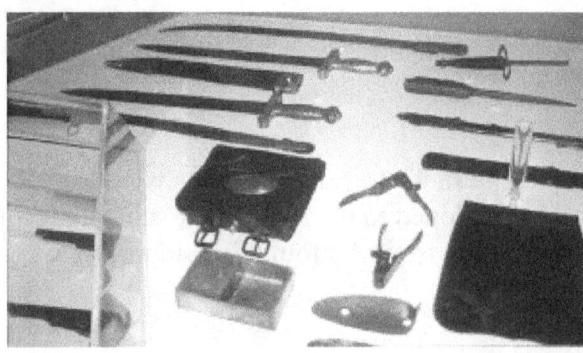

The wide variety of personal arms recovered from the Cairo bear witness to the unusual composition of the crew. It included men who originally enlisted in the army and to the scarcity of weapons early in the war.

The hand guns recovered from the Cairo ranged from the Army issued .44 caliber Colt to an assortment of 19th century pistols.

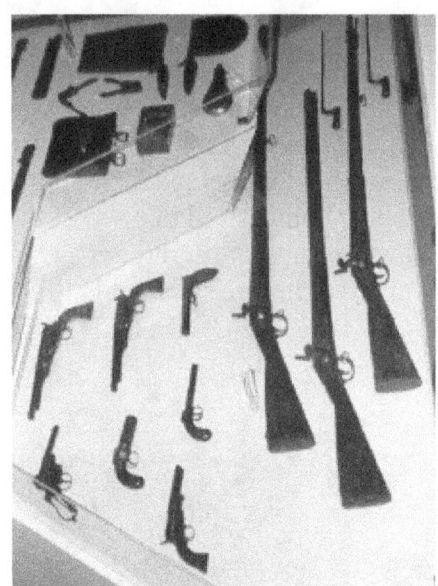

Shoulder weapons were for the most part Army muskets, but a least a few shotguns were among the weapons aboard.

Children of HENRY and MARY POLLY (EARLY) YOST Cont'd

Mary Wagner Yost born January 10, 1813

Betsy Greiner Yost born November 11, 1814

Samuel Eagon Yost born December 07, 1818, died May 4, 1861. Buried Aikman Cemetery, Williamson County Illinois, USA

Roberts Early Yost born September 30, 1820 Roberts Early Yost was the youngest of nine children born to Henry Marshall and Mary Polly (Early) Yost. His older brothers and sisters were born in Virginia. Roberts was born on "Fancy Farm" in Franklin County, Illinois, near Fort Jordon where the family had settled during or after 1819. Roberts died 1858 in Thebes, Illinois. Roberts married Nancy Jane Wilbanks December 11, 1851. Nancy was born August 1833, Jefferson, Illlinois.

Roberts and Nancy had the following children:

Emma Florida Yost born December 27, 1852, Benton, Illinois

Merit Card to Emma from her teacher dated 1864, Cairo, Illinois (Front)

Merit Card to Emma from her teacher dated 1864, Cairo, Illinois

Mary Alice Yost born December 27, 1852, Benton, Illinois

Helen Wilbanks Yost born 1854

After Mary Polly Early Yost died on September 16, 1821, Henry married Lydia Eleanor Roberts on November 12, 1822 in Franklin County Illinois.

Benton June the 16th 1845 Board of Investigation in Session

On application of Henry Yost Sen. and from his testimony with that of Simon M Hubbard it appears to the board of Investigation that the marriage License authorising any legally authorised person to solomnize and certify the rites of matrimony between Henry Yost Sen and Lydia E Roberts that was duly Solomnized and Certified by the Rev Porter on the 12th day of November 1822 and it also appears that the Record evidence of the same was consumed by Fire on the night of the 18 of November 1843 and the same having been passed uppon by the board of Investigation it is ordered that the same be Reinstated

Court on June 16, 1845 determining that Henry Yost and Lydia E. Roberts marriage was indeed valid after the original record was consumed in a fire.

At the request of Henry Yost the following Deed was Recorded February 27th 1786.

This Indenture made this Twenty fourth day of February in the year of our Lord Seventeen Hundred & Eighty Six Between Charles Beatty & Martha his wife of George Town Montgomery County State of Maryland of the one part & Henry Yost of the same Town County and State of the other part Witnesseth that the said Charles Beatty & Martha his wife for & in Consideration of the Covenants herein after Contained & expressed, on the part & behalf of him the said Henry Yost his Heirs & Assigns to be paid kept & performed, Have granted, bargained, sold aliened and confirmed, & by these presents do grant bargain sell alien & confirm unto him the said Henry Yost his Heirs & Assigns a certain Lot or portion of Ground situate lying & being in the said County & State in the addition to George Town laid off by the said Charles Beatty & a certain George Fraser Hawkins as described in the Plan thereof by number Seven, Containing in Front in width Sixty feet & back for depth One Hundred & Thirty five Feet as will appear by said Plan which is Recorded in Frederick County Records Reference being thereunto had will more fully & at large appear & all Houses Buildings Profits Commodities Hereditaments & Appurtenances whatsoever to the said Premises hereby granted belonging or in any wise appertaining & the Reversion Remainder & Remainders Issues & Profits thereof & of every part & parcel thereof To Have & To Hold the said Lot or portion of Ground Hereditaments & all & Singular the Premises before mentioned with their & every of their appurtenances unto him the said Henry Yost his Heirs & Assigns to the only proper use & behoof of him the said Henry Yost his Heirs & Assigns forever, he the said Henry Yost his Heirs & Assigns rendering & paying therefor unto him the said Charles Beatty his Heirs & Assigns upon the first day of May

Henry Yost deed transfer to P. Beatty Hagerstown, Washington County Maryland

Henry Yost deed transfer to P. Beatty Hagerstown, Washington County Maryland

262

or Assigns a Deed of Quit Claim for all the before mentioned Rent or Rents except two sixtieths of a Silver Dollar which said two sixtieths of a Silver Dollar shall be paid or received as before mentioned any thing herein contained to the Contrary thereof in any wise notwithstanding) & Lastly he the said Charles Beatty for himself his Heirs Executors Administrators & Assigns doth Covenant & agree to & with the said Henry Yost his Heirs and Assigns that the said Charles Beatty & his Heirs the said Lot or portion of Ground Hereditaments & all & singular the Premises here before mentioned with their & every of their Appurtenances unto him the said Henry Yost his Heirs & Assigns he or they paying the Rents hereby Reserved at the time & in the manner hereby directed & Performing the Covenants herein Contained against the Claim & demand of him the said Charles Beatty his Heirs or Assigns & all & every other person or persons whatsoever shall & will Warrant & defend forever by these presents. In Witness whereof the said Parties have Hereunto set their Hands & Affixed their Seals the Day & year first within mentioned

Signed Sealed & Delivered in the presence of
Richard Thompson George Creall

Cha Beatty (Seal)
M Beatty (Seal)
Henry Yost (Seal)

On the back of Which Deed was the following Endorsement Viz:t State of Maryland Montgomery County on the twenty Seventh Day of February one Thousand Seven Hundred and Eighty Six Came Charles Beatty & Henry Yost Parties to the within Instrument of Writing before us the Subscribers two of the Justices of the peace for said County & Acknowledged the same to be their Act & Deed agreeable to the Act of Assembly in such Case made & provided. At the same time came Martha wife of the said Charles Beatty before us & being privately Examined out of the hearing of her said Husband said that she freely & willingly acknowledged the within Instrument of Writing to be her voluntary Act & Deed agreeable to the Act of Assembly in that Case made & provided before Richard Thompson George Creall

40

Winchester Notes

BY

MRS. FANNY WINCHESTER HOTCHKISS

Printed at New Haven, Conn.
BY
The Tuttle, Morehouse & Taylor Co.
1912

328   WINCHESTER NOTES.

  6. SELINA WINCHESTER, married —— Robeson, and died leaving one child:
      i. SUSAN ROBESON, married Horace Hill of New Orleans.
  7. LUCILLUS WINCHESTER.
  8. JAMES WINCHESTER.
  9. GEORGE W. WINCHESTER, father of Mrs. Alice W. Person.

(*Gen. II*) MARY WINCHESTER, daughter of William and Lydia (Richards) Winchester, born Oct. 17, 1755; died Oct. 31, 1799; married —— Roberts.

  1. LYDIA ROBERTS, married —— Yost.
  2. RACHEL ROBERTS, married —— Stuart.
  3. GEORGE ROBERTS.
  4. WILLIAM ROBERTS.
  5. SARAH ROBERTS, married —— Corbit.
  6. SYDNEY ROBERTS, married —— Lytle.
  7. MARY ROBERTS, married Carneal.
  8. JOHN ROBERTS.
  9. STEPHEN ROBERTS.
  10. AMELIA ROBERTS, married —— McCarty.
  11. CATHERINE ROBERTS, married —— Scott.

(*Gen. II*) GEORGE WINCHESTER[2] (*William*[1]), son of William and Lydia (Richards) Winchester, was born March 6, 1757. A member of the Society of the Cincinnati. Killed by Indians, July 9, 1794, near Gallatin, Tenn. Never married.

George Winchester, Lieut., commissioned Jan. 1, 1779. Ensign George Winchester, commissioned April 8, 1777. (Muster Rolls of Maryland, pp. 478, 600.)

He served through the Revolutionary War and held the rank of Lieutenant in the Revolutionary Army, and was a prisoner of war at Charleston, S. C. (See Scharf's History of Maryland, Vol. 3, p. 772.)

In 1784 he, with his brother James, migrated to Tennessee and built a mill there; also purchased a large tract of land the site of the present city of Memphis. In 1794, on July 9, George Winchester was waylaid and killed by Indians near Gallatin, Tenn.

From Dr. Thomas Edward Sears, Secretary of the Society of the Cincinnati of Maryland: "The Society of the Cincinnati of Maryland records show that Lieut. George Winchester signed

Children of HENRY and LYDIA ELEANOR (ROBERTS) YOST are:

Lydia Eleanor (Roberts) Yost
(Picture courteous of Susan Vaught, Susan's 3rd Great Grandmother)
(Tim Stadler, Author's Great Great Great Grandmother)

Susan Vaught advises in an email when she sent the picture to me, "They say this is how she dressed all the time. Those are the finger-less gloves on her hands and made of lace. It doesn't show very good in this picture, it looks like she has a problem but I don't think so. This picture was an original in my grandmother's book and my cousins kindly sent to me."

John Winchester Yost born August 06, 1823 **(See John Winchester Yost's Life later in book)**

George Casper Yost born August 22, 1825 in Illinois. He married Sarah Elizabeth Morris born 1827 in New York.

George was born on Fancy Farm, Franklin County Illinois. At an early age in his youth, he went to Equality in Gallatin County, Illinois. (the closest settlement of any importance to his father's home at the time) and remained there until he learned the trade of saddler and harness maker. In 1847, he moved to Jackson Fort, Arkansas, and in May of 1848 went to Batesville, Arkansas. There he married Sarah Elizabeth Morris on November 9th, 1848. A year later he moved to Rock Island, Illinois where he spent a year, then moved back to the old Homestead of Fancy Farm where he remained until 1855. George then moved to Meolark, Iowa and in 1856 to Shelbyville, Missouri. There Robert Morris Yost was born. In 1857, George and his family moved to Utica, Missouri and in 1858 to Breckinridge in Caldwell County, Missouri. In the Spring of 1860 George continued his movements to Farmer City, Missouri and then to Sedalia in 1864 where Casper Salathial Yost was born on July 1st. George Casper was the founder of the First Masonic Lodge of Sedalia and its First Grand Master.

George Casper Yost and wife Elizabeth Morris Yost

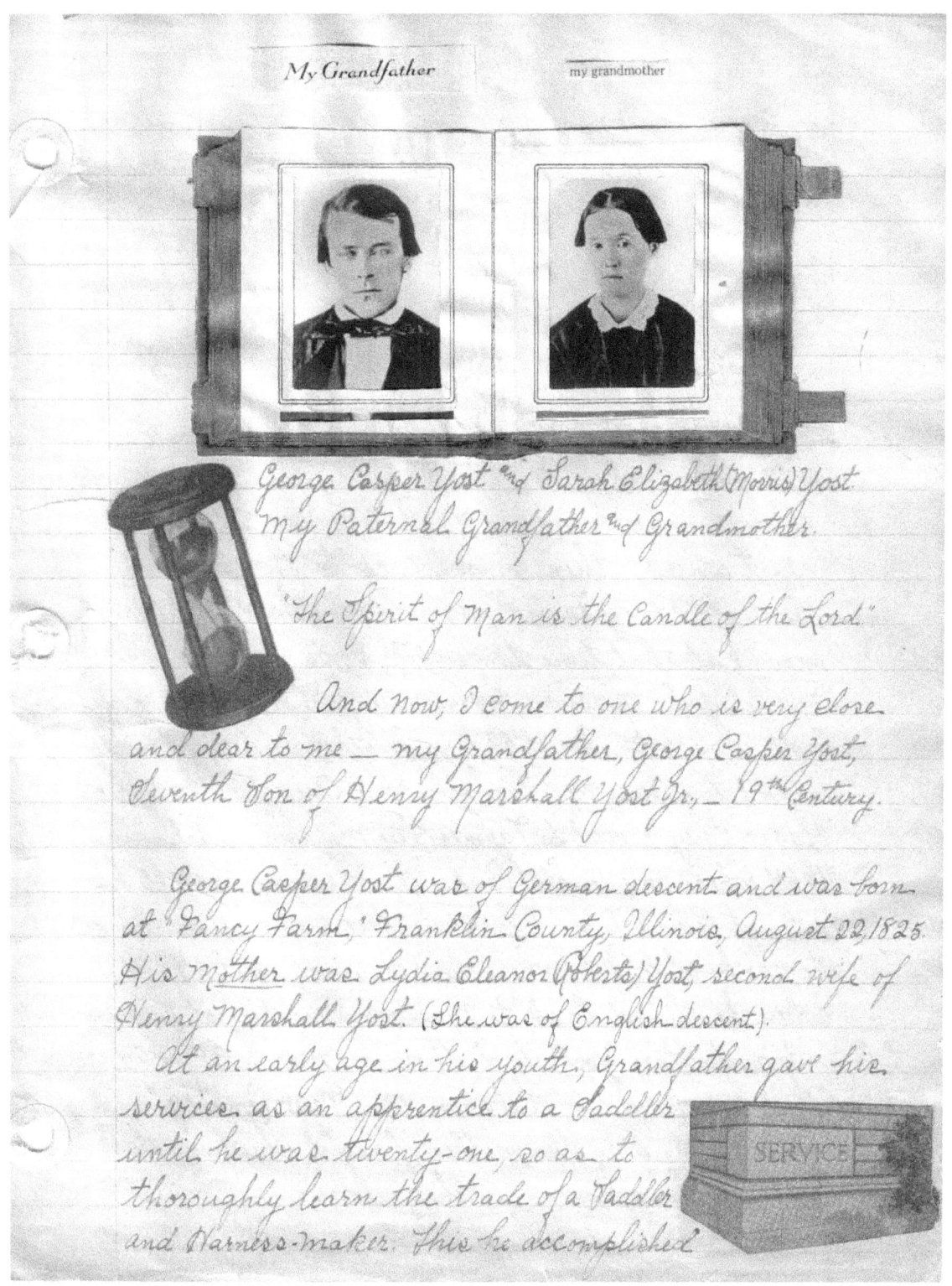

George Casper Yost and Sarah Elizabeth (Morris) Yost
My Paternal Grandfather and Grandmother.

"The Spirit of Man is the Candle of the Lord"

And now, I come to one who is very close and dear to me — my Grandfather, George Casper Yost, Seventh Son of Henry Marshall Yost Jr. — 19th Century.

George Casper Yost was of German descent and was born at "Fancy Farm," Franklin County, Illinois, August 22, 1825. His mother was Lydia Eleanor (Roberts) Yost, second wife of Henry Marshall Yost. (She was of English descent).

At an early age in his youth, Grandfather gave his services as an apprentice to a Saddler until he was twenty-one, so as to thoroughly learn the trade of a Saddler and Harness-maker. This he accomplished

Courtesy of Sallie Pritchard wrote this when she was in high school about in the late 1950's

Geo. C. Yost
to
Sarah Morris

State of Arkansas
County of Independence

I William C Curry a duly licensed and accredited Minister of the Methodist Episcopal Church do hereby certify that on the 9th day of Nov. AD 1848, at the County of Independence and State of Arkansas I did duly join in marriage George C Yost aged 23 years and Sarah Morris aged 21 years both of the county and State aforesaid according to the forms, customs or ceremonies prescribed by said Church whereof I am a minister and there and there declared them to be husband and wife.

Given under my hand this 20th day of Nov. AD 1848
Wm. C Curry L.D.

Filed & Recorded Nov. 26th AD 1848
W.R. Miller Clerk
Ex officio Recorder
By M.C. Towe Dpy Clk

Filed & Recorded Independence County Set

	Wm. Hoppies	11	M					Ill.
155 155	G.C. Yost	35	M	Clerk			500	N.Y.
	S.C. Yost	33	M					Ark.
	Mary C.	11	F					Mo.
	Rob. Morris	5	M					"
	Eliza May	1	F					Ia.
	Josephine S. Haywood	17	F	Domestic affairs				Va.

1860 George Casper Yost and family Missouri Pettis Bowling Green Census

(No. 23.)

ALPHABETICAL LIST of Persons in Division No. 7, of Collection District No. 1, of the State of Missouri, liable to a tax under the Excise laws of the United States, and the amount thereof, as assessed by John Y. P. Blair, Assistant Assessor, and by Thosfield Shipin, Assessor, returned to the Collector of said District, for the month of _____, 186_.

Assessors must be particular to fill all the blanks in this form, as far as practicable, and to number all articles and occupations upon which taxes are assessed to correspond with the entry in the Abstract.

No. of Line	Date of Demand 1865	Name	Location	Article or Occupation	No. in Abstract	Quantity	Valuation	Rate of Tax	Amount of Tax upon Particular Article	Total
1				Amt Forward						6421 86
2	April 28	Windsor I. R.	208 Bdwy	Ret Liq Deal	235			25 $	25 00	
3	"	Same	"	W S Dealer	239	Sale 8700	87 $	8700	112 00	
4	"	Wesley Petitt	83 Morgan	Photograph	228	op less 1000			15 00	
5	29	Wilson John	70 Do	Ret Deal	234			10 $	10 00	
6	"	White Thom	139 ½ 7th	Do	"			"	10 00	
7	"	Wakeman W	60 Morgan	RetLiq Deal	235			25 $	25 00	
8	May 3	Wright Jr	132 N 5 St	Manufactor	219			10 $	10 00	
9	"	Waldmer Benedict	199 Chest No	Do	"			"	10 00	
10	"	Whittaker Mary	103 Morgan	Ret Dealer	234			"	10 00	
11	8	Wasserman Anden	182 N 2 St	W S Liq Dealer	240	Sale 13700	137	137 00		
12	"	Same	"	Rectifier	233	500 bl		25 $	25 00	162 00
13	10	Wolf Joseph	22 North Wk	Butcher	195			10 $	10 00	
14	"	Wely W M D	87½ Morgan	Physician	231			"	10 00	
15	"	Wenkell Christ	15 g Morgan	Manufac	219			"	10 00	
16	12	Mann & Meek	133 Gwin	Ret Liq Deal	235			25 $	25 00	
17	17	Wensch Wm	216 Bdwy	Ret Dealer	234			10	10 00	
18	23	Waggenman Lewis	55 F av	Ret Liq Dealer	235			25 $	25 00	
19	"	Same	"	W S Dealer	239	Sale 3500	50 $	50 00	75 00	
20	24	Witte Geo	158 F av	Ret Dealer	234			10	10 00	
21	"	Westerhode N Co	160 F av	Manufactor	219			"	10 00	
22	June 3	Winter D & Co	204 F av	Ret Dealer	234			"	10 00	
23	8	Willhardt C	200 F av	Manufact	219			"	10 00	
24	"	Michard Jno	58 Cor 11 ½ May	Ret Dealer	234			"	10 00	
25	"	Same	"	RetLiq Dealer	235			25	25 00	35 00
26	"	Whittenbrook H	216 F av	Ret Dealer	234			10	10 00	
27	"	Same	"	Ret Liq Dea	235			25	25 00	35 00
28	12	W Wooldridge F	Wm b 11 ½ 6 M	Ret Deal	234			10	10 00	
29	19	Wilke R C	195 Bdwy	Ret Deal	"			"	10 00	
30	24	Winters Frank	9 Nth St	Do	"			"	10 00	
31	"	Wegmens W	7 "	Do	"			"	10 00	
32	26	Winters Joseph	12 "	Do	"			"	10 00	
33	July 3	Walter W	18 "	Do	"			"	10 00	
34										
35										
36										
37										
38	May 8	Yeager & Co	172 N 2 St	W S Dealer	239	Sale 60500	605 $	605 00		
39	23	Yost George	215 F av	Ret Liq Dead	235			25 $	25 00	
40	June 9	Yeager Frank	Corn St 11th 95	Ret Dealer	234			10 $	10 00	
41										
42										
43										6532 86

1870 George Casper Yost and family Illinois Jackson Carbondale

George Casper Yost IRS Tax Assessment Illinois 1865

Death of George C. Yost 7-1903

George Casper Yost died Saturday, July 18, at the home of his son, R. M. Yost, in Farmington, after an illness of several weeks. Mr. Yost was born in Gallatin county, Illinois, August 22, 1825. He was the last of ten children. Early in life he moved to Batesville, Ark., where he was married to Sarah E. Morris.

The deceased lived for a time after his marriage in his native State and then moved to Missouri. His wife died in 1874, and in 1879 he was remarried to Mrs. Sullivan of Richland, Mo. His second wife died in 1896. Mr. Yost was the father of eight children, five of whom are now living. The living sons and daughters are, Robert M. Yost of this city, editor of the Farmington Progress, Casper S. Yost and Mrs. F. P. Scott of St Louis, Mrs. Jno. Miner of Los Angeles, Cal., and Clarence B. Yost of Dallas, Texas.

The funeral services were conducted by Rev. R. M. Talbert at the home of Mr. R. M. Yost Sunday afternoon. The burial services were performed by the Masonic Lodge of this city at the Masonic cemetery.

Mr. Yost was a prominent and honored Mason. He was for over fifty years an ardent worker in the Christian church, being an Elder in that church.

His life was one of good works, spent in the service of God and his fellowman. His was truly a passing, nothing more. Peaceful and faithful to the last, having overcome all things on earth, he is heir to all things in heaven. His change from mortality to the immortal has made us to realize that:

"There is no death, what seems so is transition;
This passing life of breath
Is but a suburb of the life Elysian,
Whose portals we call death."

R. M. T.

George Casper Yost's Obituary

Children of George Casper Yost and Sara were:

Mary "Molly" Eleanor Yost born September 08, 1849 in Batesville, Arkansas. Died September 08, 1922 in Chihowee, Missouri. On February 24, 1876 she married Fountain Paul Scott born November 17, 1844 in Laclede County, Missouri, died November 16, 1915 in Post Oak, Missouri. They had three children, Monta Yost Scott, Morris Erritt Scott and James Paul Scott.

Fount Paul Scott and Mary Eleanor Yost Marriage Certificate

In 1870 Fountain Scott was listed as a school teacher in Laclede Co, MO, by 1880 he was a farmer, in the same County. In 1895 he's living in Kansas City and works in the Insurance Business. Interestingly, his son Morris is listed as a Newspaperman at age 16. I guess he got an early start on his career. By 1900 Fountain is in St Louis and listed as a Collector, no other details. In 1910, age 65, he's back to farming in Johnson Co, MO. His wife Mollie was a housewife.

Fountain's father, Joab Scott is considered one of the founders of Laclede Co, MO. He served as the counties first Assessor, he was their second Sheriff and later served as a County Court Justice. He was a prominent Mason.

Fountain's grandfather, Jesse Scott was a Veteran of the War of 1812 and fought at the Battle of New Orleans. He was a private in Capt Hutchins Co, 2nd TN Horse Regiment, General Coffey Brigade. He participated in the taking of Pensacola, from there to Big

Sandy and from there by forced march to New Orleans. This march is quite famous 135 miles in 3 days to support Andrew Jackson's flank. Jesse Scott married married Jennie Dial, her father was Jeremiah. Jeremiah Dial was born in 1758, in Dublin Ireland. He came to America in 1772 arriving in Charleston, SC. He died September 22, 1834 in Bedford County, Tennessee. At the outbreak of the war he enlisted as a Private and served 15 months. He reenlisted in 1780 and served to the end of the war. He fought in the battles of Blackstone and Cowpens. At Cowpens, he was one of Colonel William Washington's gallant cavalrymen.

Boston Sunday Globe July 7, 1957 reprint of cartoon by Morris Erritt Scott

Children of Mary "Molly E. Yost Scott and Fountain Paul Scott were:

Monta Yost Scott born January 4, 1877 born in Lebanon Missouri, died November 20, 1944 in Jackson Co, Missouri. Monta married May 19, 1897 Joseph E Murry born May 1872 in Missouri.

Their children were:

Burke Murry born April 8, 1890 in St Louis, MO
Julia Frances Murry born August 28, 1900 in St Louis MO

Monta then married William Best on January 2, 1911

Monta Yost Scott and William Best had the following child:

Marion Adaline Best born July 5, 1914

Morris Erritt Scott born January 25, 1879 in Lebanon, Missouri, died December 4, 1922 in Boston, MA. Morris married January 12, 1906 to Nettie Leah Romkey born July 15, 1882 in Petite Riviere, Nova Scotia, died January 4, 1940 in Boston, MA

They had the following children, Marian Aleah Scott, Walter Scott, Paul Aubrey Scott.

Morris Erritt Scott

POPULAR ARTIST OF POST DEAD

Morris Scott Gained Great Repute by Clever Work

MORRIS SCOTT.
Post artist, who died yesterday at his home, 18 Alexander street, Dorchester

Morris Scott, former Post cartoonist and sketch artist, one of the best known in newspaper circles in the country, died yesterday after a long illness at his home, 18 Alexander street, Dorchester.

WON GREAT POPULARITY

A wife, Nettie Romkey Scott, and three children, Marion, 9; Walter, 8; and Paul, 6, survive him. He also leaves a sister, Mrs. William Best, of Chilhowee, Mo.

Funeral services will be held tomorrow afternoon at 2 o'clock at his home. Burial will be at Mt. Hope.

Thousands on thousands of readers throughout the country, young and old, derived fun and enjoyment from the efforts of his pen and pencil. Of a quiet and unassuming disposition, yet possessing a remarkable sense of keenness in delving into and seeing through the humorous side of a situation, he in addition had the happy faculty of being able to put his ideas down in black and white, bringing a laugh from the most set and sedate.

Gained Fame by Sports Strip

He was an all-round sketch artist and in his 15 or more years with the Post covered news in all its varied form. His daily "sporting strip" was a feature of the Post's sporting page, and it told in a glance what would take hours to grasp through reading.

His early training was with a St. Louis paper, of which an uncle was proprietor. Born in St. Louis, the son of Morris and Mollie Scott, he was educated in the public schools and at an early age showed ability to sketch. He came East 20 years ago and his first and only newspaper connections in Boston were with the Post, where he was an acknowledged favorite.

Outside of his business his interests were of his home and family. He was not affiliated with any social organizations.

Years ago when "The Bingville Bugle," the Sunday Post's special supplement, was in its prime, "Scott" was its illustrator. His sketches for the "Bugle" were fun-provokers and brought laughter in spasms. His cow with the upturned tongue will be remembered by thousands. His knowledge of farm life was an additional asset in his sketching for the "Bugle."

In none of his sketches of prominent men of the country, and he drew the lines of many of them, did he ever offend. From more than one he received tribute for his ability to bring out their believed-hidden oddities.

One of Mr. Scott's marked traits was his devotion to his family, although far removed from father and mother and sister, he took pride and delight in contributing to their welfare.

Six years ago Mr. Scott's ill health forced him to give up active work.

Children of Morris Erritt Scott and Nettie Leah Romkey were:
Marian Aleah Scott born May 18, 1913 in Boston, MA, died September 5, 1996 in New Bedford, married May 4, 1946 to Peter Holodinski born May 4, 1915 in Manchester, NH, died October 4, 1991 in Las Vegas, NV. Marian was a school teacher for over 40 years in

the Boston Public School system. Peter was a WWII veteran and served aboard the USS Arkansas.

From Peter's son Michael,

"Peter enlisted 24 OCT 1942 in Boston as a Carpenter's Mate Third Class. Service No. 203 56 73. He was Honorably discharged in Williamsburg, VA on 01 OCT 1945 as a Carpenter's Mate Second Class. His service record reads: USNRS Boston, MA; USN Training Station Great Lakes, IL; RS Brooklyn,NY; USS Arkansas; 10:CERU NOB Argentia Newfoundland; USNAS Argentia, Newfoundland; US NH St Albans,NY; NSOTC, CAY ANX., NYNK Bayonne; ABSTC, Camp Peary, WIMVA, USNTADC, WIMVA

While looking up this info I discovered that he was a Disabled Veteran. Not sure what for. I do recall my mother telling me that he was in the hospital when his ship was getting ready to leave port. He didn't want to leave his shipmates so he left the hospital w/o permission to join the ship. Mom said he never fully recovered from his injuries. He always had great difficulty walking. Like most WWII Vets he spoke little of his experiences. He used to sing me this little ditty anytime I asked about his war experiences. "I joined the Navy to see the world; but what did I see, I saw the sea. I saw the Atlantic and the Pacific; but the Pacific wasn't terrific, and the Atlantic wasn't too very much to see." I think it's an offshoot of an Irving Berlin song."

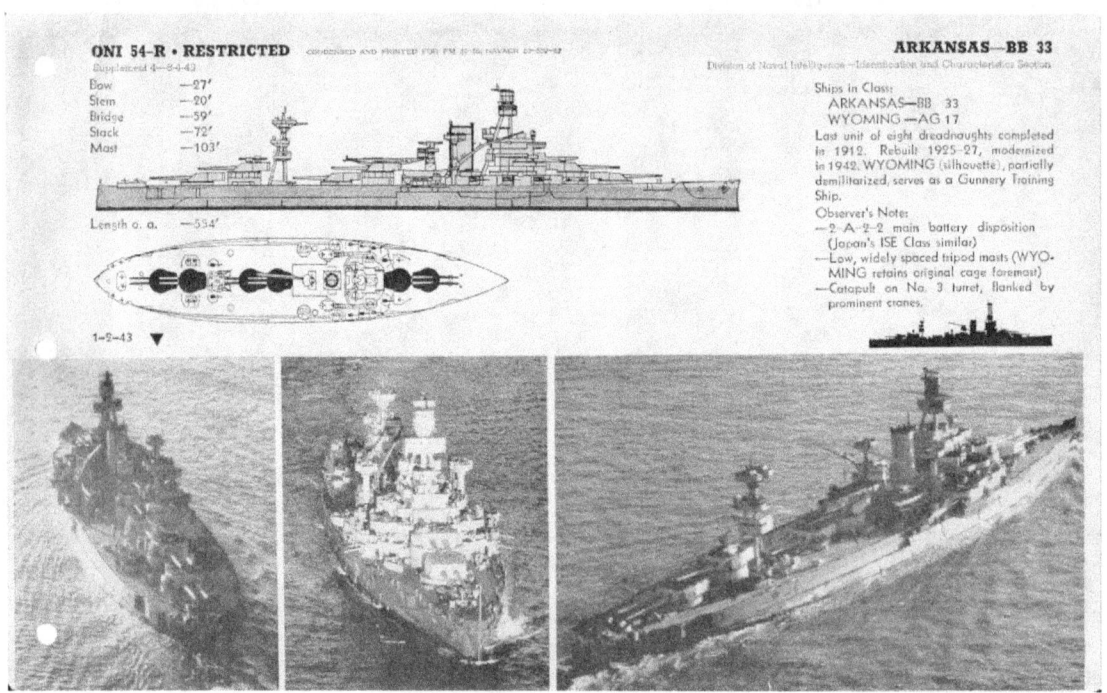

USS Arkansas World War II

World War Two

The outbreak of war with the Japanese attack upon the Pacific Fleet at Pearl Harbor found *Arkansas* at anchor in Casco Bay, Maine. One week later, on 14 December, she sailed to Hvalfjordur, Iceland. Returning to Boston, via Argentia, on 24 January 1942, *Arkansas* spent the month of February carrying out exercises in Casco Bay in preparation for her role as an escort for troop and cargo transports. On 6 March, she arrived at Norfolk to begin overhaul. Underway on 2 July, *Arkansas* conducted shakedown in Chesapeake Bay, then proceeded to New York City, where she arrived on 27 July.

The battleship sailed from New York on 6 August, bound for Greenock, Scotland. Two days later, the ships paused at Halifax, Nova Scotia, then continued on through the stormy North Atlantic. The convoy reached Greenock on the 17th, and *Arkansas* returned to New York on 4 September. She escorted another Greenock-bound convoy across the Atlantic, then arrived back at New York on 20 October. With the Allied invasion of North Africa, American convoys were routed to Casablanca to support the operations. Departing New York on 3 November, *Arkansas* covered a troop convoy to Morocco, and returned to New York on 11 December for overhaul.

On 2 January 1943, *Arkansas* sailed to Chesapeake Bay for gunnery drills. She returned to New York on 30 January and began loading supplies for yet another transatlantic trip. The battleship made two runs between Casablanca and New York City from February through April. In early May, *Arkansas* was drydocked at the New York Navy Yard, emerging from that period of yard work to proceed to Norfolk on 26 May.

Arkansas assumed her new duty as a training ship for midshipmen, based at Norfolk. After four months of operations in Chesapeake Bay, the battleship returned to New York to resume her role as a convoy escort. On 8 October, the ship sailed for Bangor, Ireland. She was in that port throughout November, and got underway to return to New York on 1 December. *Arkansas* then began a period of repairs on 12 December. Clearing New York for Norfolk two days after Christmas of 1943, *Arkansas* closed the year in that port.

1944 in the Atlantic

The battleship sailed on 19 January 1944 with a convoy bound for Ireland. After seeing the convoy safely to its destination, the ship reversed her course across the Atlantic and reached New York on 13 February. *Arkansas* went to Casco Bay on 28 March for gunnery exercises, before she proceeded to Boston on 11 April for repairs.

On 18 April, *Arkansas* sailed once more for Bangor, Ireland. Upon her arrival, the battleship began a training period to prepare for her new role as a shore bombardment ship. On 3 June, *Arkansas* sailed for the French coast to support the Allied invasion of Normandy. The ship entered the Baie de la Seine on 6 June, and took up a position 4,000 yards off "Omaha" beach. At 0552, *Arkansas*'s guns opened fire. During the day, the venerable battleship underwent shore battery fire and air attacks; over ensuing days she continued her fire support. On the 13th, *Arkansas* shifted to a position off Grandcamp les Bains.

On 25 June 1944, *Arkansas* dueled with German shore batteries off Cherbourg, the enemy repeatedly straddling the battleship but never hitting her. Her big guns helped support the Allied attack on that key port, and led to the capture of it the following day. Retiring to Weymouth, England, and arriving there at 2220, the battleship shifted to Bangor, on 30 June.

Arkansas stood out to sea on 4 July, bound for the Mediterranean. She passed through the Strait of Gibraltar and anchored at Oran, Algeria, on 10 July. On the 18th, she got underway, and reached Taranto, Italy, on 21 July. The battleship remained there until 6 August, then shifted to Palermo, Sicily, on the 7th.

On 14 August, Operation "Anvil" the invasion of the southern French coast between Toulon and Cannes, began. *Arkansas* provided fire support for the initial landings on 15 August, and continued her bombardment through 17 August. After stops at Palermo and Oran, *Arkansas* set course for the United States. On 14 September, she reached Boston, and received repairs and alterations through early November. The yard period completed on 7 November, *Arkansas* sailed to Casco Bay for three days of refresher training. On 10 November, *Arkansas* shaped a course south for the Panama Canal Zone. After transiting the canal on 22 November, *Arkansas* headed for San Pedro, Calif. On 29 November, the ship was again underway for exercises held off San Diego. She returned on 10 December to San Pedro.

1945 in the Pacific

After three more weeks of preparations, *Arkansas* sailed for Pearl Harbor on 20 January 1945. One day after her arrival there, she sailed for Ulithi, the major fleet staging area in the Carolines, and continued thence to Tinian, where she arrived on 12 February. For two days, the vessel held shore bombardment practice prior to her participation in the assault on Iwo Jima.

At 0600 on 16 February, *Arkansas* opened tire on Japanese strong points on Iwo Jima as she lay off the island's west coast. The old battlewagon bombarded the island through the 19th, and remained in the fire support area to provide cover during the evening hours. During her time off the embattled island, *Arkansas* shelled numerous Japanese positions, in support of the bitter struggle by the marines to root out and destroy the stubborn enemy resistance. She cleared the waters off Iwo Jima on 7 March to return to Ulithi. After arriving at that atoll on the 10th, the battleship rearmed, provisioned, and fueled in preparation for her next operation, the invasion of Okinawa.

Getting underway on 21 March, *Arkansas* began her preliminary shelling of Japanese positions on Okinawa on 25 March, some days ahead of the assault troops which began wading ashore on 1 April. The Japanese soon began an aerial onslaught, and *Arkansas* fended on several kamikazes. For 46 days, *Arkansas* delivered fire support for the invasion of Okinawa. On 14 May, the ship arrived at Apra Harpor, Guam, to await further assignment.

After a month at Apra Harbor, part of which she spent in drydock, *Arkansas* got underway on 12 June for Leyte Gulf. She anchored there on the 16th, and remained in Philippine waters until the war drew to a close in August. On the 20th of that month, *Arkansas* left Leyte to return to Okinawa, and reached Buckner Bay on 23 August. After a month spent in port, *Arkansas* embarked approximately 800 troops for transport to the United States as part of the "Magic Carpet" to return American servicemen home as quickly as possible. Sailing on 23 September, *Arkansas* paused briefly at Pearl Harbor en route, and ultimately reached Seattle on 15 October. During the remainder of the year, the battleship made three more trips to Pearl Harbor to shuttle soldiers back to the United States.

During the first months of 1946, *Arkansas* lay at San Francisco. In late April the ship got underway for Hawaii. She reached Pearl Harbor on 8 May, and stood out of Pearl Harbor on 20 May, bound for Bikini Atoll, earmarked for use as target for atomic bomb testing in Operation "Crossroads." On 25 July 1946, the venerable battleship was sunk in Test "Baker" at Bikini. Decommissioned on 29 July 1946, *Arkansas* was struck from the Naval Vessel Register on 15 August 1946.

Arkansas **received four battle stars for her World War II**

Photo # 19-N-77075   USS Arkansas in San Pedro harbor, California, January 1945

Photo # 80-G-231250   USS Arkansas bombarding off Normandy, 6 June 1944

Children of Marian Aleah Scott and Peter Holodinski were:

Dianne Holodinski born March 28, 1948 in Boston, MA

Michael Holodinski born March 11, 1950 in Boston, MA.

Marian Aleah Scott Holodinski, Michael Holodinski and Peter Holodinski

Michael Holodinski born March 11, 1950 in Boston, MA, married to Janice Marie Diggins born June 19, 1950 in Boston, Ma. Michael is a Vietnam veteran having served in the US Army as a Thai Linguist/ Interpreter. He is also a retired Police Captain from the City of New Bedford, MA. Janice is a Registered Nurse and works in the local hospital Emergency Room. They were married on March 20, 1971 in Boston, Ma. Their children are Melissa Holodinski born February 03, 1973 in Boston, Ma. and Michael David Holodinski born May 27, 1975 in New Bedford. They have 3 grandchildren: Ashley daughter of Michael David and Brett and Mallory, Melissa's children.

Michael and Janice Marie (Diggins) Holodinski

Children of Michael Holodiski are:

Michael David Holodinski

Melissa Holodiski

Mallory & Brett, Melissa's children **Ashley with her father Michael David**

Marilyn Holodinski born December 2, 1951 in Boston, MA, died September 8, 2005 in Las Vegas, NV

Children of Morris Errett Scott and Nettie Leah Romkey cont'd

Walter Scott born December 29, 1914 in Malden, MA
Paul Aubrey Scott born August 27, 1916 in Boston, MA

Children of Mary "Molly E. Yost Scott and Fountain Paul Scott cont'd

James Paul Scott born July 27, 1881 in Lebanon, MO, died November 2, 1939 in Warrensburg, MO

Children of George Casper Yost and Sara Elizabeth Morris Yost cont'd:

Robert Morris Yost born September 23, 1856 in Shelbyville, Missouri. He died February 21, 1916 in Los Angeles, Los Angeles County, California. He was first married to **Sallie Lynch Moore** born March 08, 1854 in Booneville, Cooper County, Missouri. They were married September 30, 1878 in Jefferson City, Missouri.

Robert Morris Yost
Courtesy of Susan Vaught

Sally Lynch (Moore) Yost
Courtesy of Susan Vaught

They had the following children, **Willie Yost** born August 30, 1879, **Maria Louise Yost** born August 27, 1881, **Sallie Moore Yost** born January 29, 1884, **Robert Morris Yost Jr.** born July 07, 1886, **Marquirite Yost** born February 01, 1889, **Kathryn "Katie" Alice Yost** born September 26, 1891, **Mamie Yost** born November 15, 1893,

Yost's Left - Sallie Moore Yost, Robert Morris Yost Jr., Maria Louise Yost
Front Kathryn "Katie" Alice Yost
Courtesy of Susan Vaught

Maria Louise Yost born August 27, 1881 in St. Louis, Missouri, died 1952. Maria married Frederick Schwartz in 1902 in St. Louis, Missouri.

Maria Louise Yost

Sallie Moore Yost born January 29, 1884 in St. Louis Missouri, died February 11, 1965 in Los Angeles, Los Angeles County, California. Sallie married Oliver Perry Schureman born March 26, 1877 in Lee Summit, Missouri. They were married June 21, 1909 in Los Angeles, Los Angeles County, California.

Oliver Perry and Sallie Moore (Yost) Schureman had the following children, Oliver Perry Schureman born April 08, 1911, Living Schureman, Baby Schureman born July 12, 1919 died the same date in So. Pasadena, Los Angeles County, California, Robert Schureman born December 24, 1920

Sallie Moore Yost (Schureman)

Sallie Moore Yost (Schureman)

Robert Morris Yost Jr. born July 7, 1886 in St. Louis, Missouri, died April 10, 1967 in Santa Monica, Los Angeles County, California. Robert married Laurie Hodge on August 11, 1915 in Los Angeles California. Laurie was born April 23, 1886 in Santa Monica, Los Angeles County, California. Robert began his career as a reporter/writer for the St. Louis (Missouri) Post-Dispatch. Later, worked for the Los Angeles Examiner and then the Los Angeles Morning Herald and the Hearst syndicate services. In 1920, was named the Publicity Director for Fox West Coast Studios and, in early 1930, was appointed head of the scenario department for Fox. Left Fox shortly after the merger of Fox Film Corporation with Darryl F. Zanuck's Century Pictures

Robert Morris Yost Jr.

Robert also became a movie and television writer. His credits include

1. Canyon City (1943)
2. Overland Mail Robbery (1943) (screenplay) (story)
3. Thundering Trails (1943) (screenplay) (story)

4. Sunset Serenade (1942) (story)

5. The Phantom Plainsmen (1942) (screenplay) (story)
6. The Carson City Kid (1940)

7. Young Buffalo Bill (1940)

8. Grand Jury Secrets (1939)

9. Tom Sawyer, Detective (1938)
10. Illegal Traffic (1938) (screenplay) (story)
11. Prison Farm (1938)
12. Tip-Off Girls (1938) (screenplay)
13. Born to the West (1937) (screenplay)
    ... aka Hell Town (USA: reissue title)
14. Thunder Trail (1937)
    ... aka Thunder Pass
15. Forlorn River (1937) (screenplay)
    ... aka River of Destiny (USA: reissue title)
16. Let's Make a Million (1936)
17. Arizona Mahoney (1936)
    ... aka Arizona Thunderbolt
    ... aka Bad Men of Arizona

18. The Arizona Raiders (1936) (screenplay)
    ... aka Bad Men of Arizona (USA: reissue title)
19. Forgotten Faces (1936/I)
20. Desert Gold (1936) (screenplay)
21. Preview Murder Mystery (1936)
22. Drift Fence (1936) (screenplay)
    ... aka Texas Desperadoes
23. Dante's Inferno (1935) (screenplay) (as Robert M. Yost)

Robert M. Yost World War I Draft Registration

CONTRIBUTIONS OF THE YOST FAMILY TO AMERICAN LITERATURE
by Sallie Pritchard

Robert M. Yost

In a study of the writers in the Yost Family one finds three dominant factors for which they stood, individually and collectively. They were almost extremists on these subjects:

PATRIOTISM--Loyalty to their Country
RELIGION--Loyalty to God and Church
EDUCATION--Loyalty to the Mind

Quite naturally their writings reflected their beliefs, whether as journalists, authors, or screen writers.

One of the successful journalists in this family was my great-grandfather, Robert Morris Yost. Of German heritage, he came from a proud and old family in Virginia. His great-grandfather, Henry Yost, settled in Ablemarle County, Virginia in 1777. While serving six months in the American forces in the Revolutionary War as a gunsmith, he made the first musket under government supervision for the United States.

Robert Yost was born in Shelbyville, Missouri to George Casper and Elizabeth Yost on September 23, 1856. His father worked for fifty years as a religious leader in welfare work, being one of the first to organize young people's meetings and Sunday Schools in the Christian Church in the Middle West.

Attending public schools and the Southern Illinois College, which was at that time much like high schools of today, he served as an apprentice in the printing trade. He became increasingly interested in newspaper work, and in 1870, at the age of fourteen, he went to work in the office of the New Era at Carbondale, Missouri. There was probably conflict in his mind, for he had run away from his home, "Funny Farm," because he did not want to help in the raising of horses.

In 1872 he became a compositor with the St. Louis Evening Journal and two years later a reporter for the Morning Journal. When barely twenty-one he was made private secretary to Governor John S. Phelps of Missouri, but after four years in politics he returned to journalism on the staff of the St. Louis Globe Democrat, of which his brother, Casper S. Yost, was editor. From 1883 to 1884 he was successively city and managing editor of the St. Louis Chronicle. He then spent several enjoyable years as literary and dramatic editor and subsequently city editor on the Missouri Republican.

In the late 1880's he became assistant secretary to the State of Missouri, but after several years returned to the Missouri Republican as Sunday editor, and in 1894 he accepted a similar place with the Post Dispatch. He joined the Scripps McCrae League of Newspapers as a special correspondent with headquarters at Cincinnati, and still later became the Jefferson City correspondent for the St. Louis Globe-Democrat. He ultimately was known as an authority on newspaper work and politics in Missouri, where he was one of the leaders of political affairs of the state and had a wide personal acquaintance and friendship with the leading men of the state for more than twenty years. Governor Dockery of Missouri appointed him commissioner to the Pan-American Exposition at Buffalo, and when this assignment was completed, he served as commissioner to the Charleston Exposition. For his work in the field of education at these expositions he was awarded a Gold Medal "for distinguished services."

After moving to Los Angeles in 1904, he was an influential figure in journalism for twelve years, as well as a man admired for his kindly character. He served as an editorial writer on the Los Angeles Times and then became managing editor of the

Morning Herald. Later he was editor to the Express for four years but was forced to relinquish his active career because of advancing ill health.

As with brilliant young writers the growing advancement was often a struggle. In Yost's early years of writing he roomed with Eugene Field. They had little money to start with and lived in an attic room. There was only one pillow, and whoever came in first got the pillow. He was also a personal friend of most of the great authors of that time. Including Robert Louis Stevenson and Samuel Clemens.

In the family now is the only unpublished letter of Mark Twain's, written to Robert Yost. In this letter Mark Twain tells of his visit with his wife in the home of Harriet Beecher Stowe, who happened to be living next door. It was not until they returned home that Mrs. Clemens reminded her husband that he had forgotten to wear his tie. She was concerned for fear Mrs. Stowe would think he did not own one. To prove that he did possess a tie, he laid one out on a large silver platter and sent it over by a servant with a note saying this really was his tie and he could bring witnesses to prove it if she so desired. Mrs. Stowe returned the tie with a note to the effect that she had examined it, and found it to be a tie, and that she would accept his word that it was really his. The tie is now incorporated into a family heirloom, a quilt made entirely of pieces of cravats, dresses, and costumes worn by famous people of my great-grandfather's day.

Yost followed the precedent set by the Great Dane of the New York Sun and had editorials reprinted in other newspapers, both here and abroad, such as the one he wrote on the sinking of the "Titanic." When he became managing editor of the Herald Express he guided and inspired his reporters so that some of them later became editors in their own right, as did his own son, Robert M. Yost, Jr.

Before my great-grandfather came to California, the secretary to the governor of Missouri offered him a number of diplomatic posts abroad. One was in Teheran, Persia. But he would not be lured from the field of journalism which was so much a beloved part of him. Today we have newsmen. In his time the best newspapermen were journalists. Newsmen are more intent upon the gathering of news and less upon its presentation. Journalists gather the news but present it in a true literary form. Robert Yost did just that, and he did so in the finest tradition.

In politics he had the ability to swing the power of the press toward the men not the party. As an example, though normally a Democrat, when William Jennings Bryant was running for President, Yost felt that he was more of an orator than administrator, and therefore staunchly refused to follow the party dictates. As he could not be bribed with money, neither could he be intimidated. One night as editor of the St. Louis Globe Democrat he was working late when a man came to see him and threatened to kill him with the gun in his hand if Yost did not cease the crusade which he was heading to clean up vice in the city. Great-grandfather, appearing outwardly calm, sat there and talked to the man for about three-quarters of an hour, finally persuading him to give up the gun.

He disliked sensationalism in newspaper work and refused to print scandalous rumors that are now so much a part of papers. He felt that honor was one of a man's most precious possessions and that the loss of it was more to be feared than the loss of his life. Upon his passing at the age of fifty-nine, February 21, 1916, obituary notices and editorials paid him great tribute. Such by-lines as "Life marked by career of sterling worth," "Many mourn loss of well-known newspaperman," and "Robert M. Yost had notable career as newspaper worker, author and educator" express fully his worthwhile life. It is obvious that he was highly respected for his ability and loved for is kindly traits of character. One editorial written in his memory speaks of him as "courteous, kindly and considerate, gentle in act and speech, charitable in judgment and quick in sympathy, having an intellectual integrity that was of his very fiber, wide knowledge of man and of events through training in his profession enriched by long experiences in many fields."

Casper S. Yost

Casper Salathiel Yost, my great-great uncle, was editor of the editorial page of the St. Louis Globe Democrat for twenty-six years and was one of the most widely known and distinguished editorial writers in the country.

The older brother of Robert Yost, he was born in Sedalia, Missouri July 1, 1854. He died at the age of seventy-seven with many and varied honors to his credit. After an apprenticeship as a printer and writer, he came to St. Louis in 1881 and for a year was employed as a reporter on the St. Louis Chronicle. Then he turned to railroading and was a telegraph operator until 1885 in Richland, Missouri. He returned to St. Louis in that year to work for three years as a reporter on the Missouri Republican. In 1889 he joined the staff of the Globe-Democrat, and this began a fifty year affiliation with this paper. He always wrote his articles and editorials in longhand, a practice he began before the days of typewriters.

Fragile and aesthetic-looking, he was a spiritual man with high and gentle idealism. The American Society of Newspaper Editors, which he founded in 1922 and of which he was the first president, called him a "practical idealist" by conceiving American rights and American liberties as enforcing a responsibility to American; "he had sought to raise the standard of the entire journalistic profession; in part through inculcating high ethical concepts, in part through demanding higher standards of training and of education."

He wrote a series of editorial which traced the history and the responsibility of the "The American Way" and these were reprinted in brochure from and distributed throughout the nation. Deeply religious, his Christmas and Easter editorials were sermonettes, beautifully written and very appealing, and he practiced the religion he so skillfully wove into his writings. He covered a wide range of subjects in his editorials and was known for his writings on national and international affairs.

Casper Yost also wrote poetry, one poem becoming well-known through President McKinley's quoting it generously in one of his greatest speeches. It was entitled "Our Destiny" and was written on his way to work one morning. It has great strength and beauty.

His books included Principles of Journalism, A Successful Husband, Carpenter of Nazareth, The Quest of God, and Patience Worth.

A number of honors were bestowed upon him, including a Liberty Ship, the S.S. Casper S. Yost, launched in 1943. Academic honorary degrees included LL.D by Lincoln Memorial University in 1926, by McKendree College in 1926 and by the University of Missouri in 1934. In 1940 the degree of Doctor of Literature was bestowed upon him by Culver-Stockton. Signa Delta Chi, national journalism fraternity, in 1936 gave him its national award for scholarship in journalism, saying that his cool and serene judgment had long been an aid n the solution of problems of municipality, state and nation, and praising him for his high ideals of journalism and his consistent contribution to its thoughtful expression.

Dorothy Yost

My great-aunt, Dorothy Yost Cummins, both in appearance and manner seems more like twenty-nine than fifty-nine. Dainty and feminine, a small brunette, bubbling with personality and *joie de vivre,* one might not realize at first the depth of her mentality and talent.

Born in Los Angeles April 25, 1899, to Robert M. Yost and Alice Kern Yost, she was a serious, Mature child. Her talent was apparent early in life when at the age of twelve she wrote an excellent group of fairy stories, one of which was entitled, "Why the Oyster has a Pearl."

At sixteen, upon the death of her father, she began newspaper work. She wanted to write murder stories, but instead was put on the society page. Later, leaving the newspaper world, she went to work for the old Triangle Company, now Metro-Goldwyn-Mayer Studios. Here she started in the reading department and in the same year began writing scenarios and adaptations, her opportunity coming quite by accident when an author became temperamental and left in the middle of a contract. She took over his work and continued to write from then on. Her first adaptation was For the Soul of Raphael, followed by, One Man in a Million. Kentucky Pride and Hills of Kentucky, were both her own stories. Although she has a wide knowledge of various types of people, she has always enjoyed writing horse stories. Kentucky Pride was one of her favorites, that being the name of the horse that starred. Several other of her early screen adaptations were Freckles, Mother, The Whip Hand, and Fangs of the Wild. The last two were her original dog stories.

While discussing this type of writing with my aunt, I learned that screen plays are not a part of the literary world, that they are a medium between books and the stage play. She feels that a screen play is actually a series of directions for the actors, the director, the set designer, the property department, the camera man, and even the electricians. "A screen play tells the story with dialogue by incorporating information to the heads of the different departments," said Miss Yost. And yet, due to the fact that screen play writers must be limited by a fixed number of pages, they learn to choose the exact word needed for any given situation. As a result, many of these scripts are literary gems in their own right.

The screen writer must write originals to fit either a star or a title or an idea which the producer may request. He is also an adapter of the work of other authors. In this particular field Miss Yost has received letters from authors thanking her for the adaptation of their work to screen. One letter was from gene Stratton Porter for her adaptation of Freckles, and the other was from Booth Tarkington for her work on Alice Adams.

With the advent of "talkies," many writers were unable to adjust their thinking from the silent screen, but Miss Yost advanced and some of her greatest successes were in that medium. The film The Gay Divorcee with Fred Astaire and Ginger Rogers was written by her with George Marion, Jr., and was chosen to be put into the archives of the Museum of Motion Picture Arts and Sciences. With her husband, Dwight Cummins, she wrote two of 20th century Fox's greatest box office successes, Thunderhead and Smoky. These pictures about horses followed one written at the beginning of her career, Kentucky Pride, which was a model for all horse racing pictures for a decade afterward.

Moving with the times from motion pictures to television she found there an even more challenging medium, buy by that time she was doing only an occasional story, while her husband forged ahead in this field.

Other well-known stars for whom she wrote include Kathryn Hepburn, Robert Preston, Edward G. Robinson, Fred MacMurray, Anne Baxter, and Ann Harding.

My aunt loves to write, and I am proud of the fact that in her writings she has always thought of the screen as a means of exerting a good influence on the public, and has tried to bring home the principles of morality. Her other writings include magazine stories, religious articles for Unity, and last but not least, No Room at the Inn, a truly beautiful Christmas play of rare quality.

Robert M. Yost, Jr.

When as a very small child, in an attempt to distinguish my great-uncle Robert Morris Yost, Jr., from a young Uncle Bob I surprised him with the greeting, "Hello, *great* Uncle Bob," he was amused and said that "Out of the mouth of babes shall come words of wisdom." His reaction is typical of this writer with a delicious sense of humor and a sunny smile.

Only son of Robert M. Yost and Sallie Moore Yost, he was born July 7, 1887 in St. Louis, Missouri. He attended St. Louis schools and moved with his family to Los

Angeles at the age of seventeen. At this young age he began his career as a newspaper man, eventually becoming a star reporter on the Examiner.

Later he was with the Oliver Morosco Stage Productions as publicity head for seven years. This was followed by a position as head of Fox Film Corporation's publicity department. From 1920-23 he was supervisor of new authors and directors who came here from New York to handle sound pictures. He wrote for Fox and Paramount and was working on a story for Will Rogers when Rogers was killed.

From the time he was a reporter until he retired he continued in the same journalistic tradition his father had inspired in him. He became the intimate friend of such authors as Don Marquis, Zane Gray, Will James, and Aldous Huxley. While in the newspaper profession, both he and his father encouraged many young authors, not merely through their interest and understanding of their work, but the more practical means of bringing them to the attention of the
public through favorable reviews and interviews.

This paper would not fulfill it's purpose without at least mentioning that the writing talent in the Yost family has continued on to Great-uncle Bob's son, the third Robert M. Yost. Although essentially a teacher, he has recently had a book on philosophy published, An Analysis of Leibits." This red-haired, boyish looking Yost is, at the age of thirty-nine, Associate Professor of Philosophy and Chairman of the department at the University of California at Los Angeles.

This proves that a talented family with homespun beginnings and lacking a well-rounded formal education was still able to pursue and work toward the goal of being good writers. The Yost family has given much to literature through various "pen and quill" fields, and today this has culminated in Dr. Robert M. Yost who has reached the apex in on of the dominant beliefs of the Yost family's philosophy:

EDUCATION--Loyalty to the Mind.

This paper was written by Sallie Pritchard, the Boyd's cousin. Sallie wrote this paper in the late 1950's when she was in high school. It has some wonderful information about the writers in the Yost family.
I personally have three of the writings by two of the Yost writers. I have the screen play, No Room at the Inn, published by Greystone Press in 1937, and the novel, Prodigal Lover, published by Samuel French in the early 1900's, both by Dorothy Yost Cummins. I also have the book, The Carpenter of Nazareth, published by The Bethany Press in 1938, by Casper S. Yost.
I just happened to see a cowboy movie, from the late 30's or early 40's, on television one evening. When it ended it said it was written by Robert Morris Yost, Jr. I knew it was my great uncle. It would be nice to get copies of these things.

Susan V.

Kathryn "Katie" Alice Yost was born September 26, 1891 in St. Louis Missouri, died February 08, 1957 in Carpendaria, California. She married Lyle Howell Boyd February 10, 1912 in Los Angeles, California. Lyle Howell Boyd was born September 12, 1889 in Forest Lake, Minnesota, died December 20, 1938 in Alhambra, Los Angeles Co., California.

Lyle Howell and Kathryn Alice (Yost) Boyd
Courtesy of Susan Vaught

Lyle Howell and Kathryn Alice (Yost) Boyd has the following children, Lyle Howell Boyd Jr. born August 16, 1915, Robert Lyle Boyd born January 25, 1917

Robert Lyle Boyd born January 25, 1917 in Los Angeles, California, died July 18, 1974 in Skilac Lake, Kenai Borough, Alaska. He married Kathryn Mary Blake on August 01, 1940 in Yuma, Arizona. Kathryn Mary Blake was born June 29, 1918 in Colorado Springs, El Paso County, Colorado.

Robert "Piper" Lyle Boyd
Courtesy of Susan Vaught

Robert Morris Yost then married Alice Roxie Kern born March 22, 1866 near Frankfort Kentucky.

Alice Roxie Kern

The Robert and Alice Roxie (Kern) Yost moved to Pasadena, California in the early 1900's. They lived on 950 Euclid Ave.

They had one child, **Dorothy Yost** born April 25, 1899.

In 1900 Robert Morris Yost was living in St. Louis Missouri with his father, George Casper Yost at 74 at the time. They had one servant Maud Royal, a black female named Maud Royal.

By 1910, Robert and his family moved out to Los Angeles California.

Dorothy Yost born April 25, 1899 in St. Louis Missouri, married Dwight Cummins born February 02, 1902 in Los Angeles California.

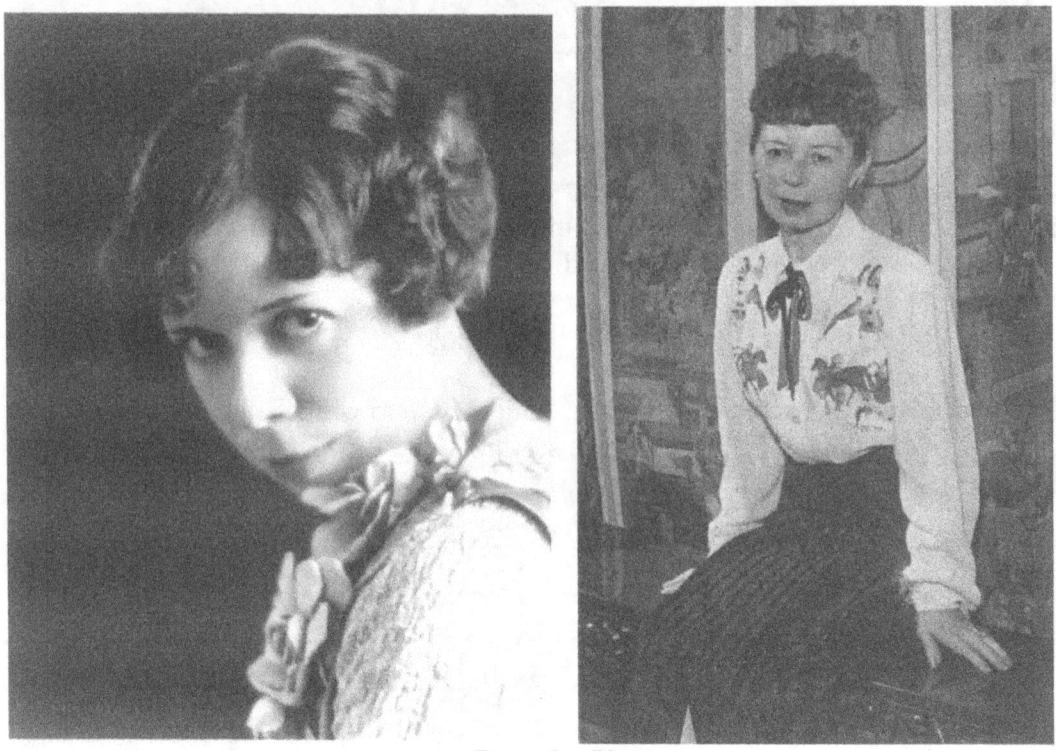

Dorothy Yost
Courtesy of Susan Vaught

By 1930, Robert Cummins and Dorothy Yost are married. Dorothy's mother Alice R. Yost is a widow and living with them. Dwight is a movie director and Dorothy is a movie and television series writer.

Dorothy Yost wrote many scripts for movies and television series along with her husband Dwight.

Writer - filmography
(1960s) (1950s) (1940s) (1930s) (1920s)

1. Smoky (1966) (1946 screenplay)

2. "Annie Oakley" (1 episode, 1954)
    - Bull's Eye (1954) TV Episode
3. Saginaw Trail (1953)

4. The Cowboy and the Indians (1949)
5. The Big Cat (1949) (screenplay)
6. Loaded Pistols (1948) (screenplay) (story)
7. The Strawberry Roan (1948) (screenplay)
    ... aka Fools Awake (UK)
8. Smoky (1946)
9. Thunderhead - Son of Flicka (1945) (screenplay)
10. Blossoms in the Dust (1941) (uncredited)
11. Hullabaloo (1940) (contributing writer) (uncredited) (contributor to screenplay construction) (uncredited)
12. Sporting Blood (1940) (screenplay)
    ... aka Sterling Metal (USA: TV title)
13. Forty Little Mothers (1940)

14. Bad Little Angel (1939) (screenplay)
15. Blackmail (1939) (story)
16. The Story of Vernon and Irene Castle (1939) (adaptation)

17. Four Girls in White (1939)
18. There Goes the Groom (1937)
19. Too Many Wives (1937)
20. Racing Lady (1937)
21. That Girl from Paris (1936) (screenplay)

22. Swing Time (1936) (uncredited)
23. M'Liss (1936)
24. Bunker Bean (1936) (screenplay)
    ... aka His Majesty Bunker Bean (UK)
25. Murder on a Bridle Path (1936)
26. Seven Keys to Baldpate (1935) (dialogue) (uncredited)
27. Freckles (1935)
28. Alice Adams (1935) (screenplay)
    ... aka Booth Tarkington's Alice Adams (USA: complete title)
29. A Dog of Flanders (1935) (adaptation)
30. Laddie (1935)
31. Roberta (1935) (uncredited) (treatment)
32. The Gay Divorcee (1934) (screenplay)
    ... aka The Gay Divorce (UK)
33. Hello, Everybody! (1933)
34. What Men Want (1930) (also adaptation)
35. The Sea Bat (1930) (story)

36. The Little Yellow House (1928)
37. The Devil's Trademark (1928)
38. Freckles (1928) (also adaptation)
39. Wallflowers (1928)
40. Fangs of the Wild (1928) (story)
41. Little Mickey Grogan (1927) (also adaptation)
42. The Harvester (1927)
43. Judgment of the Hills (1927) (also adaptation)
44. Mother (1927) (also adaptation)
45. Uneasy Payments (1927)
46. Moulders of Men (1927) (continuity)
47. Hills of Kentucky (1927) (story)
48. Wings of the Storm (1926)
49. The Millionaire Policeman (1926) (also adaptation)
50. Kentucky Pride (1925)
51. She Wolves (1925)
52. Marriage in Transit (1925)
53. The Hunted Woman (1925) (also adaptation)
54. Star Dust Trail (1924)
55. My Husband's Wives (1924)
56. Romance Ranch (1924)
57. Broadway or Bust (1924)
58. Traffic in Hearts (1924) (story)
59. Kentucky Days (1923)
60. When Odds Are Even (1923) (also story)
61. Cause for Divorce (1923)
62. The Footlight Ranger (1923)
63. Youth Must Have Love (1922) (also story)
64. The New Teacher (1922) (adaptation)

65. Little Miss Smiles (1922)
66. Winning with Wits (1922)
67. Jackie (1921)
68. Cinderella of the Hills (1921)
69. Queenie (1921)
70. Ever Since Eve (1921)
71. Lovetime (1921)
72. One Man in a Million (1921)
73. For the Soul of Rafael (1920) (scenario)
74. Smoldering Embers (1920) (scenario)
75. Flames of the Flesh (1920) (scenario)

George Casper and Sarah Elizabeth Roberts Yost children cont'd

Eliza "Lizzie" May Yost born May 04, 1859
Casper Salathiel Yost born July 01, 1864

Casper Salathiel Yost (1863-1941) was the longtime editor of the St. Louis Globe-Democrat, where he started working in 1889. He was the founder of the American Society of Newspaper Editors and was influential in developing its code of ethics. He was born in Sedalia, Missouri, and died in St. Louis.

Casper Salathiel Yost and Anna Augusta (Parrott) Yost

No. 50750

UNITED STATES OF AMERICA

STATE OF Missouri
COUNTY OF St. Louis } ss.

I, Casper S. Yost, a NATIVE AND LOYAL CITIZEN OF THE UNITED STATES, hereby apply to the Department of State, at Washington, for a passport for myself and wife, Anna A. Yost.

I solemnly swear that I was born at Sedalia, in the State of Missouri, on or about the 1st day of July, 1864; that my father George C. Yost, was born in Illinois, and is now deceased.

that I have resided outside the United States at the following places for the following periods: Never

and that I am domiciled in the United States, my permanent residence being at St. Louis, in the State of Missouri, where I follow the occupation of Editor.

My last passport was obtained from None

I am about to go abroad temporarily; and I intend to return to the United States within 4 months with the purpose of residing and performing the duties of citizenship therein; and I desire a passport for use in visiting the countries hereinafter named for the following purpose:

England, France, Belgium — Pleasure

I intend to leave the United States from the port of New York sailing on board the Albania on July 12th, 1921.

OATH OF ALLEGIANCE.

Further, I do solemnly swear that I will support and defend the Constitution of the United States against all enemies, foreign and domestic; that I will bear true faith and allegiance to the same; and that I take this obligation freely, without any mental reservation or purpose of evasion: So help me God.

Casper S. Yost

Sworn to before me this 27th day of May, 1921.

Deputy Clerk of the U.S. Court at St. Louis.

Casper Salathiel Yost Passport Application

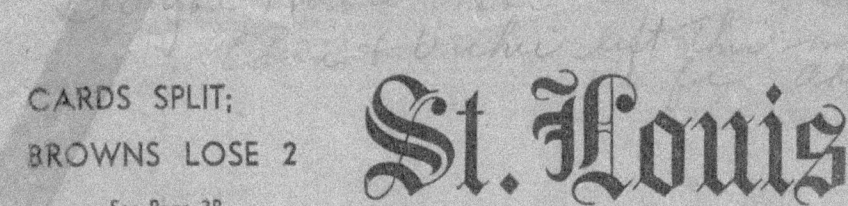

CARDS SPLIT; BROWNS LOSE 2
See Page 3B

St. Louis Glo

The Only Daily Morning New

VOL. 67—NO. 12—PART ONE   May 1941   ST. LOUIS, SATURDAY MORNING,

Casper S. Yost, Brilliant Editor, Dies

Succumbs to Heart Affliction at Jewish Hospital at 77

Casper S. Yost, for 26 years editor of the editorial page of the St. Louis Globe-Democrat and one of the most widely-known and distinguished editorial writers in the United States, died at the Jewish Hospital at 5:45 a. m. yesterday. He had been ill 10 days, an illness precipitated by a heart attack following a dinner he attended May 21, as a representative of this newspaper. Mr. Yost had been continuously on the staff of the Globe-Democrat since June 21, 1889. He was 77 years old.

Funeral services will be held tomorrow at 2:30 p. m. at the Robert J. Ambruster chapel, Clayton road at Concordia lane, with Rev. Hampton Adams, pastor of Union Avenue Christian Church, with which Mr. Yost was affiliated, officiating. Burial will be in the family plot in Oak Grove Cemetery.

Two of Mr. Yost's grandsons and four of his associates on the Globe-Democrat will serve as pallbearers. The grandsons are Robert Yost and Thomas Etter; his newspaper colleagues are Lon. M. Burrowes, managing editor of the Globe-Democrat,

DISTINGUISHED EDITOR DEAD

CASPER S. YOST.

U. S. Defense Guarded Against Sabotage

Resista British

Three Killed, 9 Hurt in Auto Crashes

St. Louis U. Teacher Dies at Springfield, Ill.; Mother, Son Victims

Start of the three-day Memorial Day holiday took the lives of three residents of St. Louis and St. Louis County in two automobile accidents late Thursday night and yesterday near the city. Nine others were injured, several seriously.

Anthony H. Montavon, 28, an instructor in biology at St. Louis University, lost his life in an accident near Springfield, Ill. Mrs. Audrey Ballmann, 32, Bellefontaine road, St. Louis County, and her son, Harvey Ballmann Jr., 11, died after a crash near Pacific, Mo.

William Jacob Yost born September 21, 1827 at Fancy Farm, Franklin County, Illinois. He dies February 24, 1840, at Metropolis, Illinois. He was a lawyer who instrumental in the building of the Southern Illinois University at Carbondale, and the reform school at Pontiac, Illinois. On February 25, 1850 he married Maria Goodner, born in 1830, died in 1867. She was the daughter of Dr. and L.T.Goodner. William and Maria had the following children:

Ella Yost died at Cairo Illinois
Ida Yost died at Cairo Illinois

Edwin Abbot Yost born June 25, 1852 at Benton, Illinois; died May 8, 1929 at La Junta, Colorado. On June 10, 1875 he married Lucy Alice Hostetter in DeQuoin, Illinois Edwin and Lucy had the following children:

Adah Hilda Yost born January 30, 1875, Duquoin, Illinois, married June 14, 1891 to Lincoln L. Jones, born March 24, 1860, Terre Haute, Indiana, died September 28, 1902

William Horace Yost born June 19, 1877 at Prentice, Illinois. On May 16, 1908 he married Grace DeMers

William Jacob Yost then married on February 25, 1889, Maria Louis Smith, widow of Thomas H. Smith who died in the civil war. William and Maria had the following children:

Henry Neil Yost born August 24, 1874, died 1930. He married on July 23, 1914 Leslie Yost, who married George N. Skinner of St. Louis, Mo. She died January 20, 1920

465

THE UNITED STATES OF AMERICA,

CERTIFICATE No. 11078

To all to whom these Presents shall come, Greeting:

WHEREAS William Yost of McLean County, Illinois has deposited in the GENERAL LAND OFFICE of the United States, a Certificate of the REGISTER OF THE LAND OFFICE at Danville whereby it appears that full payment has been made by the said William Yost according to the provisions of the Act of Congress of the 24th of April, 1820, entitled "An act making further provision for the sale of the Public Lands," for the North half of Lot number one of the North West fractional quarter of fractional Section Seven, in Township twenty one North of Range four East, in the District of Lands subject to sale at Danville, Illinois, containing Forty acres

according to the official plat of the survey of the said Lands, returned to the General Land Office by the SURVEYOR GENERAL, which said tract has been purchased by the said William Yost

NOW KNOW YE, That the **United States of America,** In consideration of the Premises, and in conformity with the several acts of Congress, in such case made and provided, HAVE GIVEN AND GRANTED, and by these presents DO GIVE AND GRANT, unto the said William Yost

and to his heirs, the said tract above described: **TO HAVE AND TO HOLD** the same, together with all the rights, privileges, immunities, and appurtenances of whatsoever nature, thereunto belonging, unto the said William Yost and to his heirs and assigns forever.

In Testimony Whereof, I, Millard Fillmore PRESIDENT OF THE UNITED STATES OF AMERICA, have caused these Letters to be made PATENT, and the SEAL of the GENERAL LAND OFFICE to be hereunto affixed.

Given under my hand, at the **CITY OF WASHINGTON,** the Tenth day of June in the Year of our Lord one thousand eight hundred and fifty one and of the **Independence of the United States** the Seventy fifth.

BY THE PRESIDENT: Millard Fillmore

By Alex McCormick A† Sec'y.

E. S. Terry, RECORDER of the General Land Office.

cepa March 5-1886

THE UNITED STATES OF AMERICA,

CERTIFICATE No. 23,477

To all to whom these presents shall come, Greeting:

Whereas William J. Yost of Franklin county Illinois has deposited in the GENERAL LAND OFFICE of the United States, a Certificate of the REGISTER OF THE LAND OFFICE at Vandalia whereby it appears that full payment has been made by the said William J. Yost according to the provisions of the Act of Congress of the 24th of April, 1820, entitled "An act making further provision for the sale of the Public Lands," for The North half of Lot numbered Two of the North West quarter of Section nineteen and the South West quarter and the South half of Lot numbered One of the North West quarter of Section Eighteen in Township One North of Range Five East, in the district of lands formerly subject to sale at Vandalia now Springfield Illinois, containing Three hundred and six acres and twenty four hundredths of an acre according to the official plat of the Survey of the said Lands, returned to the General Land Office by the SURVEYOR GENERAL, which said tracts has been purchased by the said William J. Yost

NOW KNOW YE, That the **United States of America**, in consideration of the premises, and in conformity with the several acts of Congress in such case made and provided, HAVE GIVEN AND GRANTED, and by these presents DO GIVE AND GRANT, unto the said

William J. Yost

and to his heirs, the said tracts above described: To have and to hold the same, together with all the rights, privileges, immunities, and appurtenances of whatsoever nature, thereunto belonging, unto the said

William J. Yost and to his heirs and assigns forever.

In Testimony Whereof, I, James Buchanan PRESIDENT OF THE UNITED STATES OF AMERICA, have caused these Letters to be made PATENT, and the SEAL of the GENERAL LAND OFFICE to be hereunto affixed.

GIVEN under my hand, at the City of Washington, the First day of June in the year of our Lord one thousand eight hundred and Fifty Seven and of the INDEPENDENCE OF THE UNITED STATES the Eighty-first

BY THE PRESIDENT: James Buchanan

By G. H. Jones, Secretary.

J. N. Granger, Recorder of the General Land Office.

Eleanor Matilda Yost born January 30, 1830

Francis Asbury Yost born May 13, 1832 at Fancy Farm, Franklin County, Illinois, married Mary Elizabeth Brizendine born July 18, 1834 in Kentucky. Francis died Dec. 19, 1902. He is buried at Riverside Cemetery, Hopkinsville Christian County Kentucky, USA Plot: Section OC

Pettis County Bowling Green Missouri 1860 Census

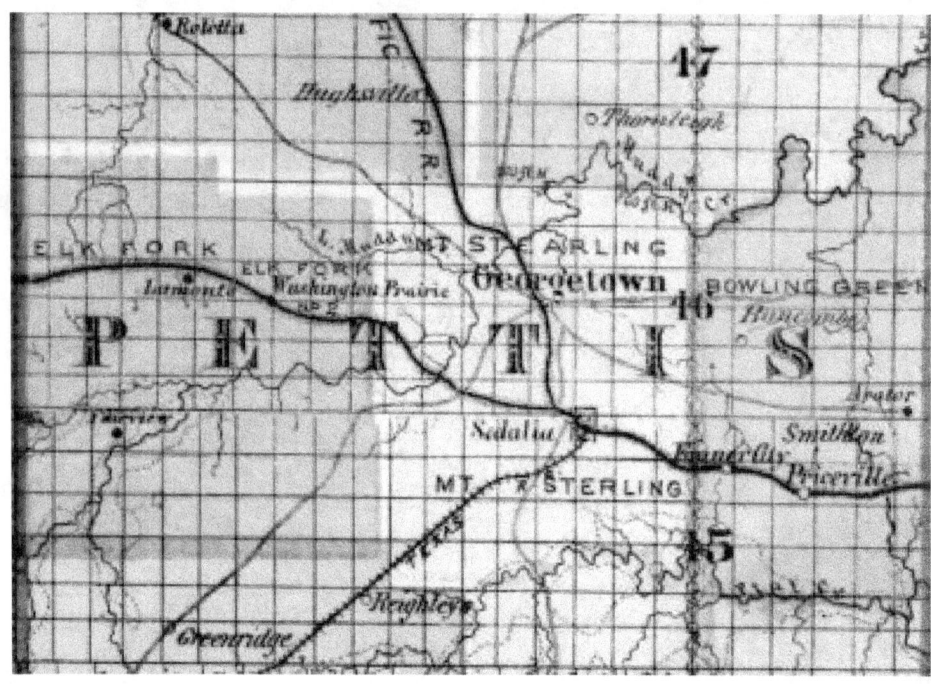

Pettis County Map 1873 at the Arator Post Office right side is where Francis Yost registered for the census

James Harvey Yost born July 23, 1835

The Yost's in Franklin County Illinois – Fancy Farm

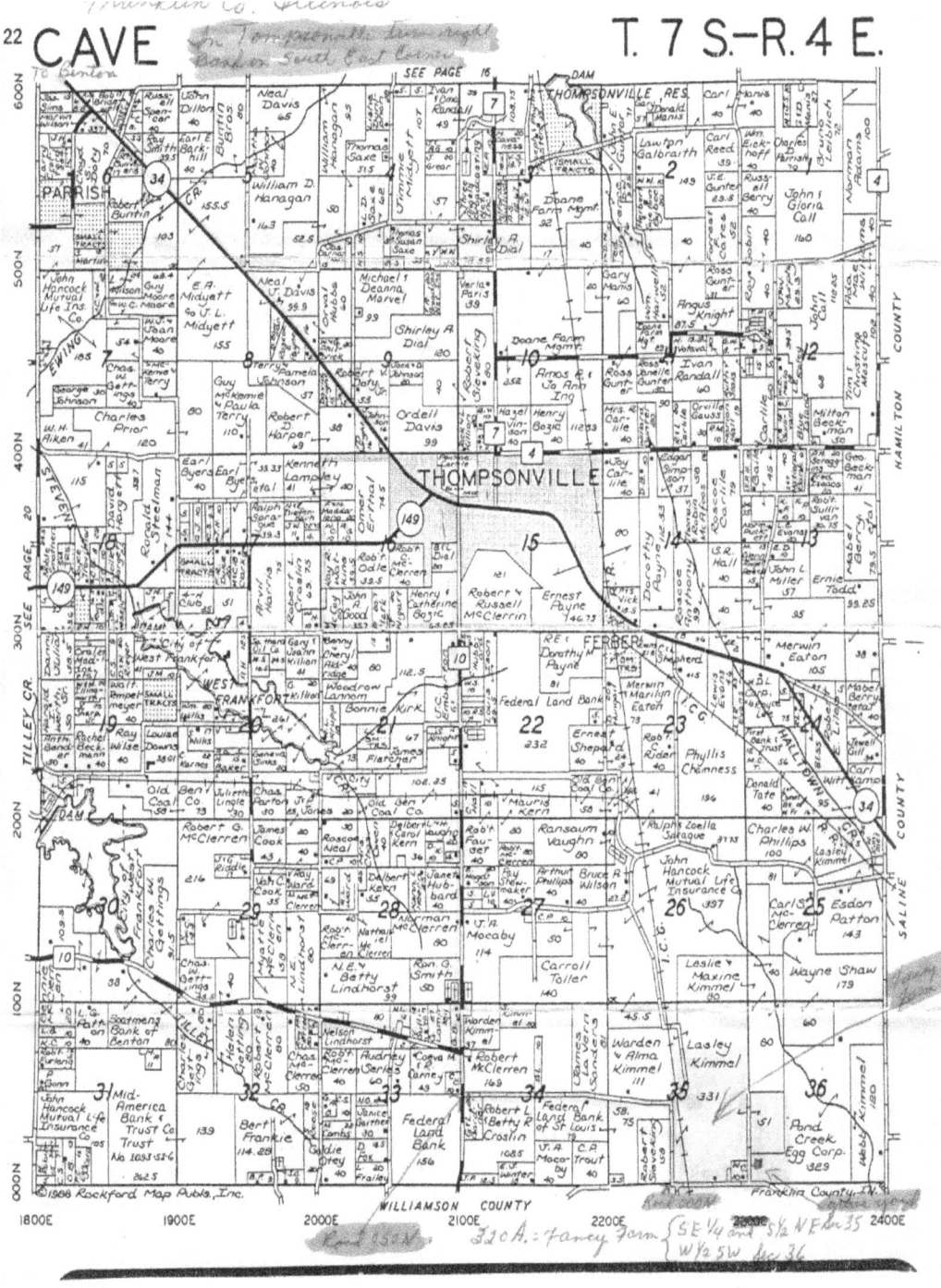

Franklin County – Fancy Farm is pointed to by the arrow at the bottom left

FANCY FARM THE HOME OF HENRY MARSHALL YOST.

I had always believed that this Land name was either an Old Spanish Grant or named in the old surveys as Spanish grants were named, but such is not the truth of Fancy Farm. Henry Yost Sr. was a meticulous extremist, and exceedingly neat and orderly both as to his person, family and property. What he did, he did well or not at all.

His farm was the show place of the County-its model in appearance and farm application. The only rail fences were the vogue in his day. Henry Yost laid them with the precision of a surveyor and kept them repaired at all times. His barn and out buildings were never allowed to become untidy.

His home inside and out was scrupulously clean. "Fancy Farm" it was named by "Old Green Mitchel" who kept the corner store on the state road, a quarter of a mile from Henrys farm. The name was originated by Mitchell in about 1825 and has stuck to that plot of ground ever since (1933) For many of the years of Henry Yost's ownership the farm was shown with pride to all new settlers. Henry YOst was a man of religious honesty and integrity. As sucess was measured in his day, he was wealthy and too generous for his own good.

Mitchell family recollections of "Polly Yost"

Legend has it that on the trip from Virginia, a stream was forded and the caravan chose the wrong place which resulted in pulling through deepwater wherin Polly in the excitement fell out of the wagon and theough saved from drowning contracted a 'cold fever' from which she never recovered and contracting another cold in the winter of 1821 was unable to resist it She is little remembered but Lydia Roberts who spent many hours in the Yost home nursing Polly and who later became Henry's second wife is remembered for her religious devotion to her step children in no less degree than her own. Lydia it seems stay on at Fancy Farm, after Henry's death until 1850 when she moved to Benton, Ill.

It was Polly Yost who brought from their old Virginia farm, many saplings of the silver leafed poplar, which made of Fancy Farm its beauty four of these trees surround the house and are very largesilver barked trees that Mrs. Whitlock, the present owner of Fancy Farm, said "I never tire of looking at them. They are beautiful in summer, so tall and spread t their shadows so far. I was born and raised under them and tho my parents haved moved to town, I remain here for I love the old place.

Fancy Farm by Vivian Ida Yost Terrel

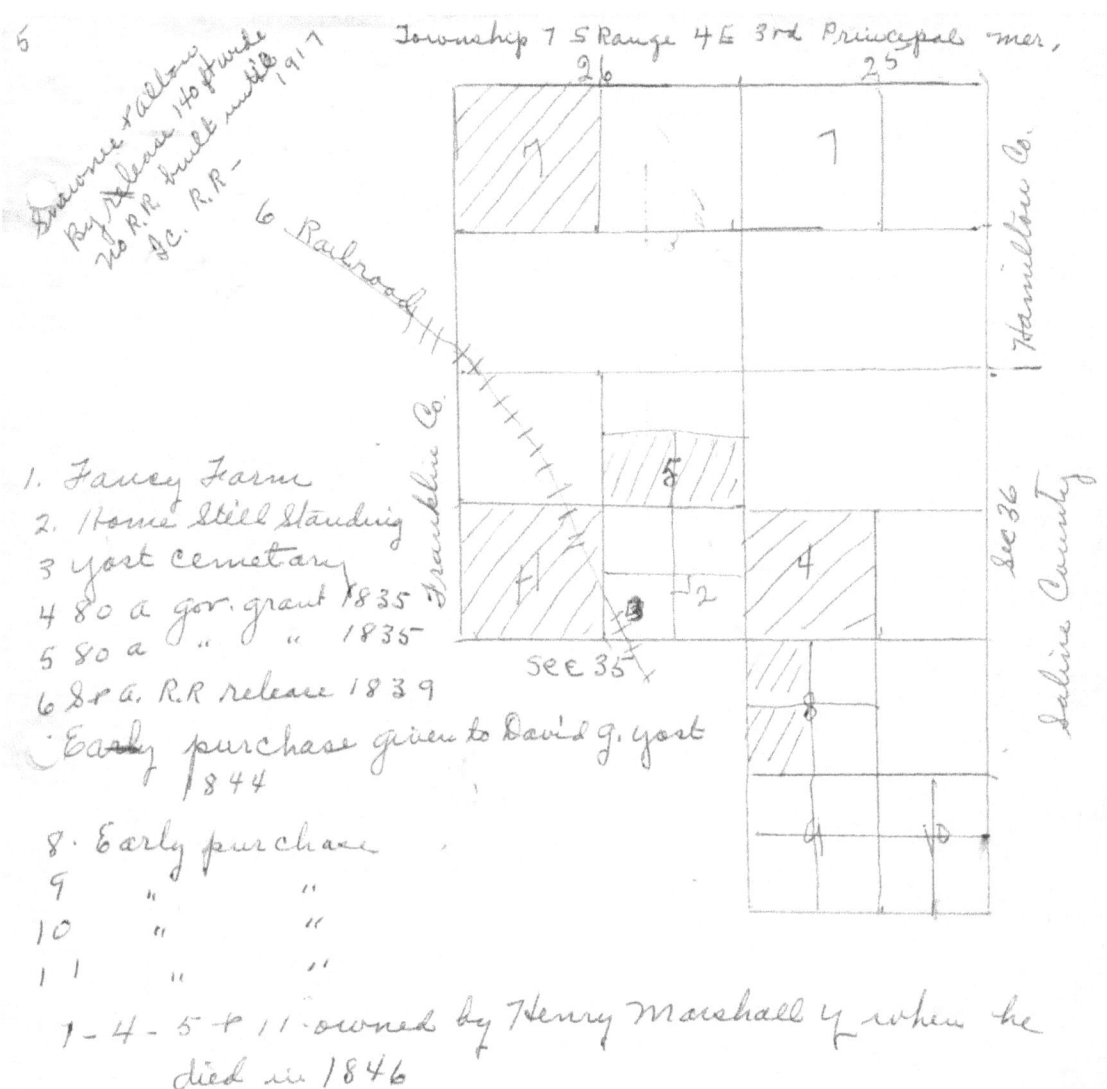

Fancy Farm Land Layout by Vivian Ida Yost Terrel

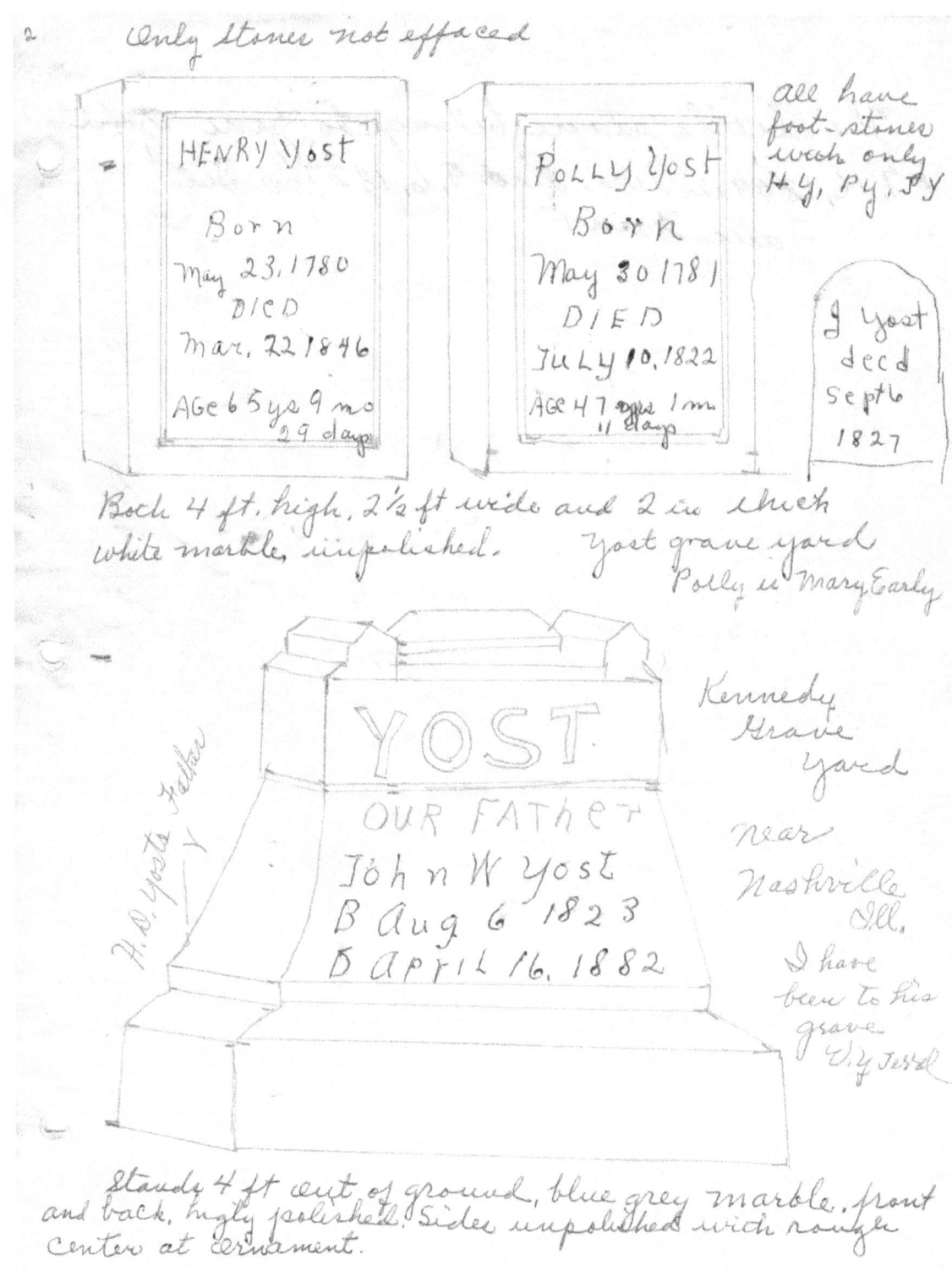

Yost Grave Marker by Vivian Ida Yost Terrell

The Jordan Settlement was made in what is now Cave Township.

John Browning returned to Tennessee in 1805, and came back to this county in 1806, and lived about two years in Jordan's fort. About this date he guarded the mail for one or two years, between Shawneetown and Kaskaskia, and afterwards assisted the government surveyors in the survey of the lands of the county. In 1820 he located on the Browning

Hill farm, and subsequently became a prominent Baptist minister, and died June 13, 1857. James K and William R Browning, twin brothers, and sons of John Browning and wife, were the first white children born in the county. They were born December 24, 1810 in the Old Jordan fort. As pioneers and settlers, few did more than John Browning and his wife. Coming here in 1804, they at once commenced to subdue the soil and raise children, becoming the parents of eighteen (three set of triplets - nine children at three births - and twins once). Two of the triplets, Joseph and Jonathon, lived to be middle aged men, and raised quite large families." Other early settlers of Cave Township were John McCreery with his family, and his son Alexander with his young wife, who came from Kentucky in 1817. The former settled in the place now known as the Fancy farm. Alexander McCreery brought his household and kitchen furniture along with him in a pair of saddle bags. He settled the farm now occupied by Judge Wm Elstun. Aaron Neal and his brother Moses, settled near the present site of Parrish in 1812. (My note: The mother of Aaron and Moses Neal was Nancy Jordan - their father Aaron Neal died in Pope County, IL) Isaac Moberly, John Hall, Nathan Clampet, John W Swafford, Nathaniel Jones, John Plasters, Wm Jackson, David Williams, James Isaacs, Thomas Lampley, J L Cantrell, John Harlow and Henry Yost, were all early settlers in the southeastern part of the county.

John Jones and his son John, and his son Wiley, the father of W R Jones, the ex-sheriff of Franklin County, came from Tennessee in 1830 and settled in Cave Township.

They People Shall be My People

Daisy Roberts Malone wrote a book titled, "They People Shall be My People" or "Elizabeth Ann and the Roberts Clan". Daisy was born in 1878. She was a member of the Daughters of the American Revolution. She spent hours and years compiling the material for this book which was published in 1939. This book contains the following excerpts in reference to our ancestors.

"I present these pages as a record of the vision, faith, and courage of those who sought to add to the great citizenry of their beloved County; but feeling my inadequacy and realizing these writings are not worthy of those to whom they are dedicated.

"Remembering" (by Douglas Mallock)

"When some old road we wind again. Some road we walked in other days; The things we seek to find again, Are flowered fields and shaded ways, Avoid the rocks that hurt our feet; And take the pathway that was sweet."

That I am grown old and look back on my years of wonderful experiences and the lives of loved relatives and friends I wish they might be recorded for our children's children to read; that they might learn to love and feel a true reverence for the God of their fathers who led them through troubles as well as along the happy paths of life and continues to guide all who trust and obey Him."

Page 3

In the early life we became members of the Methodist Episcopal Church, organized by Matheny and Glanville at Springfield the year it became the county seat. I was only twelve years old when taken into full membership.

Peter Cartright, a friend who was always welcome in our home, rode horseback over a large section of the Illinois Country, held "Camp Mettin's" aroused the impenitent, prayed for and comforted the seekers of salvation – but the rowdies who disturbed his meetings, sometimes got the thrashings they merited.

Page 9

In 1839, Father received the appointment to preach on a smaller Circuit.

That was the year of the celebrations of the Centenary of Methodism, also the year Franklin County was divided and the Southern Portion became Williamson County. It was in parts of these counties Fathers new preaching stations were located.

Mr. Henry Yost, Sr. and Mr. Sion Hunt Mitchell of the Liberty Church on the Franklin Co. side of the new dividing line and Mr. John Sutton Roberts of the Zion Church three miles South and West of Liberty Church in the new Williamson County, were attending Conference in Mt. Vernon and made the arrangements about getting Father's family moved.

Of course, we children helped, with the packing, although the older ones did the work. Mr. Henry Yost sent his team and wagon by his son Samuel, and another son Henry Yost Jr., came driving his own team.

Page 10

We were first located in a part of Henry Yost, Jr.'s house, about one half mile north of the church, on the "Worthin Trail", the farm later known as the "Spinnings Place."

It seemed almost too good to be true, that now Father could spend more time at home.

Page 14

The other boys bought land, quite cheap in those days, and filed on adjoining lands, but William Rufus Roberts went into partnership with John Wesley Yost, who was the husband of his sister Mary Jane in running a newly purchased "Carding Machine" on Wesley's farm "Cedar Hurst". He filed on this land three or four years previously. This Carding Machine was quite an innovation for the cotton growers of the Settlement and surrounding countryside.

Carding Machine

Page 15

Among the Local Preachers and Class Leaders during the first of these early nearby churches there were Richard Ratcliff, Wesley Yost, Wiliam and Robert Burns, John Roberts and son John S. Roberts, Zadock Mitchell, Alex McCreery, Henry Yost, Joseph Hendrickson, James Fowler, Solomon Motsinger, Samuel O'Neal and later Hearn Bros., Purnell and Stephen, understand these men were connected with the five churches on the charge, and their services extended over something like twenty years.

For years the nearest Post Office was at Fancy Farm, Franklin County, near the Liberty Methodist Church. A short time before the death (in 1821) of John McCreery, its first owner, Henry Yost Sr. who came from Maryland bought the farm, and give it the name Fancy Farm, it was noted for its unusual trees and shrubbery. About fifteen years later Fancy Farm Post Office was established with Yost as its first Post Master. It was his home, which stood near the through highway from Shawneetown on the Ohio River to Kaskaskia the first Capital of Illinois.

After the division of Franklin County in 1839 it was found to be South of the line in the New Williamson County.

After Henry Yost resigned as Postmaster in 1844 six appointees served during the next twenty-five years.

We frequently heard stories of the great experiences and sent out mail by the Stage-Coach, that traveled over the well known road from the Ohio River, South; to the Mississippi River, North West.

Mail was such a treat, and occassionaly they brought back news from the outside world, told by travelers who had stopped for a time at Fancy Farm, as it was customary in those days for the Yosts to accommodate any who asked for shelter.

Page 26

Then too, Mary (Roberts') Kennedy's step daughter Elizabeth married John Winchester Yost, son of Henry and Lydia (Roberts) Yost who was Mary's sister.

Page 28

When and another brother James married Hallie Roberts (sisters) their great-grandparnets were the same Rachel and John S., daughter and son of John and Mary (Winchester) Roberts of Maryland.

Page 29

On that part of "Cedar Hurst" farm, that William and my brother John had rented from Wesley Yost, William and some of his numerous cousins built us a good cabin of two rooms. Wesley's name for his farm was change to Cedar Crest in recent years, by the bride of the youngest son Dr. S.M. Mitchell who had bought it from him in 1850.

One thing about cabins built in those days, the rooms were rather large, having no closets, built-in cupboards or pantries and always a stairway to the loft rooms above they needed to be large, and twenty feet square of floor space was the common size, and large enough to a home in too.

Page 31

At the christening of our child, there were several others; baby Mary Margaret Yost, born the 16th of September, daughter of Wesley and Mary Jane Roberts Yost, then there was Tom and Elizabeth (Mitchell) Stewart's first baby, William Augustus born September 9th, of the same year. Another was Lydia Olive Roberts, William's little half-sister who was born November of that same year.

Page 34

We went over to spend a day or two at Fancy Farm, and William and the Yost cousins went deer hunting, so I had a lovely visit with Aunt Lydia.

I wish you might have known her, she had a very special something about her that I can't describe, but you knew she was always just herself; she was never, like some other folks always trying to appear different to their real selves. I suppose she was just natural; anyway there was something about her presence that caused everyone to be considerate and loving.

She was only a young girl, just returned from a year in a Seminary in Kentucky, when she married the young widower Henry Yost, but she made a good mother for the children of her friends Henry and Mary (Early) Yost.

She showed me her keepsakes, among them a beautifully made "Sampler", the material was handwoven from flax grown on her Grandfather Winchester's plantation in Old Maryland many years ago.

After feeling all the tiny stitches made by her childish fingers, my ideas abruptly changed about the size of my family, now I hoped my next baby would be a lovely little girl and I wanted her to be just like Aunt Lydia, a dainty sweet little lady and I would help her to make a sampler just like this one; so I copied it off as a pattern for the sampler of my little girl to be.

Page 35

Another time we were visiting at Fancy Farm was just after they had received word that her stepson Samuel Eagon Yost had recently married (July 1845).

He was a small boy when Aunt Lydia married his father but she loved him dearly and was happy he was married to the lady of his choice.

He rode a horse from Fancy Farm to Elizabeth Towne down on the Ohio River after his bride (the town had been named after the bride's grandmother Elizabeth McFarland) after the wedding he put her belonging into a "Poke" and she was placed on the horse to ride behind her husband to their home in Williamson County. Samuel Yost owned a Carding Machine

Here in Illinois, Lydia, a beautiful young lady became a very good girl of the Yost's at "Fancy Farm" and after the death of Mary (Early) Yost, Lydia and Henry were married (Nov. 12, 1822) by Reverent Porter. She mothered the eight children of her friends and she and Henry had a family of six. She left on them marks of her

Page 37

Not very far North of the Tom Stewart's Farm was the old Uncle George Roberts land that joined "Fancy Farm" the home of his sister and Tom's Aunt Lydia (Roberts) Yost.

The land that lay between the farms of these two brothers, John and Tom, later belonged to their younger brother, James Holiday Stewart, on down the ridge Southward was the Wesley Yost place "Cedar Hurst" and below him their fathers old homestead that their mother sold to Mardon Mitchell soon after the death of James Stewart, later it became the property of Alfred Pease, a school teacher for many years at Center and other nearby schools, a man who left his mark on the old Zion Church Community. A well-educated man, a musician and a fine Christian gentleman.

Page 40

1814

That was also the same year Illinois became a State, and at that time there were less than 16,000 acres in the county to which the settlers had a deed from the government, most of that lay around the two forts, along the Big Muddy River, the Indian Trail called "Old Path" and on the new Trail to Shawneetown in the Southeasterly direction from Fort Jordan.

The Territory of Illinois had asked Congress for an appropriation for cutting out the shortest route from Kaskaskia on the Mississippi River to Shawneetown on the Ohio, it was not completed until the year after Franklin County was organized and Illinois became a State. This road crossed the country from West to East side entering Six Mile Township crossing Big Muddy River at Plumfield, through West Frankfort over the Frankfort Hill, through Garrett's Prairie, by Ft. Jordan and Fancy Farm on to Shawneetown.

Page 42

Alex and George's father died in 1821 in Saline County, where he had located after selling his home "Fancy Farm" to the Yosts, later after the death of the mother, Alex having hired some of the slaves, went to Missouri and brought back several of them, he had considerable trouble getting some of them as they had been kidnapped from his brothers plantation to sell in New Orleans. He freed them, bought land and got all of them established as a Negro Settlement, not far from "Fancy Farm".

Among these Negroes, was exceptionally intelligent man, Richard Inge, a shoemaker, he paid for his land with labor.

This settlement was called "Little Africa", other freed Negroes there, had been brought from Kentucky by the Yost family.

"Little Africa" Sedalia Daily Democrat October 8, 1875

Page 54

William Burns, was a local preacher who with John Roberts and Richard Ratcliff had organized a "Methodist Class" this met in the homes of the Community until in 1823 they put up a church building.

The community spirit manifested in the early Settlement was largely Contributed by those most interested in becoming church people, desiring to pledge their lives in consecration to the cause for which their little "Class" organization stood, they met together for a council with Brother Launis who occasionally came to preach to them.

Before this council meeting in 1822 there had been added to their group, John Sutton Roberts, Scott, Kennedy, Jason Stewart and McCarty husbands of four daughters of John Roberts, and Zadock Mitchell and their families, then from Ft. Jordan and Fancy Farm the families of Alex and George McCreery, Henry Yost and Sion Hunt Mitchell.

Page 56

The Yosts, Sion Hunt Mitchell and McCreery families in the neighboring community, evidently retained their wholesome attitude toward religion even in this new, wild country for they too helped organize and build the Zion M.E. Church in the settlement South of the other Jordan Fort and went those six to eight miles to services often as they could, weather and road conditions prevented them attending regularly so they frequently held services in their homes.

The handicap and the increase in population in their immediate neighborhood led to the organization of the Liberty M.E. Church, and a good log building was erected by its members in 1825, not far from the Old Fort Jordan the beginning of their settlement.

Fancy Farm the home of the Yost's, continued for years to be a prominent place, it had been beautified with trees brought North and set out in a grove something a little unusual for those days in a new country. It was a stopping place for travelers on the road from Kaskaskia to Shawneetown, they frequently crowded the place to its capacity in stormy weather and there would be much clamor and bustle as beds were sometimes made down all over the house, but travelers were thankful for the hospitality of the family and appreciated the shelter.

The people for miles around there received and mailed letters on the stage coach long before there was a post office. Mr. and Mrs. Henry Yost, Sr., already had quite a family when they came there in 1820 from Virginia; but Mrs. Yost had hardly gotten accustomed to the ways of the pioneers before she died, leaving several small children who were mothered by a very dear friend Lydia Eleanor Roberts who married Mr. Yost and came to Fancy Farm to make a home for them and later her own children. Beloved by all, a good wife, mother and neighbor, no higher calling could be asked for at any time.

This family especially delighted in entertaining Missionaries and "Traveling Preachers", Henry Yost, Sr. and wife Lydia were charter members of their church "Liberty". Sion Hunt Mitchell and wife, Alex McCreery and wife, John Waller and wife are also known to have been on that list as well as having been charter members at Zion Church three years earlier.

The men of these two Jordan Fort communities were of outstanding characteristics; abolitionists, prohibitionists and conscientious puritanical Methodists.

In 1841 the Legislature created the "Fancy Farm College" Alex McCreery, Henry Yost, Sr., Sion Hunt Mitchell, Richard Cantrell, John S. Roberts and Williams Jones were made Trustees. The object of the school was to promote Science and Literature, but it seems the "College" failed to materialize, nothing remains of it, but the old farm.

After the death of Mr. Yost (1846), Henry Yost, and famiy of Zion Church Community moved in with his mother for a while and later another son came to look after things for her when Henry moved to Benton.

About eight years after her husband's death, Lydia sold Fancy Farm to Mr. George Marvel of Indiana and she too lived at Benton with her son for a time, but died in 1875 at age of seventy-nine years, at the home of her son Wm. Jacob Yost, a prominent lawyer in Metropolis.

Page 58

In time Fancy Farm was divided into three farms and lost its identity as one of the noted places in the early history of Old Franklin County, and had helped to make history for the new County of Williamson, organized from the Southern portion of that county in 1839.

Before we had been married five years, stark tragedy came into our happy home; on a clear November morning (1845) William saddled his horse hitched him to the fence near the front gate, expecting to go to his Aunt Lydia's to ask her advice and get some remedy for me, as I hadn't been well of late; he came into the house for his mitten, Henry Yost came riding fast, hesitated only long enough to call out, "Just saw a deer back a ways in the woods, get your gun! Hurry!" William took his gun off the antlers over the door and said he'd go with Henry first then go on to Fancy Farm and would be home again before night, kissed the children and me, rushed to unhitch his horse, slapped him to hurry his starting, but somehow while mounting, the gun caught on the saddle or stirrup, there was a shot, William fell; Henry hearing it hurried back. Trembling, weak with a sudden queer feeling of awful fear, for an instant my heart stood still, then trying to push away that fear of the worst; I though it simply can't be, I won't let myself think its true, I just must not let myself think of what may have happened; the very thought of losing him, the lover of my heart gripped my being with pain, with body shaking, holding back a scream it seemed my feet were lead weights as I ran to him. "O God don't let it be true, I need him so much." I knelt at his side, calling him, I prayed he'd hear me calling his name, but he only looked beyond the trees, not at me; he was dead, gone away, now he couldn't come back to me before night.

Page 61

I had often wished I might some day weave a coverlid like I saw in most every home we were in that winter, now because they wanted to do everything they could to make me happy; William's sister Mary Jane Yost suggested the children and I come to her house as soon as it was warmed up a little and she'd teach me to weave one.

So with the help of her skillful hands I became quite interested and spent hours at the loom throwing the shuttle through the web of fine linen thread to make my pretty wool coverlid, setting the "Whig Rose" design over the white web in soft blue yarn. The shuttle went back and forth across the web, the Whig Rose grew; blue flowers and threaded design upon a field of shadowy white.

Page 68

That Summer I had a good long letter from Jane Stewart Yost, you remember I told about our family living in a part of the Henry Yost home, just north of the church while the parsonage was being built for my father the new pastor of that Circuit.

Well, after the death of Henry's father he sold his farm and moved to Fancy Farm with his mother, that was the same year Father was sent to Carmi Circuit and my children and I went with him and mother. Jane wrote they lived with Aunt Lydia, Henry's mother for a few years, then moved to Benton and later to Summerfield.

George Casper Yost another son of Aunt Lydia's lived with her until she sold it to Col. Marvel about 1852, then went to a daughter at Metropolis where she passed away.

I had sweet memories of Aunt Lydia, her kindness and her hospitable home, it was such a joy to have knew such a wonderful person. The world needs such characters, so I was sorry to hear of her death.

Her son James Henry Yost married but had no children, so he and his wife took special interest in his three younger sisters. Sent Margaret Rachel and Harriet Newell to Jacksonville Women's College and Amorette to Monticello Seminary.

VIEW FROM NORTH ENTRANCE, MONTICELLO SEMINARY, GODFREY, ILLINOIS.

He died in this thirty-eighth year in Genova, Switzerland where he had gone to regain his health.

Harriet Newell Yost married William Swanwich of Kaskaskia, a grandson of Shardrick Bond first Governor of Illinois, another son, Dempsey Chase Yost was a year younger than my Leander, and he too was in the Civil War with Sherman on his March to the sea. After he returned home, he assisted in the care of his father until his death then contracted the disease and died the following month.

> **Sherman's March to the Sea** is the name commonly given to the **Savannah Campaign**, conducted in late 1864 by Major General William Tecumseh Sherman of the Union Army during the American Civil War. The campaign began with General Sherman's troops leaving the captured city of Atlanta, Georgia, on November 15, 1864, and ended with the capture of the port of Savannah on December 22.

Dempsey Chase Yost's Civil War Record

Yost, Dempsey C
Rank: Private
Company: D
Unit 48 Illinois U.S. Infantry
Residence: Nashville, Washington County, Illinois
Age: 18
Joined: February 25, 1864
Joined Where: Nashville, Illinois
Joined by Whom: Lt. Walker

Period: 3 years
Muster In: March 7, 1864
Muster In Where: Centralia, Illinois
Muster Out: August 15, 1865
Muster Out Where: Little Rock, Arkansas
Muster Out By: Captain Schlaich

The battles Dempsey Chase Yost fought in:

48th Illinois Infantry National Flag

The Atlanta Campaign

It was a swelteringly hot and clear Monday, June 27, 1864, when some of the heaviest fighting of the Atlanta Campaign occurred here. Preserved are historic earthworks, cannon emplacements and monuments. Kennesaw NBP interprets the historic events where over 5,350 soldiers were killed in the battle fought here from June 19, 1864 through July 2, 1864

Location: Fulton County
Campaign: Atlanta Campaign (1864)
Date(s): July 22, 1864
Principal Commanders: Maj. Gen. William T. Sherman [US]; Gen. John Bell Hood [CS]
Forces Engaged: Military Division of the Mississippi [US]; Army of Tennessee [CS]
Estimated Casualties: 12,140 total (US 3,641; CS 8,499)

Description: Following the Battle of Peachtree Creek, Hood determined to attack Maj. Gen. James B. McPherson's Army of the Tennessee. He withdrew his main army at night from Atlanta's outer line to the inner line, enticing Sherman to follow. In the meantime, he sent William J. Hardee with his corps on a fifteen-mile march to hit the unprotected Union left and rear, east of the city. Wheeler's cavalry was to operate farther out on Sherman's supply line, and Gen. Frank Cheatham's corps were to attack the Union front. Hood, however, miscalculated the time necessary to make the march, and Hardee was unable to attack until afternoon. Although Hood had outmaneuvered Sherman for the time being, McPherson was concerned about his left flank and sent his reserves—Grenville Dodge's XVI Army Corps—to that location. Two of Hood's divisions ran into this reserve force and were repulsed. The Rebel attack stalled on the Union rear but began to roll up the left flank. Around the same time, a Confederate soldier shot and killed McPherson when he rode out to observe the fighting. Determined attacks continued, but the Union forces held. About 4:00 pm, Cheatham's corps broke through the Union front at the Hurt House, but Sherman massed twenty artillery pieces on a knoll near his headquarters to shell these Confederates and halt their drive. Maj. Gen. John A. Logan' s XV Army Corps then led a counterattack that restored the Union line. The Union troops held, and Hood suffered high casualties.

Result(s): Union victory

Battle of Jonesborough

Other Names: None
Location: Clayton County
Campaign: Atlanta Campaign (1864)
Date(s): August 31–September 1, 1864
Principal Commanders: Maj. Gen. William T. Sherman [US]; Lt. Gen. William J. Hardee [CS]
Forces Engaged: Six corps [US]; two corps [CS]
Estimated Casualties: 3,149 total (US 1,149; CS 2,000)

Description: Sherman had successfully cut Hood's supply lines in the past by sending out detachments, but the Confederates quickly repaired the damage. In late August, Sherman determined that if he could cut Hood's supply lines—the Macon & Western and the Atlanta & West Point Railroads—the Rebels would have to evacuate Atlanta. Sherman, therefore, decided to move six of his seven infantry corps against the supply lines. The army began pulling out of its positions on August 25 to hit the Macon & Western Railroad between Rough and Ready and Jonesborough. To counter the move, Hood sent Lt. Gen. William J. Hardee with two corps to halt and possibly rout the Union troops, not realizing Sherman's army was there in force. On August 31, Hardee attacked two Union corps west of Jonesborough but was easily repulsed. Fearing an attack on Atlanta, Hood withdrew one corps from Hardee's force that night. The next day, a Union corps broke through Hardee' s troops which retreated to Lovejoy's Station, and on the night of September 1, Hood evacuated Atlanta. Sherman did cut Hood's supply line but failed to destroy Hardee's command.

Result(s): Union victory

Battle at Lovejoy's Station
Other Names: None
Location: Clayton County
Campaign: Atlanta Campaign (1864)

Date(s): August 20, 1864
Principal Commanders: Brig. Gen. H. Judson Kilpatrick [US]; Brig. Gen. William H. Jackson [CS]
Forces Engaged: Kilpatrick's Cavalry Division [US]; Jackson's Cavalry Division [CS]
Estimated Casualties: Unknown

Description: While Confederate Maj. Gen. Joseph Wheeler was absent raiding Union supply lines from North Georgia to East Tennessee, Maj. Gen. William Sherman, unconcerned, sent Judson Kilpatrick to raid Rebel supply lines. Leaving on August 18, Kilpatrick hit the Atlanta & West Point Railroad that evening, tearing up a small area of tracks. Next, Kilpatrick headed for Lovejoy's Station on the Macon & Western Railroad. In transit, on the 19th, Kilpatrick's men hit the Jonesborough supply depot on the Macon & Western Railroad, burning great amounts of supplies. On the 20th, they reached Lovejoy's Station and began their destruction. Rebel infantry (Cleburne's Division) appeared and the raiders were forced to fight into the night, finally fleeing to prevent encirclement. Although Kilpatrick had destroyed supplies and track at Lovejoy's Station, the railroad line was back in operation in two days.

Result(s): Confederate victory

The battle of Bentonville

Scene of the Last Major Confederate Offensive of the Civil War

The Battle of Bentonville, fought March 19-21, 1865, was the last full-scale action of the Civil War in which a Confederate army was able to mount a tactical offensive. This major battle, the largest ever fought in North Carolina, was the only significant attempt to defeat the large Union army of Gen. William T. Sherman during its march through the Carolinas in the spring of 1865.

Sherman Strikes into South Carolina . . .
The year 1864 ended with Sherman's grand army in possession of Savannah, Georgia, following its infamous "March to the Sea" from Atlanta to the coast. The fall of Atlanta had virtually assured the re-election of U.S. President Abraham Lincoln that November, and the tide of war further shifted in favor of the Union. Ulysses S. Grant, general-in-chief of all Federal armies, now wanted Sherman's army to unite with the Army of the Potomac, under Grant's personal supervision in Virginia. Grant wanted Sherman's men ferried by sea to the Virginia fighting front, where the combined Federal forces might deal a fatal blow to Gen. Robert E. Lee's Army of Northern Virginia. The Confederacy's principal Eastern army, on the wane after four hard years of keeping the Federals at bay, was still in position between Grant and the Confederate capital at Richmond.

But William T. Sherman had other ideas, and proposed a bold strike into the very heart of the Confederacy with 60,000 men—a march northward through the Carolinas. On Christmas Eve 1864, he explained to Grant:

I feel no doubt whatever as to our future plans. I have thought them over so long and well that they appear as clear as daylight. I left Augusta [Ga.] untouched on purpose, because the enemy will be in doubt as to my objective point . . . whether it be Augusta or Charleston [S.C.], and will naturally divide his forces . . . . [O]n the hypothesis of ignoring Charleston and taking Wilmington, I would then favor a movement direct on Raleigh. The game is then up with Lee.

Grant, who held his friend and subordinate Sherman in the highest esteem, replied on December 27:

Your confidence in being able to march up and join this army pleases me, and I believe it can be done. The effect of such a campaign will be to disorganize the South, and prevent the organization of new armies from their broken fragments . . . . If time is given, the fragments may be collected together and many of the [Confederate] deserters reassembled. If we can, we should act to prevent this . . . [Y]ou may make your preparations to start on your northern expedition without delay. Break up the railroads in South and North Carolina, and join the armies operating against Richmond as soon as you can.

As Sherman gained a lodgment in South Carolina, Fort Fisher fell to a Federal amphibious assault on January 15, 1865. This effectively closed the port of Wilmington, North Carolina—the hub of the last major supply route to Lee's army in Virginia. Wilmington itself would fall in February to the combined forces of Gen. Alfred H. Terry's Provisional Corps and Gen. John Schofield's XXIII Corps, hammering yet another nail into the coffin of the Confederacy. Grant's orders to Schofield specified that *"Your movements are intended as co-operative with Sherman through the States of South and North Carolina. The first point to be attained is to secure Wilmington. Goldsborough will then be your objective point."* Grant realized the importance of Goldsboro as the inland junction of the Wilmington & Weldon and Atlantic & North Carolina railroads. At least 425 miles of enemy territory lay between "Uncle Billy" and his ultimate destination in North Carolina, and a rendezvous there with Schofield and Terry.

Sherman's army advanced on February 1, 1865, meeting little resistance as it marched northward. General P. G. T. Beauregard did in fact divide his Confederate forces to safeguard Charleston to the east, and Augusta, Georgia to the west. This unfortunate arrangement allowed Sherman's minions to pass through the heart of South Carolina virtually unopposed, cutting a wide swath of destruction as they advanced. With the city of Columbia and much of the South Carolina countryside in ruins, only North Carolina lay between Sherman's army and a junction with U. S. Grant's army in Virginia. To make matters worse for the Southern war effort, the Army of Tennessee and other Confederate forces in the Carolinas were widely scattered. With Robert E. Lee's army bogged down against Grant in the trenches of Petersburg, and Sherman's force swiftly approaching from the south, it was a dire time for the Confederacy.

As general-in-chief of all Southern armies, Lee questioned General Beauregard's ability to oppose the Federals. As the Union juggernaut continued northward, Lee appealed to the Confederate War Department for a replacement, explaining that he knew of no officer who had so much "*the confidence of the army and people*" as Gen. Joseph E. Johnston. Lee's choice for the command was not a popular one with Confederate president Jefferson Davis, who deemed Joe Johnston a personal enemy.

In one of the great personality clashes of the Civil War, the troubled relationship between Davis and Johnston came to a head in mid-July 1864, during the Atlanta Campaign. Furious with Johnston for retreating before Sherman in Georgia instead of engaging him in a decisive battle, Davis promptly removed "Old Joe" from command of the Army of Tennessee. But the Confederate president counted few options as Sherman approached North Carolina, and with Lee's earnest request Davis gave in and reluctantly allowed the general-in-chief to call upon Johnston for his services.

On February 22, 1865, Lee sent an urgent dispatch to his old friend Johnston, who had retired to Lincolnton, North Carolina:

Assume command of the Army of Tennessee and all troops in Department of South Carolina, Georgia, and Florida. Assign General Beauregard to duty under you, as you may select. Concentrate all available forces and drive back Sherman.

Though he felt the effort to stop Sherman had come too late, a weary Johnston methodically set out to collect the scattered array of Confederate forces at his disposal. The troop concentration he would effect in North Carolina on short notice, and the resulting battle at Bentonville, would stand in sharp contrast to the general's earlier war record.

END OF DEMPSEY CHASE YOST CIVIL WAR RECORD

Daisy Roberts Malone Book Cont'd

Page 78

William's only daughter Mary Jane, was only a little seven year old girl when their parents John Sutton and Margaret Caughy Roberts came from Tennessee to Illinois and made their home in the John Roberts Settlement. She had few educational advantages, for her there was only attendance less than half of the year at the little log school house on her father's farm and what she acquired from reading and from listened to the conversations of her elders, at the age of twenty she married one of the 'Yost boys' of the neighboring Church Community (Liberty) Wesley Yost was the oldest son of Henry and Mary Early Yost of Fancy Farm, they came from Virginia in 1818; after the death of Wesley's mother his father married a dear friend of Mary's; Lydia Roberts Yost his stepmother also his Aunt by marriage.

Henry Yost

Comparison Study of the 1818 and 1820 Censuses of Franklin County, IL;
and land purchases in Franklin County, IL, by the year 1820.
by Sheila Cadwalader <scad@pinehurst.net>

Numerical columns:
White males 21 years and upwards; all other white; free people of color; servants or slaves

Yost   Henry no   Yes   2   9

Virginia State Library Archives located in Richmond Virginia

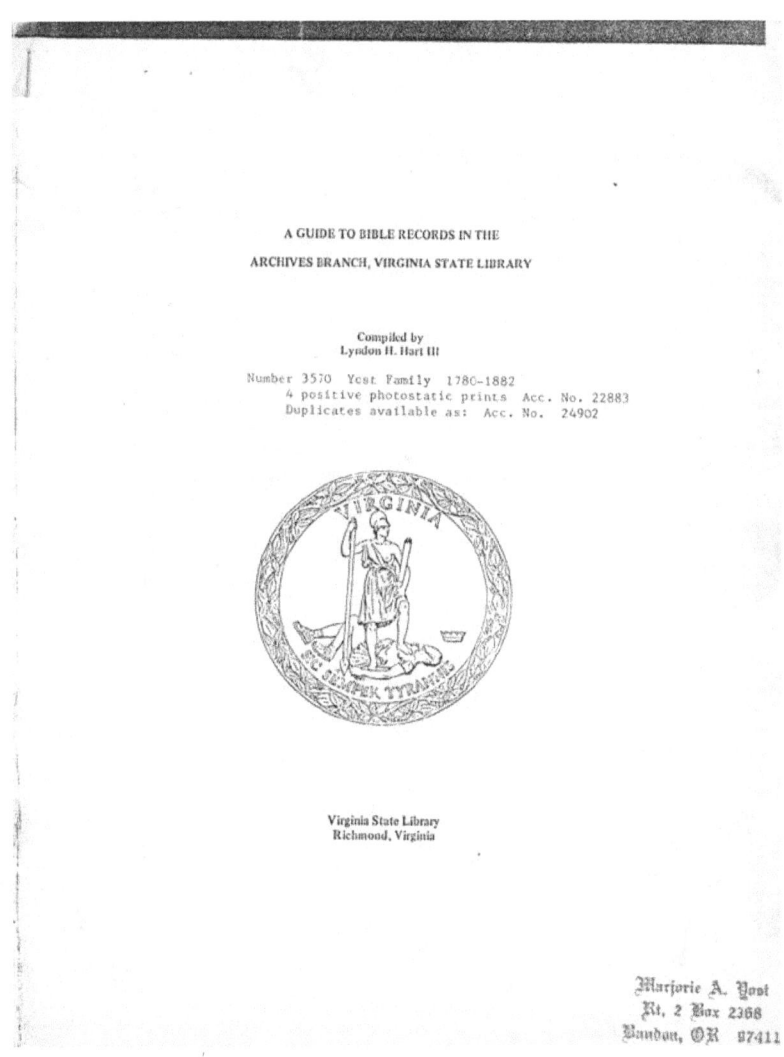

[670]

FAMILY RECORD.

BIRTHS.

Henry Yost Senior
Born May 23 1780
Polly Yost My wife
Born May 30th 1781
The age of our Children
And when Born
Nancy Mitchel Yost
Born June 26 1806
Wesley Born Sept 24 1807
Jane Born July 16th 1809
Henry Born June 24th 1811
Henry Wagner Born Jany 10th 1813
Betsy Gwinn Born Nov 11th 1814
Davies Gwinn Born March 6th 1817
Samuel Eagon Born Decr 7 1818
Roberts Carly Born Sept 30 1820
John Winchester Son of
Thomas and [illegible]
Born August 6 1823
George [illegible] Born [illegible]
[illegible] 1825
William Jacob Born Sept 21st 1827
Eleanor Matilda Born
January 30th 1830

BIRTHS.

Francis Asbury Born
May 13th 1832
James Hervey Born
July 23rd 1835

FAMILY RECORD

Births

Henry Yost Senior
Born May 23 1780
Polly Yost My Wife
Born May 30th 1781
The age of our Children
And when Born.
Nancy Mitchel Yost
Born June 26 1806
Wesley Born Sept 24th 1807
Jane Born July 16th 1809
Henry Born June 24th 1811
Mary Wagner Born Janry 10th 1813
Betsy Greiner Born Novmbr 11 1814
David Greiner Born March 6th 1817
Samuel Eagon Born Decbr 7 1818
Roberts Early Born Sept 30th 1820
John Winchester Son of
Henry and Lydia Roberts Yost
Born August 6th 1823
George Casper born August 22nd 1825
William Jacob Born Sept 21st 1827
Eleanor Matilda Born
January 30th 1830

Births

Francis Asbury Born
May 13th 1832
James Hervey Born
July 23rd 1835

[677]

FAMILY RECORD.

MARRIAGES.   **MARRIAGES.**

Henry York Married to Betty
Early Daughter of James
& Nellie Early of Botetourt County
Virginia August 18th 1835

[...] York Married to
[...] Daughter
[...]
[...] December 10th 1822

FAMILY RECORD

Marriages

Henry Yost Married To Polly
Early Daughter of James
Matten Early Botetourt County
Virginia August 18th 1805
Henry Yost Married to
Lydia E Roberts Daughter
of John and (Mary) Roberts
State of Illinois Franklin
County November 12 1822

Marriages

FAMILY RECORD.

BIRTHS.

DEATHS.

Nancy .... departed this life
December 4th 1806 aged five
Months and ten Days

Betsey G. Yost Departed
This Life Sept 7th 1821
aged five years 9 Months
and 24 Days

Mary Yost wife of
Henry Yost Departed
This Life July 14th
1822 aged Forty one
years one Month &
Ten Days and Mother
of Nine Children

James Yost Departed this
Life September 6th 1823

Eleanor Halstead
Departed this life
December 13th 1832

James Hervey Yost died
April 29th 1830
aged 4 months and 6 d[ays]

FAMILY RECORD

Births	Deaths
	Nancy M Yost Departed this life December 5th 1806 aged five months and Ten days
	Betsey G Yost Departed This Life Sep^t 7th 1821 Aged Six years 9 months and 24 Days
	Mary Yost wife of Henry Yost Departed This Life July Tenth 1822 aged Forty one years one month and Ten Days and Mother of Nine Children
	Jane Yost Departed this Life September 6 1827
	Eleanor Matilda Departed this Life December 13th 1832
	James Hervey Yost died April 29th 1836 aged 9 months and 6 days

[680]
FAMILY RECORD.

DEATHS.

Jane Early Departed This Life the 16th Day of September 1821 aged 28 Years one Month & 2 Days

Jane Early Wife of James McCarly Departed this Life the 29th Day of March 1823 age about 65 years

DEATHS.

[illegible entry]

John McChesten [?] Died April the [?] 16, 1882 Near [?] Bois Illinois Peryl[?]

FAMILY RECORD

Deaths

Jane Early Departed
This Life this 16th Day
of September 1821 aged
28 years one month &
2 days ------------

Jane Early Wife of
James M Early Departed
This Life the 9th Day of March
1823 age about 65 years

Deaths

Henry Yost Departed
this life on 22nd day
of March at the age
65 years nine months
(can't read) days

Lydia E Yost Died at
Metropolis Ill Sept 15th
1875 aged nearly 80 Years

John Winchester
Yost - Died April the
Apr 16 1882 / Near Du
Bois Illinois Perry Co

John Winchester Yost's Life

John was born August 06, 1823 in Fancy Farm, Franklin County Illinois. He died April 16, 1882 in Dubois, Washington Co. Illinois.

John married first Elizabeth Maxey Kennedy born September 19, 1827 in Washington Co. Illinois. They were married March 27, 1844 in Illinois, Washington County. They had the following children, Francis Lydia "Frank" Yost born July 27, 1849, Dempsey Dwight Yost born August 21, 1853, Eugene Lathrop Yost born April 06, 1848, Sarah Eleanor Yost born July 21, 1845, Tranquilla Richison Yost born April 06, 1848. Elizabeth died March 27, 1844 in Nashville, Washington Co. Illinois.

Demsey - Kennedy Cemetery
Beaucoup Township, Washington County, Illinois

KENNEDY, _____ ... March 15, 1828 - April 22, 1857
KENNEDY, Burrel ... June 9, 1823 - March 14, 1883
KENNEDY, Lavis M. (nee CALOWAY) ...May 19, 1825 - June 20, 1883
KENNEDY, Demsey ...March 2, 1800 - October 28, 1870
KENNEDY, Demsey S. (Son of D. & M. E. KENNEDY) ... Died February 28, 1858 graduated McKendree College in June 1856
KENNEDY, Julia E. (Wife of W. M. CASEY) ... Died January 4, 1866 *Aged 34 Y 5 M 13 D*
LYNCH, Matthew (Son of H. & M. LYNCH) ... Died December 10, 184 *Aged 32 Y 13 D*
YOST, Elizabeth (KENNEDY) (Wife of John YOST)
YOST, Sarah E. (Daughter of J. W. & E. M. YOST) ... Died October 24, 1845 *Aged 3 M 3 D*
YOST, Tranquilla R. (Daughter of J. W. & E. M. YOST) ... Died July 26, 1848 *Aged 1 Y 3 M 20 D*

Directions to the Cemetery: Coming in on Interstate 64 from St. Louis, take the Nashville exit, south to Nashville, a right turn. Come on into town about 5 miles. At the intersection of IL Hwy 127 and IL hwy 15, turn left/east. Maybe 5 miles out of town, there's a road sign for POSEN, looks like a small sub-division around there. It was actually called the Johnson Subdivision at one time and they are building some new homes there again. Turn right/south onto Posen Road, the transcript has the legal county description number on it. Maybe a block down this road, you'll see a barely maintained road that turns to the left/east. Follow this road and you'll end up in someone's back yard. Also at a little creek of sorts this road stops. Look to the right/east in the woods and you'll see the stones. One of them is 8 or 9 foot tall and easy to spot, even from the highway. I'm sure anyone living out there would point you in the right direction if you get lost.

Sarah and Tranquilla Yost Grave Marker Kennedy Cemetery

Kennedy Cemetery Beaucoup Township, Washington County, Illinois

Demsey Kennedy Grave Marker

Demsey Kennedy, Elizabeth Maxey Kennedy Yost's Father

Elizabeth Maxey Kennedy Yost

John then married Julia Hopkins Spencer on February 23, 1866. Julia was born August 26, 1837 in Dubois Illinois. She died December 04, 1926 in Norman Oklahoma. They had the following children, Herman Daniel Yost born December 04, 1866, Wreath Julietta Yost born November 22, 1875, Trevor Harlan Yost born November 11, 1869, Benton Yost born 1864, Spencer Eldredge Yost born November 10, 1873, and May Spencer Yost.

Julia Hopkins Spencer Yost

Julia Hopkins Spencer Yost's Grave Marker in Lawton, Oklahoma

NOTE: The children of Raymond John and Nora Paul Yost always suspected that the Spencer family was related to the Yost family in another way. This has been confirmed by census, that Julia Hopkins Spencer was the third child of Daniel Spencer Calvin. Daniel also had Calvin Augustus Spencer born in 1839. The 1850 census for Washington County Illinois shows that Daniel Spenser and his family including Calvin lived just two farms away from Dempsey Kennedy. The 1870 census for Washington County Illinois reveals Calvin Augustus Spencer married to Francis Lydia "Frank" Yost, the daughter of John Winchester Yost.

A 1894 letter from Julia to Trevor Harlen and Clara Yost:

Mr. T. H. Yost and Wife
Dear Children, Your welcome letter rec - I am always glad to hear from you. I was glad to learn that Clara got well but I don't want her to smash her thumb any more. First sick then smashed thumb, no wonder I do not hear from her any more. enough of that. I have not felt well today, had to lay down a little while. Esta washed and Ironed yesterday but was too much for me. I went to town this morning and helped Esta pick her a lovely ******** at 50 cents per yd. Fawn color - I will send you a piece. Well Bandover is to be married a week from next Sunday in the South Methodist Church publically to a girl from Tuscahoma. She lives here now. Well the cold has eliminated my fruit entirely., peaches all gone, Cherries and pears also killed, Strawberries killed in bloom. Todays report says about a 3rd of apple crop yet alive. All my canned fruit I hauled from Wichita frozen and broke, I lost 24 jars of fruit but jellie and preserves did not freeze.My lettuce, radishes, beets is all up but freeze did not hurt them. Ed Guild is here on his way to Fort Smith for a few days and is look up some kind of business here or further south. He is a nice young man I believe and a splendid worker.Gets up and kindles fire every morning and seekps the kitchen. He has cut up a cord of wood for cook stove. Well Mr. Doug is all right. Mad dog scar is over and dogs can run at large. Pug is as happy as a king, he dug out twice during his confinement, he is so fat and lazy he is laying on my feet now. He has not slept out doors one night since we cam ehere. Clara is your Caludrum Bulb sound yet? Mine here all froze and rotted. I have lost all but my eagle claw that Trevor sent to me. I am going to close now and eat something. Mother

1850 Census — Household 848

Dwelling	Family	Name	Age	Sex
848	848	Daniel R Spencer	46	M
		Lavina "	35	F
		William C "	17	M
		Elizabeth D "	16	F
		Judith H "	13	F
		Calvin A "	11	M
		John M "	9	M
		Margaret D "	7	F
		Nancy P "	5	F
		Roswell H "	4	M
		Edward "	2	M
		Infant "	½	M
		Joshua Hatcher	25	M
849	849	Lewis Morrison	46	M
		Sarah "	35	F
		Thomas "	18	M
		Eliza "	15	F
		Sidney "	12	M
		Susana "	8	F
		Elizabeth M "	7	F
		Lewis W "	5	M
		Joseph S "	2	M
		Henry Haston	19	M
		Louisa Walker	21	F
850	850	Dempsey Kennedy	50	M
		Mary E "	51	F
		James H "	20	M
		Julia E "	18	F
		Dempsey S "	15	M
		Mary C " (twins)	14	F
		Eleanor A "	14	F
		Sarah B "	12	F
		Lydia C "	7	F
		William Eason	26	M
		Samuel Shuttleworth	21	M
		Moctuma Logan	20	M

1850 Daniel Spenser Calvins dad Illinois Washington with Dempsey Kennedy living two farms away

1870 Census

Dwelling	Family	Name	Age	Sex	Race	Occupation
85	85	Spenser Calvin	32	M	W	Farmer
		Frances	21	F	W	Keeping House
		Era May	1	F	W	
		Houltlien Charles	16	M	W	Works on Farm
		John	14	M	W	"

1870 Calvin Spenser and Aunt Frank Yost Illinois Washington

John Winchester Yost

REGISTERED VOTERS OF CENTRALIA PRECINCT.

True Henry	Yost J W
Trieb John	Yandell John
Thompson D B	Zick B
Taylor Joseph	Zick F H
Torgerson Ole	Zick F J
Taylor Jos G	Zick John
Tate R E	Zehntmeier Nich
Van Cleve W S	Zeh John

We, the undersigned, composing the Board of Registry for Election District, Centralia Precinct, in the county of Marion and State of Illinois, do certify, that the foregoing is a correct list of the voters in said District, to the best of our knowledge.

J. C. COOPER,
M. C. KELL.

Dated May 15, 1867.

29 April 1882 BARTON'S FREE PRESS

During the preparation for the burial of Mr. John W. YOST on Monday at the Kennedy burying grounds, a few miles east of Nashville, it was thought by some that perhaps his life was not extinct, because during the services at Beaucoup Church the face of the deceased was covered with drops of perspiration. As a measure of precaution, the body was not buried, but brought to the house of Mr. JACK, in Nashville, and there kept until the following day. Doctors HENRY(?) and TROUT applied an electric battery but they detected no signs of life. A thorough examination was made by those competent to judge, and all doubts were removed as to the death of Mr. YOST. As is always the case at such times, there were all kinds of rumors afloat which, being traced up, had no foundation in fact. The appearance of the body was such as is sometimes seen after sudden death where the person had been in general good health, and the physicians had no doubt in their minds as to the reality of death in this case. Mr. YOST was buried on Tuesday by the side of his first wife, who was the daughter of the late Dempsey KENNEDY. Nashville Journal.

Yost Family Spoon it is said, was brought over by Hans Casper Yost as a set of silver coins. John Winchester Yost used his skill with metals to make several spoons out of the silver coins. It is also rumored that the original coins were to be used as a signal back in Germany or France to obtain the family land and possessions back that had been taken. (Note the Y at the top of the handle)

John Winchester Yost Book Case

(At Vivian Yost Terrel's home Enid, OK in 2008)

**John Winchester Yost's
Encyclopedia of Religion Published 1865
Handed down to Herman Daniel Yost**

**John Winchester Yost's
Encyclopedia of Religion Published 1865
Handed down to Herman Daniel Yost
Inside Cover**

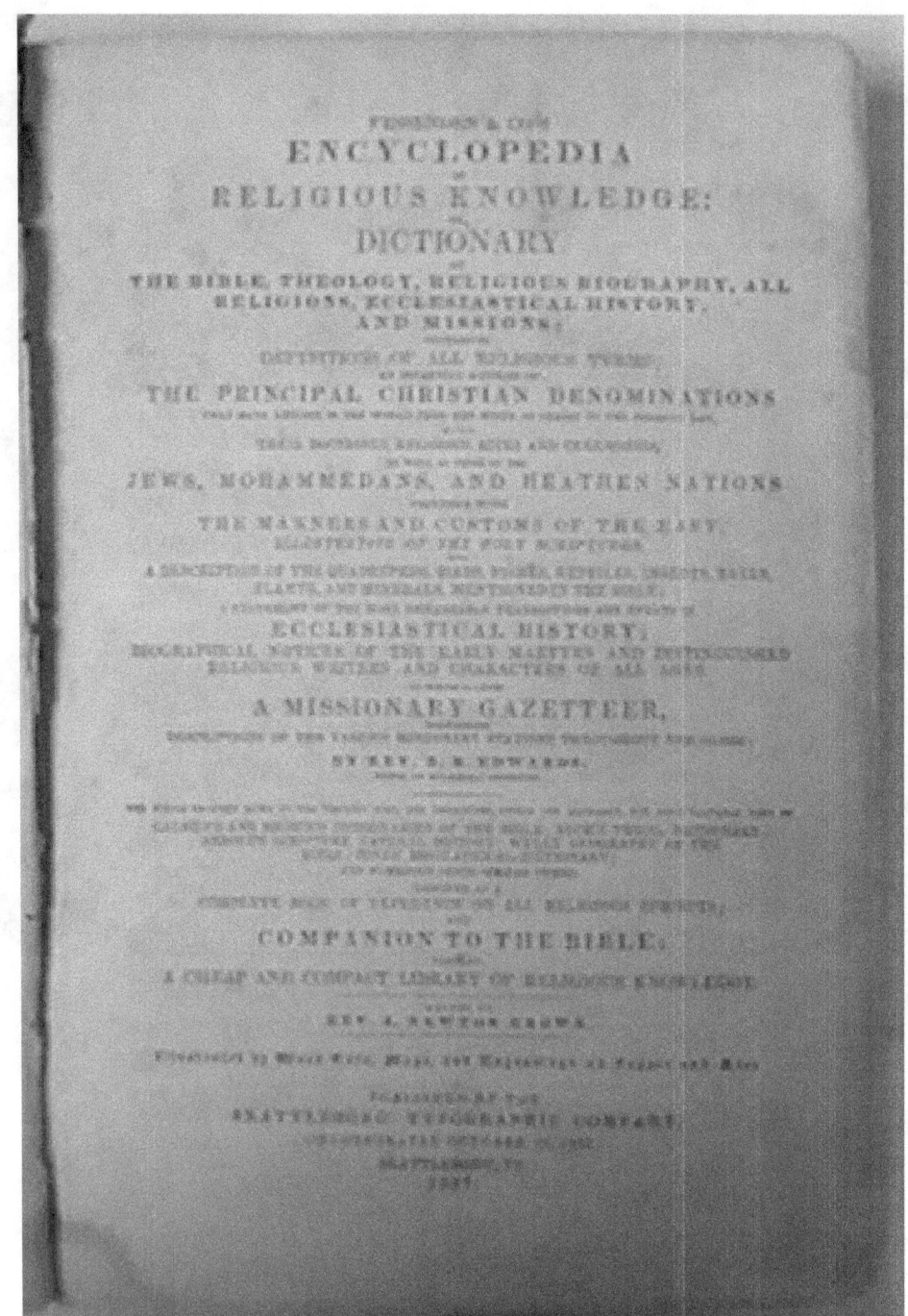

John Winchester Yost's
Encyclopedia of Religion Published 1865
Handed down to Herman Daniel Yost

Illinois Public Land Purchase Records

Name:	**YOST JOHN**
Section:	NENW
Price:	125
Total:	5040
Date:	13 Dec 1836
Volume:	031
Page:	081
Type:	FD
Sect:	31
Township:	13S
Range:	02W
Meridian:	3
Acres:	4032
Corr-Tag:	0
ID:	278924
SocStat:	
Blank:	
Reside:	091

Name:	**YOST JOHN**
Section:	SWSE
Price:	125
Total:	5000
Date:	3 Dec 1836
Volume:	031
Page:	080
Type:	FD
Sect:	30
Township:	13S
Range:	02W
Meridian:	3
Acres:	4000
Corr-Tag:	0
ID:	278925
SocStat:	
Blank:	
Reside:	091

Name:	**YOST JULIA H**
Section:	NWNE
Price:	600
Total:	24000
Date:	9 Apr 1879

Volume:	794
Page:	271
Type:	RR
Sect:	34
Township:	02S
Range:	02W
Meridian:	3
Acres:	4000
Corr-Tag:	0
ID:	503974
SocStat:	F
Blank:	
Reside:	000
Name:	**YOST JOHN W**
Section:	LOT1BL127
Price:	00000
Total:	12500
Date:	10 May 1866
Volume:	796
Page:	026
Type:	RR
Sect:	18
Township:	01N
Range:	01E
Meridian:	3
Acres:	000000
Corr-Tag:	0
ID:	516173
SocStat:	
Blank:	
Reside:	000
Name:	**YOST JOHN W**
Section:	LOT2BL129
Price:	00000
Total:	11500
Date:	20 Jul 1866
Volume:	796
Page:	026
Type:	RR
Sect:	18
Township:	01N
Range:	01E
Meridian:	3
Acres:	000000
Corr-Tag:	0
ID:	516174

SocStat:
Blank:
Reside: 000

Name: **YOST JOHN W**
Section: LOT4BL129
Price: 00000
Total: 11500
Date: 20 Jul 1866
Volume: 796
Page: 026
Type: RR
Sect: 18
Township: 01N
Range: 01E
Meridian: 3
Acres: 000000
Corr-Tag: 0
ID: 516175
SocStat:
Blank:
Reside: 000

Name: **YOST JOHN W**
Section: LOT1BL129
Price: 00000
Total: 11500
Date: 20 Jul 1866
Volume: 796
Page: 026
Type: RR
Sect: 18
Township: 01N
Range: 01E
Meridian: 3
Acres: 000000
Corr-Tag: 0
ID: 516176
SocStat:
Blank:
Reside: 000

Name: **YOST JOHN W**
Section: LOTALLBL124
Price: 00000
Total: 53000
Date: 11 May 1866
Volume: 796

Page:	026
Type:	RR
Sect:	18
Township:	01N
Range:	01E
Meridian:	3
Acres:	000000
Corr-Tag:	0
ID:	516177
SocStat:	
Blank:	
Reside:	000

THE UNITED STATES OF AMERICA

CERTIFICATE No. 3824

To all to whom these Presents shall come, Greeting:

WHEREAS John Yost of Union County, Illinois has deposited in the GENERAL LAND OFFICE of the United States, a Certificate of the REGISTER OF THE LAND OFFICE at Kaskaskia whereby it appears that full payment has been made by the said John Yost according to the provisions of the Act of Congress of the 24th of April, 1820, entitled "An Act making further provision for the sale of the Public Lands," for the South West quarter of the South East quarter of Section thirty, in Township thirteen South, of Range two West, in the District of Lands subject to sale at Kaskaskia, Illinois, containing forty acres

according to the official plat of the survey of the said Lands, returned to the General Land Office by the SURVEYOR GENERAL, which said tract has been purchased by the said John Yost

NOW KNOW YE, That the United States of America, in consideration of the Premises, and in conformity with the several acts of Congress, in such case made and provided, HAVE GIVEN AND GRANTED, and by these presents DO GIVE AND GRANT, unto the said John Yost and to his heirs, the said tract above described: TO HAVE AND TO HOLD the same, together with all the rights, privileges, immunities, and appurtenances of whatsoever nature, thereunto belonging, unto the said John Yost and to his heirs and assigns forever.

In Testimony Whereof, I, Martin Van Buren PRESIDENT OF THE UNITED STATES OF AMERICA, have caused these Letters to be made PATENT, and the SEAL of the GENERAL LAND OFFICE to be hereunto affixed.

GIVEN under my hand at the CITY OF WASHINGTON, the first day of August in the Year of our Lord one thousand eight hundred and thirty eight and of the INDEPENDENCE OF THE UNITED STATES the Sixty third

BY THE PRESIDENT: Martin Van Buren

By M. Van Buren Jr. Sec'y.

Jos. S. Wilson Acting Recorder of the General Land Office.
ad interim

THE UNITED STATES OF AMERICA.

CERTIFICATE No. 3904

To all to whom these Presents shall come, Greeting:

WHEREAS John Yost of Union County, Illinois has deposited in the **GENERAL LAND OFFICE** of the United States, a Certificate of the REGISTER OF THE LAND OFFICE at Kaskaskia whereby it appears that full payment has been made by the said John Yost according to the provisions of the Act of Congress of the 24th of April, 1820, entitled "An Act making further provision for the sale of the Public Lands," for the North East quarter of the North West quarter of Section thirty one, in Township thirteen South, of Range two West, in the District of lands subject to sale at Kaskaskia, Illinois, containing forty acres and thirty two hundredths of an acre

according to the official plat of the survey of the said Lands, returned to the General Land Office by the **SURVEYOR GENERAL**, which said tract has been purchased by the said John Yost

NOW KNOW YE, That the United States of America, in consideration of the Premises, and in conformity with the several acts of Congress, in such case made and provided, HAVE GIVEN AND GRANTED, and by these presents DO GIVE AND GRANT, unto the said John Yost and to his heirs, the said tract above described: TO HAVE AND TO HOLD the same, together with all the rights, privileges, immunities, and appurtenances of whatsoever nature, thereunto belonging, unto the said John Yost and to his heirs and assigns forever.

In Testimony Whereof, I, Martin Van Buren PRESIDENT OF THE UNITED STATES OF AMERICA, have caused these Letters to be made PATENT, and the SEAL of the GENERAL LAND OFFICE to be hereunto affixed.

GIVEN under my hand at the CITY OF WASHINGTON, the first day of August in the Year of our Lord one thousand eight hundred and thirty eight and of the INDEPENDENCE OF THE UNITED STATES the Sixty third

BY THE PRESIDENT: Martin Van Buren

By M. Van Buren Jr Sec'y.

A. S. Wilson, Acting RECORDER of the General Land Office. ad interim

468

Copd Mar 28/74

THE UNITED STATES OF AMERICA,

CERTIFICATE
No. 16,434

To all to whom these Presents shall come, Greeting:

Whereas John W. Yost of Washington County, Illinois

has deposited in the GENERAL LAND OFFICE of the United States, a Certificate of the REGISTER OF THE LAND OFFICE at Kaskaskia whereby it appears that full payment has been made by the said

John W. Yost according to the provisions of the Act of Congress of the 24th of April, 1820, entitled "An act making further provision for the sale of the Public Lands," for

The South East quarter of the South West quarter of section Twenty three in Township Two South Range Two west in the District of Lands subject to sale at Kaskaskia Illinois containing Forty acres

according to the official plat of the Survey of the said Lands, returned to the General Land Office by the SURVEYOR GENERAL, which said tract has been purchased by the said John W. Yost

NOW KNOW YE, That the **United States of America**, in consideration of the premises, and in conformity with the several acts of Congress in such case made and provided, HAVE GIVEN AND GRANTED, and by these presents DO GIVE AND GRANT, unto the said

John W. Yost

and to his heirs, the said tract above described: **To have and to hold** the same, together with all the rights, privileges, immunities, and appurtenances of whatsoever nature, thereunto belonging, unto the said

John W. Yost and to his heirs and assigns forever

In Testimony Whereof, I, Franklin Pierce PRESIDENT OF THE UNITED STATES OF AMERICA, have caused these Letters to be made PATENT, and the SEAL of the GENERAL LAND OFFICE to be hereunto affixed.

GIVEN under my hand, at the CITY OF WASHINGTON, the first day of November in the year of our Lord one thousand eight hundred and fifty one and of the INDEPENDENCE OF THE UNITED STATES the eightieth.

BY THE PRESIDENT: Franklin Pierce
By H. C. Baldwin, Secretary

J. N. Granger, Recorder of the General Land Office.

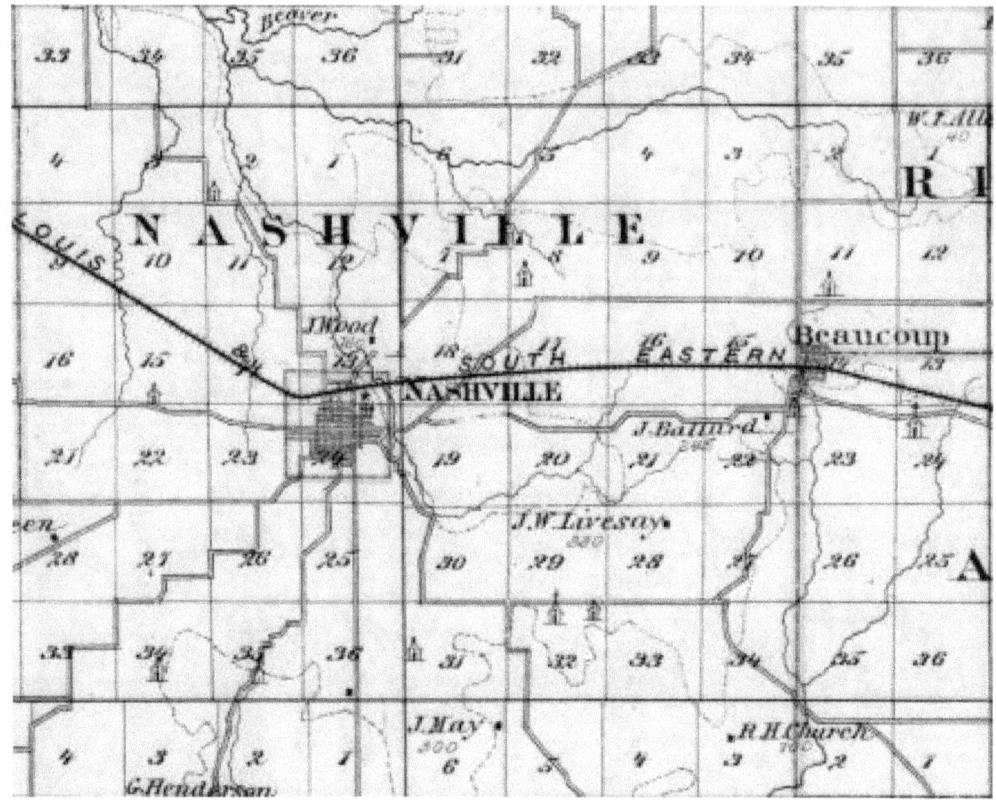

1867 Washington County Illinois Map
(Sections 18, 30, 31, and 34 John Winchester Yost Purchased land for his family)

Children of John Winchester Yost and Elizabeth Maxey Kennedy are:

Francis Lydia "Frank" Yost, born July 27, 1849; died 1930. Francis married Calvin Augustus Spencer and later married Colonel Frederick HAHA. Frederick died September 26, 1906.

The Civil War History of Frederick HaHa

American Civil War Soldiers
Name: Frederick Haha,
Enlistment Date: 06 June 1861
Distinguished Service: DISTINGUISHED SERVICE
Side Served: Union
State Served: Ohio
Unit Numbers: 1908 1908
Service Record: Enlisted as a Private on 06 June 1861 at the age of 25
Enlisted in Company G, 6th Infantry Regiment Ohio on 06 June 1861.
Transferred Company G, 6th Infantry Regiment Ohio on 15 November 1863
Transfered in on 15 November 1863.

Civil War Pension Index: General Index to Pension Files, 1861-1934
Name: Frederick Haha
State Filed: Kansas
Widow: Frances L. Haha

Uncle Fred Haha is buried at the Central Wisconsin Veteran's Memorial Cemetery he was at the Wisconsin Veteran's Home (G.A.R. Home) - N2665, Hwy. QQ., in the State of Wisconsin, County of Waupaca, City of King. Lot 3 Section 8. Uncle HaHa's grave has a Military Headstone.

Frederick HaHa Civil War awards: Distinguished Service Award and Civil War Campaign Badges for the

Battle at Shiloh: 6-7 Apr 1862
Battle at Chickamauga: 16 Aug - 22 Sep 1863

6th Regiment, Ohio Infantry

Organized at Camp Dennison, Ohio, June 18, 1861. Moved to Fetterman, W. Va., June 29-July 2. Attached to 1st Brigade, Army of Occupation, West Virginia, to September, 1861. Reynolds' Command, Cheat Mountain, W. Va., to November, 1861. 10th Brigade, Army Ohio, to December, 1861. 10th Brigade, 4th Division, Army Ohio, to September, 1862. 10th Brigade, 4th Division, 2nd Corps, Army Ohio, to November, 1862. 3rd Brigade, 2nd Division, Left Wing 14th Army Corps, Army of the Cumberland, to January, 1863. 3rd Brigade, 2nd Division, 21st Army Corps, Army of the Cumberland, to October, 1863. 2nd Brigade, 3rd Division, 4th Army Corps, to June, 1864.

SERVICE.-At Grafton, W. Va., July 2, 1861. March to Philippi July 4. West Virginia Campaign July 6-21. Laurel Hill July 8. Carrick's Ford July 13. Pursuit of Garnett's forces July 15-16. Duty at Beverly till August 6. Camp at Elkwater, foot of Cheat Mountain, August 6-November 19. Operations on Cheat Mountain against Lee September 11-17. Cheat Mountain Pass September 12. Reconnaissance up Tygart Valley September 26-29. Moved to Louisville November 19-30. Duty at Camp Buell till December 9, and at Camp Wickliffe, Ky., till February 14, 1862. Expedition down Ohio River to reinforce Gen. Grant at Fort Donelson, thence to Nashville, Tenn., February 14-25. Occupation of Nashville February 25, the first Regiment to enter city. Camp on Murfreesboro Pike till March 17. March to Savannah, Tenn., March 17-April 6. Battle of Shiloh, Tenn., April 6-7. Duty at Pittsburg Landing till May 24. Siege of Corinth, Miss., May 24-30. Occupation of Corinth May 30. Pursuit to Booneville May 30-July 12. Moved to Athens, Ala., and duty there till July 17. Ordered to Murfreesboro July 17, thence to McMinnville and duty there till August 17. March to Louisville, Ky., in pursuit of Bragg August 17-September 26. Pursuit of Bragg into Kentucky October 1-22. Battle of Perryville October 8. March to Nashville, Tenn., October 22-November 7, and duty there till December 26. Advance on Murfreesboro, Tenn., December 26-30. Battle of Stone's River December 30-31, 1862, and January 1-3, 1863. Duty at and near Murfreesboro till June. Actions at Woodbury,

Tenn., January 24 and April 4. Middle Tennessee or Tullahoma Campaign June 23-July 7. At Manchester till August 16. Passage of Cumberland Mountains and Tennessee River, and Chickamauga (Ga.) Campaign August 16-September 22. Battle of Chickamauga September 19-20. Siege of Chattanooga, Tenn., September 24-November 23. Reopening Tennessee River October 26-29. Brown's Ferry October 27. Chattanooga-Ringgold Campaign November 23-27. Orchard Knob November 23-24. Mission Ridge November 25. March to relief of Knoxville, Tenn., November 28- December 8. Operations in East Tennessee till April, 1864. About Dandridge January 16-17. Garrison at Cleveland, Tenn., April 12-May 17, and at Resaca, Ga., guarding Railroad Bridge over the Oostenaula River, till June 6. Ordered to the rear for muster out June 6. Mustered out at Camp Dennison, Ohio, June 23, 1864, expiration of term.

Regiment lost during service 4 Officers and 82 Enlisted men killed and mortally wounded and 2 Officers and 56 Enlisted men by disease. Total 144.

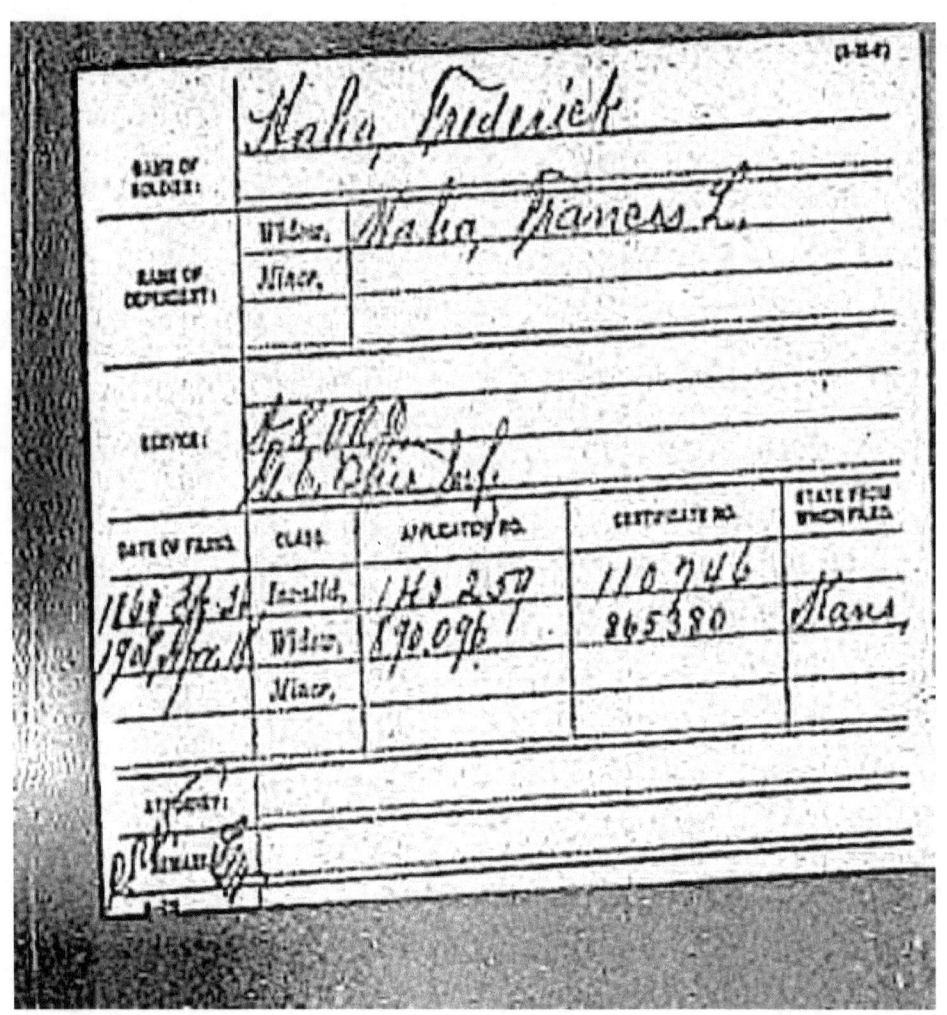

Uncle Frederick HaHa's Civil War Pension to Aunt Frances L. Yost HaHa

**Uncle Fred Haha with Elzina Yost sons Top: Marcus, Ralph, Herman
Bottom: Frank, Ray**

Dempsey Dwight Yost, born August 21, 1853, Fancy Farm, Franklin County Illinois; died January 28, 1924, Quapaw, Ottawa Co. Oklahoma.

Eugene Lathrop Yost, born April 06, 1848. On June 06, 1847, she was baptized by Elder James.

Sarah Eleanor Yost, born July 21, 1845; died October 24, 1845. She died without having been baptized.

Tranquilla Richison Yost, born April 06, 1848; died July 26, 1848. On June 06, 1847, she was baptized by Elder James

Children of John Winchester Yost and Julia Spencer are:

Herman Daniel Yost, born. December 04, 1866, Centralia, Illinois; died March 13, 1957, Enid, Oklahoma. Herman Daniel Yost married Ida Qualls born September 13, 1867 in Dubois Illinois; died February 15, 1924 in Rabourn Cemetery Located about 12 miles west of Sedalia. They were married September 28, 1886 at her father Samuel Qualls residence in Washington County Illinois.

**Mrs. H.D. (Ida) Yost 81 years old Garfield County Pioneer died Monday morning at her home at Gentry, Arkansas. She had been ill several months. Mrs. Yost had lived at Covington till nine years ago having come there from Illinois soon after the opening of the Cherokee Strip.
She is survived by her husband H.D. Yost, four children, Mrs. Vivian Yost Terrel of Enid, Oklahoma, Victor Yost of Houston, Texas, Vesta Yost of the home, and Velma Green of Tulsa, Oklahoma. 4 grand-children, three great grand children.
Funeral services will be held at 2 p.m., Tuesday in Gentry at the Methodist Church and grave side rites will be at Covington, 1:30, Wednesday.**

Herman and Ida Yost Homestead Covington Oklahoma

H. I. Yost
1930 — Straw shed on farm when we came in 1897.

Covington Farm Home

Herman and Ida Yost Home in Gentry Ark during retirement

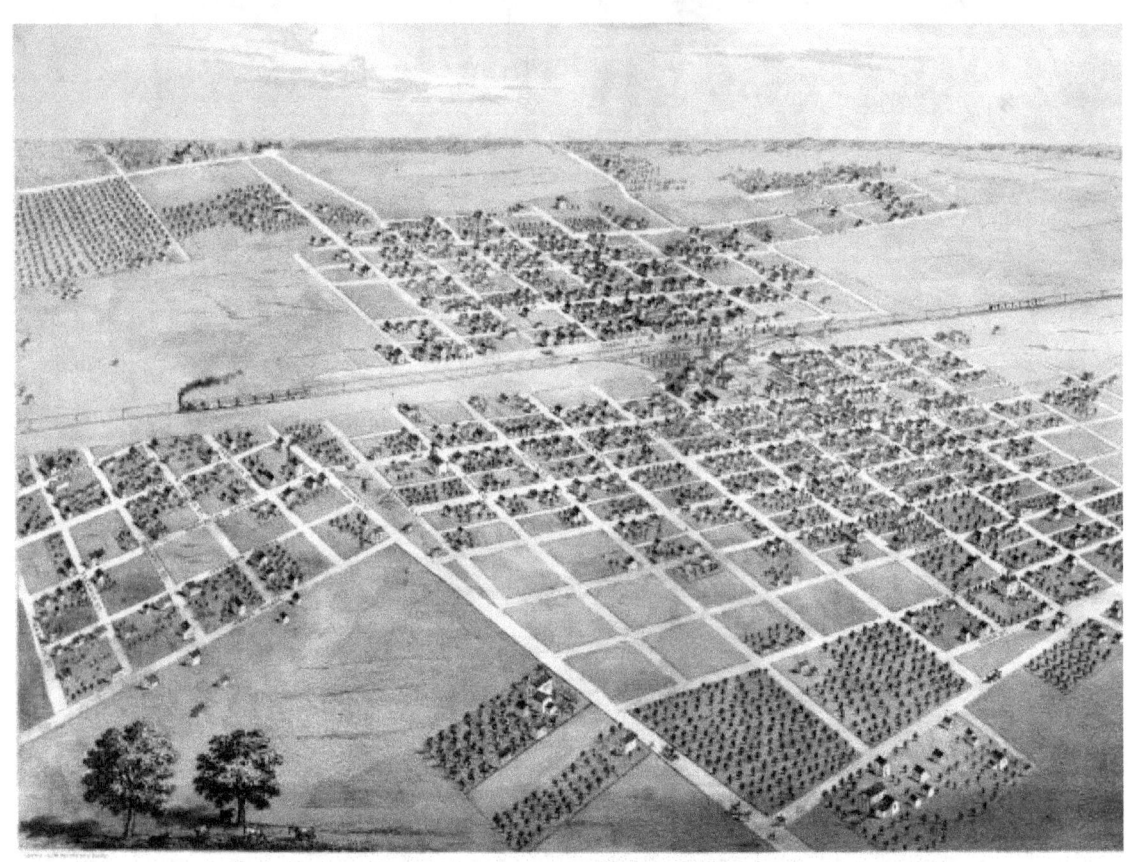

Centralia Illinois 1867

Below is an actual copy of their marriage Register

1. No. of License. 2. Date of License.	1. By whom affidavit, if any, is made. 2. By whom consent to Marriage given.	1. Full Name of Groom. 2. Place of Residence. 3. Occupation.	1. Age next Birthday. 2. Race or Color. 3. Place of Birth.	1. Father's Name. 2. Mother's Maiden Name. 3. No. of Groom's Marriage.
1. 122 2. Sept 28/86	1. 2.	1. Herman D Yost 2. Perry County 3. Farmer	1. 20 years 2. Wh Caucasian 3. Marion Co.	1. John W. Yost 2. Julia H Spencer 3. First

1. Full Name of Bride. 2. Maiden Name, if a Widow. 3. Place of Residence.	1. Age next Birthday. 2. Race or Color. 3. Place of Birth.	1. Father's Name. 2. Mother's Maiden Name. 3. No. of Bride's Marriage.	1. Where and when Married. 2. Witnesses. 3. By whom Certified, Name and Office.	1. Date of Return. 2. When Registered.
1. Ida Qualls 2. 3. Washington Co.	1. 20 years 2. Wh Caucass 3. this County	1. Samuel Qualls 2. Dillia Cranton 3. First	1. at S. Qualls res this County Sept 29, 1886 2. S D Qualls, Lizzie Lewis 3. J.B. Curlee M G	1. Oct 2/86 2. Nov 9/86

MISSOURI STATE BOARD OF HEALTH
BUREAU OF VITAL STATISTICS
CERTIFICATE OF DEATH

No. 5178

1. **PLACE OF DEATH**
   - County: Pettis
   - Township: Elk Fork
   - Registration District No.: 664
   - Primary Registration District No.: 5883
   - Registered No.: 54

2. **FULL NAME**: Ida Yost
   - Length of residence in city or town where death occurred: 56 yrs.

PERSONAL AND STATISTICAL PARTICULARS

3. Sex: Female
4. Color or Race: White
5. Single, Married, Widowed or Divorced: Married
5a. Husband of (or) Wife of: H. C. Yost
6. Date of Birth: Nov 25 – 1867
7. Age: 56 years, 2 months, 20 days
8. Occupation: Housewife — Her Own
9. Birthplace: Pettis Co. Mo.
10. Name of Father: Geo McKinley
11. Birthplace of Father: Indiana
12. Maiden Name of Mother: Matilda Stevens
13. Birthplace of Mother: Moniteau Co. Mo.
14. Informant: H. C. Yost, La Monte Mo R.R.
15. Filed Feb 20, 24 — G.R. Shelley, Registrar

MEDICAL CERTIFICATE OF DEATH

16. Date of Death: Feb 15, 1924
17. I hereby certify that I attended deceased from Dec 4, 1921 to Feb 15, 1924, that I last saw her alive on Feb 15, 1924, and that death occurred on the date stated above at 8:10 a.m.

The CAUSE OF DEATH was as follows:
Malignant tumor of right abdominal cavity
(duration) 7 yrs.
Contributory: 53 E ever

18. Did an operation precede death? No
    Was there an autopsy? No

(Signed) H. A. Hite, M.D.
2/15, 1924 Address: Green Ridge Mo

19. Place of Burial: Rayburn Cemetery — Date of Burial: Feb 16, 1924
20. Undertaker: B. F. Parker, La Monte Mo.

Ida Qualls Yost Death Certificate

Left Victor Ida Vivian Vesta Herman Daniel Yost

Yost farmhouse, 1901. H.D. Yost, Ida Yost, Vivian, Victor and Vesta. Also pictured, surrey with fringe on top horses Eva K., Firefly and Starlight; dogs – Shepherd – Nails; Bird dog – Lee. Compliments: Vivian Yost Terrel

Marie, Roselie and Louise was buried at sea.

Gottfried, was born in Canton Bern, Switzerland on March 12, 1851. He was 14 years old when he came to America with his family. He died on January 3, 1941 at almost 90 years of age. He farmed 3 miles south of Fairmont for many years, and upon retirement, moved into town. He and his wife, Marie had nine children, all born in Nebraska. One daughter, Maria lived one week. The other eight children all moved to Oklahoma. The eldest was 18 and the youngest 2 years.

Marie Berghorn, was born August 28, 1855 in Neundorf, Hanover, Germany. She came to America with a wealthy family who had employed her as their housekeeper. She had lovely golden blond hair which she braided into two heavy braids. Her employer promised to bring her to America with them if she would sell her braids and also work for them for one year after they arrived here. She did this, and of course her hair grew back again. Her braids were still partly blond when she died on September 9, 1937 at age 82 years. She was 26 years old she came to America. From oldest to youngest their children were: Henry, William (Bill), Gottfried II, John, Carl, Dorothea (Dora), Carolina (Lena) and Amelia.

Three of the sons moved to the Covington area where they farmed the land.

Bill, married Alvina Kriethe, and their five children are Eldo, who married Berniece Bartels, Ervin (deceased), never married, Elvira, married Joe Funk, Wilbert, married Virginia Funk, and Kenneth married Gladys Mack Baker.

Gottfried II, (also called Godfrey) married Anna Schulze and their eight children are Ottilie, not married, Edna (deceased), married Edwin Bohlmann, Walter (deceased), married Lorene Whiteneck, Erna married Bill Steinert, Melvin married Alice Friday Gerbitz, Renata married Herold Schweer, Leroy married Dorothy Spillman Mossler – (divorced), and Viola married Cledith Gregg.

John, married Frieda Peters and their six children are Arthur (deceased), married Mary Louise Kaiser, Leona married Vilah Thorp, Mildred married Wilfred Burk Jr., Irma married Walter Fischer, John Jr. (deceased), married Shirley Link Coombs and Mary married John Knecht.

YOST, H.D. AND IDA (QUALLS)

F229

On Nov. 2, 1897, H.D. Yost and wife Ida Qualls Yost with their two children, Vivian Ida and Victor H. ages 8 and 6, left DuBois Ill. Nov. 2, 1897 with their neighbors John W. and Minnie Fischer with their two children Etta and Arthur to come west to make their homes.

My Grandmother (TO-Mamma) Julia Hopkins Yost Burns had made a payment down on this farm N.E. ¼ of Sec. 7 Township 21 Range 3, Garfield Co. to hold it till we could get here and Dad could file on it. We paid 500.00.

We drove in a covered wagon, driving two bays, Luther and Charlie, and two big sorrel mules, Mike and Jack, at least 16½ hands

Yost farmhouse, 1901. H.D. Yost, Ida Yost, Vivian, Victor and Vesta. Also pictured, surrey with fringe on top horses Eva K., Firefly and Starlight; dogs – Shepherd – Nails; Bird dog – Lee. Compliments: Vivian Yost Terrel

high, and mother's saddle mare, Eva K. We pitched a tent and cooked all our meals. Mrs. Fischer baked light bread in a little wood range stove we set up every night. We came through East St. Louis driving two and leading two behind the wagon. Dad leading the way on the pony and keeping all together across the Mississippi River. On Eads bridge the horses tyed behind the wagon would turn crosswise and the Street cars would have to stop to keep from hitting them.

We camped that night in Forest Park. The dust was about 3 inches deep. We lost our good blood hound dog that we were bringing for protection. Later we came upon a rabid dog that bit our other two dogs and they had to be killed.

We were traveling light, driving the horses through so there would be room in the box car that came later, with cows, chickens, guineas, farm machinery, furniture and our square piano, which we still have with some other pieces of furniture in our homes now at this time, 75 years later Dec. 15, 1971.

H.D. had just gotten over typhoid fever, in fact we were detained about starting on account of his health, but he was a very discerning and capable person. He would ride ahead on a pony and find a place to camp for the night. There were no bridges. We had to ford all the streams, but with our four draft animals hitched to the wagon we could go over the Ozark Mts. and rivers easily.

Our extra wagon sheets and the tent would be frozen when we got up and we had to wait for them to thaw out.

One night one of the animals snorted and woke us up and all but one was untied (9 in all) and there was a vehicle going by, we thought they had been untied so some one could get away with them.

After we got to the Indian Territory we could hear the Indian drums beating. One Sun. noon we stopped along the roadside. The grass was too tall and heavy to have a fire and we were eating a cold lunch of home made light bread and molasses. Some Indians came along and wanted to eat with us, we divided with them.

I was afraid and hid in the wagon, I don't think I got much lunch that day.

We came on to Perry, (dad's) H.D.'s brother, T.H. Yost, lived 14 miles west of Perry. We got there the evening of the 29th. of Nov. We were on the road 27 days.

The next day Dad and his brother T.H. came to Enid and filed on the farm, 1 mile north of his place (this is ½ North and 1½ East of the town of Covington, which wasn't there then) without Mother or any of us seeing it. After 75 years the farm belongs to the heirs and will remain that w memorial to H.D. and Ida Yost fo years. The square piano and som furniture, dishes, all heirlooms, are i sion of some of the family.

We had one room about 16 by 16 dugout and half boards and shingle r a little attic. Then we built a room on half with sod and dirt roof. Two ye we built a five room house (1899). V born that year Oct. 17, 1899.

That is the first year I can re raising wheat, it was stored in one roo house.

Dad had built a crib to hold the c soon built a large barn over it with way, wheat bins and stalls for 8 hors we had a surrey with the fringe on the surry in "Oklahoma" then a carr a one seated buggy.

My Dad would hitch a team to th and put side curtains on it and brother and me and the neighborh dren to school and come and get school was out.

In 1897 Fred Wilson was my first I was in the third grade; Victor in th sister Mabel Wilson was a pupil, I cri knew Johnny and Ralph Mouts, t Uncle Trevor's wife's sisters fam teacher told me to go back and sit wi and Gertie Jayne, they were big gi They were all nice to me and I soon of them. There was about 8 from th families. 5 were from the Lum Jayn I believe they are all deceased, Edward and Albert were the only were in school at that time. Etta an Fischer (Arthur is deceased) B (deceased), Norcie Jackson, Donna vel Pitts. The 3 Walker boys, Ray later Ray Keltner. Mrs. John C taught the year 1899 and brought girls with her. Mildred was my age were good pals. She was associated w Lookout", a church paper for many

by Vivian Yost

YOST, HERMAN DANIEL

Herman Daniel Yost was born D 4, 1866 in Centralia, Illinois to Jo chester Yost and Julia Hopkins Yost. The Yost ancestors have bee back to Jacob Yost, Mainz, German 16th century, a great-great-grandfa great-grandfather was Lt. Henry Y along with his brother John ha Factory, making guns for the Gov during the Revolutionary War.

He attended a private Boys S Centralia, Illinois and later went to dale, now known as Illinois Univer

He married Ida Qualls on Septe 1886 at DuBois, Illinois. She w September 13, 1867 to Samuel D. an Courtney Qualls. They moved on t farm consisting of 220 acres in thi area after his father died, and farm mould board walking plow for a few 1890 they moved to Mt. Vernon, where he operated a dray busines wagons, two horses, and two mules,

YOST, H.D. AND IDA (QUALLS)

F229

On Nov. 2, 1897, H.D. Yost and wife Ida Qualls Yost with their two children, Vivian Ida and Victor H. ages 8 and 6, left DuBois Ill. Nov. 2, 1897 with their neighbors John W. and Minnie Fischer with their two children Etta and Arthur to come west to make their homes.

My Grandmother (TO-Mamma) Julia Hopkins Yost Burns had made a payment down on this farm N.E. ¼ of Sec. 7 Township 21 Range 3, Garfield Co. to hold it till we could get here and Dad could file on it. We paid 500.00.

We drove in a covered wagon, driving two bays, Luther and Charlie, and two big sorrel mules, Mike and Jack, at least 16½ hands

Yost farmhouse, 1901. H.D. Yost, Ida Yost, Vivian, Victor and Vesta. Also pictured, surrey with fringe on top horses Eva K., Firefly and Starlight; dogs – Shepherd – Nails; Bird dog – Lee. Compliments: Vivian Yost Terrel

high, and mother's saddle mare, Eva K. We pitched a tent and cooked all our meals. Mrs. Fischer baked light bread in a little wood range stove we set up every night. We came through East St. Louis driving two and leading two behind the wagon. Dad leading the way on the pony and keeping all together across the Mississippi River. On Eads bridge the horses tyed behind the wagon would turn crosswise and the Street cars would have to stop to keep from hitting them.

We camped that night in Forest Park. The dust was about 3 inches deep. We lost our good blood hound dog that we were bringing for protection. Later we came upon a rabid dog that bit our other two dogs and they had to be killed.

We were traveling light, driving the horses through so there would be room in the box car that came later, with cows, chickens, guineas, farm machinery, furniture and our square piano, which we still have with some other pieces of furniture in our homes now at this time, 75 years later Dec. 15, 1971.

H.D. had just gotten over typhoid fever, in fact we were detained about starting on account of his health, but he was a very discerning and capable person. He would ride ahead on a pony and find a place to camp for the night. There were no bridges. We had to ford all the streams, but with our four draft animals hitched to the wagon we could go over the Ozark Mts. and rivers easily.

Our extra wagon sheets and the tent would be frozen when we got up and we had to wait for them to thaw out.

the heirs and will remain that way as a memorial to H.D. and Ida Yost for many years. The square piano and some of the furniture, dishes, all heirlooms, are in possession of some of the family.

We had one room about 16 by 16 feet half dugout and half boards and shingle roof, with a little attic. Then we built a room on half and half with sod and dirt roof. Two years later we built a five room house (1899). Vesta was born that year Oct. 17, 1899.

That is the first year I can remember raising wheat, it was stored in one room of the house.

Dad had built a crib to hold the corn, and soon built a large barn over it with a drive way, wheat bins and stalls for 8 horses. Later we had a surrey with the fringe on top, like the surry in "Oklahoma" then a carriage and a one seated buggy.

My Dad would hitch a team to this surry and put side curtains on it and take my brother and me and the neighborhood children to school and come and get us when school was out.

In 1897 Fred Wilson was my first teacher, I was in the third grade; Victor in the 1st. His sister Mabel Wilson was a pupil, I cried. I only knew Johnny and Ralph Moats, they were Uncle Trevor's wife's sisters family. The teacher told me to go back and sit with Mabel and Gertie Jayne, they were big girls to me. They were all nice to me and I soon was one of them. There was about 8 from the Jayne families. 5 were from the Lum Jayne family, I believe they are all deceased, I believe Edward and Albert were the only ones that were in school at that time. Etta and Arthur Fischer (Arthur is deceased) Basil Cain (deceased), Norcie Jackson, Donna and Marvel Pitts. The 3 Walker boys, Ray Walker, later Ray Keltner. Mrs. John Covington taught the year 1899 and brought her three girls with her. Mildred was my age and we were good pals. She was associated with "The Lookout", a church paper for many years.

by Vivian Yost Terrel

HERMAN AND IDA YOST'S RECORD OF THEIR TRIP TO OKLAHOMA

John Fischer and family and the H.D. Yost family, left DuBois, Ill. for Okla. Territory. Went and took dinner at Johanas on first day. Left Tues. afternoon for the west. Camped first night one mile south of Nashville, Ill. Nov. 3rd. camped at Okan, ate dinner 7 miles west of Nashville. Passed New Venedy. Shumbach camped for the night. Nov. 4th drove through Fayetteville and took dinner ½ mile off Freeburgh. Went through Belleville 4 miles and camped passed first toll gate. This Nov. evening crossed St. Louis Bridge at noon. It rained on us in camp last night. Drove through Forest Park, lost Drum (Dog) in Park. Camped one mile west of Park. Nov. 6th we passed Pond Post office, Oak Grove, Kirkwood and got about 5 miles into Franklin Co. and camped for the night. On the morning of the 7th we saw it rained in the night and was still raining at noon. Nov. 8th we camped at Labadie. It rained in the night and till noon. Ida took sick headache and had to lay up all morning. Nov. 9th, nice morning. Went through St. Claire and Stanton. Camped on top of Ozark Mts. Nov. 10th, wind blew hard in night. Drove through Sullivan, Burbon, Cuba drove 23 miles. Nov. 11th, camped. Fine day. Drove through St. James and Rollo 25 miles. Camped on a little creek, two miles down the hill. Nov. 12th, drove 22 miles through Arlington, Vest Post Office, Little Pine River and drove to Big Pine River. Nov. 13th, camped. Climbed Hoozier, turned back, drove 5 miles. A mad dog ran amuck among our dogs biting them and I had to kill him. Drove to Wayne Ville on Rubudu River, took dinner. Drove 5 miles and killed our dogs.

Drove to Union Springs and camped. This is where the Union Soldiers camped. Nov. 14th, got up and drove to Gasconda River, had dinner and started on our road. Began raining and rained till night. Camped in about 2 miles of Lebanon.

Nov. 15th, started and drove through Lebanon and ate dinner 7 miles out. On the other side about 8 miles it began raining

One night one of the animals snorted and woke us up and all but one was untied (9 in all) and there was a vehicle going by, we thought they had been untied so some one could get away with them.

After we got to the Indian Territory we could hear the Indian drums beating. One Sun. noon we stopped along the roadside. The grass was too tall and heavy to have a fire and we were eating a cold lunch of home made light bread and molasses. Some Indians came along and wanted to eat with us, we divided with them.

I was afraid and hid in the wagon, I don't think I got much lunch that day.

We came on to Perry, (dad's) H.D.'s brother, T.H. Yost, lived 14 miles west of Perry. We got there the evening of the 29th. of Nov. We were on the road 27 days.

The next day Dad and his brother T.H. came to Enid and filed on the farm, 1 mile north of his place (this is ½ North and 1½ East of the town of Covington, which wasn't there then) without Mother or any of us seeing it. After 75 years the farm belongs to

Yost family, friends and neighbors in Oklahoma. Alex, Dora, Lora Cain; Emma, Ruth, Blanch, Dick, Mary and Mrs. Charles Feger; Beatrice and Charles Brown; Sallie Clack; Laura King; Iola and Vesta Yost; Minnie and Walton Moats; Mrs. Jim Pitts and boys; Cora Hoagland; Mrs. Bill Terrel and Blanch. Compliments: Vivian Yost Terrel

Drove 3 miles in rain and went into camp. Rained and froze the ground. Nov. 16th, drove 16 miles through Conway and to the sand springs. Put up for night. Nov. 17th, morning, ground frozen hard enough to hold up a wagon, drove 10 miles. Nov. 18th took dinner then drove to Springfield, camped on Commons. Nov. 19th drove through Springfield and through Republic about 20 miles. Nov. 20th drove through Billings and Vernon. Drove 28 miles through Phelps, Arvilla down to 1½ miles of Spring River on 2 miles. Nov. 21st, drove to Spring River, watered and drove to Carthage and down by Oranka down by Spring. Nov. 22nd drove across Spring River, down through Crestline, through Columbus about 10 miles on west and camped. Nov. 23rd, day drove 18 miles of Coffeeville and 2½ miles in territory line and camped. Nov. 24th drove through Coffeeville and down in territory 8 miles to the Timber Hills and camped. Nov. 25th crossed Amon River. Drove across Kaney River, drove 22 miles through Bartlesville and camped. Nov. 26th drove down on Sand River, ate dinner, then to Pawhuska, and camped. Nov. 27th, drove through Pawhuska and by two mission schools and two Government stores and by two Indian grave yards and a town by the name of Grayhorse, went about a mile out to a spring and camped. Nov. 28th, morn, drove down and crossed Arkansas River about 9 o'clock Sunday morning through Pawnee about 8 miles in country; put up for the night. Indian Buck, Squaw and papoose took dinner with us. Nov. 29th, through one or two little towns and through Perry and put up for the night in city limits. Nov. 30th got up and got breakfast some trading in Perry at one o'clock and got to T.H. Yost's at dark.

by Herman and Ida Yost

ILLINOIS TO OKLAHOMA TERRITORY, 1897

The following story was started by H.D. Yost in DuBois, Illinois, November 2, 1897, when he and his family started for Oklahoma Territory, and completed upon his arrival in Oklahoma.

DuBois, Ill. November 2, 1897

I, H.D. Yost and wife Ida, and our two children, Vivian and Victor got in our Prairie Schooner with four horses hitched to same with saddle horse leading, and started for Oklahoma Territory. Accompanying us was John Fisher and wife Minnie, and their two children, Etta and Arthur, as well as their nephew, Johnny Wintz.

The second day we crossed the Mississippi River at St. Louis. We had our dogs, as is the custom whenever a move is made. I had one Hound, ½ Blood and ½ Fox, which we lost in Forrest Park, St. Louis.

We left St. Louis behind and followed the old wire road as it was called. It was the road the Government used to haul freight from St. Louis to Fort Smith, Arkansas. The trees were blazed at that time, and there were hardly any bridges so we forded the streams.

We had a tent and a cook stove with us. At night we would strike camp, put up the tent, jerk out the cook stove, and Mrs. Yost and Mrs. Fisher would commence to mix dough and we would have biscuits or pancakes — just whatever they would decide on for that meal. We had an extra tent with us so when the weather was bad, as it was quite a lot of the time, we would put our wagons up side by side and throw the extra tent over both wagons. It rained, snowed, and hailed on us at different times.

At times I would take the saddle horse and gun and hunt while the wagons were going. Other times I would take the horse and go ahead and buy feed, or hunt a good camp site as we camped out every night.

One night we camped on Big Pinie River 25 miles from Waynesville. The folks were hauling corn that 25 miles and selling it for .25¢ per bushel, but they asked me .35¢, just to show you how some people will do, but we kept feed ahead all of the time except hay. The next morning we hitched up and started on West. The first thing we did was climb the "hill". It was called "Horses Turn Back" as it was reported there that quite a good many people turned back. When we got to the top it was something like a mile.

I was on a saddle pony and out squirrel hunting when a mad dog came up from behind just as our dogs got to the wagons, and bit all of the dogs before I caught up with the wagons. I killed the mad dog about four feet from Fisher's lead team. That was in the morning. We traveled until noon, ate our dinners, held a caucus and agreed the best thing to do was to kill our dogs. After dinner we hitched up and drove some three or four miles till we came to timber. Fisher and I took our guns and three dogs and went over the hill out of sight of the wagons. Our dogs treed squirrel. We never looked up in the trees, but we killed our dogs and went back to the wagons. When we got back there were two women and four children crying, and I came back very near crying myself.

We crossed Missouri, and the first town in Kansas was Baxter Springs. We went West as far as Coffeyville, then dropped into Oklahoma Territory. The first town we came to was Bartlesville and it consisted of some seven or eight houses and the old Bartlesville Store. We forded the Canie straight up and down, the Grey Horse, and on to Pawnee and Perry.

We landed at Perry November 27, 1897 after dark and struck camp. We had to have water. I saw a house with a light close to camp which was on the Commons, so I took my bucket and go up to the front door. I knocked two or three times as I could hear someone talking inside. Got no answer to my knock so I listened and it was a Negro praying as it was a Negro Church.

Next day we hitched up and drove to my brother's, T.H. Yost, so we stayed with them a few days. Then I filed on the place where I now live, NE¼ 7-21-3W.

by H.D. Yost

Victor Aorta Uncle Herman Vivian Vesta Yost

More about HERMAN DANIEL YOST:

Written by Vivian Yost Terrel

Nov.2,1897;

H.D.Yost and wife Ida Qualls Yost with their two children Vivian Ida Yostand Victor Hermanyost,ages 8 and 6 left DuBois,Ill.Nov.2,1897 with their neighbor John W. Fischer and wife Minnie Kroeger Fischer and their two children Etta and Arthur to come west to make their home

My grandmother (To-mamma,Julia Hopkins Yost Burns (Dad's mother had made a payment down on this farm.N.E.quarter of Sec.7,township 21, range 3,to hold it till we could ger here and could file on it.we paid 500 dollars for it.

We drove a covered wagon,driving two big bay horse,Luther and Charlie and two big bay mules,Mike and Jack 16 hands high,and mothers saddle mare,Eva K..we pitched a tent and cooked all our meal. Mrs.Fischer baked Light bread in a little wood stove we set up every night.We came through St.Louis driving two and leading two behind the wagon,Dad leading the way and keeping all together acroo the Mississippi River,on Eads bridge the horses leading behind the wagon would turn crosswise and the street cars would have to stop to keep from hitting them.

We camped that night in Forest Park.the dust was 3 inches deep.we lost our good blood hound dog that we were bringing for protection,however later we came upon a rabid dog that bit our other two dogs and they had to be killed.

We were traveling light driving the horses through so there would be room in the box car that came later with the cowws,chickens, guineas.farm machinery and of course the square piano.

We have the piano and some of the furniture in our homes now at this time 75 years later(Dec,15,1971)

H.D.(my father) had just gotten over typhoid fever in fact we were detained about starting on account of his health.but he was a very determined and capable person,he would ride ahead on the pony and find the best route to take and find a place to camp.for the night,there were no road maps and no bridges,so we had to ford all atreams,but with our four draft animals hitched to the wagon we could go over the Ozark mountains and rivers easily.

Our extra wagon sheet and the tent would be frozen when we got up and we had to wait for them to thaw out.

One night one of the animals snorted and woke us up and every one but one was untied(8 in all and there was a vehicle going by we thought they had been untied by some one who was trying to steal them.

After we got in the Indian Territory we could hear the Indian drums beating one Sunday we stopped along the roadside,the grass was too tall and heavy to have a fire,we were eating a cold lunch,home made bread and mollasses,and some Indians came along and wanted to eat withus we divided with them,

I was afraid and hid in the wagon,I don't think I got much lunch that day.

We came to Perry.N.D.'s (my father) brother T.H. Yost lived 13 miles west of Perry and we got there the evening of Nov.29,1897.we were on the road 27 days.

The next day N.D.and brother T.H. went to Enid and filled on the f farm,1 mile north of Trevors place.without mother or us seeing it. afte 75 years the farm belongs to the heirs and will remain that way as a memoral to N.D. and Ida Yost for many years.

The square piano and some of the furniture and dishesare in posession of the family.

We had one room about 16 by 16 feet.half dugout and half boards and shingle roof,with a little attic,then we built a sod room on half ha and half with sod and dirt roof.Two years later in 1899 we built a 5 room house ,Vesta Wreatha was born that year,Oct 17,1899.

That is the first year I can remember raising wheat.we stored it i one room of the house,

We had built a crib to hold the corn and soon built a large barn w with a drive way and wheat bins and stall for 8 hOrses,

Later we had a surrey with the fringe on top.like the surrey in "Oklahoma" then a carriage and a one seated buggy.

My dad would hitch a team to this surrey and put side curtains on take my brother(Victor) and me and the neighborhhood childreb to school and come and get us when school was out.

In 1897 Fred Wilson was My first teacher,I was in the third grade and Victor was in the first, his sister Mabel Wilson was a pupil, I cried I Only knew Johnny and Ralph Moats, they were Uncle Trevor's wifes sisters children and the teacher told me to go back and sit with Mabel and Gertie Jayne. They were big girls to me, They were all nice to me and I soon became one of them. There were about 8 from the Jayne families 5 were from the "Lum" Jayne family, I believe Edward and Albert are th only ones living who were in school at that time.

Etta and Arthur Fischer(Arthur is deceased)Basil Cain (Deceased) norcie Jackson, Donna and Marvel Pitts the three Walker boys, Ray Keltner

Mrs. John Covington(The town of Covington was named after her husband)taught the year of 1900 and brought her three girls with her, Nolene Mildred was my age and Mario, we were good pals.

Mildred was associated eith "The Lookout Magazine" a church paper for many years.

Sylvester, Chester and Ray Walker attended school at that time the new school was built in 1900.

Vivien Yost Terrel.

He attended a private Boys School in Centralia Ill. and later went to Carbondale now known as Illinois University. On November 2, 1897, H.D. Yost and wife Ida Qualls Yost with their 2 children, Vivian Ida and Victor H. ages 8 and 6, left DuBois Ill. with their neighbors John W. and Minnie Fischer with their 2 children Etta and Arthur went west headed for Oklahoma Territory. They drove a covered wagon, driving two bays, Luther and Charlie, and two big sorrel mules, Mike and Jack. They crossed the Mississippi River and from there on had to ford all streams to Perry Oklahoma, arriving on November 29, 1897 at his brothers home. His brother Trevor, had settled on a farm 14 miles straight west of Perry on "Y" Street. The next day her and his brother went to Enid, Oklahoma and filed on the Northeast Quarter of 7-21-3, Wood Township, Garfield County. Julia Hopkins Yost Burns had made a payment down on this farm N.E. 1/4 of Sec. 7 township 21 Range 3, Garfield Co. to hold it till H.D. and Ida could get there. They paid 500.00.

The Frisco Railroad's direct line from St. Louis to San Francisco was built in 1903 and the town of Covington was formed and named for a neighbor, John Covington who had three daughters and no sons; this way his name would be remembered.

The farmers built a Co-op Elevator in 1903 and Herman Daniel operated it until 1906, the year the green bugs "completely devastated" the crop and the Elevator closed.

Herman Daniel Yost had a sale in 1907 and quit farming but kept the farm. In 1907 a state election was held and Indian Territory and Oklahoma Territory became the 46th State of the Union. He stayed until after the election and then moved to Rogers Arkansas, along with his brother, Trevor Harlan Yost and their families. Their children attended public schools and Vivian and Vister attended The Rogers Academy, a Congregational Church School in 1907 and 1908.

PUBLIC SALE
TUESDAY, SEPT. 25

HAVING SOLD MY FARM, I WILL SELL AT PLACE 2 MILES NORTHWEST OF GENTRY, ARK., ON THE WPA ROAD, THE FOLLOWING PROPERTY, BEGINNING AT 10:00 A. M.:

HORSES

Two horses, 9 and 10 years old, 12 and 14 hands high, weight 1300 and 1500 lbs.

23 COWS AND HEIFERS

One Guernsey cow, 8 years old, gives 5 gallons when fresh.

One roan cow, 7 years old, gives 5 gallons when fresh.

Two White Durham cows, 4 years old, give 4 gallons when fresh.

Two White Durham cows, 3 years old, give 3 gallons when fresh.

One Guernsey cow, 5 years old, gives 4 gallons when fresh.

One spotted Guernsey cow, 4 years old, gives 4 gallons when fresh.

Two roan Durham cows, 2 years old.

These are all good cows and breeding dates will be given day of sale.

One Roan Durham heifer, 1 year old.

One red Durham heifer, 1 year old.

Two Guernsey heifers, 1 year old.

One Guernsey male, 1 year old.

One roan steer, 1 year old.

Seven whiteface calves.

FARM TOOLS

One 2-horse plow. One 1-horse plow.
One 14-tooth strawberry plow.
One double shovel. Some calf chains.
One set double harness. One set fly nets.
One wagon. Three steel cables.
One 1-horse and one 2-horse springtooth.
Pitchforks, rakes, shovels, grubbing hoe, saws, sledges, iron wedges, etc.
One corn sheller. Five drums.
One horse mower. One wheelbarrow.

HOUSEHOLD GOODS

Two kitchen cabinets. One buffet.
Two library tables. One desk.
One coal or wood cook stove.
One circulator heater.
One King-O-Heat heater.
One violin. One set kitchen scales.

MISCELLANEOUS

Four 10-gallon milk cans. One strainer.
Some milk buckets. Some lamps.
Some garden tools. Six bee gums.
One vise. One anvil. One cold cut.
Two garden plows. Some pipe tools.
Two Irish pasture fences. 200 ft. of rope.
Some $1\frac{1}{2}$ and $2\frac{1}{2}$ inch rope.
Some 1 inch and 1x4 lumber.
One house jack. One Cyclone seeder.
Five or six ricks of cook wood.
One lantern. One ladder.
Some bedsteads, dishes, fruit jars, linoleums, rugs and other things too numerous to mention.

LUNCH BY BOZARTH CLUB   TERMS CASH

H. D. YOST, Owner

They moved back to the farm at Covington, Oklahoma in 1909 and Herman Daniel managed the Perry Mill Elevator at Covington for several years. He also served as Deputy Sheriff for several years, as well as being part owner of a garage and services station for many years. He retired in 1937 and moved to Gentry, Arkansas. His wife died there January 3, 1947, and in 1951 Herman moved to Enid, Oklahoma, along with his daughter Vesta. He passed away March 13, 1956 in Enid.

Herman and Ida Yost

YOST, HERMAN DANIEL

F230

Herman Daniel Yost was born December 4, 1866 in Centralia, Illinois to John Winchester Yost and Julia Hopkins Spencer Yost. The Yost ancestors have been traced back to Jacob Yost, Mainz, Germany in the 16th century, a great-great-grandfather. His great-grandfather was Lt. Henry Yost who along with his brother John had a Gun Factory, making guns for the Government during the Revolutionary War.

He attended a private Boys School in Centralia, Illinois and later went to Carbondale, now known as Illinois University.

He married Ida Qualls on September 29, 1886 at DuBois, Illinois. She was born September 13, 1867 to Samuel D. and Delilah Courtney Qualls. They moved on the family farm consisting of 220 acres in the DuBois area after his father died, and farmed with a mould board walking plow for a few years. In 1890 they moved to Mt. Vernon, Illinois, where he operated a dray business of two wagons, two horses, and two mules, and also a riding mare. He sold the dray business in 1893, moving back to the DuBois farm.

On November 2, 1897, Herman and his wife Ida, and two children, Vivian and Victor started for Oklahoma Territory in a covered wagon with two big mules and two big bay horses. They crossed the Mississippi River on the "Toll" Ead's Bridge and from there on had to ford all streams to Perry, Okla. arriving there November 29, 1897, at his brother's home. His brother, Trevor Yost had settled on a farm 14 miles straight West of Perry on "F" Street.

On December 1, 1897, he and his brother went to Enid, Oklahoma, and he filed on the Northeast quarter of 7-21-3, Woods Township, Garfield County. He proved his claim five years later and President Teddy Roosevelt signed the deed. This farm is still in the family and is located one-half mile North and one and one-half mile East of Covington. Their first house was built half in the ground and half out with a shingle roof, and a straw shed for their stock. They built a five room house in 1899, and raised their first wheat crop that year, hauling it to Perry, Okla.

Later two more children were born, Vesta and Velma.

The Frisco Railroad's direct line from St. Louis to San Francisco was built in 1903. The 25 mile track from Covington to Enid was considered to be the longest straight track at that time.

Herman Daniel Yost

by LaVelle Sheffer

COVINGTON SHERIFF GETS THREE BANDITS

Captures Men in Car Belonging to Guthrie Banker—Trailed Through Cornfield

Three auto bandits were captured near Covington Thursday morning when Deputy Sheriff H. D. Yost, of Covington spotted the men driving a Cole Eight automobile belonging to a banker of Guthrie.

Yost saw the car in Covington when the thieves were getting gasoline and oil.

Levelling a shot gun at the bandits as he passed their speeding car, Yost demanded that they halt. They stopped the car, but before Yost could apply the brakes to stop his own car, the men escaped into a cane field.

The car was recovered. With aid of a posse the men were tracked into the cane patch Thursday morning and captured.

They were taken to Guthrie, and turned over to county officers there by Deputy Sheriff Yost.

Herman Daniel Yost

Herman Daniel and Ida Qualls Yost Grave Stone in Covington, Oklahoma

Children of Herman Daniel Yost and Ida Qualls are:

Infant Son born October 18, 1887 and died November 30, 1887

Vivian Ida Yost, born. December 15, 1888, Dubois Illinois; died July 24, 1991, Enid Oklahoma. She married Parker Marion Terrel November 25, 1914 at Covington Oklahoma. Parker was born January 27, 1890 at Woodlawn, Kansas. He died July 9, 1946 in Enid Oklahoma, buried at Covington, Oklahoma.

Parker Marion and Vivian Ida Yost Terrel

More about Vivian Ida Yost:

In 1897, she came to Oklahoma in covered wagon. Member of the Daughters of the American Revolution. Attended Rogers Congregational Academy in Rogers Arkansas

Vivian Ida Yost

TERREL, VIVIAN YOST
F204

Vivian Yost Terrel

Vivian Ida Yost was born December 15, 1888, in Dubois, Illinois to Herman D. and Ida Yost. She attended school in Dubois before moving with the family in a covered wagon to Oklahoma Territory in 1897. Her father filed on a claim December 1, 1897, one-half miles East of Covington. This farm has remained with the family down through the years, and after the death of her father, she purchased it from the heirs. The family lived in a house built half in the ground and half out with a shingle roof, and had a straw shed for the livestock, until a five room house was built on the farm in 1899.

She married Parker Marion Terrel November 25, 1914, and to this union were born two children, Cloyd Elwyn and Lois LaVelle. They owned and operated the Terrel Furniture Store in Covington for many years at the same location where the Terrel Blacksmith Shop had been. She gave music lessons in Covington, and she and her sister-in-law Thelma Terrel also had a Variety Store. She and her husband were also co-partners with her father H. D. Yost and brother Victor, in the Albert Pike Garage located on Main Street in the 1920's.

Her son Cloyd was born June 12, 1916, attended Covington Grade and High School, graduating from High School with the class of 1937. He attended Northern Oklahoma Junior College in Tonkawa, Okla. and took some special classes at Oklahoma State. He served in World War 2. He married Anna Lauline Estes from Nash, Okla. and they live in Enid, Okla. Their children and grandchildren are as follows: Janice JoLene Terrel born February 18, 1942. She graduated from Enid High School and attended Oklahoma University. She married Virgil Nell Schroeder of Cleo Springs, Okla. and they have three children as follows: Terrel Lee Schroeder born August 19, 1967; Jakki JoLene Schroeder born March 8, 1971; and Michael Cory Schroeder born June 13, 1973. They reside in Oklahoma City. Dennis Lee Terrel born August 20, 1948, and died March 10, 1967. He graduated from Enid High School and attended Okla. State University

Her daughter, LaVelle was born December 2, 1927, attended Covington Grade School, graduating from Enid High School in 1945, then went to Enid Business College where she received an Executive Business Degree. She is married to John William Sheffer of Garber, Okla, and they live Northeast of Garber. John served in World War 2, making the initial landing at Normandy, with the 4th Infantry Division of the 1st Army and the 377th Artillery.

Their daughter, Janene Kay Sheffer was born September 12, 1955. She graduated from Garber High School, attended Oklahoma State University, and graduated Cum Laude from California State University in Pomona, Calif. She married Lynn Marcus Yost in Arlington, Texas, May 16, 1992.

Vivian Terrel has lived in Enid forty-one years and is still living in her home at 506 South Harrison at 97 years of age. She has worked for years on the family genealogy and has traced her family back to Mainz, Germany in 1600, and England in 1620 when her ancestors came to America on the Mayflower. The genealogy also establishes the family connection with Louisa May Alcott. She is a member of Central Christian

Vivian Ida Yost Terrel's Story

Vivian Ida Yost Terrel holding the Yost Family Bible in Enid, Ok

PAGE F-6   SUNDAY, DECEMBE

Vivian Terrel

Vivian Terrel Marks 95 Years

Vivian Yost Terrel, 506 S. Harrison, celebrated her 95th birthday Thursday at a family gathering in her home.

Mrs. Terrel was born Dec. 15, 1888, in DuBois, Ill. She came with her parents to a homestead northeast of Covington in 1897. She still owns the farm. She attended school in Covington and Lawton High School, where she stayed with an aunt because Covington had no high school. She also attended Rogers Congregational Academy in Rogers, Ark. She and P.M. Terrel were married in 1914.

Mrs. Terrel moved to Enid in 1942. She worked in the supply room at University and Bass Hospitals for 18 years. She is an active member of Central Christian Church, Christian Women's Fellowship and pianist for Women's Bible Class. She is a member of DAR, Order of Eastern Star Chapter 36 and a life member of Rebekah Lodge. Her hobbies are genealogy, crocheting, making quilts and growing flowers.

Mrs. Terrel's children are Cloyd and Laudine Terrel, Enid, and John and LaVelle Sheffer, Garber. She has three grandchildren and six great-grandchildren.

Children of Vivian Yost and Parker Terrel are as follows, Vivian was the daughter of Herman Daniel Yost:

Cloyd Elwyn Terrel, born June 12, 1918 in Covington Okahoma, died August 24, 1998. Cloyd served in the Army during World War II. He married Anna Laudine Estes, born June 2, 1919 in Nash, Oklahoma, died January 11, 2006. They were married April 13, 1940 in Perry, Oklahoma. From this union were born a son, Dennis Lee Terrel, born August 2, 1948, in Oklahoma City, died March 10, 1967. A daughter, Janice Jolene Terrel, born February 18, 1942.

Cloyd Elwyn and Laudine Estes Terrel

Janice Jolene Terrel married Virgil Neal Schroeder, born February 18, 1942 in Enid, Oklahoma. They married on November 20, 1964 in Cleo Springs, Oklahoma.

Virgil Neal and Janice Jolene Terrel Schroeder

Virgil, Jolene, Cory, Jakkie, Terrel Schroeder – 2007

Children of Janice Jolene Terrel and Virgil Neal Schroeder are:

Terrel Lee Schroeder born August 19, 1967 in Enid Oklahoma. Terrel married Melody Martin.

Terrel Lee Schroeder and Melody Martin had the following children:

Parker Neal Schroeder born May 29, 2001 in Oklahoma City, Oklahoma.

Parker Neal Schroeder – July 2007

Jakki Jolene Schroeder born March 8, 1971 in Oklahoma City, Oklahoma.

Michael Cory Schroeder born June 13, 1973 in Oklahoma City, Oklahoma. Michael married Christy Horne.

Michael Cory Schroeder and Christy Horne had the following children:

Madison Grace Schroeder born April 26, 2007.

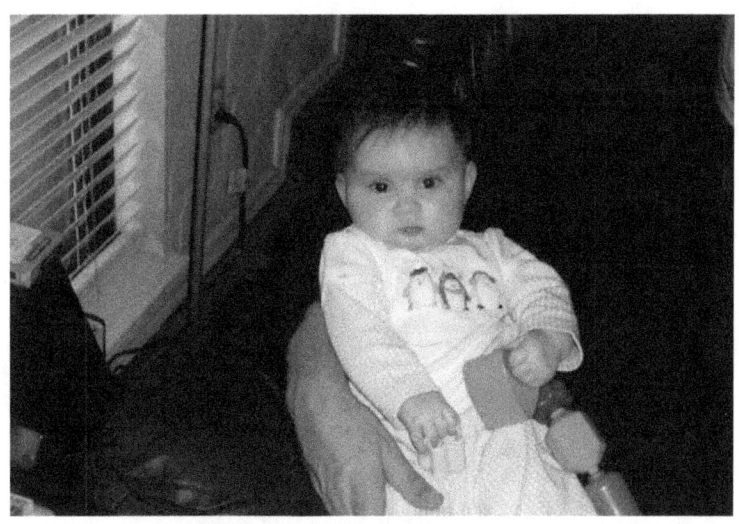

Madison Grace Schroeder - 2008

Cloyd Elwyn Terrel

Dennis Lee Terrel born August 20, 1948, died March 10, 1967

Dennis Lee Terrel

Lois Lavelle Terrel, born December 02, 1927, Covington, Oklahoma. She married Eugine Leroy Sheffer born January 31, 1923 in Hunter Oklahoma. Eugene Leroy Sheffer died August 29, 1949 They were married August 2, 1947. Lois Lavelle Terrel then married John William Sheffer of Garber, Oklahoma, on May 21, 1954. Lois Lavelle Terrel and John William Sheffer had on child, Janene Kay Sheffer born September 12, 1955 in Enid, Oklahoma. Janene married Lynn Marcus Yost, born March 29, 1961 in Wichita, Kansas. They were married May 16, 1992 in Arlington, Texas.

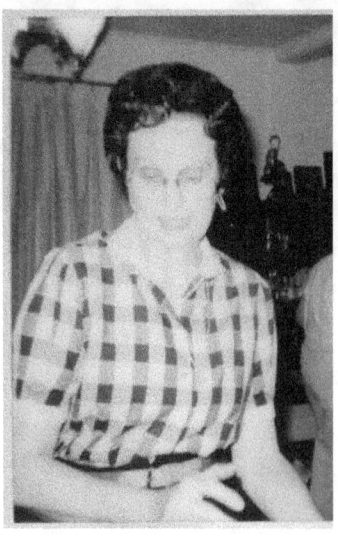

Lois Lavelle Terrel

Eugine Leroy Sheffer and Louis Lavelle Terrel had one child:

Janene Kay Sheffer born September 12, 1955 in Enid Oklahoma. Janene married Lynn Marcus Yost. (see picture later in book under Lynn Marcus Yost.)

Janene's father died August 26, 1949 just North of Garber:

Young Garber Farmer Died of Fire Burns

Eugene (Gene) Sheffer, 26, a farmer living six miles north of Garber, was burned fatally Saturday while overhauling a tractor at his farm. His death occurred at 7 o'clock Monday morning in an Enid Hospital where war had been waged to save his life after severe burns were suffered.

Sheffer had completed work on the tractor and asked his helper, Gatland Potter to turn the motor over. As this operation occurred, a spark apparently ignited gasoline fumes about the motor and clothing of Sheffer and he was immediately enveloped in flames.
The Former Marine farmed at Covington for a time, but had lived on the place north of Garber since getting out of the service.

Surviving are his wife, the former LaVelle Terrell of Covington; his parents, Mr. And Mrs. Therman E. Sheffer, a sister Mrs. W.A. White of Hunter, Oklahoma, and two brothers John and Alvin of Tonkawa.

His body was removed to the Anderson Funeral Home of Garber, pending completion of arrangements for funeral service.

Burial was in Covington Cemetary. The body was later removed to The Memorial Cemetery at Enid.

Victor Herman Yost, born April 23, 1891 in Mt. Vernon, Illinois, died May 24, 1975 in Houston, Texas. He married Edna Faubion in Enid Oklahoma. Edna was born November 5, 1903 in Frederick, Oklahoma. Victor served in World War 1 from July 1918 until being medically discharged in November of 1918. He attended grade and High School and then attended Wichita Business College in Wichita Kansas.

Victor Herman Yost

Victor Herman Yost World War 1

Victor Herman Yost with mother Ida Yost World War

Herman Daniel Yost and son Victor Herman Yost

They had Vickie Van Yost born December 18, 1921. She married Floyd Franklin born April 22, 1916. Vickie died April 27, 1969 in Dallas, Texas. She is buried in Houston. Vicki and Floyd has one child, Chloe Shi Franklin born December 21, 1944 in Oklahoma City, Oklahoma. Chloe married Dennis Owen Reed born January 10, 1942. They had two children:

> Dennis Owen Reed born November 4, 1963 in Houston, Texas
> Devin Burton Reed born January 28, 1966 in Houston, Texas

Victor Vickie Van Franklin Herman Clie Sho Franklin Ida Yost

Vesta Wreatha Yost, born October 17, 1899 in Covington, Oklahoma; died March 3, 1978 Covington Oklahoma, House caught on fire smoke inhalation. She attended grade school and graduated from Phillips University High School. She then attended College at Phillips University in Enid, Oklahoma. She also attended the University of Oklahoma and Oklahoma College for Women at Chickasha, Oklahoma. She received an Oklahoma State Life Teachers Certificate and taught school for a numbers of years. She is buried in I.O.O.F. Cemetery in Covington with her parents

Vesta Herman D Velma Palmer Victor H Yost

Fire Victim's Funeral Set

Miss Vesta Yost, 78, died in a pre-dawn fire Friday that broke out in her two-story apartment house at 1308 W. Oklahoma.

Firemen answering the 4:20 a.m. alarm reported the wood structure was in flames. Miss Yost was found in the living room of the upstairs apartment.

She apparently died of carbon monoxide or smoke inhalation, according to Dr. Cecil Reinstein, county medical examiner.

"We took a blood sample, but the results have not come back yet. We're almost certain that she died of either asphyxiation or smoke inhalation."

Fire officials said the fire apparently originated in the living room of the upstairs apartment and spread rapidly. Damage was estimated at $5,000, according to reports at the central fire station. Cause of the fire is still under investigation.

The fire was discovered by a juvenile living in the upstairs apartment, according to Enid police detectives, Dennis Madison and Ted Jones. The youth told officers he awoke and smelled smoke, then went downstairs to notify Miss Yost. He called the fire department while she went upstairs presumably to check on the cause.

Miss Yost's funeral will be at 10 a.m. Monday in the chapel of the Henninger-Allen Funeral Home. Dr. Irving L. Smith, pastor of the First United Methodist, will officiate and burial will be in the Covington Cemetery.

Miss Yost was born northeast of Covington Oct. 17, 1899, on the farm her parents had homesteaded at the Opening of the Cherokee Strip, and which she and her sister still owned.

She attended Covington Schools, the Oklahoma College for Women at Chickasha, the University of Oklahoma and received her life teaching certificate from Phillips University.

Miss Yost taught in the Garber-Covington area for several years before moving with her parents to Gentry, Ark., then moved back to Enid in 1951.

She was an active member of the First United Methodist Church, was secretary-treasurer of the Trinity Sunday School Class and Circle Eight. Miss Yost was also active in the Women's Christian Temperance Union and the Enid Genealogical Society.

She is survived by a sister, Mrs. Vivian Y. Terrel, Enid; three nieces and nephews, Mrs. John (LaVelle) Sheffer, Garber, Cloyd E. Terrel and Mrs. Maurice (VesStella) Olds, both of Enid. A brother and sister died earlier.

Enid Okla
Mar 18-78

Dear Cousins Leon & Sally: -

I do not know how to begin to tell you of this tragedy that has happened to us. Vesta had rented her upstairs apt to a young man he woke up came down woke her up said he smelled smoke he called fire dept. and she went up to investigate was overcome by inhalation of smoke and burned badly. We could not see her, had to have an autopsy and a lot of red tape. For the service we got a beautiful casket & vault and had lovely flowers and a beautiful service.

Uncle Trevor Yost's sons Bennie Harlan & Tommie & wife & son were here the girls were not

able to come (Faye & Juanita)
I am out with LaVelle & John
will try to go home this wk end
and stay if I stay away to long
I won't be able to go home.

We saved most of Vesta's
genealogy records (I mean the
Children did) I have not been over
they won't let me go.

They worked so hard to take
care of what was left. The
upstairs was a complete loss
and down stairs flooded and
frozen water & debris.

She called me 6:30 Thurs evening
again at 8:00 Thurs evening, and
was coming over that day
(March 3—Fri 4:20 in morning)
for me to roll her hair up.
when her watch stopped.

I just don't feel like I can
go on with out her
write to Edith please and
write me   love Vivian

The Lord is my shepherd: I shall not want.
He maketh me to lie down in green pastures. He leadeth me beside the still waters.
He restoreth my soul. He leadeth me in the paths of righteousness for his name's sake.
Yea, though I walk through the valley of the shadow of death, I will fear no evil: for thou art with me; thy rod and thy staff they comfort me.
Thou preparest a table before me in the presence of mine enemies: thou anointest my head with oil; my cup runneth over.
Surely goodness and mercy shall follow me all the days of my life: and I will dwell in the house of the Lord for ever.

In Memory of
Miss Vesta W. Yost
1899   Mar 3 1978
           4:20 a.m.

Place and Time of Services
Henninger-Allen Chapel
March 6, 1978   10:00 a.m.

Clergyman
Dr. Irving L. Smith

Final Resting Place
Covington Cemetery

Under Direction of
HENNINGER-ALLEN
Enid, Oklahoma

Vesta Yost and sister Velma Weatherbee Grave Stone

Velma Burns Yost, born October 18, 1904 in Covington, Oklahoma. She married Noah Palum on May 23, 1925 in Enid, Oklahoma. Noah was born February 12, 1900, died July 14, 1941. Velma died July 15, 1954 in Enid, Oklahoma. She is buried in Covington, Oklahoma.

    Noah Palum and Velma Burns Yost had the following children:

Daniel Albert Palum born October 17, 1929
Vestella Palum born July 10, 1933

Children of John Winchester Yost and Julia Spencer continued:

Wreatha Julietta Yost, born November 22, 1875, Beaucoup, Illinois; died January 10, 1967, Lawton, Oklahoma She married RICHARD SCOTT NANCE October 18, 1896. Wreatha, her husband Richard and daughter LeVeta were among the pioneers who settled in Oklahoma at the opening of the Kiowa, Commanche and Apache Reservation in 1901, and they homesteaded a quarter section in Commanche County.

Letters received by Dewitt Yost from Wreatha J. Yost Ruland regarding Yost family history:

Lawton, Oklahoma
June 3, 1933

My dear Cousin,

 Your most interesting letter read and records forwarded at once. I sure wish to thank you for your promptness. If every letter sent out brought as quick results, the labor of gathering data for this "History" would be greatly decreased, but unfortunately only about 1 out of 6 reply, some probably through lack of time but more through procrastination, others being unable to answer all questions at once, do not answer any.
 I doubt if any of us realize what this genealogy will mean to "Posterity". At the time I wrote you I sent a letter to your Father seeking data of his own family, as well as of his sons families, but I haven't heard from him yet. I hope you can help me on this as I have so little regarding his family. I also wrote the same day to Ollie S. Yost, Greenville, Texas and Iva F. Yost Alexander, but have received nothing from either of them. A letter to Lem Jones, Altus, Oklahoma, where I was informed Charlotte Janette Yost Jones died, was returned to me. I am enclosing this hoping you know where to send it and thus avoid delay. Our time is growing so short now that every mail counts.
 There are many records still lacking of the descendants of W. H. Yost. Robert Earley

Yost, the last of the family of Wesley Yost passed away Feb. 27, 1933 at his home in Manchester, N.H. He was a half brother of W. H. Yost.

And now, let me tell you of some relatives who live in Dallas with whom I am sure you will find much in common, should you visit them. Mrs. Pearl Yost Williams and her two brothers, Clarence Casper and Virgil Morris Yost. 3911 Shenandoah is her address. Mr. Williams and Virgil are both accountants, and C. C. is an advertising publicity man. Your wife no doubt will find Pearl very interesting, as she too is a University woman. Their grandfather - George Casper Yost, your great grandfather - Wesley Yost, my father - John Winchester Yost, were brothers, sons of Henry Marshall Yost.

   Your cousin,

   Wreatha J. Ruland

Lawton, Oklahoma
July 9, 1933

My dear Cousin,

I am again indebted to you for data along the W. H. Yost lineage. Thanks to you and some others we are now in possession of a nice little record.
I have not heard from Ollie Yost yet, so probably will not hear unless you can spur him into action. I am very much interested in his wife's lineage, as she was a Nance, and my first husband (the father of my children) was a Nance. So we have two Nances marrying Yosts, however at widely separated dates. I married first in 1896.
I am so glad you enjoyed your visit with our Cousins in Dallas. I have since had a letter from them and they too enjoyed the visit and looked forward to more visits being exchanged between your families.
I am enclosing a brief Outline of our genealogy which will give some of the information you requested. The Historical parts are not in my records, as they are mostly confined to data along later generations. I am following the lineage of my Father's brothers' families.
I have found this work very interesting, and it has become quite a hobby with me. I have also worked up my Mother's lineage which antedates the Yost lineage in America by 100 years. I have a brother living in Oklahoma City and one in Covington, Oklahoma. They each have families and grandchildren.

   Your cousin,

   Wreatha

Lawton, Oklahoma
July 19, 1933

My dear Cousins,

I am really glad you called my attention to the errors in the records I sent to you. I am enclosing corrected statements and some additional data from a later record.

Al C. Yost of St. Louis is continually sending me records which I copy and forward to a cousin in California who returns them to Al. We have been working this way for nearly 3 years and each of us reaching out in every direction in our effort to contact as many Yosts as we can. It is quite a job, I assure you, and when we reach someone willing to help we certainly appreciate it.

I have the date of William H. Yost born - January 6, 1832, Franklin County, Illinois, died January 12, 1887, Bosque County, Texas. These dates were sent by Mrs. French. No letter from Cousin Ollie yet, so I doubt very much if we hear from him. However, our History may be delayed on account of Cousin Al's brother who is lying at the point of death and will naturally greatly interfere with the final work. He (Robert Yost) has been very very sick since in April when the surgeons started to operate and found a condition making an operation useless. They pronounced it tumor on the liver, and sewed him up to die by inches. Each day he lives seems a miracle to the attendants. Thus we go down the Valley one by one. Yet I love to think of death with the Poet.

Death is only an old door, set in a garden wall.
On gentle hinges it gives at dusk when the thrushes call.
Along the lintel are green leaves. Beyond, the light lies still.
Very willing and weary feet go over that sill.
There is nothing to trouble any heart, nothing to hurt, at all.
Death is only a quiet door, in an old wall.

    Sincerely, your cousin

    Wreatha

Child of Wreatha Yost and Richard Nance is:

    Laveta Agness Nance, born 1897.

Trevor Harlen Yost, born November 11, 1869, Beau Coup Illinois. . He married Clara Agnes McNally born September 1874 in Iowa.

30 Nov, 1892 ,
Mulhall, Logan Co., Oklahoma Territory Letter from Trevor to future wife Clara:

Written on paper from Atchison, Topeka & Santa Fe' Railroad Company (Trever's Employee) Mullhall, OT (Okalahoma Territory) November 30th, 1892

Dear Clara

Once more I have the pleasure of writing to you, although I haven't much to write=but could say lots if we were together. Got home in good shape Sunday night at 10:10pm. I turned off at Arrington and went south to miss those two gates west of town that I opened the first time I was out to your home. The bridge is out here at the creek. That is why we went via Orlando you remember. This U. S. Marshalls shot a fellow near Orlando this morning. He was wanted for robbing a bank in western Kansas. He is also supposed to be one of the men who has been doing the train robbing at Wharton. He was fatally shot but haven't heard yet if he is dead or not.

Miss Lowe quit our hotel Monday morning and Ruth Dishan done the same thing. Bell Lowe went home and Ruthy took Lizzie's place at the Hotel Kralleys. Lizzie came in Monday but went home again. I never got to see her. Mrs. Bryant is Chief cook at our house now. We have a grass widow in Ruth's placeat our house now but she is no good to cook either. She is not less than 50 years old. I expect you know her but I forget her name.

I saw Hugh and I gave him a talk that he will remember, I think. I told him that I did not think his intentions were bad. But he would have to do quite different in the future. I will tell you more about this subject when I see you, if you will mention it to me. Elmer got back Monday night at 12 o'clock and came over to see me. He had not seen me since Saturday night and thought I had died or you had stolen me.

Well Dear, I don't know what more to write, as news are scarce here so I will close. Hoping to hear from you at your earliest convenience

I remain "Forever Yours'

T H Yost

Letter from Marquis L. Burns
Mar 30, 1894 , Sent to Mulhall, Oklahoma

Rogers Arkansas
March 30th, 1894

Trevor and Clara (Yost)

Your Mother requested me to write and answer your kid letters. This is Friday night & Wreatha and Edward J Gould have gone to church. You will remember him at the opening of the Strip, (OK Indian Territory) We are all well, as Julia is complaining some. Hope she will soon feel all right again. We have had very cold weather lately.

We thought all kinds of fruit were killed but fruit men san there will be one half crop of apples yet not killed. If the apple crops does reasonably well, Rogers will improve more this year than she has for several years. There has been quite a number of good houses put up since you was here. I am very sorry have have had trouble with railroad men. Hope you was not to blame and will come out all right. You must let us know more about it came about or who caused the trouble. I am glad some railroad men say you was not to blame so we believe you will hold your place. Your mother is writing to you and my paper is out so I will stop. Be sure and write soon and often. Mulhall (OK) is a better place than anywhere I have been in the Strip. I like Mulhall very well and I like Rogers too.

Your Pa M. L. Burns

1900 Trevor Harlan Yost Oklahoma Garfield Wood Census

1910 Trevor Yost Missouri Wright Hart Census

1920 Trevor Yost Oklahoma Oklahoma City Census

1930 Trevor Yost Oklahoma Oklahoma City Census

Trevor Harlen Yost as teen

Trevor Harlen Yost Spring 1890 about 21 years old

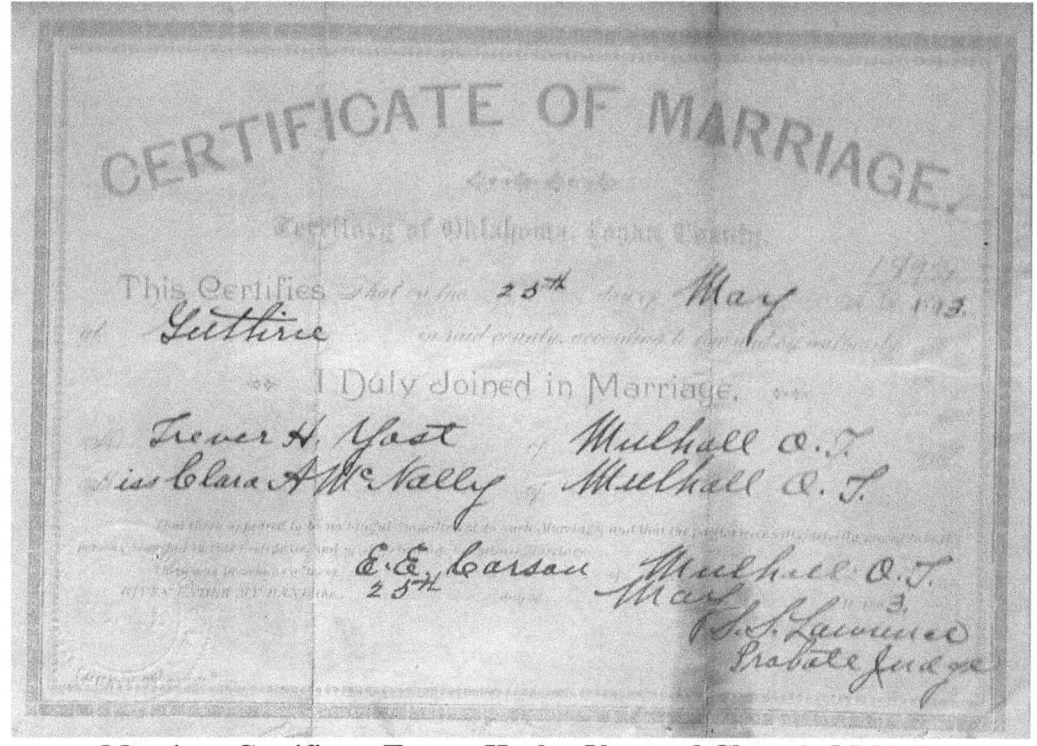
**Marriage Certificate Trevor Harlen Yost and Clara A. McNally
May 25, 1893 in Guthrie Oklahoma**

Front: Herman Daniel Yost and Trevor Harlan Yost
Back: Wreatha Julietta Yost and their moth Julia Yost

Trevor Harlen and Clara Agnes Yost with family

Trevor Harlen Yost

Clara Anges McNally Yost

Trevor Harlen and Clara Agnes Yost

Trevor Yost Home in Oklahoma City

Bappie Burns with beard, Julia Burns Yost, Trevor and Clara Yost at back others unknown

Trevor Harlan and Clara Yost Grave Stone in Covington, Oklahoma

Children of Trevor Harlan Yost and Clara A. are:

Julia Lafay Yost, born October 1894, Oklahoma.

Julia Lafay Yost

Julia LaFaye Yost and cousin Edyth Hougland

Julia Lafay Yost as adult

Marquis "Marcus" L. Yost, born January 1897, Oklahoma.

Marquis "Marcus" Lamont Yost

Marquis Lamont Yost and Julia LaFaye Yost

Marquis LaMont Yost and Julia LaFaye Yost in Oklahoma

Marquis LaMont Yost

Baby Son Yost born Oct. 28, 1899 died Dec. 17, 1899

Covington Cemetery Garfield County Oklahoma

Thomas H. Yost, born 1916, Oklahoma.

William Harlan Yost, born 1901, Covington, Oklahoma, died May 9, 1980, Oklahoma City, Oklahoma.

William Harlan Yost

William Harlan Yost, Rose Hill Burial Park Oklahoma City Oklahoma County Oklahoma, USA

Juanita D. Yost, born 1905, Oklahoma.

Julia LaFaye Yost with sisters Juanita and Helena

Helena Arkoma Yost, born January 26, 1908, Rogus, Arkansas, died April 8, 1975, Bishop, Texas. Helena married Frank Pierce Norcross on January 6, 1930 in Oklahoma City, Oklahoma. Frank Pierce Norcross born September 25, 1905, Austin, Texas, died March 21, 1975, Fort Worth, Texas.

Juanita Agnes Yost and Helena Arkoma Yost

Helena Arkoma Yost

Frank and Helena on wedding day

Helena Arkoma Yost and Frank Pierce Norcross had the following children:

Barbara Clara Norcross born November 16, 1931
LaVene Marie Norcross born August 15, 1933
Franklin Helena Norcross born January 6, 1938
Shirley Jean Norcross born December 1, 1944

Bennie E. Yost, born 1911, Missouri.

1910 U. S. FEDERAL CENSUS: Wright County, Missouri, Hart Township, NARA Series T624, Roll 828, page 164, Enumeration District: 136, Sheet Number: 7A, Enumeration Date: 21 April 1910. Line 1, dwelling 120, family 120: Trever H. YOST, head, age 40, married once 17 years, farmer, general farm, birthplace: Illinois, father's birthplace: Illinois, mother's birthplace: Illinois. Clara A., wife, age 37, married once 17 years, mother of 6 children, 5 children now living, birthplace: Iowa, father's birthplace: Ohio, mother's birthplace: Ohio. Children were born in Oklahoma. LaFay J., daughter, age 15, house keeper, home house. Marcus L., son, age 13, farm laborer, home farm. Harlen W., son, age 9. Waneta A., daughter, age 5. Halena A., daughter, age 2.

1920 U. S. FEDERAL CENSUS: Oklahoma County, Oklahoma, Oklahoma City, NARA Series T625, Roll 1475, page 116, Enumeration District: 157, Sheet Number: 19B, Enumeration Date: 20 January 1920. Line 62. 422 West Chicasan (?), dwelling 274, family 526: Trever H. YOST, head, age 50, cream checker, packing plant, birthplace: Illinois, father's birthplace: Illinois, mother's birthplace: Illinois. Clara A., wife, age 46, birthplace: Iowa, father's birthplace: Ohio, mother's birthplace: Ohio. Marcus L., son, age 23, birthplace: Oklahoma, shipping clerk, barbers supply. Wm. H., son, age 19, birthplace: Oklahoma, shipping clerk, rubber shop (?). Juanita A., daughter, age 15, birthplace: Oklahoma. Helena A., daughter, age 11, birthplace: Arkansas. Bennie E., son, age 9, birthplace: Missouri. Thomas H., son, age 4 years 5 months, birthplace: Oklahoma.

1930 U. S. FEDERAL CENSUS: Oklahoma County, Oklahoma, Oklahoma City, NARA Series T626, Roll 1920, Enumeration District: 122, Sheet Number: 5B, Enumeration Date: 11 April 1930. Line 61, family 163: T. H. YOST, head, age 60, married at age 23, bookkeeper, furniture company, birthplace: Illinois, father's birthplace: Illinois, mother's birthplace: Illinois. Clara A., wife, age 56, married at age 19, birthplace: Iowa, father's birthplace: Ohio, mother's birthplace: Ohio. Thomas H., son, age 14, birthplace: Oklahoma.

Benton Yost, born 1864.

Spencer Aldredge Yost, born. November 10, 1873; died January 30, 1875.

Dempsey Dwight Yost's Life

Dempsey Dwight Yost was born August 21, 1853 in Fancy Farm, Franklin County Illinois, and died January 28, 1924 in Quapaw, Ottawa Co. Oklahoma. He married **Ella Elzinee** White November 18, 1878 in Missouri, daughter of Samuel White and Nancy McLean. They had the following children, Marcus Otto Yost born November 15, 1885, Frank N. Yost born June 22, 1894, Ralph Yost born November 10, 1882, Edith Yost born December 11, 1899, Raymond John Yost born May 15, 1890, Harry P. Yost born September 1897, Maybelle Yost born 1881, Herman "Hurbert" Willis Yost born January 1885.

Dempsey Dwight Yost

Ella Elzinee White and daughter Edith Elzina Yost

Quapaw Okla
Jan 28 1924

Dear Uncle & Aunt:—

Now I wish I might have been spared the sad news I must try to tell you for God alone knows who and what we have lost. Father died on the 24th we buried him by Herman and his little girl in the Miami Cemetery. He had been sick almost three weeks with the flue the Dr said when the fever left him his heart was too weak. It was an aful shock to us we though he was getting better I helped him to rase up on the side of the bed when he fainted Mother dashed a little cold water on his he came to we sent for the Dr but he seemed to just weak, he took his medicine and ate some soup it was almost an hour after he fainted that he ask Mother if the Dr. had come and she said she would send again. she ask him what hurt him he said he did not hurt any where but his heart fluttered. that was he last word and seemed the last breath two Dr came but could do nothing this is all I can stand to write now.

Your Niece
Edith

Letter from Edith Elzina Yost to her Aunt and Uncle advising Dempsey Dwight Yost had passed away

**Yost Family Stone
GAR Cemetery Miami, Oklahoma**

Dempsey Dwight Yost Grave Marker
GAR Cemetery, Miami, Oklahoma

Elzina Yost Grave Marker
GAR Cemetery, Miami, Oklahoma

Marriage Certificate Dempsey D Yost and Ella White

Dempsey D. Yost and Ella White Court Marriage Record

Children of Dempsey Dwight Yost and Ella White are:

Marcus Otto Yost, born November 15, 1885, Kansas; died November 25, 1930, Spurgeon Newton County Missouri buried Miami Oklahoma. He married Isa Lina Galena Chambers December 24, 1908 in Joplin, Missouri.

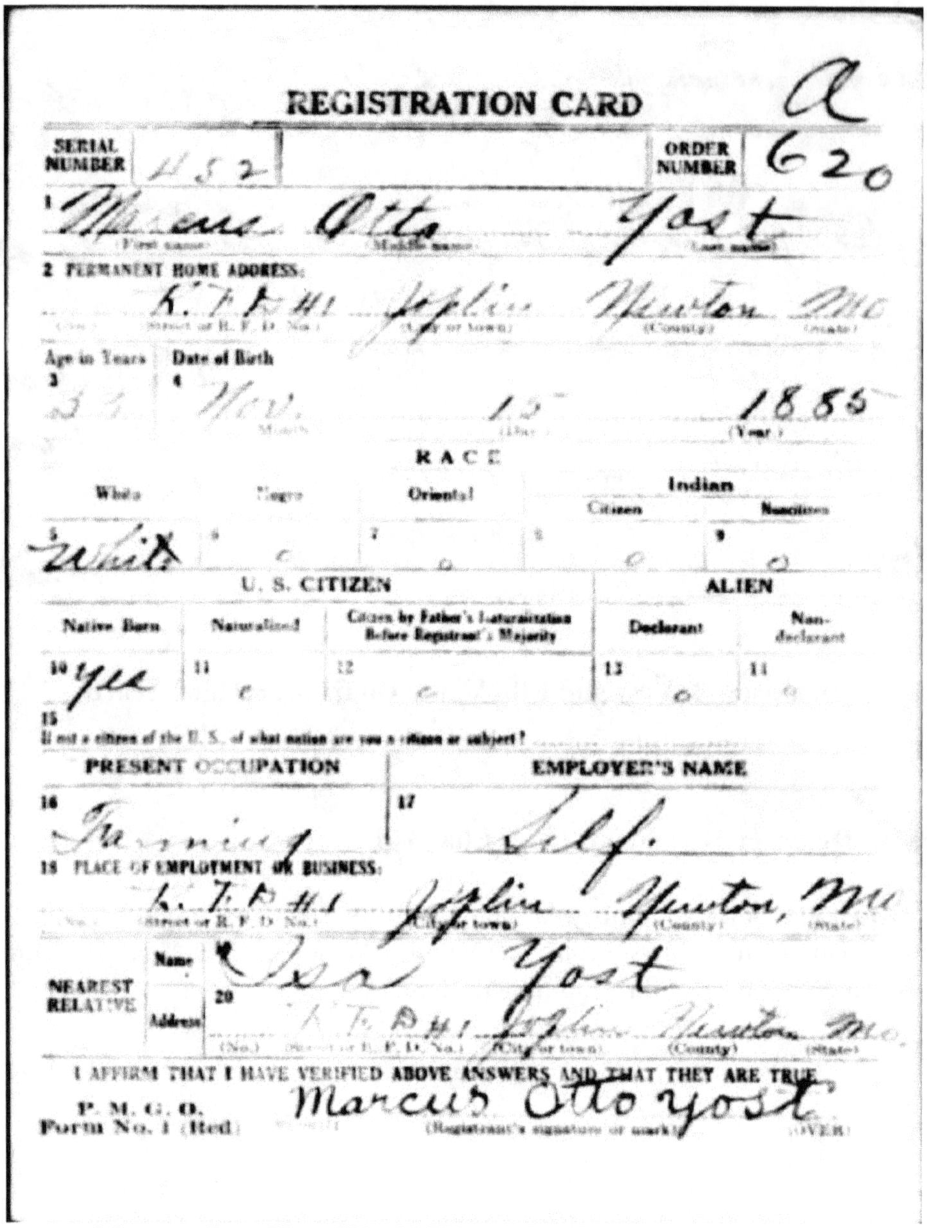

REGISTRATION CARD a

SERIAL NUMBER 452 ORDER NUMBER 620

1 Marcus Otto Yost
(First name) (Middle name) (Last name)

2 PERMANENT HOME ADDRESS:
R. F. D. #1 Joplin Newton Mo
(No.) (Street or R. F. D. No.) (City or town) (County) (State)

Age in Years 3	Date of Birth 4		
32	Nov.	15	1885
	(Month)	(Day)	(Year)

RACE

White	Negro	Oriental	Indian: Citizen	Indian: Noncitizen
5 White	6 o	7 o	8 o	9 o

U. S. CITIZEN: Native Born	U. S. CITIZEN: Naturalized	U. S. CITIZEN: Citizen by Father's Naturalization Before Registrant's Majority	ALIEN: Declarant	ALIEN: Non-declarant
10 yes	11 o	12 o	13 o	14 o

15 If not a citizen of the U. S., of what nation are you a citizen or subject?

PRESENT OCCUPATION	EMPLOYER'S NAME
16 Farming	17 Self.

18 PLACE OF EMPLOYMENT OR BUSINESS:
R. F. D. #1 Joplin Newton, Mo
(No.) (Street or R. F. D. No.) (City or town) (County) (State)

NEAREST RELATIVE
Name 19 Isa Yost
Address 20 R. F. D. #1 Joplin Newton Mo.
(No.) (Street or R. F. D. No.) (City or town) (County) (State)

I AFFIRM THAT I HAVE VERIFIED ABOVE ANSWERS AND THAT THEY ARE TRUE.

P. M. G. O.
Form No. 1 (Red) Marcus Otto Yost
(Registrant's signature or mark) (OVER)

Marcus Otto Yost World War 1 Draft Registration card

Marcus Otto Yost Death Certificate

Marcus Otto Yost
GAR Cemetery, Miami, Oklahoma

Children of Marcus Yost and Isa Chambers are:

Winifrid Lily Yost, born. January 03, 1910, Badger, Kansas; died December 31, 1994, Tipton Ford "Diamond" Missouri.

Wilford "Wilfred" Marcus Yost, born 1912, Spurgeon Newton County Missouri; died July 31, 1945, Joplin Missouri; married Goldie Nutz, October 22, 1933.

**1900 Census Missouri, Newton County, Neosho Dempsey Yost and family.
Elzina White Yost's mother Nancy White living with them**

The Wilfred operated Yost Dairy south of Joplin Missouri. Their deliver truck had the following on it's side:

Yost Dairy
You can whip our Cream but you can't beat our Milk

Wilford Yost and his Yost Dairy Truck

Yost Dairy Bottle Cap

Yost Dairy Farm near Neosho Missouri

Yost Dairy Farm Building

Yost Dairy Cow Stalls

K. C. S. TRAIN-TRUCK COLLISION INJURES 2

Wilfred Yost, Dairyman, in Serious Condition—Wife Also Hurt in Crash on East 12th Street.

Wilfred Yost, operator of the Yost dairy south of Joplin on route 2, was in a serious condition early today in St. John's hospital, suffering from injuries he received at 6:30 o'clock last night when a light panel delivery truck he was driving and the northbound Southern Belle, crack Kansas City Southern railroad streamlined train, collided at a crossing at Twelfth street and Minnesota avenue. Mrs. Yost, who was with her husband, also suffered cuts and abrasions about her body and possible internal injuries.

Yost suffered a deep gash on his throat, extending from the lobe of his left ear downward under his left jaw and across his throat upward to the right side of his chin. He also suffered a deep cut on his left arm and other cuts and abrasions.

Yost was driving the truck west at Twelfth street. Mrs. Yost said she saw the train approaching the crossing from the south only a few seconds before the collision occurred. Theer is no warning signal at the crossing.

The truck was dragged by the train about 40 feet north on the tracks and finally thrown into a ditch on the west side of Minnesota avenue, where it was demolished.

Mr. and Mrs. Yost were taken in a Hurlbut ambulance to the hospital.

The greatest tonnage increase in steelmaking capacity since the beginning of the war has occurred in and around Pittsburgh.

Joplin Globe July 29 1945, Wilford "Wilfred" Yost and wife Goldie in accident with train

Wilford, Winifred, William,

Winola Isa Juanita Yost

STATE BOARD OF HEALTH OF MISSOURI
STANDARD CERTIFICATE OF DEATH

State File No. 27672
Filed AUG 18 1945
Primary Registration District No. 2001
Registrar's No. 351

1. PLACE OF DEATH:
(a) County: Jasper
(b) City or town: Joplin
(c) Name of hospital or institution: St. Johns Hospital
(d) Length of stay: In hospital or institution: 3 days; In this community: lifetime

2. USUAL RESIDENCE OF DECEASED:
(a) State: Missouri (b) County: Jasper
(c) City or town: Joplin
(d) Street No.: 1214 Missouri Ave
(e) Citizen of foreign country?: No

3. (a) PRINT FULL NAME: Wilford Yost
(b) If veteran, name war: —
(c) Social Security No.: —

4. Sex: M
5. Color or race: W
6. (a) Single, widowed, married, divorced: married
6. (b) Name of husband or wife: Goldie
6. (c) Age of husband or wife if alive: —
7. Birth date of deceased: Sept 18 1912
8. AGE: Years 32 Months 10 Days 13
9. Birthplace: Newton County, Mo.
10. Usual occupation: Yost Dairy
11. Industry or business: Wholesale milk
12. Father Name: Marcus Yost
13. Birthplace: Okla
14. Mother Maiden name: Isa Chambers
15. Birthplace: Kansas
16. (a) Informant: Goldie Yost
(b) Address: 1214 Missouri
17. (a) Burial (b) Date thereof: 8-2-45
(c) Place: burial or cremation: Ozark Memorial
18. (a) Signature of funeral director: Thornhill Dillon
(b) Address: 305 W. 4th St.
19. (a) Date received local registrar: 8-1-45

MEDICAL CERTIFICATION
20. DATE OF DEATH: Month July day 31 year 1945 hour 3:50 P.M.
21. I hereby certify that I attended the deceased from ____, 19__, that I last saw h__ alive on ____, 19__, and that death occurred on the date and hour stated above.
Immediate cause of death: Skull fracture, internal bleeding
Due to: Auto hit by K.C.S. train
Other conditions: —
Major findings: Of operations: — Of autopsy: —

22. If death was due to external causes, fill in the following:
(a) Accident, suicide, or homicide: Accident
(b) Date of occurrence: 7/28/45 12:2_
(c) Where did injury occur: Joplin, Jasper, Mo.
(d) Did injury occur in or about home, on farm, in industrial place, in public place? Public Place
While at work? No
Signature: [signed] M.D.
Address: Joplin
Date signed: 8/1/45

INQUEST INTO DEATH OF W. YOST TONIGHT

Joplin Dairyman Dies of Injuries Suffered in Collision of Truck and K. C. S. Streamliner.

An inquest into the death of Wilfred Yost, Joplin dairyman, who died at 1:30 o'clock yesterday afternoon in St. John's hospital of injuries suffered Saturday in a truck-train collision, will be conducted at 8 o'clock tonight at the Thornhill-Dillon chapel, Coroner Dawson W. Derfelt announced last night.

Yost suffered a deep gash across his throat, extending from the lobe of the left ear to the right side of his chin, and numerous other cuts and abrasions.

Married a Week.

His wife, Mrs. Goldie Yost, to whom he was married July 22, was the only other occupant of the truck. She suffered several fractured ribs in the accident and is still a patient at the hospital, but her condition is not believed to be serious.

Yost was driving a light panel delivery truck, which collided with the Kansas City Southern streamliner, Southern Belle, at Twelfth street and Minnesota avenue. The truck was dragged 40 feet by the train before being thrown into a ditch and demolished.

Surviving besides his widow are his mother, Mrs. Isa L. Yost; a brother, William Yost and a sister, Mrs. E. D. Shilling, all of Joplin route 2, and two other sisters, Mrs. C. W. Shilling of Diamond route 1 and Mrs. Ralph Hood of Neosho route 1.

Yost operated the Yost dairy, south of Joplin on route 2. He was a member of the Assembly of God church.

Funeral plans are incomplete.

Wilfred Yost dead August 1 1945 Joplin Globe

> We express our thanks and appreciation in this way, publicly, to those who have been with us in the death of Wilford Yost. The words of Rev. S. K. Biffle and Rev. Thurman Kelly will strengthen us in our grief and for the floral offerings of friends and neighbors and the music and to the Pallbearers and Thornhill-Dillon mortuary for their kindly services, we thank you one and all.
> MRS. WILFORD YOST,
> MRS. ISA YOST AND FAMILY.

Wilfred Yosts wife thanks public August 3 1945 Joplin Globe

SUES K. C. S. FOR $25,000 IN DEATH OF HUSBAND

Suit for $25,000 judgment as damages for the death of her husband and injuries to herself in a grade crossing accident at Twelfth street and Minnesota avenue July 28 was filed yesterday in circuit court by Goldie Yost against the Kansas City Southern railroad.

Mrs. Yost, who was a bride at the time of the accident, sued for $10,000 for the death of her husband, Wilford Yost, a dairyman, who was fatally injured, and $15,000 for serious injuries she said she received.

Wilfred Yost's wife sues Train August 21 1945 Joplin Globe

> LOST—Eisenberg pin, between Fifth and Joplin and Bartlett Bldg. Reward Mrs. Wilford Yost, 1214 Missouri.

Wilfred Yosts wife lost pin during accident Sep 14 1945 Joplin Globe

Juanita "Waunita" Fern Yost, born July 18, 1914. Married Clarence William Shilling born April 01, 1933 in Tipton Ford "Diamond" Missouri.

Juanita Yost and Husband Clarence Shilling 50th Wedding Anniversary in 1983

Juanita Yost Shilling

A miscellaneous shower was given last week at the home of Mrs. Carl Chambers in honor of Mrs. Donald Chambers. Games were played and refreshments were served. Many gifts were presented to the honoree. Those present were J. F. Gilstrap, Mrs. Lillie Gilstrap, Mrs. Ruth Brown, Mrs. Helen Tieso and son, Andrew, Mrs. Alpha Gilstrap and daughter, Dorothy Jean, Mrs. Hazel Gilbert, Mrs. Grace Vaughn, Mrs. June Van Horn, Mrs. Wanda Lee Page, Mrs. Fred Benton, Mrs. Stalla Collins, Mrs. Daisy McGee, Mrs. Delpha Moffett, Mrs. Savella Evans, Mrs. Fern Hunt, Mrs. Lola Carpenter, Mrs. Clara Schwrieweis, Mrs. Lucille Harlan and daughters, Loy Lea and Lela Carol, Mrs. Junetta Fisher and children, Sula Mae, Dona Kay, Carl Dean and Connie Jo, Mrs. I Yost, Mrs. Doris Yost and daughter, Billy Jean, Mrs. Waunetta Schilling and children, Clarence Donald, Dale and Shirley, Mrs. Pearl Gilstrap and daughter, Violet, Mrs. Sula Chambers, Carl Chambers, Melvin Chambers and Avery Chambers.

Mrs. Isa Chambers Yost, Mrs. Doris Jean Domitz Yost, and Waunetta Schilling attend a baby shower for Mrs. Donald Chambers on August 27 1946, Joplin Globe

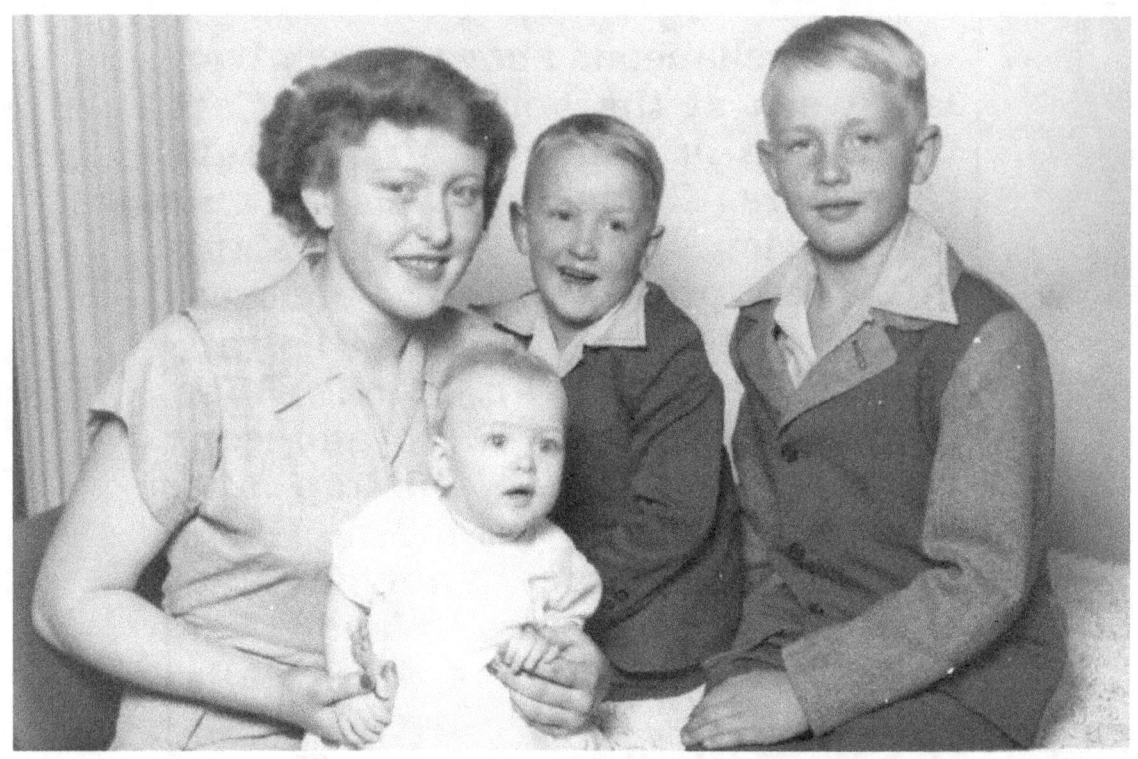

1949 June Robert Danny bottom Linda Shilling

The Story of the Yost Dairy Farm and Family:

Written by Waunita Schil June 2- 2001 at Yost Reunion at Vinita

① Marcus Otto & Isa Chambers 1908 —

The early part of their marriage was financed by Marcus working in the mines and Isa raising garden and making butter to sell from their small Dairy herd. Their first child Winifred Lily was born in 1910 Jan 3., she was blond and blue eyed. Marcus kept meat on the table by hunting and butchering hogs in winter.

The second child was Wilford Marcus borned in 1912 Sept 18 at this time Marcus was taking a load of ore in Joplin, and he spent the money for 15 heifer calves for Isa to raise on the two Jersey Cows they already had. She did just that — Therfore our Dairy started from this —. In 1914 Isa had her 2nd girl Waunita was borned on July 18, 1914 She was a husky 8 lb. and ready for what life had to offer. She still is at 87.

In 1922 Marcus bought a new ford called a model T. We bought crates to pack milk in and ice to keep it cold

2) The Yost Family had another girl in 1917. She was Winola Wretha named for an indian girl in a book Isa was reading to their children. We called her Bud because Marcus said she was his buddie.

We all worked together and it was not bad work.

For the next four years we had a very good milk business and then we were preparing for a new member to the Yost family. Little Bill was born March 10, 1921. He weighed 5 lbs and was a real bundle of joy for everyone. He was named William Wilburn after Isa's oldest brother. He was a very independant person and grew up that way. When he was 5 years old our dad died and we had a real sad time. Marcus had pneumonia and died in St Johns Hos.

Isa Yost was a real manager and she had Wilford quit school in his senior year to deliver the milk for Yost Dairy

3) One of our brothers had to go to army Bill voulenteered to go, so Wilford and Winifred Winola and Harold Yost run the dairy. Opal and Andy Yost also lived with at one time.

Waunita met Clarence Shilling and after 2 y they planned a Wedding for April 1, 1933 Winifred Married Edgar Shilling in Oct 22 1933 in our home. Edgar and Winifred started a Dairy. Winola, Leon Yost Harold helped and operated dairy until 1940. Winola married Ralph Hood and Bill got home from the army

Wilford was killed in train truck accident and Bill faithful, Isa run the dairy 6 year. They hired enough help to keep going Waunita and Clarence bought the dairy place from Mrs Marcus Yost and have been owners since. Isa bought realeste in Joplin and moved in one of her houses.

Isa Yost lived until July 6 1979. She had a good realeste business going and had helped countless people on her way We all lost a lot when she went home She was ready To, and all her family fallow

This is an aerial view of the Yost Diary Farm South of Joplin Missouri. Owner Isa Lina Galena Chambers Yost and Marcus Otto Yost

James Yost flew his airplane over Dairy and took this picture when he came to the Yost Family on June 2, 2001. Reunion for Edith Yost Sutton and daughter Verla, and Juanita "Waunita" Fern Yost and husband Clarence William Shilling bought the dairy farm when Isa moved to Joplin Missouri

Winola "Wilola" Retha Yost, born September 18, 1916, Newton County Missouri, Joplin Rural Route.

Willliam Wilburn Yost, born March 10, 1921, Newton County Missouri, Joplin Rural Route.

Service Info.:	PVT US ARMY WORLD WAR II
Birth Date:	10 Mar 1921
Death Date:	9 Aug 1998
Cemetery:	Ozark Memorial Park Cemetery
Cemetery Address:	415 N St Louis Ave Joplin, MO 64804

Neosho Daily News   Wednesday, July 28, 1982-

FAMILY GATHERING—Part of Mrs. Edith Yost Sutton's nieces and nephews gathered together recently and the family picture was taken. In the front (from the left) are Winifred Shilling, Waunita Shilling, Bill Yost, Jeffrey Yost and Rhonda Yost; second row, Donna Shilling and escort; Winola Hood, Mrs. Edith Sutton (the honoree), Glenna Yost, Bud Yost Sr., Edith Yost, Ronnie Yost and Roxanne Yost; third row, Dana Shilling and escort, Edgar D. Shilling Jr., E.D. Shilling Sr., C. Don Shilling, Mrs. Bud Yost Jr., Roberta Haff, Edith Yost, Bill Yost, Irene Rush; fourth row, Daniel Scorse, Edgar Daniel II, Perry Yost, Bill Vandiver, Debbie Vandiver, James Yost, Bud Yost Jr. and John Rush.

Mr. and Mrs. Jewell Hunt, 228 Maiden Lane, gave a lawn party and shower Sunday in honor of their son, J. C. Hunt, Jr., and Miss Betty Hinderliter of Okmulgee, Okla., who will be married June 7. Assistant hostesses were Mrs. Blanche Downs, Mrs. J. D. Staves and Mrs. Earl Stevens. Miss Rayma Jean Rowland was in charge of the entertainment. Games were played and contest prizes were won by Mrs. Jantra and J. C. Hunt, Jr. A prayer was given by the Rev. A. L. Todd. Refreshments were served. Many gifts were presented from the following: Mr. and Mrs. J. D. Staves, Mrs. Downs, Mrs. Josephine Hunt, Mr. and Mrs. E. O. Hunt, Mr. and Mrs. Earl Stevens, Bonnie Jo Stevens, Ronald Stevens, Mrs. Winters, Thelma Winters, Clara Mae Gassaway, Martha Rose Gassaway, Mr. and Mrs. LeRoy Pierce, Jackie Pierce, Mr. and Mrs. E. F. Rowland, Rayma Jean Rowland, Mr. and Mrs. W. A. Ford, Dr. and Mrs. E. J. Visek, Maurice Morgan, Shelly Morgan, Mr. and Mrs. Glenn Orem, Mr. and Mrs. Gene Wasson, Mr. and Mrs. William Beeler, Jonell Beeler, Loretta Beeler, Mr. and Mrs. Charles Domitz, Mr. and Mrs. William Yost, Billie Jean Yost, Ronnie Yost, Mrs. Lillian Rowlette, the Rev. and Mrs. A. L. Todd, Beverly Joan Todd, Mrs. Jantra, Mr. and Mrs. Dwight Vaughn, Mr. and Mrs. Robert Hightower, Mr. and Mrs. Alvin Potter, Shirley Potter, Mrs. Gladys Rea, Pat Rea, Mr. and Mrs. Oscar Carroll, Mr. and Mrs. Wayne Jackson and the following from out of town: Mrs. Richey, Glen Richey, Josephine Richey, Alice Richey, Myrtle Richey and Carroll Richey of Webb City, Mr. and Mrs. Roscoe Barnes and Terry Lane Barnes of Kansas City, Mrs. C. W. Hinderliter of Okmulgee and Mrs. Charles Keefer of Detroit.

William Yost and family May 28 1952

Noah "Frank" Yost, born June 22, 1894 in Missouri, died April 07, 1970 in Shasta California.

Noah "Frank" Yost World War I draft registration card

Relatives say Frank Yost lived in California. He chased Nora Jane Paul and Raymond John Yost when they were on a date.

Ralph Dempsey Yost, born November 10, 1882, Neosho, Missouri. He married Marietta E. Maretta, born August 20, 1883 in Jasper County, Joplin, Missouri.

Ralph Dempsey Yost World War I Draft Registration Card

Ralph and Wife Ollie Yost

Ralph Dempsey Yost
GAR Cemetery, Miami, Oklahoma

Mariette E. Yost
GAR Cemetery, Miami, Oklahoma

1910 Ralph Yost Missouri Newton Shoal Creek

1930 Ralph Dempsey Yost Oklahoma Ottawa County, Quapaw

Children of Ralph Yost and Ellie E. Maretta are:

Paul Yost born 1905 in Kansas

Mark W. Yost born 1907 in Oklahoma

Ralph Yost born 1909 in Missouri

Elmer Yost, born 1911, Oklahoma.

Mrs Fred Ford was complimented at a surprise party Tuesday afternoon at the home of Mrs C. A. Hopkin, 326½ Grant street The affair was in observance of Mrs Ford's birthday. Games were enjoyed, after which refreshments were served Guests were Mrs Ray Matthews, Mrs. William Lanman Mrs Ivy Flecther Mis Kenneth Copeland, Mrs. Elmer Yost and Mrs. Dannie Samuels

Mrs. Madge Stottle was hostess to unit No 1 of the Federation of Presbyterian Women Tuesday night at her home on Clinton street. Miss Edith Harker was in charge of devotions Miss Elizabeth Pfiffer discussed the missionary topic which described progress made in various activities of the church throughout the world Mrs J R. Williams, president of the federation, told of increased activities in Christian education in both national and foreign fields Announcement was made of a dinner meeting of business and professional women of the Carthage presbyterial to be held at 6 o'clock Tuesday night, April 26 at the First Presbyterian church in Joplin. This meeting is one of the sessions of the presbyterial which meets next Tuesday in Joplin Miss Jennie Robertson and Miss Leona Fletcher were assistant hostesses

Mrs Elmer Yost April 24 1949 Joplin Globe

Edith May Yost, born July 31, 1914, Ottawa Oklahoma; died December 18, 1985, Commerce Oklahoma.

Edith May Yost
GAR Cemetery, Miami, Oklahoma

Children of Dempsey Dwight Yost cont'd

Edith Elzina Yost, born. December 11, 1899, Missouri; died September 17, 1983. She married John Sutton.

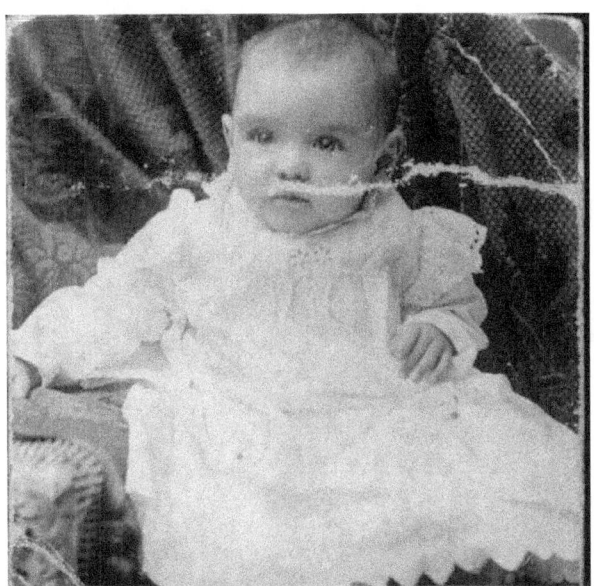
Edith Elzina Yost Age 1

Edith Elzina Yost Age 12

Edith Elzina Yost

Edith Elzina Yost on left

Edith, according to Aunt Roberta Yost Haff fell in love with an Indian boy. They had a child, "Virla" before they had a chance to get marriage. The father ran off upon hearing she was pregnant. Virla's family changed her name back from Virla Grand to Virla Yost.

Winifred Lily Yost   Edith Yost Sutton   Juanita Waunita Fern Yost

Photo taken on Marcus and Isa Yost home(Yost Dairy) south of Joplin Missouri
Front: Perry Yost, Edith Yost Sutton, Verla Yost, Roberta Yost Haff
Back: James Yost, Irene Yost Rush

FAMILY GATHERING—Part of Mrs. Edith Yost Sutton's nieces and nephews gathered together recently and the family picture was taken. In the front (from the left) are Winifred Shilling, Waunita Shilling, Bill Yost, Jeffrey Yost and Rhonda Yost; second row, Donna Shilling and escort; Winola Hood, Mrs. Edith Sutton (the honoree), Glenna Yost, Bud Yost Sr., Edith Yost, Ronnie Yost and Roxanne Yost; third row, Dana Shilling and escort, Edgar D. Shilling Jr., E.D. Shilling Sr., C. Don Shilling, Mrs. Bud Yost Jr., Roberta Haff, Edith Yost, Bill Yost, Irene Rush; fourth row, Daniel Scorse, Edgar Daniel II, Perry Yost, Bill Vandiver, Debbie Vandiver, James Yost, Bud Yost Jr. and John Rush.

History is recalled as former resident visits

Mrs. Edith Yost Sutton, 82, Burbank, Calif., an old time Newton County resident, returned recently for a visit and especially to see the children of her six brothers.

She came to the home of Clarence and Waunita Shilling, where an open house was held in her honor on Sunday, July 11. Invitations had been sent to all of her brothers' descendants. More than 60 people attended the event. One nephew who lives in Texas flew his own plane up, left it at the Joplin airport, and upon leaving in the evening, flew over the Shilling farm taking pictures of the celebrating relatives.

Mrs. Sutton, the daughter-in-law of Dr. J.R. Sutton of the booming town of Spurgeon in the early 1900's, recalled many exciting things that happened in her school days at Shaumburn School, south of Spurgeon.

The old Yost residence was between Racine and Spurgeon. The Yost family traded eggs, butter and fresh vegetables to the Parker Grocery at Spurgeon for other needed supplies.

Ralph and Janice Van Dorn gave a tour of Mrs. Sutton's old home place, now know as the Earl Kraft farm. At one time the farm belonged to Dempsey and Alzina Yost. Their chilren were Ralph, Herman, Marcus, Ray, Frank, Harry and Edith. Most of the boys died while living in the four state area. Marcus was the only one to remain in Newton County to establish one of the first four Grade A dairies to sell bottled milk in Joplin. Marcus died in 1930, leaving a wife and five children, who operated the dairy many more years. Wilford, his oldest son, took over the deliver route. He was killed in 1942 when a train struck the milk truck. His four other children are Mrs. E.D. Shilling, Tipton Ford, Mrs. Clarence Shilling, of the old Yost Dairy Farm, Mrs. Ralph Hood, Route 1, and William Yost, Route 4, Joplin.

Mrs. Sutton arrived with her oldest daughter, Verla Noel, and a granddaughter, Holly Kay Gaston. Representatives from most of the Yost families came to the reception.

Others Mrs. Sutton visited were the Bud Yost family, Webb City; Bill Yost, Route 4; Edith Yost (her namesake), Commerce, Okla.; Agnes Routledge family, Joplin; Richard Van Dorn, Route 4, Joplin; E.D. Shilling, Route 2; Ralph Hood, Route 1; Bonnie Wydick, Commerce, Okla.; Willard Murphy, Quapaw, Okla.; Dorsa Shilling Main, Route 1, Diamond. She also visited the George Washington Carver National Monument.

In recalling family history, the Yost family, father and sons, all mined in Spurgeon. Mrs. Sutton told of the time a man, Mr. Frazier, who disappeared in the mines, near Spurgeon. Everyone in the area turned out to move a chat pile where he was reported to be buried. Mrs. Sutton visited with Bonnie West about this. Miss West found a picture of the incident showing buggies, surreys, wagons and people walking to help dig. They finally moved the entire chat pile but never found the man.

Mrs. Sutton returned to Burbank the following Monday after the reception and reported that she was "tired but happy with her Missouri visit."

Edith Yost Sutton returns to Missouri

THE LORD is my shepherd; I shall not want. He maketh me to lie down in green pastures: He leadeth me beside the still waters. He restoreth my soul: He leadeth me in the paths of righteousness for His name's sake. Yea, though I walk through the valley of the shadow of death, I will fear no evil; for thou art with me; thy rod and thy staff they comfort me. Thou preparest a table before me in the presence of mine enemies, thou anointest my head with oil: my cup runneth over. Surely goodness and mercy shall follow me all the days of my life; and I will dwell in the house of the LORD for ever.

Psalm 23

In Loving Memory Of

EDITH E. SUTTON

BORN
December 11, 1899 - Neosho, Missouri

PASSED AWAY
October 13, 1983 - Burbank, California

SERVICES
Saturday, October 15, 1983 - 1:00 P.M.
Pierce Brothers Little Country Chapel

OFFICIATING
Pastor Will Strong
Overcomers Faith Center
Burbank, California

INTERMENT
Valhalla Memorial Park - N. Hollywood, California

DIRECTORS
PIERCE BROTHERS VALHALLA MORTUARY
10621 Victory Blvd. - North Hollywood, California - 763-9123

Edith Elzina Yost

Children of Edith Yost and John Sutton are:
Joan Sutton, born February 06, 1940.

Joan Sutton and husband Bill Gaston

Mary Lou Sutton.

Children of Dempsey Dwight Yost cont'd

Harry P. Yost born September 1897 in Missouri married Martha E. Fudge born 1902 Missouri.

Harry P. and Martha E. Yost had the following children:

Pauline M. Yost born 1920

William O. Yost born 1923

Thomas E. Yost born 1924

Geraldine R. Yost born 1930. Harry worked Northeast of Miami Oklahoma at the Iron Works.

Maybelle Yost born 1881 in Missouri, died 1881 in Missouri

Herman "Hurbert" Willis Yost born January 1884 in Neosho Missouri, died March 13, 1918. Herman married Ada Buno born 1890 in Kansas.

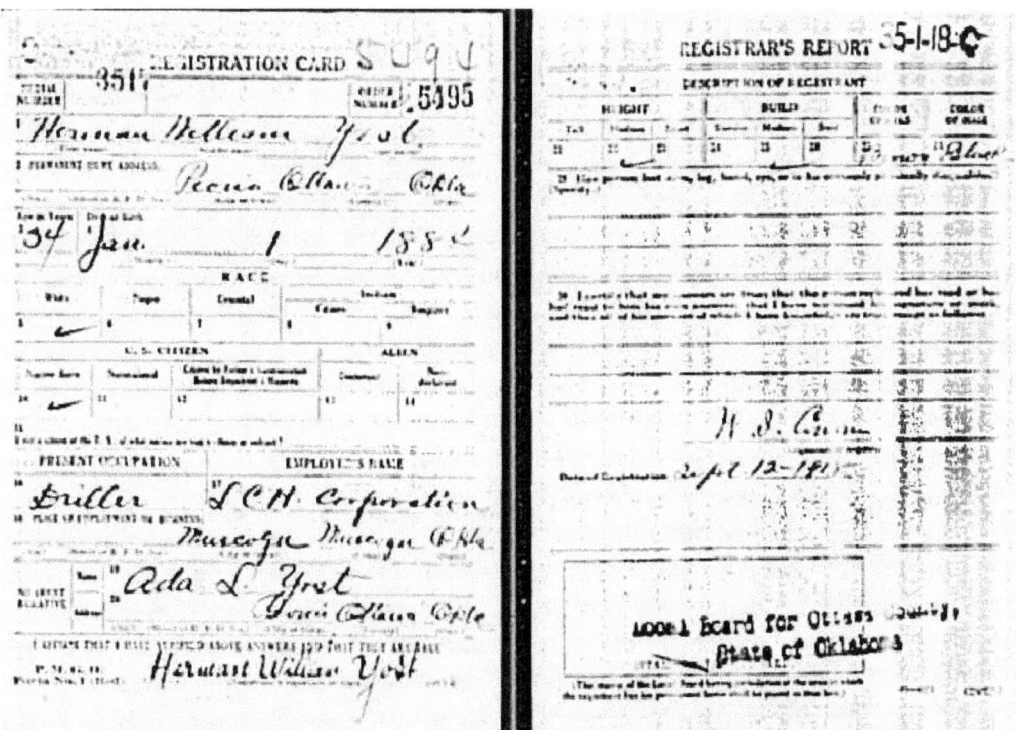

Herman William Yost World War I Draft Registration Card

Herman Willis Yost Grave Marker

Herman and Ada Yost had the following children

Bonnie Yost born 1908

Thelma Yost born October 16, 1912, died March 17, 1914 in Joplin, Missouri

Thelma Yost Death Certificate

Raymond John Yost, born May 15, 1890, Galena Cherokee County, Kansas; died March 06, 1941, Picher Miami, Oklahoma. He married **Nora Jane Paul** January 07, 1912 in Marcus Yost's Residence Joplin Newton County Missouri, daughter of Golby Paul and Clara Kraft. The word passed down is that Nora was at a pie supper in Joplin when she met Raymond.

MINER'S BANK
The oldest bank in the city.

Joplin Missouri 1913

Uncle Leon Ralph Yost wrote the following before his death:

Ray John Yost
    He was a quiet soft-spoken person, tall-over 6 feet, dark brown eyes and coal black curly hair. His sunny disposition prevailed most of the time; however, he had an incendiary temper that could flare when things went wrong. He had plenty of patience with the little ones. In fact, he was a nice guy to have around when you got an earache and was 7 years old. He would load up his old pipe and light it, push the stem in your ear and blow gently on the bowl. The warm air and tobacco smoke would stop the ache real quick.

He called himself a miner, but he had plenty of know how in a lot of areas. He was one of the best at operating a thrashing machine separating wheat, oats, and beans from the straw. He was thoroughly qualified at operating a drill rig, cable tool walking beam type, drilling water wells or prospecting for ore. He drilled the well for the Baker School East of Ketchum, Oklahoma when I was 9. I helped fire the boiler, putting in wood and coal, watching the water level in the boiler and adding water when it got low. Some of the more up to date boilers had a high pressure pump to add water. The one we had had a steam injector, very temperamental but after he had taught me to operate the injector I became a wizard at it. When he and my older brother Cleve had given up getting it to take water and started running to let the boiler blow-up, I would jump upon the platform, spin the valves two or three times and flue would burn thru and blow off. The water escaping would usually put out the fire and we pulled the grates and Dad went in, to install a new flue, not waiting for it to cool. I always thought he would get burned really bad, but he never did.

I recall once coming home from town, the rear axel on the wagon broke. He sent me to the nearest house to borrow an axe. He cut a pole and put one end under the broken axel and tied the other end up to the front of the wagon box. I took the axe back and we went home on 3 wheels and a pole runner. He made a new axel.

I can recall the County Road Commissioner coming to get him to do some blasting with dynamite. He was really god with "powder", another time a neighbor had a mean stallion that he wanted shoes put on. The local blacksmith refused. Dad told the man he would shoe the horse. He took a rope and tied the foot to be shoed to the horse's tail. The guy said, 'won't he kick his tail off?' Dad said, 'I am worried more than about him kicking mine off.'"

Patricia Shanahan Yost often quoted her mother-in-law (my grandmother, Nora Yost), who said "When the Lord sets you free, he sets you free indeed." Recently Patricia realized that this was a Bible verse. (She previously thought it was just something Grandma said!)

In researching exactly where Nora Yost's home in Vinita came from, I asked Aunt Birdy, Roberta Yost Haff. She told me the following:

Nora Yost's brother Walter Paul was fairly well to do. He loaned his sister $600 to $800 to purchase the farm outside of Vinita. Walter later met a lady in Alabama and moved by Montgomery. Her son Maurice, who was back from the War, assisted the family by purchasing food all the time using the money he earned in the mine. Maurice also fixed the home up and re-built the barn. When Nora Yost sold the farm and moved into town in 1953 to 1954. At that time she paid her brother back for the loan. Below is a picture of Walter Paul

Walter Paul

Grandma Yost lived in a home on the north side of Vinita Oklahoma. I would like to take this time to bring back some memories of Grandma and the visits to her home. I remember the hug and kiss we always got upon our arrival. I remember she always kept cookies in breadbox in the kitchen. We were always welcome to one upon our arrival for a visit. I remember her rocking chair in the middle of the living room, which always faced towards the bedrooms. I remember her back-enclosed porch that led to the backyard where her black dog was. I don't remember the name of her dog, do you? I remember playing in her back yard and going to the back fence and looking down the alley wandering what was at either end. I remember her garage that always had the door closed. I wondered what neat things were inside. I remember going shopping with her, we always took a cab. I remember going to the local swimming pool with my brother and sister. But one thing that to this day I enjoy the memory of, was when I would get to spend the night, I would lay in bed beside the window (front window on the side of the house in the picture below), the sun still going down, and hearing the train come through town, the whistle, the sound of the wheels on the track. It gave me such a relaxed neat feeling having lived in the city all my life. I do remember somewhere in the living room was a picture of Jesus our Lord and Savior, but I can't remember where, do you?

Nora Yost's home in Vinita

Nora Jane Yost backyard of her home, Vinita Oklahoma

Nora Jane Yost's Poem

Nora Jane Yost at home, Vinita Oklahoma

Grandma Yost's last days before going home

I remember when Grandma Yost came to my home from St. Francis hospital just before she died. I remember it was a trying time because the doctors said there was nothing wrong with her. But I think she knew she was getting ready to go home to the Lord. One evening my mother Janice Clara Yost Stadler was at work, we kids and dad were at home. Grandma was staying in me and my brother's room. She asked my father, Edward Purdy Yost to come pray with her. Dad went back and got on his knees beside her bed. I was in the living room and could hear Grandma praying for the Lord to bring her home. She had lived a good life, I truly believe she knew the Lord was calling her and she had lived a good life raising 13 kids by herself, she is sitting with her husband at the table of the Lord in Heaven as I write these words.

I write the following words not to hurt anyone's feelings, but to simply tell the truth for the generations to come who like me wonder about their wonderful family history. My mother Janice Clara Yost Stadler could get no sleep while Grandma waited for her last days. I remember the decision was finally made to move her to my Cousin Peggy Haff's home in Sand Springs Oklahoma. I do not remember the actual move; I only remember hearing that a short time after Grandma Yost moved to Peggy's home, she went to be with our Lord. To this day I have to give my father credit, he knelt with my grandmother as she prayed for the Lord to take her.

I was at Grandma's funeral; it was there that I heard the most beautiful song there ever was. At her funeral the song "Amazing Grace" was played. I believe all Yost descendants should have this song played at their funeral.

DEATHS

Nora Yost

Nora Yost, 79, Vinita, passed away Wednesday evening in a Tulsa hospital.

She was born April 3, 1896, near Neosho, Mo., and had lived in the Vinita area since 1945. She was a member of the Ironside Assembly of God Church.

Surviving are six daughters, Mildred Andrews and Irene Rush, both of Vinita, Roberta Haff, Sand Springs, Beatrice Prine, Bluejacket, Janice Stadler, Tulsa, and Kathryn Gardner, Houston, Tex.; five sons, Leon Yost, Grass Valley, Calif., Maurice Yost, Locust Grove, Perry Yost, Muldrow, James Yost, Fort Worth, Tex., and Clyde Yost, Springfield, Ill.; two brothers, Walter Paul, Stevenson, Ala., and Clarence Paul, Joplin, Mo.; two sisters, Mrs. Viola Lampe, Los Angeles, Calif., and Della Stoots, Joplin, Mo.

She is also survived by 42 grandchildren, 48 great-grandchildren and two great-great-grandchildren.

Services are pending and will be announced later by Luginbuel Funeral Service of Vinita.

Nora Jane (Paul) Yost Passes away

Nora Paul Yost Death Certificate

Children of Raymond Yost and Nora Paul are:

Irene Agnes Yost, born August 09, 1914, Yost Farm; died December 09, 2002, Vinita Oklahoma.

Maurice Ray Yost, born October 15, 1922, Ketchum, Oklahoma; died September 06, 2006, Pryor, Oklahoma   Military Funeral buried Spavinaw-Strang Cemetery.

Cleve Woodrow Yost, born January 24, 1913, Joplin, Missouri; died June 28, 1952, Vinita, Oklahoma. Buried Fairview Cemetery Vinita Oklahoma

Harold John Yost, born August 23, 1916, Marcus Yost's Residence Joplin Newton County Missouri; died April 19, 1964, Hockerville Oklahoma buried Gar Cemetery Miami Oklahoma.

Leon Ralph Yost, born February 13, 1918, Joplin, Missouri; died August 08, 1991, Eugene, Oregon   Buried at Sea by United States Coast Guard of the Pacific Coast.

Clyde Lee Yost, born November 14, 1935, Vinita, Oklahoma; died October 12, 1989, Virden, Illinois.

Beatrice Viola Yost, born December 11, 1920, Quapaw, Oklahoma; died November 27, 2006, Vinita, Oklahoma. Buried Pheasant Hill Cemetery, north of Vinita Oklahoma.

Mildred Pauline Yost, born December 29, 1924, Miami, Oklahoma, died July 7, 2009.

Perry Kenneth Yost, born September 08, 1926, Cardin, Oklahoma; died November 30, 2001. Military Funeral buried Spavinaw-Strang Cemetery.

Roberta Ruth Yost, born October 28, 1928, Spavinaw, Oklahoma.

James Dillard Yost, born February 20, 1932, Cleora, Oklahoma; died April 01, 2003. Buried Fairview Cemetery Vinita Oklahoma

Kathryn Johanna Yost, born November 02, 1933, Cleora, Oklahoma.

Janice Clara Yost, born February 16, 1938, Cleora Oklahoma; died January 24. Buried beside her father at the Grand Army of the Republic Cemetery in Miami Oklahoma.

Raymond John Yost's Life

Raymond John Yost, born May 15, 1890, Galena Cherokee County, Kansas; died March 06, 1941, Picher Miami, Oklahoma.

Raymond and Nora Yost Wedding Picture

IN THE RECORDER'S OFFICE OF NEWTON COUNTY MISSOURI

MARKRIAGE LICENSE.

STATE OF MISSOURI,
County of Newton

THIS LICENSE AUTHORIZES any Judge of a Court of Record or Justice of the Peace, or any Licensed or Ordained Preacher of the Gospel, who is a citizen of the United States, or who is a resident of and a pastor of any church in this State, to SOLEMNIZE MARRIAGE between Ray J. Yost of Spurgeon in the County of Newton and State of Missouri who is over the age of twenty-one years; and Nora Paul of Greece in the County of Newton and State of Missouri who is over the age of eighteen years. J. R. Paul and Mrs. J. L. Paul, parents of Nora Paul, having given their consent to this marriage in writing.

WITNESS my hand as Recorder of Deeds, with the seal of office hereto affixed, at my office in Neosho, Mo. this 8th day of January 1912. L. H. Keller, Recorder of Deeds.

By _____ Deputy.

STATE OF MISSOURI,
County of Newton

This is to certify that the undersigned Wm. D. Cox, Justice of the Peace did, at R. J. Yost in said County, on the 2nd day of January A.D. 1912 unite in Marriage the above named persons. And I further certify that I am legally qualified under the laws of the State of Missouri to Solemnize Marriages.

Wm. D. Cox, Justice of the Peace

The foregoing Certificate of Marriage was filed for record in my office, on the 11th day of January A.D. 1912.

L. H. Keller, Recorder of Deeds

By _____ Deputy.

COUNTY OF NEWTON } ss.
STATE OF MISSOURI,

I, Leland L. Berry, Clerk of the Circuit Court and Ex-Officio Recorder of Deeds within and for Newton County, Missouri, hereby certify the above and foregoing to be a true copy of the MARRIAGE LICENSE------RAY J. YOST AND NORA PAUL as the same appears in Book ___0___ Page ___3___ in my office.

WITNESS my hand as Clerk and Seal of said Court.

DONE this __10th__ day of __March__ A.D., 19_78_, at Office in Neosho, Missouri.

Raymond John Yost and Nora Jane Paul Marriage License

Raymond John Yost World War I draft registration card

Farm in Missouri between Joplin and Neosho

Back: Unknown, Unknown, Unknown, Raymond John Yost holding Leon Yost
Middle: Wheat Hand, Edith Yost Raymond's sister,
Bottom: Unknown, Unknown, Elzina White Yost, Irene Yost, Dempsey Yost, Cleve Yost, Nora Paul Yost holding Harold Yost

Craig County Home Demonstration Club members at a state conference in Stillwater, August, 1949. Front Row: Elaine Inman, Claudia Jenkins, Home Demonstration Agent Thelma Bennett, Mrs. Woolman, Mrs. Graves, Mrs. Odell. 2nd Row: Mrs. Rose, Mrs. Hattie Robertson, Mrs. Howard Tyler, Mrs. Trott, Mrs. Chester Simms, Juanita Dason, Mrs. Phillips. 3rd Row: Mrs. Bert Oskison, Mrs. Ruth Blackwell, Mrs. Youst, Mrs. Caprillica (Simms) Hughes.

Nora Paul Yost back row Center wearing glasses

Nora Jane Yost at Roberta Yost Haff's Home

Nora Jane Yost at Roberta Yost Haff's Home in Sand Springs Oklahoma

FAMILY HISTORY CONTINUED

CHILDREN

NAMES	PLACE BIRTH	DATE	DEATH DATE
Cleve Woodroe Yost	Joplin Mo R2	Jan 24, 1913	1951
Irene Agnes Yost	Neosho Mo R1	Aug 9, 1914	Dec 9, 2002
Harold John Yost	Joplin Mo R2	Aug 23, 1916	April 19, 1964
Leon Ralph Yost	Joplin Mo R2	Feb 13, 1918	Aug 8, 1991
Beatrice Viola Yost	Inapan Okla	Dec 11, 1920	
Maurice Ray Yost	Ketchum Okla	Oct 15, 1922	
Mildred Pauline Yost	Miami Okla R2	Dec 29, 1924	
Perry Kenneth Yost	Cardin Okla	Sept 8, 1926	Nov 30, 2001
Roberta Ruth Yost	Spavinaw Okla	Oct 28, 1928	
James Dillard Yost	Cleora Okla	Feb 20, 1932	April 1, 2003
Kathryn Johanna Yost	Cleora Okla	Nov 2, 1934	Oct 1989
Clyde Lee Yost	Vinita Okla	Nov 14, 1936	
Janice Lou Yost	Cleora Okla	Feb 16, 1938	

NAMES	BAPTISM CHURCH	DATE	CONFIRMATION CHURCH	DATE
Beatrice		July 1933	Holliness	
Mildred		July 1433	Holliness	
Cleve			Baptist	

FAMILY HISTORY CONTINUED

CHILDREN

NAMES	EDUCATION	MARRIAGE
Cleve W Yost	Common	Lona
Irene A Yost	11th grade	John Rush
Harold G Yost	Comm-n	Violet
Patricia V Yost	12th grade	Ed Prine
Mildred P Yost	11th grade	Jessie Moore / Jr Andrews
Perry R Yost	Graduate	Sue
Roberta R Yost	Graduate	Herman Haff
Leon R Yost	Graduate	Sal

GRANDCHILDREN

NAMES	BIRTH DATE	NAMES	BIRTH DATE
Wayne Rush	Dec 26, 1935	Eleanor Delores Yost	May 1942
James Ray Yost	Aug 6, 1937	Carolyn Sue Moore	
Judy Anne Prine	Feb 5, 1942	Velma Yost	Oct 31
Jessie Ray Moore	June 30, 1944		
Johnny Lee Moore		Cheryl Sue Yost	Dec 47
John Eugene Rush	Nov 8, 1947	Mildred Anne Moore	
Linda Sue Prine	Dec 6, 1949	Peggy Lyn Haff	1950 Jan 28
Tommy Joe Rush	Aug 25, 1951		

Raymond and Nora Yost Bible Page 2

FAMILY HISTORY CONTINUED

GREAT-GRANDPARENTS

NAMES	BIRTH PLACE	DATE	DEATH DATE
HUSBAND'S GRANDPARENTS			
Kennedy			
John Yost	Illinois		
Nancy McClain			
WIFE'S GRANDPARENTS			
Adam Kraft	Germany		
Louise Kercher	Michigan		
Joseph Paul	Georgia		
Jane Knox			

GRANDPARENTS

NAMES	BIRTH PLACE	DATE	DEATH DATE
HUSBAND'S PARENTS	Illinois		
Demsey W. Yost			
Elzina			
WIFE'S PARENTS			
G. K. Paul			
Clara L. Kraft	Missouri		

Raymond and Nora Yost Bible Page 3

Falling Pump Arm Is Fatal To a Miner

Picher, Okla., March 6.—Ray J. Yost, 50 years old, was killed instantly when an arm of a walking-beam pump fell and struck him on the head at the old Molsberry mine east of Hockerville, shortly before 9 o'clock this morning.

Yost was placed in a motor car by a brother, Ralph Yost, and brought to Picher hospital, where he was pronounced dead. The body then was removed to the Mitchelson funeral home at Commerce.

The miner's skull was crushed by the heavy timber, although it fell but a few feet. The pump was being dismantled to be moved to a coal mine near Bluejacket.

Yost lived near the Prairie Dog mine, between Picher and Quapaw. He is survived by his widow, Mrs. Nora Yost; seven sons, six daughters and a brother.

T. Ray J.—Joplin News Herald, Thursday, March 6, 1941

Joplin News Herald, Thursday March 6, 1841 Raymond Yost died in accident

Raymond John Yost
Miami, Oklahoma (G.A.R. Cemetery)

In 1910 Raymond John Yost was living with his brother Herman "Hurbert" Yost and his family in Jasper County Missouri in the town of Joplin.

In 1920 years later, after Nora and Raymond were married and had kids, they were living in Newton County Missouri in the town of Neosho.

By 1930, Nora, Raymond and their children had moved to Delaware Count Oklahoma in the township of Jay

Name		Relation					Sex	Race	Age	MS
Yost	John R	Head	R				M	W	40	M
	Nora	Wife H				X	F	W	34	M
	Clare	Son				X	M	W	17	S
	Irene	Daughter				X	F	W	16	S
	Hazel	Son				X	M	W	13	S
	Leon	Son				X	M	W	11	S
	Beatrice	Daughter				X	F	W	9	S
	Maurice	Son				X	M	W	7	S
	Mildred	Daughter				X	F	W	5	S
	Perry	Son				X	M	W	3	S
	Roberta	Daughter				X	F	W	1	S

In 1900 Nora Jane Paul was living with her parents Golby Knox and Clara Newton County Missouri in the township of Neosho.

Paul	D. K.	Head	W	M	Apr	1867	33	M
	Clara	wife	W	F	Dec	1870	29	M
	Benjamin	son	W	M	Aug	1893	6	S
	Nora	daughter	W	F	Apr	1894	5	S
	Della	daughter	W	F	May	1894	5	S

The 1930 census shows Golby Knox Paul and wife Clara Louise Kraft was in 1930 when Raymond and Nora Yost's daughter Irene was found to be living with them in Ottawa County Oklahoma township of West Georgia.

		daughter			W	F	W	25	S
Paul	B. K.	Head	R		W	M	W	63	M
	Clara	wife-H			X	F	W	59	M
	Walter F	son			X	M	W	29	S
	Clarence	son			X	M	W	27	S
Yost	Irene	Granddaughter			X	F	W	15	S

SPAN cotten mules. Nora Yost, one mile northeast Quapaw to K. O. & G. track, turn north, third house.

May 14, 1944, Joplin Globe News Paper - Nora Yost selling Span Cotton Mules

**Left Front: Melissa Yost (James daughter), Jesse Lee Haff, Nora Jane Paul Yost, Roberta Yost Haff, Beartice Yost Prine, Hazel Haff(Loyd's wife)
Back: Patricia Yost (James Wife), Lynn Ray Yost (James son), Herman Haff, Loyd Haff (Herman's brother)**

Light Bread Rolls

Heat 1½ cups milk just scald put ¾ cup lard 3 level teaspoons of salt ½ cup sugar — all these ingredients into hot milk let cool to luke warm while above ingredients cool put 2 pkgs dry yeast to soak in ½ cup warm water

Put all these ingredients into flour in pan to mix. But first stir & beat all ingredients in small pan then put into flour in pan and beat with fork until you can handle with hands if to sticky put a little grease on hands also grease bowl and then put dough in pan let rise until double its size

then work down & make into rolls the size you want & let rise & cook at 400 degrees about 20 minuets last few minuets turn oven to 300 degrees

Nora Yost's famous Light Bread Rolls Recipe written down June 1965 for Roberta Ruth Yost Haff in Nora's own hand writing

Yost Family Reunion September 30 1995 Tulsa Oklahoma – LaFortune Park

Yost Brothers, Leon, Clyde, Maurice, James

Yost Family Reunion 2006

Tim Stadler, Steven Stadler, Janice Yost Stadler, and Brian Stadler at Nora Jane Yost's grave in Vinita Oklahoma

The Children of Raymond John Yost and Nora Jane Paul

Cleve Woodrow Yost, born January 24, 1913, Joplin, Missouri; died June 28, 1952, Vinita, Oklahoma. Cleve is buried in Fairview Cemetery, Vinita, Oklahoma, plot SR3-13A. On April 04, 1934 he married Louise Breedlove in Smith County Texas. Oma was born April 12, 1919 in Rusk County Texas. Oma died March 31, 1981 in Austin, Travis County, Texas.

Fairview Cemetery Vinita, Oklahoma

According to Aunt Mildred, they were working on an oil rig down in Texas. A worker at the top dropped something heavy and hit Cleve in the head. It was so heavy after hitting his head it traveled on down and cut off his thumb that they re-attached.

Obviously there was severe damage to Cleve's skull. I am sure like when he got back up to Vinita, he was acting totally strange down there after the accident. Apparently Louise's dad couldn't handle it so he called Cleve's dad Raymond Yost and told him to come get him before he killed him.

Grandpa Yost sold a bunch of his hogs off and took a train down there and got Cleve and brought him back. When he got back here they took him to the Mayo Hospital in Joplin Missouri. They then brought him back to Grandpa and Grandma Yost's house. Apparently his skull was crushed in, in the back and basically soft. Cleve wondered away from the farm. The Yost's and the Sheriff and relatives such as Aunt Edith went out to find him.

They found him in a field walking in circles saying he was walking back to Texas. They then placed him in Eastern State Hospital. Mom and sisters would go and see him. Eventually he died in 1951 according to the sisters.

After Nora Yost passed away, Aunt Mildred Yost Moore purchased a grave marker for Cleve's grave.

James Ray "Jimmie" Yost after he grew up visited Aunt Mildred, after his dad's death. He asked Aunt Mildred why Grandma Yost never came to see him growing up. Aunt Mildred told him that at the time he was born, 1936, she (Grandma Yost) was busy raising little children, Janice Clara Yost was not born until 1938 and she was the youngest of the 13. Apparently Jimmie was mad because he was always told by his mom that his dad, Cleve, was dead, when in fact he didn't die until 1951.

Nora Jane Paul Yost
Fairview Cemetery Vinita, Oklahoma

Children of Cleve Woodrow Yost and Louise Breedlove.

James Ray "Jimmie" Yost born August 06, 1936.   Cleve and Louise divorced and eventually after Cleve died, Louise married Logan Edmond Fields. She died March 31, 1981. Jimmie died December 21, 2003 in Canton, Van Zandt, Texas.

Louise holding Jimmie Ray Yost

(Oma) Louise Breedlove and son James Ray "Jimmie" Yost

Rose and Jimmie Ray Yost 1944-45

Jimmie Ray Yost

James Ray "Jimmie" Yost Fields Army Picture
Jimmie Yost served in the United States Army and was in the War in Korea.

Jimmie Ray Yost (compare this photo to Anthony Edward Stadler they are like brothers, much like Lynn Yost)

Jimmie Ray Yost and sister Bee

Jimmie Ray Yost and wife

Jimmie Ray Yost and family

Sister-in-law Sandy Jo Hornsby, m. to Tom Ethan Fields Ron's son Tom Fields Thomas Edward Fields Jims stepbrother Ron Fields with the beard as a kid he went by Ronny and Jimmie Ray Yost Fields

Irene Agnes Yost, born August 09, 1914, Yost Farm; died December 09, 2002, Vinita Oklahoma. Irene Agnes Yost married John Rush on April 29, 1935 in Craig County, Oklahoma. John Rush born August 24, 1912 in Arkansas, died March 10, 1997 in Vinita, Oklahoma. John Rush enlisted in the Army July 19, 1945 for World War II. They had Tommy Joe Rush born August 25, 1951, Johnny Eugene Rush born November 09, 1947 in Vinita, died January 1983 in Vinita, and Wayne H. Rush born December 26, 1935 in Vinita, Oklahoma, died October 18, 2005 in Grandview, Missouri, Lees Summit Cemetery.

Irene Agnes Yost 1934

Wayne married Martha? And they had the following children: Larry Rush, Rene Rush, and David Rush.

Irene Agnes Yost Rush and Wayne H. Rush

Wayne Rush

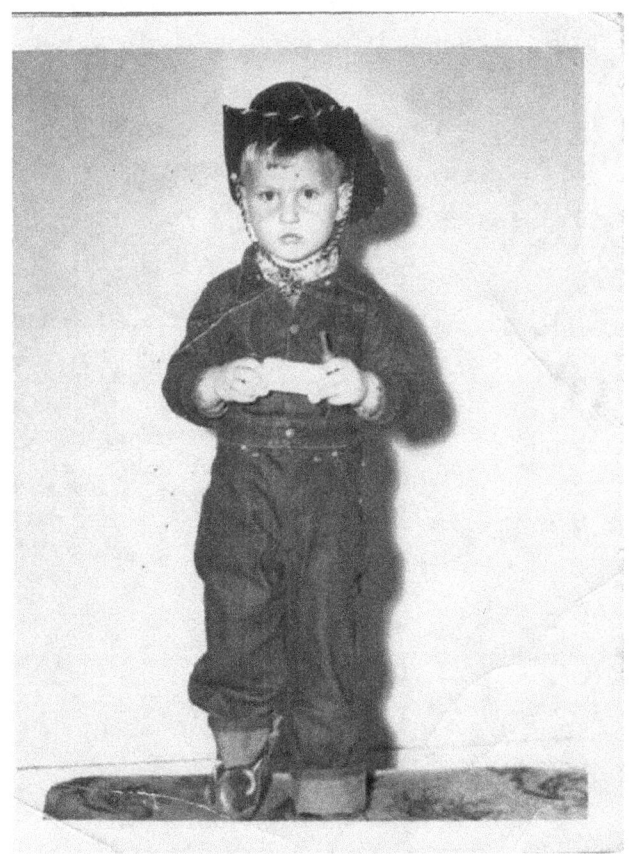

John Eugene Rush age 3

RUSH TREATED AT SILL

Wounded Vinitan Back From War

Sgt. John E. Rush, a Vinita soldier, has returned to the United States via hospital plane after receiving serious leg wounds in battle in Vietnam.

Serving with the U.S. Army, Rush suffered the wounds when shot five times in the right leg and foot by enemy forces on Aug. 4. After treatment in a series of hospitals, he now is at Ft. Sill Army Hospital, Okla.

He is the son of Mr. and Mrs. John Rush, 302 S. Brown St.

Rush, who received his basic training at Ft. Polk, La., where he was awarded the expert marksmanship medal, later won the Bronze Star and other medals while fighting.

After Ft. Polk, he was stationed at Ft. Ord, Calif., as office personnel and truck driver before transfer to Mannheim, Germany with the U.S. 595th Transit Co., HT, where he drove 25-ton trucks transporting tanks over Europe and received the truck driver's medal.

The unit was then sent to Vietnam and Rush drove an 8,000 gallon tanker carrying water to troops in the war zone. He completed Claymore mine school and helicopter school and also is a 1967 graduate of the U.S. Army School at Chu Chi, 25th Infantry Hdq., Vietnam.

The 19-year-old Vinitan then was sent into the air cavalry and missions included fire fights into the war zone where his feats won the medals, his mother said.

He was promoted to sergeant in Vietnam on July 10, and rode in the command ship in the war, she added.

Sgt. Rush was given leaves here before going to California and again while en route to Vietnam. He is a member of the First Baptist Church here.

It still is not known how long the young veteran will be hospitalized or to what extent his treatment will be, Mrs. Rush said.

SGT. JOHN E. RUSH

John Eugene Rush Vietnam War

John Eugene Rush, Vinita Oklahoma

John Eugene Rush, Vinita Oklahoma

Tommy Joe Rush, Vinita Oklahoma

Irene had an 11th grade Education and her religion was Baptist. I always remember Aunt Irene having a smile when we visited and had her arms open for a big hug.

Irene Agnes Yost Rush with family, grandson right and son far right

Wayne Rush Football Vinita High School 1953

Clyde Yost and Wayne Rush

Irene Yost Rush

Irene Yost Rush Age 62

Irene Yost Rush age 80 in 1994

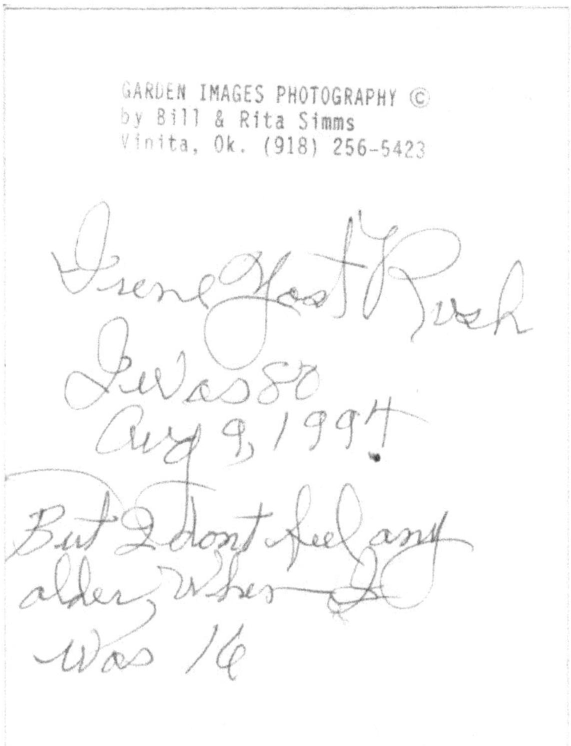

Page 389

> GARDEN IMAGES PHOTOGRAPHY ©
> by Bill & Rita Simms
> Vinita, Ok. (918) 256-5423
>
> Irene Yost Rush
> I was 80
> Aug 9, 1994
> But I dont feel any
> older when I
> was 16

Irene Yost Rush age 80 in 1994 Back of Picture

In Remembrance Of

Irene A. Rush

In Celebration of the Life of

Irene Agnes (Yost) Rush

Entered This Life
August 9, 1914
Neosho, Missouri

Entered Eternal Life
December 9, 2002
Vinita, Oklahoma

Service
First Baptist Church
10:00 A.M., Saturday, December 14, 2002

Officiating
Rev. Henry "Skip" McClain

Music
Marvin McBee

Songs
Sweet Bye & Bye
How Great Thou Art

Pallbearers
J.C. Coombes / Dee Robinson
Lee Hale / Ken Flaming

Interment
Fairview Cemetery
Vinita, Oklahoma

Twenty-third Psalm

The Lord is my Shepard, I shall not want.
He makes me lie down in green pastures;
He leads me beside quiet waters.
He restores my soul;
He guides me in the paths of righteousness
For His name's sake.
Though I walk through the valley of the
Shadow of death, I fear no evil;
For thou art with me;
Thy rod and Thy staff, they comfort me.
Thou dost prepare a table before me
In the presence of my enemies;
Thou hast anointed my head with oil;
My cup overflows.
Surely goodness and loving kindness will follow me
All the days of my life,
And I will dwell in the house of the Lord
Forever.

Irene Agnes Yost Rush
Fairview Cemetery, Vinita, Oklahoma

John Houston Rush

Raymond John and Nora Jane Yost's children
Front Bottom: James, Irene, Beatrice
Middle: Janice, Kathryne
Back: Clyde, Roberta, Leon

NEWTON COUNTY FARMERS HOLD A BASKET SUPPER

The Newton County Balanced Farming Association held a basket supper at the Don Sheppard farm in the Wanda community on June 26. Approximately 60 persons were present and all brought well-filled baskets. After the supper, get acquainted games were played. The following were present:

Mr. and Mrs. Jack Buzzard and family; Mr. and Mrs. Lewis Raines; Mr. and Mrs. J. C. McGhee; Mr. and Mrs. Jim Stone; Mr. and Mrs. Earl Kraft and family; Mr. and Mrs. Frank Kraft; daughter, Mary; Dorothy Spence; Irene Moore; Mrs. Gerald Teagarden and son, Danny; Mrs. Teagarden of Phillipsburg, Kansas; Mr. and Mrs. Doyle Cooper; Mr. and Mrs. R. K. Hailey; Mr. and Mrs. Bob Hailey and son; Mr. and Mrs. Harold Ames; Mr. and Mrs. Mr. and Mrs. G. M. Smith and Charlie Sheppard; Mr. and Mrs. Virgil Burch and son, Jimmie; Mr. and Mrs. Harry Landreth; Jessie Philliber; county agent, Marvin Vines and family; Miss Floy Hood, 4-H Club agent; associate county agent, Lincoln Kerby and wife; Mr. and Mrs. Don Sheppard and children, Nana Jo and Teddy.

Joplin Missouri Globe July 6, 1947

Happy Birthday
(1)
They took my picture at Church a few days ago Oct. 23, 1990
Dear Roberta,
  I think about you a lot, and all my Sisters and Brothers. But all these years we all haven't took time to talk much. So go set down in a chair and read what I say. It's a True Story about me. And now you know I was 76 the 9th Aug 1990. Mama and I were real Close and she told me before I was born a Woman she knew told her to have an Abortion. Mama said No. There a lot people in Mo Close to Bee Yost farm. Where Papa and Mama was living in the Big 2 story house with Grandma and Grandpa Yost and rest the family. Well lot the people had small Pox and some died and they Burned Part the houses where they died. Mama said all the Yost went to Dr and got Vaccinated and didn't take Mama. Then Mama took the small Pox and When I was Borned I was brake out with small Pox. I still have a scar on 1 arm. and at school when I was 10 all kids was Vaccinated + me to on the other arm

(2)

and the Kids all got sick and Clene and Harold and Leon to. But I didnt, and when we got home from school, Mama said I didnt need to be Vacurnated for small Pox Because I'd had it.

Roberta the midWife Mrs Demasters, that took care mama when I was borned Was scared afraid she would take small Pox from me, and went got Vaccinated and didnt take small Pox. Roberta you know by Bible Record I gave you and Janet. Clene Was Born 24th Jan. 1913 And I Was Born 9th Aug, 1914. And when I was setting by Cook stove. It Was Winter, papa Went out side and talked to a man and drank something Mama Was making Bread and meat was frying on stove. Papa came in threw the bread out at door and throwed hot meat and grease all on me. It like to Kill me it hurt so bad. Mama pick up her rolling Pen, and broke end it off on papas head. He sure went out of it then. But I think he was still drunk. That is why our rolling had its end broke off. I quess it burned up in fire out there We lived in Gray Hollar a little ways

(3)

from Dripping Springs, where the lake came up. And people jump off nocked sometimes in to the lake.
Mama had some Mentholatum and put some on. I was burned so bad. It's a wonder I'm not blind today.
Well I grew up with my Sisters and Brothers I loved, and boys had a good time. playing Basket-Ball, Base Ball, going to partys & dances. And since I got married I've played Ball at North Park and South Park here in town. I even played foot-Ball at Celina.
Roberta I knew Grandma Paul folks got the Big Yost farm. And Uncle Clarence told me a little over a year ago the Kraft that got Yost farm build a house right over the well that was in the yard.
Bonnie West told Clarence and I the thrasher house was still there where we lived when Mamas Baby died after the house caught on fire. and Mama drawed water out the well, so that Clene & other people carried the water and put the fire out.
It is a 2 story house. I still wonder where Papa buried the Baby. That is between Leon and Beatrice

(4)

Mama said to me you take Leon and Harold. And I run to the Big Barn I was afried of that fire. But Martha made me came and take care them. While she drawed water out the Well. A few years ago when We Was at Waunita. and Aunt Edith Was there Waunita's girl Janice took Aunt Edith over to Yost farm Where Aunt Edith used to live. And she said flowers Was still growing there, that was there when she was a Kid

One I ask mama Why did you name me Irene — She said there was a family she Knew. Had a girl named Irene And she was good to help take care the rest the Kids.

Irene Yost Rush

Roberta Ing rode trains, But never planes But When I was holding you in back of the wagon with Leon, Beatrice, Maurice, Mildred and Perry. And Mama and Papa sit on the Wagon seat. And that Nash 8 Car hit side wagon and tain't all aff. North 10 mile Corner, We both Went high

March 3, 1988

Dear Roberta,

John & I were so glad you came here with Janice. Both of you look so good. Come & see us anytime. Wayne came not long after you left. He stayed all night and went back to Kansas City about noon Sunday.

Then Mildred came and talk to us and showed us some pictures.

Sunday evening I went to church. There was a lot of people there. I go to the Ball games past time. The Vinita School gives any one over 65 Gold Key ticket free to be used to see foot-Ball or Basket-Ball or any thing going on at school. They gave John & I Gold Key Tickets. Some of the Boys and girls on the Basket-Ball team that I know Mama took care of them, when they were little. And some of the kids Mama and Dad went to school with Johnny & Tommy. You can see I had a picture made for you and copys of Family names in my old Bible you wanted. Janice gave me money to have it done for both of you, and I am sending these other pictures with it. I got a good letter from Perry. He said there was snow up there. It is snowing here to-night. Lots of Love Irene

Harold John Yost, born August 23, 1916, Marcus Yost's Residence Joplin Newton County Missouri; died April 19, 1964, Hockerville Oklahoma buried G.A.R. Cemetery Miami Oklahoma. Harold married Helen Rozella Mitchell on November 11, 1938. She died June 02, 1992. Harold also married Violet Douthitt.

Harold John Yost

Harold John Yost Grand Army of the Republic Cemetery in Miami, Oklahoma

The following is from the transcript of the preliminary hearing for the murderer of Harold John Yost. I believe that in writing this book, everyone needs to know what happened to my Uncle. No matter what different opinion I have heard growing up, of my Uncle Harold, no one deserves what happened to him based on the eyewitness account.

On April 19, 1964, Harold John Yost was murdered by his next door neighbor, Robert Edward Williams in Hockerville, Oklahoma. Seventeen year old eye witness David Edward Johnson's testified at the Preliminary Hearing for Robert Edward Williams on May 19, 1964 before Ottawa County Judge George G. Russell at the Ottawa County Court House on a charge of murder. His testimony is as follows:

Q – David, on or about April the 19th, 1964, you were at Bob Williams house, is that correct?
A – Yes

Q – About what time did you arrive there?
A – Seven thirty or eight – around seven thirty to eight o'clock.

Q – And what, if anything, did you do while there?
A – We loaded up a stove and some pipe to sell it.

Q – And where did you load it?

A – We loaded one next to the house next to his and loaded the pipe right there at his house.

Q – And in what did you load it?
A – In his pick-up

Later in the questioning

Q – Now David, while you were there, did it come to your attention of any trouble involving Mr. Williams' neighbor?
A – Yes

Q – Will you please tell the Court here, David, what that was?
A – They was in it over a fence.

Q – David, what happened there that morning in regard to the trouble?
A – Bob's little girl was coming from her grandma's and Mr. Yost jumped on to her about the fence, and said he was going to shoot his calf, and he sent her back up there and told her to tell him to fix the fence himself because he cut it down, and she come back bawling, and he sent her back up there, and he jumped her again, and she come back and he went up there.

Q – And what did he – you said he sent his daughter back up there David, to tell him something. What was it he told her to tell him?
A – Told him to fix the fence himself.

Q – Were those his exact words David?
A – No, he said to tell the son-of-a-bitch to fix the damn fence himself.

Q – Now then, David, did you leave his house at any time that morning?
A – No

Q – Did you ever get into Mr. Williams' pick-up?
A – Yes, when we started to go sell the pipe. First we started to fix the fence.

Q – Okay, Did you ever see a gun that morning?
A – Yeah, he brought it out of the house just before we started to leave.

Q – This was just – you had already loaded the pick-up truck?
A – Yes

Later in the questioning

Q – Did he make any statement about why he was putting the shot gun in the pick-up truck?
A – I think he said if Mr. Yost started to jump him he was going to shoot him.

Later in the questioning

Q – And what happened then, if you will tell it in your own words please?
A – He got out to fix the fence, and Mr. Yost come out and he called him and asked him why he jumped his girl.

Q – Now, who called who out there?
A – Mr. Williams asked Mr. Yost to come up there.

Q – Okay. What happened then?
A – Mr. Yost come up where he was and Mr. Williams went to the pick-up truck and got his gun and shot him.

Later in the questioning

Q – Then what did Mr. Yost do?
A – He grabbed himself and he went back seven or eight feet and fell.

Q – And then what happened? If anything?
A – Mr. Williams reloaded the gun and shot him again.

Q – How close was he to him then?
A – He had the gun up to his head.

Q – And then what happened David?
A – He went and got in the pick-up truck. He said he had to take the kids home and let me out, and he put the gun in his truck, and he went up to his ma's and he come back and waited for the police.

The final statement of the court on the matter:
It appearing to the Court that the offense of Murder has been committed, and the Court having reason to believe the Defendant, Robert Edward Williams, probably guilty thereof binds him over to the District Court on the 22nd day of May, 1964. The Defendant is remanded to the custody of the Sheriff without bond.

It should be known, that I was told growing up, that several of the Yost brothers went to Harold's widow, and offered to "do away with Mr. Williams." Mrs. Yost declined the offer saying enough bad had happened. She was a kind lady. I think most men who have descended from the Yost's have had the same, "what if thoughts" about their family, particularly their children. My conclusion of what I would have done is this, "if he was already in custody and I couldn't get to him, I would tell the court, you ever let him out, and he will be gone."

Harold John Yost's Grave

Children of Harold John Yost and Helen Rozella Mitchell are:

Nancy Yost born August 17, 1939
Joan Yost

Children of Harold John Yost and Violet Douthitt are:

Harold Yost Family

Harold Yost Family Nora Jane Paul Yost on Right

Harold and Violet daughter Velma and son Gene Yost

Elenore "Dee" Deloris Yost

Elenore Deloris Yost

Elenore Dee Deloris Yost Widger and Bob Widger November 2004

Left Dave Ciano Larry Yost Ciano Leons daughter Bob Widger Deloris Widger Harold Yost daughter

Left Carolyn Moore Mildreds daughter Larry Kaye Leons daughter Deloris Widger Harold daughter

**Kevin, Leslie, Johnathan, Carmen, Megan
Center back is Kathleen Widger McDowell with children**

Hello from Idaho 2006
The Widger Family

Yes it's been awhile since you have heard from us. January and February 2005 we went to Australia to visit Carmen and Chris. They took us to Melbourne, Canberra and all over Sydney, where they lived. We celebrated our 47th anniversary while we were there. Australia is beautiful. In Sydney they have wonderful transportation; you can walk out the front door and catch the bus to the train station. The train will take you to downtown where you can catch any number of boats up the river or across the Bay. You only have to buy one ticket that costs $15 AUS dollar and you can ride all 3.

Sydney is a city of five million people and on any given day there are a million visitors. They come by either flying or by cruise ship. It is a long flight from here but most visitors are flying in from much closer. Our first flight was a total of 16 hours, only about 13 hours from Los Angeles to Sydney.

During March I came down with some type of virus that has had me in and out of the hospital. I also had a heart attack in April. I've not been back to work as the museum gift shop manager since. In August this year we again visited Australia, Leslie came a few days after us due to school. This time it was in Queensland, north of Sydney. The kids live in a little town called Aroona. We went to the Steve Irwin Australia Zoo just after he died. What a place to visit! The employees are so well trained and work with the animals like they are kittens. It's a wonderful zoo, a man's dream that will be continued by his wife and children.

We waited for 24 days for a little girl by the name of Chloe Rose Kovac. She was 8 pounds and 18 ½ inches long. She was due on August 30, but was not born till September 14th in Nambour Queensland, Australia. She will have dual citizenship when all the paper work is done, Australia and USA. We may have to wait a bit for her to visit us as she needs to get a passport for each. It was really hard for us to leave. We had so much fun with Chris as a new daddy and Carmen as the new mommy. They were planning on coming home for a month at Christmas but they had to send back the birth certificate as it was printed wrong so it may not be till middle of next year.

We missed the Yost Family Reunion due to illness. During this year we have lost 4 loved ones, Uncle Paul Douthit – Violet's brother, Uncle Maurice Yost, Aunt Bea Yost Prime, and John Gale – Bob's cousin.

On to happier news, Mike and Kathleen presented us with another baby girl on April 20. Her name is Rowan Dorothy McDowell was born 7 pounds and 10 ounces and 19 ½ inches. She is a loving little blue-eyed red head. So that is 3 for her, her oldest is a boy Quinlan, he is 4 this year and Rhiannon is 2. They are coming home in January for a visit with all the kids. Kathleen and Rowan came to visit in November when I was in the hospital the last time for kidney problems, due to another virus.

Belinda and Carl live in Missouri. I am a great grandma by Cheryl who is 32 this year; she has 2 children a boy Jared and a girl Brittaney. Donald is doing well still working as a chef; he is engaged to be married to Tracy who has 2 children of her own. Elaina has a beautiful little girl named Tympson and is living in Missouri as well.

Angela and Charlie live in Caldwell, Idaho with their 4 children. All the children are in school this year and we don't get to see them that often unless we go to their house. Kevin is almost 16 and is now in high school. Megan is 13 and in junior high, Johnathan will be 11 in April still in grade school. Lindsay started school this year and was so excited she is in the afternoon class. Charlie hauls trailers all over the west coast and Canada. Angela and the kids have gone with him a few times so they get little mini vacations when the kids are not in school.

Leslie is in college currently enrolled at ITT Tech where she is learning how to fix computers and how to create the programs for them. She will graduate in March 2008, so 1 more year of working and studying. She is living with us, which makes for a long drive before she gets home from school.

In 2007 with our health now dictating what and where we go, remember it was the money before. We plan to go visit friends and family from coast to coast, so be ready for a surprise visit. Carmen, Chris and Chloe and maybe Mama will travel with us in the summer. Which means we will need to buy a new van as ours has over 134,000 miles on it. That is our project after Christmas.

We wish everyone a Merry Christmas and a Wonderful New Year.

With our Love
Bob, Eleanor and Leslie

We have changed addresses again so please update your address book. Since we have not been home a lot we got a larger box at the post office. Please do not send anything to the physical address as we have not moved the mail box to other side of road where mail comes from now Thank You.
P.O. Box 116
Murphy, Idaho 83650

(208) 495-2292 is our number if you want to give us a call.

Velma Bertha Yost born October 30, 1945

Harold Eugene "Gene" Yost Jr. born September 25, 1952

Infant Dies.

Miami, Okla., Aug. 30.—Har[old] Yost, jr., infant son of Mr. a[nd] Mrs. Harold Yost, sr., of west M[i]ami, died at 7:30 o'clock Tuesd[ay] night in the Bradshaw hospital [at] Welch, Okla.

Surviving besides the pare[nts] are two sisters, Delores Yost a[nd] Velma Yost both of the home; [the] paternal grandmother, Mrs. N[ora] Yost of Vinita and the mater[nal] grandmother, Mrs. Bertha D[ou]thitt of Treece, Kan.

Harold Eugene "Gene" Yost Junior

Gene Harold Yost, born September 25, 1952 in Pitcher Oklahoma. Died March 24, 2011 at his home in Kent Mart Waskington. Gene Harold Yost married Bonney Lake. They had the following children, Sydney, Ashley, and Danai Yost.

Gene Yost and daughters Sydney 10 Ashley 8 Janai 6 in 1994

Gene Harold Yost Gene Yost died at his home in Kent March 24th. Born in Pitcher, Oklahoma September 25th 1952, Gene moved to Tacoma in 1964 and graduated from Washington High School in 1971. Gene then went to Olympic College and Central Washington University. Gene worked as a logger, commercial fisherman, longshoreman, and teamster in his early years. Later in life he worked in indoor and outdoor sales at Proctor Sales and Harrington Plastics. Gene enjoyed watching Fox News, football, and golf, along with listening to the Beatles, Billy Joel, Johnny Cash, and Lyle Lovett. He was a faithful attendee of his daughter's volleyball games, always wearing his pink and purple MC Hammer pants. His pride and joy was spending time with his mother, daughters, and most of all his grandchildren. Gene was preceded in death by his father Harold and brother Harold Jr. Gene is survived by his mother Violet, daughters Sydney, Ashley, and Danai, their mother Holly, and grandchildren Madalynn, Isabelle, and Wyatt. Gene is also survived by his sisters Dee Widger, Vel Klatt, and Nancy Miller and their families. Gene leaves behind many lifelong friends that treasure the memories of the good times they had. A memorial service will be held at Bethany Lutheran Church, 26418 Mountain Highway East, Spanaway, WA 98387, on Thursday, March 31st, 2011 at 1pm, with a reception to follow. Please make donations to Seattle Children's Hospital.

Gene Yost died at his home in Kent March 25th. Born in Pitcher Oklahoma September 25th 1952, Gene and his mother Violet moved to Parkland to be closer to his older sister Dee after his fathers death. Gene attended Keithley Junior High. Gene and his friends would take the bus downtown for school clothes shopping. Gene was fond of his yellow skip wide-wale cords and his two tone Beatle boots. Gene outgrew that phase and went on to be a standout football player for the first graduating class of Washington High School in 1971. Gene played football for two years at Olympic College before transferring to Central Washington University where he graduated. As a young man, Gene worked for Gildersleeve Logging near Ketchikan Alaska before a career as a shrimp fisherman in Kodiak and later a king crab fisherman in the Bering Sea. He returned to Tacoma, got married and started a family in their home in Bonney Lake. Gene worked for Associated Grocers for many years before leaving to pursue a sales career at Proctor Sales he then moved on to be an outside sales representative for Harrington

Plastics. Gene enjoyed spending time watching Fox News, football and golf, along with listening to Beatles, Billy Joel, Johnny Cash and Lyle Lovett. He was faithful attendee of his daughters volleyball games where you could always spot him in his pink and purple mc hammer pants. His pride and joy was spending time with his mother, daughters and most of all his grandchildren. Gene was preceded in death by his father Harold, and older brother Harold, Jr. Gene is survived by his mother Violet, daughters Sydney, Ashley, and Danai and their mother Holly grandchildren Madalynn, Isabelle and Wyatt. All of western Washington. Gene is also survived by his sisters Dee Widger, Vel Klatt and their families. Gene leaves many lifelong friends that treasure the memories of the good times they had. A funeral service will be held at Bethany Lutheran Chruch 26418 Mountain Highway East Spanaway, WA 98387 on Thursday March 31st 2011 at 1pm with a reception to follow. Interment will be at Bethany Cemetery. Please make a donation in his name to Seattle Childrens Hospital.

Tributes to Gene Harold Yost:

April 15, 2011
I don't know where to begin when talking about how incredible Dad was.. He was one of a kind in every way to say the least! I couldn't begin to put into words how much I miss him and our times we had together!! Reading all of these posts about him puts a smile on my face, seeing those that cared and loved him is truly touching!

Dad your story telling was unlike anyone's I have ever met!! You would give every possible detail to make sure I would get the WHOLE picture! I don't think you ever told a short story (Which I loved!!) We would go for car rides usually rocking out to Bruce Springsteen or Johnny Cash as loud as the car stereo could possibly go! We would watch movies like Jackie Brown and Pulp Fiction while eating steak dinners! I remember whenever My Girl or Shawn Michaels Theme Song came on in either of our cars we would call each other and leave music messages if one of us didn't answer.. And Whenever I did something stupid you were there asking me if I had rocks in my head?!

I miss your stories, our drives together, movie nights, and playing phone tag leaving each other music messages!! I wish we were still adding to those memories and times we had together!! But I am so thankful for ALL of the memories and things you have given to me to remember! I feel lucky to know I have you as my guardian angel always looking out for me and protecting me like you always have!! I love you and miss you DA!!

Love, Nay
~
Danai Yost,
Portland, Oregon

April 09, 2011

We've had some time now after the services to reflect on it all. Very many people have contacted me to say what they appreciated most was how like a family Gene, his Mom Violet, kids and their kids are with so many of us that have shared our lives with them over the decades. Lifelong close friendships I believe are rare, but I count myself lucky to be in one with Gene, Violet and his girls.

I don't consider our friendship to be over. Gene is buried next to my brother Steve and my Mom - like all good family members be. One day, others of us will join them there. Those three are looking down on us all and wanting nothing more than for us to go forward with our lives and to remember the times shared. There are reunions to be had beyond WHS 1971.

Paul mentioned Gene's Dardanelles shirt. Yes, he still had it, along with his sports letters from Keilthley and Washington. But those in the Knecht basement will recall Gene wanted us to be the "Whiporills" Luckily Sharp and I read the definition of Dardanelles from the Webster's. I ask you to do the same, because Dardanelles was an apt description for those young men of Parkland.

See you around Geno - but maybe not too soon.

Love,
Jay
~
Jay Page,
Anchorage, Alaska

March 31, 2011
Gene was always a rough cut diamond with a heart of gold for that we all know, he will be missed by many so sorry for the family and friends.
~
SKIP Fletcher,
Nisqually, Washington
March 31, 2011
My thoughts and prayers go out to you and your family. I am Kenny Lang's sister and he always spoke so highly of Gene. A great friend.
~
Laurel McMahon,
Dublin, California
March 31, 2011
I will really miss Gene. He always made me laugh. We played football together at both Keithley Jr. High and Washington High. Gene was an excellent player and great teammate. Whenever we got together we would rehash the games, discuss ways we could have won and laugh. I loved his wit and sense of humor. I too was looking forward to seeing Gene at this years 40th reunion. Gene was kind, thoughtful and was very proud of his daughters. I will miss him so.
~

Bryan Gaume,
Lakewood, Washington
March 30, 2011
Thank you Gene for sticking up for me when we were kids and for the long conversations that we shared as adults.
Rest in Peace my friend.

~

Sly Boskovich,
Tacoma, Washington
March 30, 2011

My heart and prayers go out to his entire family. I had the honor and pleausre of knowing Gene only for a short while during his tenure at Harrington Industrial Plastics. He was a great man who loved his family and his job and was compasionate in all that his did. I'll miss his smile and his friendship he truly was one of a kind. May God bless the Yost family and lay his hand upon them.

~

Ryan Brumpton,
Everett, Washington

Leon Ralph Yost, born February 13, 1918, Joplin, Missouri; died August 08, 1991, Eugene, Oregon   Buried at Sea by United States Coast Guard. He married Marjorie Anne Powell Nelson. She had one child already, Louis Carl Nelson Yost. Together, Leon and Marjorie "Sally" had one child Larrie Kay Yost:

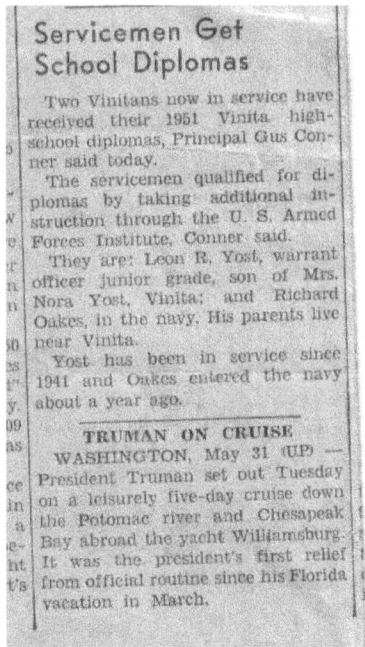

Leon Ralph Yost gets H.S. Diploma

Leon's service to his country and his life during World War II and his military service in the Air Force. While in World War II, he fought in East Indies, Air Offensive Japan, China, Papua, Luzon, New Guinea, Western Pacific, Southern Philippines, Eyukas. His decorations include the Philippine Liberations Ribbon, and Good Conduct Medal.

Leon Ralph Yost

HONORABLE DISCHARGE

1. LAST NAME - FIRST NAME - MIDDLE INITIAL	2. ARMY SERIAL NO.	3. GRADE	4. ARM OR SERVICE	5. COMPONENT
Yost Leon R	19 059 754	M Sgt	AAF	AUS

6. ORGANIZATION	7. DATE OF SEPARATION	8. PLACE OF SEPARATION
63d Bomb Sq (H)	9 Nov 45	Separation Center Ft Leavenworth Kans

9. PERMANENT ADDRESS FOR MAILING PURPOSES	10. DATE OF BIRTH	11. PLACE OF BIRTH
R 2 Vinita Oklahoma	13 Feb 1918	Joplin Mo

12. ADDRESS FROM WHICH EMPLOYMENT WILL BE SOUGHT	13. COLOR EYES	14. COLOR HAIR	15. HEIGHT	16. WEIGHT	17. NO. DEPEND.
See 9	Brown	Brown	5' 7"	169 LBS	0

18. RACE	19. MARITAL STATUS	20. U.S. CITIZEN	21. CIVILIAN OCCUPATION AND NO.
WHITE X	SINGLE X	YES X	Automobile Mechanic 5-81.010

MILITARY HISTORY

22. DATE OF INDUCTION	23. DATE OF ENLISTMENT	24. DATE OF ENTRY INTO ACTIVE SERVICE	25. PLACE OF ENTRY INTO SERVICE
	17 Dec 41	17 Dec 41	Seattle Wash

26. SELECTIVE SERVICE DATA REGISTERED	27. LOCAL S.S. BOARD NO.	28. COUNTY AND STATE	29. HOME ADDRESS AT TIME OF ENTRY INTO SERVICE
YES NO X	Idaho	Idaho	Box 195 Quapaw Ottawa Co Okla

30. MILITARY OCCUPATIONAL SPECIALTY AND NO.	31. MILITARY QUALIFICATION AND DATE
Airplane Maint Tech 750	Carbine Marksman 4 Aug 44

32. BATTLES AND CAMPAIGNS: GO 33 WD 45 East Indies Air Offensive Japan China Papua Luzon New Guinea Western Pacific Southern Philippines Ryukyus

33. DECORATIONS AND CITATIONS: Good Conduct Medal Philippine Liberation Ribbon

34. WOUNDS RECEIVED IN ACTION: None

35. LATEST IMMUNIZATION DATES				36. SERVICE OUTSIDE CONTINENTAL U.S. AND RETURN		
SMALLPOX	TYPHOID	TETANUS	OTHER	DATE OF DEPARTURE	DESTINATION	DATE OF ARRIVAL
1Feb44	8May45	5Aug44		25 Sep 44	APT	16 Oct 44
				21 Oct 45	USA	28 Oct 45

37. TOTAL LENGTH OF SERVICE				38. HIGHEST GRADE HELD
CONTINENTAL SERVICE		FOREIGN SERVICE		
YEARS	MONTHS DAYS	YEARS	MONTHS DAYS	
2	9 19	1	1 4	M Sgt

39. PRIOR SERVICE: None

40. REASON AND AUTHORITY FOR SEPARATION: Convenience of Government RR 1-1 (Demobilization) AR 615-365 15 Dec 44

41. SERVICE SCHOOLS ATTENDED		42. EDUCATION (Years)
Airplane Mech Course Chanute Fld Ill	Sep 42	Grammar 8 High School 0 College 0
B-17 Transition Course AAFTS Amarillo Field Tex	Jul 44	

PAY DATA

43. LONGEVITY FOR PAY PURPOSES	44. MUSTERING OUT PAY		45. SOLDIER DEPOSITS	46. TRAVEL PAY	47. TOTAL AMOUNT, NAME OF DISBURSING OFFICER
YEARS MONTHS DAYS	TOTAL	THIS PAYMENT			4597
3 10 23	$300.00	$100.00	240.00	103.85	957.26 L B WACHS Captain FD

INSURANCE NOTICE

IMPORTANT: IF PREMIUM IS NOT PAID WHEN DUE OR WITHIN THIRTY-ONE DAYS THEREAFTER, INSURANCE WILL LAPSE. MAKE CHECKS OR MONEY ORDERS PAYABLE TO THE TREASURER OF THE U.S. AND FORWARD TO COLLECTIONS SUBDIVISION, VETERANS ADMINISTRATION, WASHINGTON 25, D.C.

48. KIND OF INSURANCE	49. HOW PAID	50. Effective Date of Allotment Discontinuance	51. Date of Next Premium Due (One month after 50)	52. PREMIUM DUE EACH MONTH	53. INTENTION OF VETERAN TO
Nat. Serv. X U.S. Govt. None	Allotment X Direct to V.A.	30 Nov 45	31 Dec 45	$6.70 10 000	Continue Continue Only Discontinue

55. REMARKS: Lapel Button Issued ASR Score (12 May 45) 77
1. Tonsilectomy Jan 43 2. LD yes

57. PERSONNEL OFFICER: D E SLOSSBERG 1st Lt AGD Asst Adjutant

Leon Yost (left) with buddy standing by Ernie Pyle Monument during WWII

In August and September of 2007, Sally Yost was in the Hospital in California. I asked Lou to have Aunt Sally describe how she and Leon had met. The following is his description of her answers.

I talked to Sally about those episodes today and I'll relate the answers in time order.

We know he left home at age 14 with his brother Harold who was 16 because there wasn't enough to eat. That would be in 1932. They hitchhiked and followed the harvest working at that for a while. We don't know when they separated and the next thing we know is that Leon worked at a gold mine in Idaho. It was there that he went swimming in the tailings pond or some such and lost all his hair. He later lost all his teeth in Bermuda due to Gingivitis.

Next thing we know Leon was working in Idaho for International Harvester as an engine mechanic on large equipment when Pearl Harbor was attacked. He immediately got on a bus to Seattle Washington and enlisted in the Army. Here's where it gets strange. At the end of his initial processing he didn't go to basic training (he never really learned to march). Instead, he found himself on the flight line working on aircraft engines. Very soon he was training others to maintain engines and he was promoted to Master Sergeant in slightly less than one year. Amazing. Of course he made Warrant Officer long before the war ended. He stayed in the US on various bases (somewhere in Texas included) almost until the end of the war. He finally got sent overseas to the Philippines so you can see it was truly near the end.

Sally lied about her age and started work at Douglas Aircraft in late 1942 or early 1943 at age 16 in the Long Beach plant where they assembled C-47s for the Army Air Force. That's the military version of the DC-3 and they built 10,000 of them in WWII. At first, her job was to install wiring harnesses in the fuselage, and later she was promoted to testing them during test flights over Long Beach. She worked between 1.5 and 2 years at Douglas altogether.

The really exciting part came soon after she started going on test flights. On the 3rd or 4th flight, the plane caught on fire! It was bad enough that she and 2 other testers had to jump out of the airplane with parachutes. I asked if she jumped or was pushed and she said she jumped. They had turned the plane so that the jumpers landed on the camouflage netting that covered the plant. That's much better than having completely untrained people land on the ground. She said that she bounced and bounced on the netting and hurt her back. Since she was already pregnant with me, I guess I've made a parachute jump! She got home very late that night (she was working swing shift) and found her parents walking the floor. When they asked what delayed her, she told them that she was busy. She didn't fess up until the 1980s.

The three crew members stayed on board until they made sure the plane would go down in the ocean and then they jumped.

Sally went on 8 or 10 more flights afterwards and then quit work because my grandmother didn't think Sally should be pregnant and working. Very soon after that they moved to Bakersfield where I was born.

She met Leon at Travis Army Air Base near Sacramento in the chow line of the NCO club the first time, while still married to Louie, my father, who was in Leon's maintenance squadron and, in fact, worked for Leon. She met Leon again briefly at Travis about a year after she left Louie, but hadn't yet divorced him. She had moved back home to live with her parents in Bakersfield and sometime later, Leon stopped by to see how she was doing while on his way to New Mexico, taking some wings to another base. She didn't say so, but I think he was quite taken with her already and no one in the squadron liked the way Louie had treated her.

Sally's father and older brother got along very well with Leon, and her father really liked that Leon was a mechanic and would go out and work alongside him on his cars.

Leon started coming down on weekends from Travis and they would go on dates for dinner and a movie. He liked me so that was a plus too. One night, he arrived very late, after 11pm, sat down next to her and asked if she would like to go to the Philippines with him. She said, "What kind of girl do you think I am?!" He said, "Well I thought we would get married first." That was her marriage proposal. She accepted, but she was still married to Louie.

The problem was that she was very poor. When she first came back to Bakersfield, she borrowed her father's car and went to Reno to file for divorce, but couldn't meet the residency requirement. After Leon proposed, he took her to Carson City, and gave her enough money to refile and stay in Carson City the required 6 weeks to establish residency. She said she wouldn't have sex with Leon until after they were married. Leon, Sally's parents and I met her in Carson City the day her divorce was granted and after she got the decree they got a license at the courthouse and immediately got married. I was best man and Sally said I thought I was a big man that day. They honeymooned at the Ahwanee hotel in Yosemite. Expensive stuff. I was sent back to Bakersfield with my grandparents. Then Leon got orders to go to Bermuda so he went ahead and Sally and I followed later.

On October 9, 2007, I received the following email from Aunt Sally Yost's son, Louis Carl Nelson Yost, "Sally passed at 8:50am this morning, October 9, 2007. The hospice nurse was with her when it happened and told me the passing was very peaceful.
Lou".
I emailed back Lou the following Prayer for Sally and all of us who knew and loved Sally Yost, "Lou,

I have informed Aunt Birdy and mom, they are passing the word to everyone else. By the Grace of God, Aunt Sally did not suffer. She is now with Uncle Leon in the Glory of Heaven.

May God comfort each of us in this time of sorrow.

I think the best words are from my book as follows:

"Jesus Christ, Lord of the living and dead: with each generation your body of believers grows and grows. Thank you for all who have gone before us, for what they achieved and what they learned. Give us strength to do your will to be your body now. Amen."

Tim C. Stadler

Left to Right: Sally, Larrie Kay, Louis Carl Nelson, Leon Yost

Leon holding his father's pipe and equipment presented by his brothers and sisters

Leon Yost with William Herman Haff, Roberta Ruth Yost's husband in Sand Springs, Ok

Leon and Sally Yost

Kathryn Johanna Yost Gardner, Jim Gardner, Roberta Ruth Yost Haff, Leon Ralph Yost, Marjorie Anne Powell Nelson Yost

Children of Leon Ralph Yost and Marjorie Anne Powell Nelson:
Larrie Kay Yost born August 24, 1950 in St. Georges, Bermuda. Larrie Kay married David Anthony Ciano born May 03, 1945 in Los Angeles California.

Larrie Kay Yost

Larrie Kay Yost Ciano daughter of Leon Ralph Yost and Marjorie Anne Powell

Larrie Kay Yost Ciano beside her fathers grave stone she purchased

**Kathryn Yost Gardner, Larrie Kay Yost Ciano, Carolyn Moore Monfort
August 20, 2006**

Front: Waydene Moore, Dave Ciano Vicki Moore
Back: Ed Prine, Jess Moore, Larrie Kay Yost Ciano, Johnny Moore

Kathryn Yost Gardner, Larrie Kay Yost Ciano, Dave Ciano, Jim Gardner

Larrie Kay Yost Ciano and Dave Ciano had one child, Roger David Ciano born June 01, 1976 in San Luis Obisto, California. Roger David Ciano married Catherina Ching Fu on May 15, 2004.

Catherina Ching Fu and Roger David Ciano
May 15, 2004

Dave Ciano, Catherina Ching Fu Ciano, Roger David Ciano, Larrie Kay Yost Ciano

Beatrice "Bea" Viola Yost, born December 11, 1920, Quapaw, Oklahoma; died November 27, 2006, Vinita, Oklahoma. She married Edgar Prine born April 26, 1922 in Cleora Oklahoma, died June 29, 2009 in Bluejacket, Oklahoma. Beatrice Viola Yost Prine and Edgar Prine had the following children, Judy Ann Prine born February 05, 1942, Linda Sue Prine born December 16, 1945, Deborah Jo Prine born September 19, 1952.

How Edgar Prine and Beatrice Viola Yost met:

Uncle Ed Prine, in 1938, took neighbor lady out to rodeo, Uncle Ed saw Aunt Bea, asked who she was, but you didn't see her for another year. At age 16 Uncle Ed says Aunt Bea again at the school. At age 17, Uncle Ed would pay Palmer Smith to drive them all to the movie on Saturday, he would pay for everyone's, movie and dinner. They would then go to the Grand Café by the Post Office in Vinita. Aunt Bea was 19 years old at the time.

It should be known by one and all, that the description of "Uncle Ed" was best described by Ken Omazawa. Ken's parents owned the land that Ed's home was on for years. I met Ken at William's company in Tulsa, and when talking we realized that we both use to go up and see Ed as young children growing up. Ken was no relationship to the Yost's but his words fit "Uncle Ed" so perfect when he said, "Ed Prine is a man's man."

On June 29, 2009, I received word that Uncle Ed had passed on to heaven to be with his with his wife, my Aunt Bea. Uncle Ed was found in his horse barn. His daughters used to tell him that they would find him passed away in his horse barn because he was always there taking care of his horses he loved so much. I learned to ride a horse at that horse barn. My boys and me used to always visit that horse barn and Uncle Ed's horses. Uncle Ed was a indeed, "A man's man." Uncle Ed passed on to heaven as every Cowboy Rancher should, at the ripe old age of 86 and with "his boots on". Ranchers like Uncle Ed made the State of Oklahoma as Great as it is. Uncle Ed will be missed very much by us all.

A little insight on Uncle Ed for the Yosts, when his beloved wife became ill, he made absolutely sure she was taken care of, she was a Yost. He used to tell me on the phone just how much the doctors, the nursing cost. He would make it clear. He did not care. He used to talk about how my Aunt Bea would ask him when she could go home. I could tell in my heart how much it hurt him to not be able to take her home. I used to tell him, from the Yost perspective; he did exactly what I would do. He did his part, he did what every man should do. My Aunt Bea needed to be in a nursing home to be taken care of. My Uncle Ed was a "Man's man".

I am sure that the rest of Uncle Ed and Aunt Bea's nephews and nieces would agree, one the greatest times we had growing up was our visit's to Uncle Ed's farm to see the horses, chickens, and cattle. Seeing Aunt Bea ring a chickens head off for dinner, and the trip to his pond where we would catch a fish every time. Were all times at that time great. Well, me and my brother took a switching from Aunt Bea when we were in front of the house throwing rocks at each other. Did we deserve it. Absolutely. Did it teach us a life lesson on how to behave and treat each other, you better believe it.

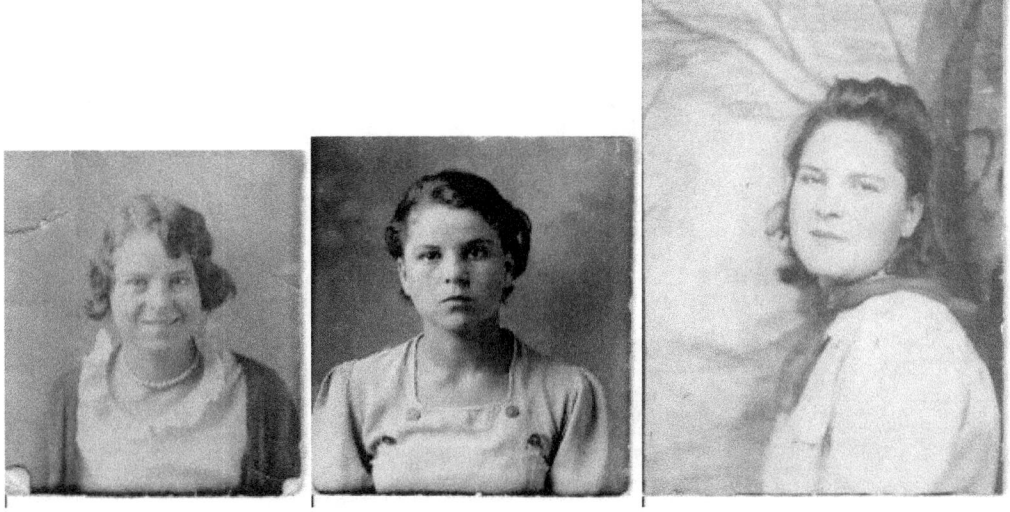

Beatrice Yost age 13   **Age 14**   **High School**

Bea and Mildred Yost in Cleora Oklahoma

Ed and Bea Prine a week after wedding

Judy, Beatrice, Deborah, and Linda Prine

Judy, Bea, Ed, Deborah, Linda Prine

Ed and Bea Prine

Back: Edgar Prine, Beatrice Yost Prine, Nora Jane Paul Yost, Janice Clara Yost Stadler
Front: Alice Gertrude "Trudy" Stadler, unknown, Anthony Edward "Tony" Stadler

**Front Left Marissa Doggett, Edgar W. Prine, Beatrice Yost Prine, Janet Spaulding
Middle Row Deborah Jo Horn, Judy Prine, Jerry Spaulding, Darin Shope, Angela Spaulding, Jerry Todd Spaulding
Back Row Will Doggett, Linda Brown, Lowell Brown, Charlie Diaz, Marcia Diaz
May 1989**

Beatrice Mildred Roberta Janice Yost

Leon Yost, Beatrice Yost, Kathryn Yost, Roberta Yost, James Yost, Mildred Yost, Maurice Yost at Roberta Yost Haff's home in Sand Springs Oklahoma

Beatrice Yost Prine, Tim, Steven, Janice, Brian Stadler at Nora Clara Paul Yost's Grave in Vinita

Debbie, Ed, Will (Ed's Grandson)

**Brian Tim Steven Stadler Mildred Yost Moore Beatrice Yost Prine Irene Yost Rush
1997**

Psalm 100
Make a joyful noise unto the Lord,
All ye lands.

Serve the Lord with gladness: come before his presence with singing.

Know ye that the Lord he is God: it is he that hath made us, and not we ourselves; we are his people, and the sheep of his pasture.

Enter into his gates with thanksgiving, and into his courts with praise: be thankful unto him, and bless his name.

For the Lord is good; his mercy is everlasting; and his truth endureth to all generations.

In Memory Of
Beatrice "Bee" Viola Prine
December 11, 1920
November 27, 2006

Funeral Service
Friday – 2:00 p.m.
December 1, 2006
First Baptist Church of Welch

Officiating
Pastor C. G. Gilmore

Congregational Music
"The Solid Rock" - #406
"Faith Is The Victory" - #413
"It Is Well With My Soul" - #410
Accompanist – Randy Henry

Casket Bearers
Marvin Coats, John Barnes, Allen Hency
Duane Tucker, Dewey Tucker, Jim Hext

Honorary Bearers
Pat Campbell, Jeff, Jimmy & Jamie Williams

Final Resting Place
Pheasant Hill Cemetery
Vinita, Oklahoma

Luginbuel Funeral Home
Vinita, Oklahoma
www.honoringmemories.com

Beatrice "Bee" Viola Yost Prine

Children of Edgar Prine and Beatrice Viola Yost are:

Judy Ann Prine born February 05, 1942 in Vinita Oklahoma, married Jerry Spaulding born December 26, 1941 in Vinita Oklahoma. They were married May 27, 1960 in Vinita Oklahoma.

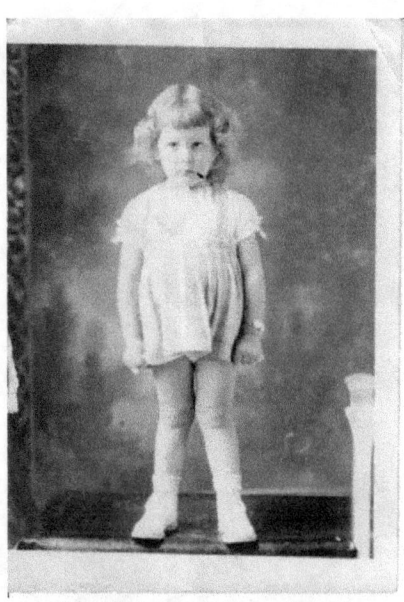

Judy Ann Prine Age 3

Judy Ann Prine and Deborah Sue Prine

Children of Judy Ann Prine Spaulding and Jerry Spaulding are:

Marcia Spaulding born October 24, 1961 in Okmulgee, Oklahoma. Marcia married John Charles Diaz. They had the following children:

Robin Allison born April 16, 1991 in Houston Texas.

Robin Allison Diaz

Robin Diaz Sophomore Attendant

Todd Spaulding born April 25, 1963 in Miami, Oklahoma, married Janet Lori Townsend born May 1, 1962. They had the following children:
   Angela Lori Spaulding born July 1, 1988 in Wellington, Kansas.

Mellisa Spaulding born February 05, 1967 in Pittsburg, Kansas. Mellisa married Darin Lee Shope, born October 23, 1962. They had the following children:
   Tyler Isaac Shope born June 7, 1991 in Joplin, Missouri
   Jordan David Shope born March 16, 1994 in Joplin, Missouri
   William McGee Shope born August 20, 1997 in Joplin, Missouri

Linda Sue Prine born December 16, 1945 in Vinita Oklahoma, married Robert Lee Wright born January 7, 1938 married March 29, 1968 Stillwater.   Then married Lowell Clark Brown born June 11, 1940. They were married April 11, 1980 in Oklahoma City, Oklahoma.

Linda Sue Prine

Deborah Jo Prine born September 19, 1952 in Vinita Oklahoma, married John Otis Doggett July 4th, married in Miami, Oklahoma.

Children of Deborah Jo Prine Doggett and John Otis Doggett are:

John "Will" Wilton Doggett born May 17, 1974 in Tahlequah, Oklahoma, married Joy Williams born January 1, 1975.

Marissa Prine Doggett born April 3, 1977 in Tahlequah, Oklahoma.

Marissa Prine Doggett High School Graduation

Maurice "Morris" Ray Yost, born October 15, 1922, Ketchum, Oklahoma; died September 06, 2006, Pryor, Oklahoma   Military Funeral buried Spavinaw-Strang Cemetery. "Morris" married Fern Paul. Fern Paul was born July 26, 1936 in Strang Oklahoma. Fern died July 25, 2004.

Fern L. (Paul) Yost in Spavinaw-Strang Cemetery

Maurice Ray Yost and Fern L. Paul Yost had the following children; Grant Yost, Susie Yost, and Wiatt Yost, Joe Yost:

Wyatt Ernie Yost born June 16, 1957 in Pryor Oklahoma

Name:	Wyatt E Yost
Birth Date:	16 Jun 1957
Address:	Spav Ck Brdg Spr Pm, Spavinaw, OK, 74366
Name:	Wyatt E Yost
Birth Date:	16 Jun 1957

Maurice Grant Yost born December 28, 1958 Pryor Oklahoma

Joseph Paul Yost born in August 1961 in Pryor Oklahoma. Joseph died in a mini-bike accident in October 1971.

Joseph Paul Yost in Spavinaw-Strang Cemetery

Growing up with my mother being the sister of Joseph's dad, after he was killed in the mini-bike accident we were forbidden from owning, riding, or touching a motorcycle. I remember mom telling me the reason was we had a cousin who was killed riding his mini-bike on a country dirt road and hit by a drunk driver.

V. Sue "Sue" Yost born October 8, 1962 in Pryor Oklahoma, married Daniel Morgan Davis born August 14, 1957, died march 10, 1996. Sue and Daniel were married on November 23, 1983.

Sue Yost Davis and Daniel Morgan Davis had the following children:

Marc Daniel Davis born October 27, 1986 in Midwest City Oklahoma

Matthew Morgan Davis born February 14, 1991 in Midwest City Oklahoma

Son Marc Daniel Davis, mom Sue Yost Davis, Matthew Morgan Davis

Johnny Keith Yost born October 29, 1970 in Pryor Oklahoma. Johnny married Missy Trundle born June 15, 1968.

Johnny and Missy had the following children:

Tyler Yost born October 30, 1990 in Claremore Oklahoma.

Maurice Ray Yost – World War II hero

Morris served in the 3rd Army during World War II where he landed at Normandy. He then fought in the Battle of Bulge. Johnny Lee Moore talked to Maurice one time about his war experience. Maurice told Johnny he was the head of his company in Germany going down a dry creek bed. Maurice was point man. He went around curve about 110 yards ahead of every one else. As he rounded the corner, he found he was facing a machine gun nest. German gun cut loose on Maurice. He started running backwards zig zagging through the rocks. All of a sudden he took a thirty foot step. A German round had hit the bottom of his left foot gone through the ball of his foot and blew off his big toe. Maurice said, "When I hit the ground I was still running, ran around curve out of the line of fire." All of Maurice's service records were burned up in the Kansas City Military Storage record fire of 1973. However, using the records that were still in existence at the Veteran's Hospital in Muskogee, his War Medals were able to be obtained. They are as follows:

The 3rd Army in World War II

General Patton said to the 3rd Army, "I've been given command of the Third Army for reasons which will become clear later on (he was referring to Operation Overlord, the code name for the D-Day invasion on the Normandy beaches). I'm here because of the confidence of two men; the President of the United States and the Theater Commander. They have confidence in me because they don't believe a lot of lies that have been printed about me and also because they know I mean business when I fight. I don't fight for fun and I won't tolerate anyone on my staff who does."

"You're here to fight. Ahead of you lies battle. That means one thing. You can't afford to be a fool, because in battle fools mean dead men. It's inevitable for men to be killed and wounded in battle. But, there's no reason why such losses should be increased because of the incompetence and carelessness of some stupid S.O.B. I don't tolerate such men on my staff."

"We're here because some crazy Germans decided they were supermen and that they had a right to rule the world. They've been pushing people around all over the world, looting, killing, and abusing millions of innocent men, women, and children. They were getting ready to do the same thing to us. We have to fight to protect ourselves."

"Another reason we're here is to defeat and wipe out the Nazis who started all of this trouble. If you don't like to fight, I don't want you around. You had better get out before I kick you out. There's one thing you have to remember. In war, it takes more than the desire to fight to win. You've got to have more than guts to lick the enemy. You also must have brains. It takes brains and guts to win wars. A man with guts but no brains is only half a soldier. We whipped the Germans in Africa and Sicily because we had brains as well as guts. We're going to lick them in Europe for that same reason."

"That's all. Good luck."

Third Army's battle record began on August 1st, 1944 at 1200 hours. That was when the Third Army was officially operational as a combat army.

In nine months and eight days of fighting, the Third Army compiled a great record. Not only did the Third Army astonish the world, but it's deeds, in terms of statistics, challenged the imagination. The Third Army gave a new meaning to fluid warfare. The Third had only one general order from Patton; "Seek out the enemy, trap him, and destroy him."

The Germans never knew what to expect from Patton. His methods of operation were very different from British General Montgomery and the more conventional American generals. Patton's Third Army tore open the German lines of defense and trapped thousands of German soldiers. Most of them were either killed or they surrendered.

The history of the Third Army is a story of constant attack. They drove on in fair weather or foul, across favorable terrain or across mud, ice, and snow.

The soldiers in the Third Army knew the value of teamwork. Aircraft and artillery teamed with infantry and armor to a perfection that amazed not only the enemy but other Allied Armies. The XIX Tactical Air Command's bombing and air cover, coupled with the Artillery's timed, precision barrages, wrecked all enemy hopes to profit by American inexperience.

The Third Army was an army on wheels. Thousands of trucks driven by soldiers who called themselves the Red Ball Express carried tons of supplies to the army to keep it fighting and on the move. The Red Ball Express also set up special convoys that carried nothing but gasoline just to keep Patton's tanks rolling toward Germany.

One of the Third Army's greatest assets was American ingenuity. American soldiers were creating new instruments of war on the spot to overcome new problems encountered day after day.

Third Army had an excellent command structure. Each level of command had a special job and each did the best job they could. The planners who told the soldiers what to do also made every effort to help them do it.

Of course, a war cannot be won without hard fighting and personal courage. The Third Army had more than its share of courageous front-line fighting men; infantry, tankers, tank destroyers, engineers, all of them were soldiers who met every new challenge with courage and endless endurance.

Not all soldiers were part of combat teams, though. Many important jobs were done by administrative soldiers. It was these soldiers who backed up the front-line soldier, making sure he had the tools he needed to fight; food, weapons, ammunition, gasoline, and clothing. As General Patton once said, "No matter how small your job might seem, it's important in the vast scheme of things. Every job is important."

It was this type of teamwork which enabled each single squad to capture and hold a piece of ground taken from the enemy.

In terms of speed of advance, in amount of ground liberated or captured, and in terms of losses inflicted upon a powerful enemy there was never before anything like the Third Army's lightning quick sweep across France.

Breakout

After Lieutenant General Courtney H. Hodges' First Army punched a hole in the German defenses at a French town called St. Lo, the Third Army began roaring through the hole with their Sherman tanks. They began an attacking advance that moved in every direction on the compass; north, south, east, and west, all at the same time. There was no stopping them once they got started.

They went east toward Le Mans, south and southwest through Laval, west toward Brest, and north toward St. Malo.

Third Army was not a defensive army. General Patton didn't believe in defensive tactics, he believed in attacking. He often told his soldiers, "When in doubt, attack." They knew that to defeat the Germans, they had to be on the offensive at all times. Like a boxer, they understood that once you got your opponent on the ropes, you had to keep at him until he went down. You couldn't let up and give him a chance to rest.

The soldiers of the Third Army took the fight to the enemy. They swept over the Brittany Peninsula before the enemy knew what was happening. Two tank columns of the Sixth Armored Division, commanded by Major General R.W. Grow, forced the Germans to withdraw into the fortified ports of St. Malo, Lorient, St. Nazaire, and Brest.

Threatened with a severed supply line where it narrowed to a ten mile wide strip at Avranches, the soldiers of the Third Army delivered those needed supplies despite nightly air attacks. At the same time they repulsed a vicious German counter-attack at Mortain.

Facing complete encirclement, the Germans quickly withdrew to the east. Although the Third Army had almost surrounded the German Seventh Army, they were not allowed to close a gap that existed between the towns of Argentan and Falaise. They were told to wait and let General Bernard L. Montgomery close the gap with his British Second Army.

Montgomery moved too slowly. He failed to close the gap until almost a week later. Because of this the Germans were able to continue their retreat from this pocket and they managed to save a large portion of their armor. They did, however, suffer a great loss of men and materials.

This Argentan-Falaise Pocket later became a very controversial issue. Many people claimed that the Third Army could have closed the gap themselves and they could have destroyed the complete German Seventh Army. If this had happened, the war might have been won much sooner than it was.

The Germans desperately raced toward the Seine River while being chased by the Third Army's spearhead units. Fearing a second encirclement west of the Seine River, the Germans fought to save their dwindling escape routes. All during their escape, they were hit with a never ending barrage of air and artillery bombardment which took a fearful toll of their lives and material.

In Pursuit

With their fast moving armored columns racing toward Paris and to the northeast of the French capital, the Third Army had to give up control of the XV Corps commanded by Lieutenant General Wade H. Haislip. Along with the Corps, the Third Army relinquished the Corps area to command of First Army. Always on the move, the Third Army continued to advance to the south, southeast, and southwest of Paris while continuing to fight.

The enemy was under continuous attack by both the Third Army's infantry and tank forces and Brigadier General O.P. Weyland's XIX Tactical Air Command's fighter-bombers. At this point, the enemy lost all hope of regaining the initiative.

The speed of the Third Army's advance forced the Germans to break into a hap-hazard, hasty retreat. The Third Army gave the Germans no time to occupy any natural defense lines or strong-points. It just kept punching it's way toward victory.

The German's retreat continued until only the Moselle River and the German built Siegfried Line lay between the Third Army and German soil. As the month of August drew near to a close, there was much evidence that the Third would have to actually slow down it's advance so that the other Allied armies could catch up with them.

Amazingly, despite shattered communications and huge losses, the Germans had not collapsed. They remained to be good soldiers and hard fighting professionals.

Out Of Gas

In September 1944, General Eisenhower decided to let British General Montgomery put together a massive attack called Operation Market Garden. Because of this, a large part of all available supplies were diverted to the British Second Army. This included supplies that should have gone to the Third Army.

Eisenhower's decision created a shortage of gasoline and other necessary supplies that were badly needed by the Third Army to keep up its fast-paced advance. Without these supplies the Third Army was forced to slow down and finally to halt its rapid advance.

This was another decision made by Eisenhower and his officers at SHAEF (Supreme Headquarters Allied Expeditionary Force) that would become very controversial later. Many people thought, and still think, that if the Third Army had not been stopped when it was, it might have been able to bring the war to a close by the end of 1944, instead of the middle of 1945.

One thing was for certain; General Montgomery's plan was a failure. It not only failed to encircle and trap the Germans, it also failed in that it lost and wasted thousands of tons of supplies that could have been used by other armies (especially the Third Army) to continue their successful attacks. Because none of the plans were accomplished, it was also a waste of many soldier's lives. Lastly, it caused unnecessary destruction in the Netherlands. After it was all over, Prince Bernard of the Netherlands said, "My country can never again afford the luxury of another Montgomery success."

Since the Germans opposing General Patton's soldiers were not stupid, they were took full advantage of the opportunity given to them by Eisenhower's orders to stop the Third Army.

Without the Third Army chasing them, destroying their equipment, and killing them, German soldiers now had enough time to reinforce their battle lines with hastily reorganized units. The reorganization included non-battle tested, untrained troops who had never before performed non-combatant duties.

The Germans dug in and entrenched themselves in a frantic effort to stabilize their front lines. One counter attack followed another as the Germans sought to gain valuable time to strengthen the favorable terrain with fortifications. Even with all of their efforts, however, they failed to stop the Third Army from forcing the line of the Moselle River.

Helped by the greatest possible use of artillery, Third Army units pushed across the Meurthe River and then established important bridgeheads across the Moselle River. Progress was slow and costly because of the shortage of supplies, but at least it was positive. Even though the Third Army wasn't gaining ground at the speed it had been just weeks before, at least they weren't losing ground. Some terrible and vicious battles were fought along the Moselle River as the Third Army battled to break through the outer defenses of the city of Metz.

Even though German losses in personnel and materiel were high they did manage to firm up their front lines after the Third Army was ordered to hold it's positions. During this period there was not only a shortage of gasoline, but also a shortage of ammunition.

As usual, the Third Army refused to waste their time by doing nothing. As General Patton often told them, "There's always something you can do. There's never any excuse for being lazy." Bridgeheads over the Moselle River were improved so that when they got their badly needed supplies they would be ready to immediately start their offensive again.

Although the Third Army was expected to do nothing but patrol their lines during Operation Market-Garden, they always patrolled aggressively. This was one of General Patton's terms for a lot of small attacks. This aggressive patrolling kept the soldiers sharp and kept the Third Army moving forward.

Third Army continued to build up supplies, ammunition, and much needed winter clothing. This forced rest period and buildup continued through October and the first week of November.

Metz and Mud

Finally, on November 8th, the waiting was over. The Third Army once again had been given a green light from Eisenhower. That is just what Patton and his soldiers had been waiting for. The soldiers of the Third Army knew that, as Patton had told them, "The road home is through Berlin." After their long delay, they started their first big fight by attacking the German city of Metz.

Patton had gone through the ordeal of a trench war in World War One. He knew how bad the effects of a stalemate could be. It was exactly that type of trench warfare he wanted to avoid with his rapid, motorized war of continual advance. "Never let the enemy rest," he told his men, "once you have them on the run, keep them on the run."

Major General Walton H. Walker, commander of the XX Corps, and Major General Manton S. Eddy, commander of the XII Corps, managed to establish bridgeheads across the Saar River because of bold attacks. Both of these generals knew how important it is to surprise the enemy so they started battles during weather so bad the Germans didn't think it was possible to attack.

As usual, because of their boldness, the Third Army achieved a tactical surprise. They were becoming famous for being able to do the impossible.

During these attacks, heavy rains left the terrain muddy and the rivers at a record flood level. These conditions called for more than average performance by the bridge building engineers.

The wet and cold weather caused a trenchfoot epidemic among Third Army troops, but a program of individual foot care was ordered personally by General Patton. This lowered the casualty rate and broke the epidemic.

The severe weather helped the Germans to prevent a complete breakthrough, but they still had to withdraw into Germany and take defensive positions behind the Siegfried Line. In spite of fanatic German resistance, Metz was captured for the first time since 451 A.D. The Third Army entered the city on November 18th after it was completely encircled.

The Battle of the Bulge

After capturing Metz, General Patton ordered a powerful drive into the Siegfried Line, which he called, "A monument to the stupidity of mankind." Using this attack, he planned on fighting its way into the coal mining region of Germany. The Third Army was forced to give up this attack because of a problem that developed in the First Army's area to the north.

German General Von Rundstedt started an attack against the First Army's VII and VIII Corps on the 16th of December. Von Rundstedt's forces hit quickly and gained the element of surprise. Because of this, his soldiers were making excellent progress.

Eisenhower and his staff at SHAEF began to worry that they had underestimated the ability of the Germans. They feared that the Germans might be able to use this massive offensive to go to the north and west to capture the cities of Liege and Antwerp.

Liege was extremely important because the Allies had large supply dumps there. If the Germans managed to seize those supplies, they could possibly push the Allies back to the coastline, causing them to lose all the ground they had gained.

Antwerp was important because it was a port city. If captured, the Germans could use it to bring in badly needed supplies.

At a special meeting of all the highest ranking generals in the American, British, and Canadian armies, it was decided that the toughest job would go to General Patton and his

Third Army. They would have to relieve the soldiers who had been surrounded by the Germans at the Belgian city of Bastogne.

After the meeting, Eisenhower, who had just been promoted to the five-star rank of General of the Army, was talking with General Patton. He remarked, "George, every time I get promoted I get attacked." Patton shot back with the comment, "And every time you get attacked, I pull you out!"

The 101st Airborne Division, commanded by Major General Maxwell D. Taylor, was holding out and fighting off the fierce attempts by the Germans to overrun Bastogne.

The Third Army had to stop a full scale attack they had started to the east, pull back the entire army, swing around ninety degrees to the north, and then begin another full scale attack on the southern flank of the German forces. Nothing like that had ever been done in the history of warfare. Everyone thought it was impossible except General Patton. He knew his men could do the impossible.

It only took three days for the Third army to perform that massive maneuver. Today, military historians readily admit that only Patton's Third Army could have accomplished a maneuver like that and make it look easy. Patton always demanded more from his soldiers than other commanders did and they never let him down.

One of the reasons the Third Army performed so well is because they expected the German attack. While Eisenhower and his friends were playing cards in London and the First Army turned part of their area into a R & R (Rest and Recuperation) area, Patton's intelligence officers were hard at work.

The events leading up to the Battle of the Bulge have, like the Falaise Gap and Operation Market-Garden, become controversial issues. Many people believe that Eisenhower's staff at SHAEF made poor decisions when they ignored Third Army reports about a possible German offensive in the Ardennes.

Colonel Oscar Koch, head of Third Army's G-2 Intelligence department, had sent intelligence reports warning SHAEF that the Germans were probably planning a major attack against the First Army's R&R area. His report was ignored. They refused to believe the Germans could collect the mass of weapons, men, and material to launch a large attack. It was a classic case of under-estimating the enemy. At Colonel Koch's suggestion, General Patton gave the order for his staff to design two separate plans in the event of a German attack. General Patton believed Colonel Koch and considered him to be the best G-2 in the European Theater of Operations.

When Patton attended the meeting with the other Allied commanders he told them he could attack in two days with at least two divisions. Everyone thought he was crazy, but he told them that he had already set plans in motion before he left his headquarters. All he had to was place a phone call. When it was finally decided that he should attack as soon as possible, he phoned his headquarters and said, "Nickel." The attack was on.

The General never returned to his headquarters. Instead, he and his driver, Sergeant Mims, began traveling along the roads where he knew he would meet his soldiers heading north. He gave orders on the spot and told everyone he met to head north and kill Germans. Sergeant Mims once said to Patton, "General, the army is wasting a lot of money on your staff officers. You and I can run the whole war from your jeep."

While watching his men heading toward the Germans surrounding Bastogne, he said, "No other army in the world could do this. No other soldiers could do what these men are doing. By God, I'm proud of them."

On the 26th of December a 4th Armored Division Task Force, commanded by Major General H.J. Gaffey, made contact with the soldiers at Bastogne.

By this time, urgently needed snow camouflage for both troops and vehicles was being quickly supplied. Because of the problem of tanks slipping on the icy terrain, supply troops had installed special cleats on the treads of the tanks, much like the cleats on athlete's shoes.

The Germans threw everything they had into the attack against Bastogne. It was their last chance against the Allies. They made every attempt to smash and close the corridor the 4th Armored Division had opened to Bastogne. When failure was certain they began to withdraw their armor behind the Siegfried line for the second and final time. Badly hurt by the beating they had taken, the Germans used what was left of their infantry to screen their movements.

Although they were handicapped by bitterly cold weather, ice, and snow, the Third Army continued it's pressure on the south flank of the enemy penetration. By the end of December, the enemy had succeeded in saving what armor had not been destroyed. The bulge slowly became a wedge and the wedge finally disappeared. Finally, another bulge appeared except this time it was on the German side of the front lines.

Officially, on the 28th of January, the Battle of the Bulge was over and Von Rundstedt's Ardennes Offensive (as the Germans called it) had lost all of the ground that it had originally won. The enemy was now completely pushed back into German territory.

The soldiers of the First Army had fought gallantly and bravely throughout the entire Battle of the Bulge. Although they were to be commended for their courage and fighting ability, the truth is that they would have lost the battle without the help of the Third Army.

It was General Patton's Third Army that performed the most crucial role in stopping the Germans. Without their quick and decisive maneuver and attack, the Battle of the Bulge would have been a massive disaster for the Allies.

What cannot be understood was General Eisenhower's attitude toward General Patton and the Third Army. General Bradley, 12th Army Group Commander, and General Hodges,

First Army commander, received Distinguished Service Medals for their poor leadership. It was also partly due to their lack of discipline among their soldiers that the Germans were able to get so far in their attack. Yet, General Patton, whose Third Army was mostly responsible for saving they day, was never even thanked by Eisenhower.

Patton, however, didn't have time to worry about such small things. He was getting ready for another drive into Germany. After The Bulge became history, the Third Army began a powerful advance to the Kyll River. It was during this advance that the Third Army captured the German city of Trier.

The Beginning Of The End

There's a funny story about the capture of Trier that shows the differences between General Patton and General Bradley and their ability to judge a military situation. After the battle was already won and the Third Army had taken the city, General Patton received a message from General Bradley. The message said, "Bypass Trier. It would take too many divisions to capture it." Patton's humorous reply to Bradley was, "Have already taken city, do you want me to give it back?"

By this time, Germany's manpower problem was becoming very evident to the Allies. All units of the Third Army was meeting great numbers of rear echelon German troops. Among these were many Volkssturm (German militia) troops.

After their defeat at Bastogne, the Germans were now totally incapable of stopping the Third Army in it's sweep across the Rhine River. Parts of eleven German divisions were trapped between the Third Army in the south and the First Army in the north. They were being chopped to pieces with only a very few of them managing to escape. The enemy was all but whipped and they knew it. They were becoming more demoralized as each day passed.

By driving quickly to the Rhine River, the Third Army exposed the enemy's right flank. This created the opportunity for Patton's men to reopen a devastating war of movement for the first time since the fighting they had done in France. This was Patton's favorite kind of war. He liked to hit hard and fast. He never stopped to regroup his forces the way General Montgomery did with his British 2nd Army.

After crossing the Moselle River south of Koblenz, Third Army's 4th Armored Division ripped across the enemy's rear. They were followed closely by XII Corps Infantry units who did the mopping up. Shortly afterwards, XX Corps armored units plunged through the Siegfried Line and they, too, raced toward the Rhine River. When the XX Corps linked up with the XII Corps units, they had trapped the remaining Germans in the Hunsruck Mountains.

While the Third Army was busy cleaning out the Hunsruck Mountains, the American Seventh Army, commanded by Lieutenant General Alexander Patch, attacked to their north through the Siegfried Line. There was no safe place for the Germans and there was no place for them to hide.

By now, the Germans were panic-stricken. They tried, but failed, to hold a line of defense against the Third Army's unstoppable armor west of Mainz and Mannheim.

Third Army's 4th Armored Division penetrated deeply into Germany territory and into the Seventh Army's zone of operations. Major General W.H.H. Morris' 10th Armored Division and Major General R.R. Allen's 12th Armored Division pushed the enemy eastward toward the Rhine.

The German withdrawal was completely disorganized and confused. It was quickly becoming a complete rout. The enemy was making a mad dash for the city of Speyer. It was the only city they could get to that still had an open crossing to the Rhine River.

During this period, the enemy lost the greater part of two entire armies. They were chopped to pieces by the powerful armor rushing on him from three different directions.

From the air, the XIX Tactical Air Command, commanded by General O.P. (Opie) Weyland, attacked the Germans relentlessly with their P-47 and P-51 fighter-bombers. On the ground, they were pursued closely by Third Army infantry. In addition to losing a large part of two armies, more than 81,000 German soldiers were captured as prisoners of war during this campaign.

To the north, at Remagen, General Montgomery was planning a major assault. Montgomery never believed in attacking unless he had such overwhelming odds in his favor that he was assured of victory simply by the weight of his attack. His massive preparations for crossing the Rhine River included landing craft, air support, artillery, and large numbers of troops. All of the materials, supplies, and manpower he planned on using was almost equal to that used by the Allies during their landings in Normandy on D-Day.

Montgomery's crossing of the Rhine was supposed to be a spectacular invasion of Germany. It was meant to be an earth-shaking event that would be broadcast throughout England over the BBC radio network. Monty had even invited the Prime Minister of England, Winston S. Churchill, to be present at the crossing.

Meanwhile, very quietly, and without any great fanfare or massive preparations, Patton's Third Army was already crossing the Rhine and driving toward the heart of Nazi Germany.

Patton's men were just following his basic order to, "Kill the enemy before they kill you." The soldiers of the Third Army gave the Germans no chance to recover from the beating they were taking.

Third Army quickly moved two bridgeheads over the Rhine River within five days. Patton had often warned his men that, "Many battles have been lost because of an army stopping on the wrong side of a river."

The 5th Infantry Division, under Major General S. Leroy Irwin, made a perfectly executed assault crossing of the Rhine early on the morning of March 23rd. They had received no artillery or air support and the Germans offered little or no resistance at all.

Third Army's VIII Corps made a second assault crossing of the Rhine south of Koblenz on the 26th of March. The Third Army's bridgeheads were expanded rapidly. The enemy's high losses and his concern over First Army's bridgehead at Remagen left him with totally inadequate forces to contain the Third Army. Advancing to the Main River, the Third Army seized bridgeheads over that river in the vicinity of Hanau and Aschaffenburg on the 25th of March. The enemy's attempt to contain the Main River bridgeheads ended in utter failure. The Third Army broke through and by March 28th, the 4th Armored Division had swiftly driven thirty miles northward to join forces with the First Army. Their movement had again trapped thousands of German troops in the Wiesbaden and Bingen area.

When General Patton was ready to cross the Rhine, he did it on foot. He got out of his jeep and walked across the river on a pontoon bridge built by his Third Army Engineers. When he reached the half-way point he stopped and urinated into the German river. He then continued his walk to the other side of the bridge and got back into his jeep. Patton always enjoyed being dramatic.

Advancing as quickly as their tracks could carry them, the Third Army again gave the enemy no time to build defense lines. Armor and troops drove swiftly down both sides of the Werra River, across the Fulda River, and twenty miles beyond, ruining any hope the enemy had of making a strong stand.

They met strong enemy resistance only at the town of Kassel. By the 10th of April, the Third Army was pushing toward the Mulde River in a five day drive that gained them eighty miles. This campaign ended on the 21st of March. While the Third Army was getting ready to advance east of the Mulde River, they once again were ordered by Eisenhower to halt

After four days of preparation and regrouping (which Patton called the curse of warfare) the Third Army was given a new mission. On the 22nd of March they were to advance to the southeast into Bavaria to attack what SHAEF called the National Redoubt area. Patton protested this order claiming that the National Redoubt existed only in General Eisenhower's imagination. As it turned out, Patton was right again.

Patton had wanted to turn his Third Army north and head for Berlin before the Russians got there. Eisenhower, however, failed to understand the importance of the German Capital and he refused permission.

It was later discovered that Eisenhower had sent unauthorized messages to some Russian generals. He had taken upon himself the authority to make strategic decisions which were not his to make.

By now, enemy resistance appeared to be on the point of total collapse. Final victory was in the air. On the 4th of May, the 11th German Panzer Division surrendered unconditionally to the Third Army.

It became very clear that the Germans had no desire at all to defend the so-called Redoubt area. Germans were surrendering in ever increasing numbers.

Third Army's final campaign across the Danube River, into Czechoslovakia and Austria, was halted with the official end of the war in Europe at 0001 hours (one minute after midnight) on May 9th, 1945.

The Germans had officially surrendered all of Germany on May 8th, 1945, a date which would become known as V.E. Day or Victory In Europe Day.

1944 - 1945
Facts and Figures

Reduced to cold, statistical figures, the feats of the Third Army were astonishing. The Army liberated or captured 81,522 square miles of territory. An estimated 12,000 cities, towns, and communities were liberated or captured, including 27 cities of more than 50,000 in population.

Third Army captured 765,483 prisoners of war. 515,205 of the enemy surrendered during the last week of the war to make a total of 1,280,688 POW's processed.

The enemy lost an estimated 1,280,688 captured, 144,500 killed, and 386,200 wounded, adding up to 1,811,388. By comparison, the Third Army suffered 16,596 killed, 96,241 wounded, and 26,809 missing in action for a total of 139,646 casualties. Third Army's losses were only 12.97 percent of the German losses. That is only about 13 American soldiers for every 100 German soldiers.

Third Army aircraft and artillery dropped or dispersed by shell 31,552,700 psychological warfare leaflets to enemy troops.

XIX Tactical Air Command completed 1,767 tactical reconnaissance missions and 77 photo reconnaissance missions which resulted in 3,205,670 aerial photographic prints being distributed.

XIX Tactical Air Command flew 7,326 missions and 74,447 sorties during the 281 days of fighting.

Third Army's air support dropped 17,486 tons of bombs, 3,205 napalm tanks, and launched 4,599 rockets.

The Air Command destroyed 1,640 enemy planes and only lost 582 of it's own from all causes.

Targets destroyed or damaged by the XIX Tactical Air Command included:

Tanks and armored cars 3,833
Motor vehicles 38,541
Locomotives 4,337
Railroad lines cut 2,585
Marshaling yards 974
Towns and villages 816
Factories 3,664
Supply dumps 220
Military installations 1,730
Gun installations 2,809
Highway and railroad bridges 285
Miscellaneous naval vessels 654
Miscellaneous targets 3,010

Third Army artillery fired 5,870,843 rounds of ammunition during the fighting.

Tank destroyers with the Third Army knocked out 648 enemy tanks and 211 self propelled guns. At the Maginot Line and the Siegfried Line, they eliminated 801 pillboxes. They fired a total of 101,178 rounds of ammunition on direct fire missions and 231,998 rounds on indirect fire missions.

Within the Army area, 2,186,792 tons of supplies were transported a total of 141,081,336 miles by trucks in the transportation pool. A total of 2,092 miles of railway track was reconstructed and placed into operation.

The Army repaired 99,114 general purpose vehicles, 21,761 combat vehicles, 11,613 artillery pieces, 125,083 small arms, and 32,740 instruments.

Third Army Engineers constructed 2,498 bridges with a total footage of 255,520 feet, almost 48 and one half miles of bridging. They built or maintained an average of 2,240 miles of road.

Third Army's nine chemical mortar companies expended 349,097 rounds of 4.2 inch mortars, including 189,095 rounds of high explosive and 160,002 rounds of white phosphorous. Chemical warfare supplies included 32,454 gallons of flame thrower fuel and 335,944 grenades.

Third Army Signal Corps personnel laid 3,747 miles of telephone wire. The Third Army message center handled a total of 7,220,261 code groups and switchboard operators handled an average of 13,968 telephone calls daily.

Military personnel in the Third Army were paid a total of $240,539,569 from the 1st of August, 1944 until the 30th of April, 1945.

The forward echelon of the Third Army (code named Lucky Forward by General Patton) traveled 1,225 miles while making 19 complete moves during combat.

The decorations awarded to soldiers of the Third Army were:

Medal of Honor 19
Distinguished Service Medal 44
Distinguished Service Cross 291
Legion of Merit 159
Silver Star 4,990
Soldier's Medal 247
Bronze Star 29,090

Normal promotions numbered 6,464; battlefield promotions totaled 1,817; and combat appointments totaled 848.

The correspondents of the Third Army and soldier correspondents wrote 30,326 stories totaling 7,010,963 words. They submitted 7,129 photographs about the Third Army's combat fighting.

A total of 11,230,000 soldiers attended motion picture shows at the Third Army. The USO shows played to 650,000 soldiers, and the soldier talent shows played to a total of 625,000 soldiers.

General Patton was right when he said, "It sure takes a lot to kill a German."

In this way, the Third Army played it's proud part in helping to crush the Nazi war machine. When men talk of the Second World War the name of the Third U.S. Army and of it's commander will awaken a special thrill of courage and adventure.

Perhaps more than any other group of soldiers in the European Theater, the soldiers of the Third Army deserved the praise of the Supreme Allied Commander Eisenhower when he said, "Working and fighting together in a single indestructible partnership you have achieved perfection in unification of air, ground, and naval power that will stand as a model in our time."

Page **457**

Bronze Star

Purple Heart

WWII Campaign

European African Middle Eastern Campaign with 3 Stars

Good Conduct Medal

Presidential Unit Citation

Expert Rifleman   Combat Rifle w/Cluster   WWII Lapel Pin

In Vinita Maurice was not known by his God given name. He was known all over town as "Tuffy Yost". As you can see by the pictures, Morris was not a large man. However, after Morris came back from World War II, he was walking down the street in Pitcher at night. I man stuck something in his back and robbed him of his money. Morris then turned around pulled the man into the alley, and beat "the living crap" out of the man and took his money back.

Later, a Yost sister was in Chubb's bar east of Vinita. She asked the bartender if she knew any of the Yost boy's. The bartender/owner said, "Yea, a big guy and a little guy come in here to drink. The big guy is named Perry and the little guy is named Morris. Sometimes they get a little loud and I will go over and whisper in Perry's ear, they need to quiet down. Onetime I did, and the little guy came out of the booth fixing to kick my butt wanting to fight. I had to calm him down to keep there from being a fight."

In 1962 when Johnny Lee More was 16, he got a call from Morris to come get him. He was at the filling station at the south end of Langley Oklahoma. When Johnny arrived he found Morris was wrinkled up, nose broke, eye swollen, hit by a pipe, slid skin back on head. Morris got in the truck and asked Johnny to take him downtown. Johnny asked him, "What happened, I need to take you to the hospital." Morris replied, "Nah…"

Morris had been in the bar and got into fight with 5 guys at once, Morris said, "I think I hurt 3-4 or pretty bad." One went down alley and got a pipe and came out and began hitting Morris in the head with it. The old boys thought they had killed him so they threw him in a truck bed, and drove him to the bridge. The dropped him off the side of the bridge into the water thinking he would float down river.

Morris said, "When I hit the river, I woke up, and was on the bottom. He said he made it back up. He exclaimed, "I was sure needed some air." He swam to shore, and walked from bridge to Langley at gas station.

Johnny took Morris on home where he sewed his own head up, refusing to go to the hospital. Morris's last words on the subject were, "I know the old boys....I'll get them back."

One thing I have learned in my journey to write this book, is the genes are very strong. Aunt Mildred who told me the stories of Morris said, "I never picked a fight, but if someone wanted to fight, I didn't stop until the end." This statement and the story of Morris is very ironic, in raising my two boys, I always told them, "You never start the fight, but when it starts, you end it." And several times during my boys raising, there were several times that I would get called to the Union Public Schools. The counselor would tell me that my boy had been in a fight. That he did not start it, but after the other boy started it, my son beat the crap out of the kid. The school would tell me, we don't tolerate fighting. I would tell them, "I have raised my boys to never start a fight, but when it starts, you beat the crap out of the kid and end the fight." On one occasion, I received a call reference Steven beating a kid up. I asked what happened, and he informed me that the other boy pushed Steven by the door. Steven slung the kid into the wall and beat him up. In this case, Steven received no punishment because he did not start it. On another occasion, my youngest son Brian had another kid picked on him by pushing him in the hallway. Pushed the boy down and stood over him ready to throw punches. The boy stayed down. The Principal told me Brian did not start it, but he would have to have 2 days suspension. I advised the Principal, "That is fine, but I will tell you now, you better advise that boy and his parents, if he picks on Brian again, and Brian will do the same thing and worse the next time." The schools in Union did not necessary like me; because I never have believed that a boy or man should not be able to defend themselves. It must be in the genes.

Maurice Yost

Maurice Yost

Violet Yost (Harold Yost's wife) Maurice Yost, Bob Widger, Deloris Yost Widger (Harold Yost's daughter), Mildred Yost Moore

Nora, Maurice, Gene, Ed, Debbie, Delores Yost Widger 1972

IN LOVING MEMORY OF
Maurice R. Yost

BORN
October 15, 1922 in Ketchum, Oklahoma

ENTERED INTO REST
September 6, 2006 at Pryor, Oklahoma

SERVICES WITH MILITARY HONORS
Monday, September 11, 2006 at 10:00 AM
Pentecostal Church Of God

OFFICIATING
Reverend Junior Mullin
Jan Yost Stadler

MUSICAL SELECTION
Military Hymns

Pledge Of Allegiance
Spencer Haff

American Veteran's Honor Guard Salute
Jan Yost Stadler

PLACE OF INTERMENT
United States Army Honor Guard
Spavinaw-Strang Cemetery
Spavinaw, Oklahoma

Shipman's Funeral & Cremation Service

"Old Soldiers Never Die
They Just Fade Away."

General Douglas
MacArthur

Maurice Ray Yost Memoriam

Maurice Ray Yost in Spavinaw-Strang Cemetery

Obituary for Maurice Ray Yost by niece Ma'lisa Yost Mann

Mr. Maurice Yost was one of 13 children born to Ray and Nora Yost. He served in the Army Infantry during World War II and was injured during the Battle of the Bulge. At different points during his lifetime, he was a miner, an electrician and a rancher. He had a great love of horses and competed in rodeos.

Mr. Yost was preceded in death by his mother and father; his sister Irene Rush; and his six brothers: James Yost, Cleve Yost, Harold Yost, Leon Yost, Clyde Yost and Perry Yost. He is survived by his sons and daughter, Suzie Davis of Oklahoma City, as well as five sisters: Kathryn Gardner of West Point, Texas; Janice Stadler of Tulsa, Roberta Haff of Sand Springs, Okla.; Beatrice Prine of Bluejacket, Okla.; and Mildred Andrews, also of Bluejacket.

My mother, Patricia Shanahan Yost often quoted her mother-in-law (my grandmother, Nora Yost), who said "When the Lord sets you free, he sets you free indeed." My mother just realized recently that this was a Bible verse. (She previously thought it was just something Grandma said!) I thought perhaps you or the minister could use this in some way.

By the way, my grandfather, Ray Yost, died after a mining accident and my uncle Maurice was apparently there at the time of the accident. Several of the Yost children were grown, but several were still at home and my grandmother raised them by herself. She lived to be 80 years old and was quite an exceptional woman. I like to think she passed her tenacity and life force along to her 13 children and many grandchildren and great-grandchildren…

Ma'lisa Yost Mann,
Daughter of James Yost

Mildred Pauline Yost, born December 29, 1924, Miami, Oklahoma, died July 7, 2009 in Tulsa, Oklahoma. She married Jesse Lenard Moore who was born August 8, 1919 in Hoggervile Oklahoma. He died May 7, 2956 in Peoria Oklahoma died of Heart Attack. Jesse Moore and Lenard had the following children, Jesse Ray Moore born June 30, 1943, Carolyn Sue Moore born September 06, 1944, Johnny Lee Moore born July 11, 1946, Mildred Anne "Mickey" Moore born December 06, 1948.

Milred Pauline Yost

Mildred and Sister Birdy Yost

Mildred Pauline Yost in 8th Grade Quapaw Oklahoma

Mildred Pauline Yost and Jesse Lenard Moore

Mildred and Jesse at home

Left: Larie Fry Jesse ½ sister   Daughter Carolyn Moore   Mother Mildred Pauline Yost Moore   Anne "Mickey" Moore   Father Jess Lenard Moore   Son Johnny Lee Moore   Son Jesse Ray Moore

Jesse Leonard Moore, G.A.R. Cemetery in Miami, Oklahoma

Mildred Pauline (Yost) Moore, G.A.R. Cemetery in Miami, Oklahoma

Mildred Pauline Yost then married Clyde Edward Andrews born September 7, 1921 in Rocky Ford, Colorado. They were married on September 28, 1957 in Miami, Oklahoma. Mildred and Clyde had the following children, Ricky Dale Andrews born September 19, 1959, Teresa Jane Andrews born January 21, 1962.

This picture was taken in the mid 1960s and shows the last buildings on Hockerville's main street. This is taken south from where the first picture (above) was taken. You can see the old bank building and the pole standing in front of it. Also, the railroad track is visible. Zine (Jesse Moore's sister) worked the only telephone in town. This building is the wooden structure on the left and also served as the Post Office. The town store is the white building on the right.

Monument to war veterans at Hockerville, Oklahoma

Jesse Moore's name on the monument for service in World War II

In the words of Larrie Kay Yost" I was 7 years old, and we were living in Ardmore, OK. Butch and I went on the bus to visit Aunt Mildred and the kids. This was after Jess' death. Must have been summer of 1957. Butch and I stayed about 3 weeks, and I remember it being one of the best times of my childhood.

One night Mildred drove us to see the spook light, and I sat next to her and hid my head in her lap. Butch was going to get out of the car and investigate, but he changed his mind when the time came!"

Mildred Pauline Yost

Mildred Yost Moore, Janice Yost Stadler, Kathryn Yost Gardner, Maurice "Morris" Yost, Herman Haff at Yost Reunion

Great Grandchild Nicholas Wilson, Mildred Yost Moore, Great Grandchild Kaile Brock

Kim Wilson, Lance Wilson, Kevin Brock, Kaile Brock Nicholas Wilson, Mandy Brock, Mildred Yost Moore Grand and Great Grand Children

Mildred Yost Moore and Janice Yost Stadler Mildred's 82nd Birthday in front of flowers sent by Larrie Kay Yost Ciano

Children of Mildred Pauline Yost and Jesse Lenard Moore are:

Jesse, Carolyn, Johnny, Mickie

Jesse Ray Moore born June 30, 1943 in Vinita Oklahoma. Jesse married Waydene Taylor on April 15, 1960 in Miami Oklahoma. Jesse and Waydene had the following children, Sherry Jean Moore born January 03, 1961, Ronda Sue Moore born September 26, 1963.

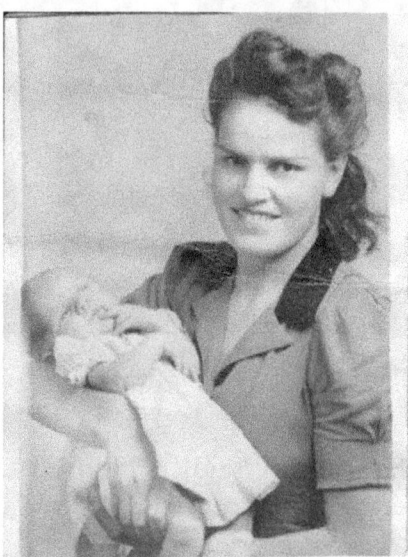

Mildred Pauline Yost Moore and son Jesse Ray Moore

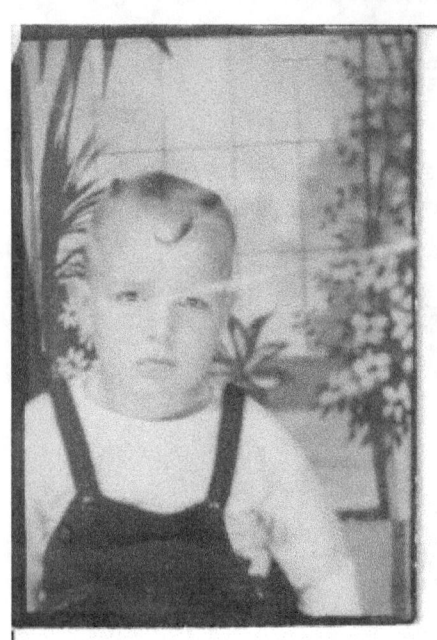 

Jesse Ray Moore

Jesse Ray Moore School Pictures

Jesse's wife Waydene at Family Reunion

Sherry Jean Moore born January 3, 1961 in Vinita, Oklahoma. Sherry married Brad hall.

Sherry Jean and Brad Hall had the following children:

Mathew Hall born July 11, 1982 in Vinita, Oklahoma
Jessica Dee Hall born April 6, 1985 in Vinita, Oklahoma

Brad Hall, Sherry Moore Hall, son Matt Hall, grandson Brenan Lee Hall, daughter Jessica Hall

Ronda Sue Moore born September 26, 1962 in Vinita, Oklahoma. Ronda married Dale Brookshire born May 24, 1963.

Ronda Sue and Dale Brookshire had the following child:

Kelsey Jo Brookshire born August 31, 1988 in Miami, Oklahoma

Carolyn Sue Moore born September 06, 1944, in Baxter Springs Kansas

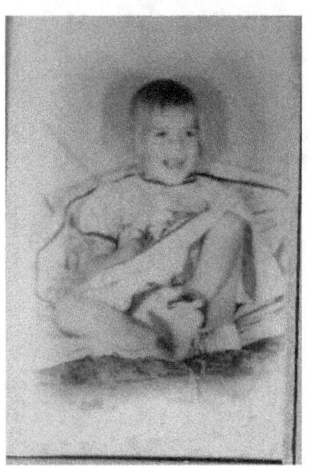 

Carolyn Sue Moore age 4   **Carolyn Sue Moore School Picture**

Carolyn Sue Moore

Carolyn Kimberly Amanda and Amandas son Travis

Carolyn Sue and Eustice Kelly Jenkins had the following children:

    Kimberly Kay Jenkins born September 11, 1963. Kimberly married Kevin Wilson. Kimberly and Kevin had the following children, Lance Lee Wilson born July 10, 1991 and Nicholas Todd Wilson born September 30, 1995.

    Amanda Lea Jenkins born September 4, 1966. Amanda married Mark Allen Brock born November 11, 1960. Amanda and Mark had he following children, Travis James Brock born November 9, 1987 and Kaylea Hope Brock born October 31, 1996.

Carolyn Sue Moore married Charles Henry Pressler born July 17, 1941 in Hurou, Ohio.

Carolyn Sue and Charles Henry Pressler had the following children:

    Christopher Allen Pressler born December 28, 1972 in Miami, Oklahoma

Carolyn Sue Moore married Morris Richard Monfort born September 19, 1931

Carolyn Sue and Morris Richard Monfort had the following child:

    Christopher Allen Monfort born December 28, 1971

Dave Ciano, Larrie Kay Yost Ciano, Carolyn Moore Monfort, and Dick Monfort at Sand Luis Obispo January 2006

Great Granddaughter Kaile Brock, Granddaughter Mandy Brock, Mildred Yost Moore, Carolyn Sue Moore Monfort

Kaile Brock, Kevin Brock, Amanda Lea Jenkins Brock's children

Johnnie Lee Moore born July 11, 1946 in Baxter Springs, Kansas. Johnnie died April 12, 2010 in Tulsa, Ok, St. John's Hospital after a stroke. Johnnie Lee Moore married Donna Rae McKinney born February 23, 1948 in Vinita Craig County, Oklahoma. They were married in 1967. Johnnie Lee Moore then married Vicki Lena Young born December 20, 1953 in Smithville, Missouri. They were married April 27, 1987 in Miami Oklahoma.

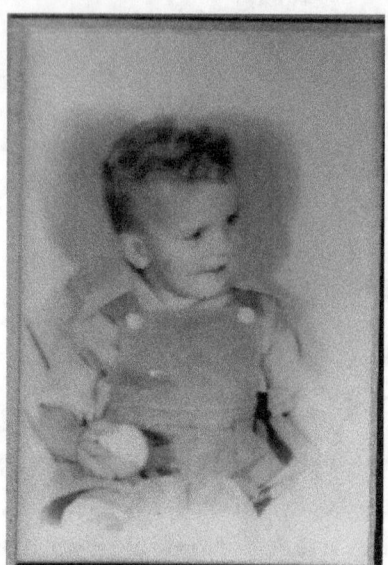

Johnny Lee Moore

Johnny Lee Moore Vietnam

Johnnie Lee and Donna Rae Moore had the following children:

Gena Lee Moore born September 12, 1968. Gena married Scott Bullard

Gena Lee and Scott Bullard had the following children:

   Lindsey Kay Bullard born October 23, 1987

Will Rogers Memorial Rodeo Queen
Lindsey Bullard
2004

Lindsey Kay Bullard Rodeo Queen

Ben Heston Bullard born August 16, 1989

Kerry Lynn Moore born February 3, 1970. Kerry married David Eidson. She then married Jon Page.

Kerry Lynn and David Eidson had the following children:

    Cale Johnathan Eidson born May 21, 1991
    Chandler Brook Eidson born December 28, 1992

Sheila Ann Moore born August 21, 1972. Sheila married Eric Curley

Sheila Ann and Eric Curly had the following child:

    Madison Renee Curley born November 27, 1995

Johnnie Lee and Vicki Lena Young Yost had the following children:

Lacy Tyler Moore born April 16, 1986 in Grove Oklahoma.

Lee Haff and John Moore cooking fish at Roberta Yost Haff's home in Sand Springs Oklahoma

Johnny Lee Moore's Service to his country in Vietnam

Jonnie Lee Moore in Vietnam

Johnnie Lee Moore in Middle with buddies

ARMED FORCES OF THE UNITED STATES REPORT OF TRANSFER OR DISCHARGE

PERSONAL DATA
- LAST NAME, FIRST NAME, MIDDLE NAME: MOORE, JOHNNIE LEE
- SERVICE NUMBER: RA 18 713 792
- SOCIAL SECURITY NUMBER: 444 46 0653
- DEPARTMENT, COMPONENT AND BRANCH OR CLASS: ARMY RA — INF
- GRADE, RATE OR RANK: SP4 (P)
- PAY GRADE: E-4
- DATE OF RANK: 21 Feb 66
- PLACE OF BIRTH: Baxter Springs, Kansas
- DATE OF BIRTH: 11 Jul 46
- SEX: [X] Male
- DATE INDUCTED: NA

SELECTIVE SERVICE DATA
- SELECTIVE SERVICE NUMBER: 34 18 46 57
- LOCAL BOARD: LB # 18, Vinita, Oklahoma 74301

TRANSFER OR DISCHARGE DATA
- TYPE OF TRANSFER OR DISCHARGE: Transferred to USAR (See #16)
- STATION OR INSTALLATION: Fort Sill, Oklahoma
- REASON AND AUTHORITY: AR 635-200 SPN 201 Exption of term of service
- EFFECTIVE DATE: 9 Nov 67
- LAST DUTY ASSIGNMENT AND MAJOR COMMAND: 4th Bn, 30th Inf — FOURTH US ARMY
- CHARACTER OF SERVICE: HONORABLE — Transferred to USAR
- TYPE OF CERTIFICATE ISSUED: NONE
- DISTRICT, AREA COMMAND OR CORPS TO WHICH TRANSFERRED: Control Group (Reinforcement) USAAC St. Louis, Missouri 63132
- REENLISTMENT CODE: 1
- TERMINAL DATE OF RESERVE OBLIGATION: 9 Nov 70
- SOURCE OF ENTRY: [X] ENLISTED (First Enlistment)
- SERVICE: 3
- DATE OF ENTRY: 10 Nov 64
- PRIOR REGULAR ENLISTMENTS: NONE
- GRADE AT TIME OF ENTRY: PVT E-1
- PLACE OF ENTRY INTO CURRENT ACTIVE SERVICE: Oklahoma City, Oklahoma
- HOME OF RECORD AT TIME OF ENTRY: Route # 1, Vinita, Oklahoma 74301
- SPECIALTY NUMBER & TITLE: 11B20 Lt Wpns Infman
- RELATED CIVILIAN OCCUPATION: NONE

STATEMENT OF SERVICE (YEARS | MONTHS | DAYS)
- NET SERVICE THIS PERIOD: 3 | 0 | 0
- OTHER SERVICE: 0 | 0 | 0
- TOTAL: 3 | 0 | 0
- TOTAL ACTIVE SERVICE: 3 | 0 | 0
- FOREIGN AND/OR SEA SERVICE: USARV 1 | 5 | 25

DECORATIONS, MEDALS, BADGES, COMMENDATIONS, CITATIONS AND CAMPAIGN RIBBONS AWARDED OR AUTHORIZED:
NDSM CIB RVCM w/Dev-60 Expert (Rifle)
VSM w/Bronze Star (1) O/S Bar (1) (Vietnam)

TRUE COPY OF ORIGINAL/CERTIFIED
Date Recd. 351 2-27-02
Date Original Returned 2-27-02
Veterans Benefits Counselor
4505 AUTHORITY

EDUCATION AND TRAINING COMPLETED: Battle Indoc   Code of Conduct   Mil Justice   Non Jud Pun

VA AND SGLI SERVICE DATA
- NON-PAY PERIODS TIME LOST: NONE
- DAYS ACCRUED LEAVE PAID: 10
- INSURANCE IN FORCE: [X] NO
- AMOUNT OF ALLOTMENT: NA
- MONTH ALLOTMENT DISCONTINUED: NA
- VA CLAIM NUMBER: NA
- SERVICEMEN'S GROUP LIFE INSURANCE COVERAGE: [X] $10,000

REMARKS
10 Years - General
Blood Group: "A"
Item 6: Date of appointment 21 Feb 67

PERMANENT ADDRESS AFTER TRANSFER OR DISCHARGE:
Route # 3
Vinita, Oklahoma 74301

Signature: Johnnie L Moore

TYPED NAME, GRADE AND TITLE OF AUTHORIZING OFFICER:
E. P. VAUGHN, JR., CW4, USA, ASST AG

FORM 214

Mildred Anne "Micky" Moore born December 06, 1948 in Baxter Springs, Kansas. Mildred Anne married Jeffrey Michael Myers.

Mildred Anne "Mickey" Moore

Carolyn and Mickie

Mildred Anne "Micky" Moore

Mildred Anne and Jeffrey Michael Myers had the following children:

Michael Shawn Myers born July 31, 1968

Shannon Lynn Myers born March 29, 1977. Shannon Lynn married Jason Simon Coan born August 26, 1976.

Shannon Lynn and Jason Simon Coan had the following children:

Breya Madyx Myers-Coan born November 13, 2003

Shannon married Michael Sean Myers

Shannon and Michael had the following children:

Kylie MacKenzie Myers born July 10, 2000
Maryann Myers
Troy Michael Myers

Mildred Pauline Yost and Clyde Edward Andrews had the following children:

Ricky Dale Andrews born September 19, 1959 in Vinita, Oklahoma
Teresa Jane Andrews born January 21, 1962 in Vinita, Oklahoma

Perry Kenneth Yost, born September 08, 1926, Cardin, Oklahoma; died November 30, 2001. Perry Kenneth Yost married Marjorie Sue Fanning.

Kenneth Perry Yost

Perry Kenneth Yost – Navy – Age 18

U.S. Naval Training Center – Farragut, Idaho – December 1, 1944
Perry Kenneth Yost - 3rd Row, 5th Sailor from the left

NOTICE OF SEPARATION FROM U.S. NAVAL SERVICE
NAVPERS-553 (REV. 8-45)

1918

1. SERIAL OR FILE NO. / 2. NAME (LAST) (FIRST) (MIDDLE) / 3. RATE AND CLASS/OR RANK AND CLASSIFICATION / 4. PERMANENT ADDRESS FOR MAILING PURPOSES

677 29 28
Y O S T, Perry Kenneth
Seaman, first class
V-6 USNR.
Rt. #2
Vinita, Craig Co., Okla.

5. PLACE OF SEPARATION
PSC-Norman, Oklahoma.

6. CHARACTER OF SEPARATION
Honorable Discharge

7. ADDRESS FROM WHICH EMPLOYMENT WILL BE SOUGHT
Rt. #2
Vinita, Craig Co., Okla.

8. RACE: W **9. SEX:** M **10. MARITAL STATUS:** Single **11. U.S. CITIZEN:** Yes **12. DATE AND PLACE OF BIRTH:** 9-8-26, Cardin, Okla.

15. HOME ADDRESS AT TIME OF ENTRY INTO SERVICE: Quapaw, Okla.

13. REGISTERED: No **14. SELECTIVE SERVICE BOARD OF REGISTRATION:** —

16. MEANS OF ENTRY: X Enlisted **DATE:** 5-5-44

17. DATE OF ENTRY INTO ACTIVE SERVICE: 5-15-44

18. NET SERVICE (FOR PAY PURPOSES): 1 yr. 10 mos. 13 days

19. PLACE OF ENTRY INTO ACTIVE SERVICE: NRSS Tulsa, Okla.

20. QUALIFICATIONS, CERTIFICATES HELD, ETC.:
See Rating Description Booklet
Gunner's Mate, third class

21. RATINGS HELD: AS; S2c; S1c(GM).

22. FOREIGN AND/OR SEA SERVICE WORLD WAR II: X Yes

23. SERVICE SCHOOLS COMPLETED / WEEKS:
Gunner's Mate Sch, Farragut, Idaho — 14

24. SERVICE (VESSELS AND STATIONS SERVED ON):
NTC Camp Wallace, Tex.
USS Sitkah Bay (CVE-86)

25. KIND OF INSURANCE: NSI **26. EFFECTIVE MONTH OF ALLOTMENT DISCONTINUANCE:** 5-46 **27. MO. NEXT PREMIUM DUE:** 4-46 **28. AMOUNT OF PREMIUM DUE EACH MONTH:** 6.40 **29. INTENTION OF VETERAN TO CONTINUE INS.:** Undecided

30. TOTAL PAYMENT UPON DISCHARGE: $20.67 **31. TRAVEL OR MILEAGE ALLOWANCE INCLUDED IN TOTAL PAYMENT:** $8.30 **32. INITIAL MUSTERING OUT PAY:** 100.00 **33. NAME OF DISBURSING OFFICER:** A.W. Johnson Lt. (SC) USN

34. REMARKS:
Point System
Victory Medal
American Campaign Medal
Asiatic-Pacific Campaign Medal
1-Star

35. SIGNATURE (BY DIRECTION OF COMMANDING OFFICER):
Frank E. Couch
FRANK E. COUCH
Lieut., USNR.
Ass't. Personnel Officer.

36. NAME AND ADDRESS OF LAST EMPLOYER: General Power Inc., Quapaw, Okla.
37. DATES OF LAST EMPL'MT: FROM 3-44 TO 5-4-44
38. MAIN CIVILIAN OCCUPATION AND D.O.T. NO.: Farmer

39. JOB PREFERENCE: Farmer Oklahoma
40. PREFERENCE FOR ADDITIONAL TRAINING: High School

41. NON-SERVICE EDU.: GRAM.: 8 H.S.: 1½ COLL.: —
42. DEGREES: —
43. MAJOR COURSE OR FIELD: Gen.

47. DATE OF SEPARATION: 3-17-46
48. SIGNATURE OF PERSON BEING SEPARATED: Perry Kenneth Yost

TO: BUREAU OF NAVAL PERSONNEL

Perry's commendations during World War II were, the Victory Medal, American Campaign Medal, Asiatic-Pacific Campaign Medal with 1 Star. The Star meaning he saw action as you will see in the details that follow.

Perry served aboard the USS Sitkoh Bay Aircraft Carrier during World War II. He was assigned to the 3rd Division. The 3rd Divisions jobs were the upkeep of armament, aviation ordnance, magazines, bombs, torpedoes, fire control equipment, look-outs come under the cognizance of the 3rd Division. All gunners' mates are attached to this division.

Back Row (left to right): Yost, P. K., S1c; Robinson, K. E., S1c; Young, M. A., FC3c; Contrell, J. W., S1c; Boone, E. W., S1c; Shatzer, J. W., GM3c; Herman, J. L., S1c; Black, A. A., S1c; Atwood, H. E., S1c; Mc Donald, E. L., S1c; Hartsock, L. N., S1c; Branum, R. D., S1c.
Middle Row (left to right): Bowling, H. B., GM3c; Saufley, C. W., FC1c; Rooney, G. (n)., GM3c; Fielder, C. J., GM2c; Wood, T. G., GM1c; Lt. (jg), E. F. Dyroff; Ens. L. "H" Van Buskirk; Richey, R. F., GM1c; Hancock, W. J., GM3c; Ashburn, W. T., GM2c; Cook, W. J., GM3c; Hepler, D. B., GM3c.
Front Row (left to right): Bergstrom, L. B., S1c; Farrow, B. R., S1c; Carlstedt, J. A., S1c; Snowden, H. E., S1c; Mc Dowell, A. J., S1c; Roberts, C. C., S1c; Hefferman, S. F., S1c; Bolinger, E. R., S1c; Burt, R. F., FC3c; Whitaker, E. H., S2c; Wickman, W. F., S2c; Crowley, B. (n), S1c

Perry Kenneth Yost is standing on the top row, left hand corner of the picture above.

NAVPERS-995A
(Revised October 1943)

Page 19

MUSTER ROLL OF THE CREW

of the U. S. S. SITKOH BAY (CVE-86)

for the quarter ending 1 July 1945, 1945

NAMES (Alphabetically arranged without regard to ratings, with surname to the left and the first name written in full)	SERVICE NUMBER (The service number must under no condition be omitted.)	Present Rating	DATE OF ENLISTMENT			Date first received on board
			Day	Month	Year	
WOODWARD, Samuel Benjamin	269 55 79	S2c				19 June 1945
WOOLDRIDGE, Wesley (n)	962 36 99	S2c				19 June 1945
WORKMAN, Richard Stuart	554 44 00	S2c				2 June 1945
WORLEY, Noel Douglas	393 80 27	S1c				28 Mar. 1944
WORTHINGTON, Charles Albert	987 45 99	S2c				19 June 1945
WYDLER, Alfred Asa	336 36 90	RT1c				28 Mar. 1944
WYRICK, Charles William	613 94 19	S2c				19 June 1945
YORK, James Alfred	551 82 68	S2c				19 June 1945
YOST, Perry Kenneth	677 29 25	S1c(GM)				31 Dec. 1944

Muster Roll U.S.S. Sitkoh Bay – Perry Yost last entry

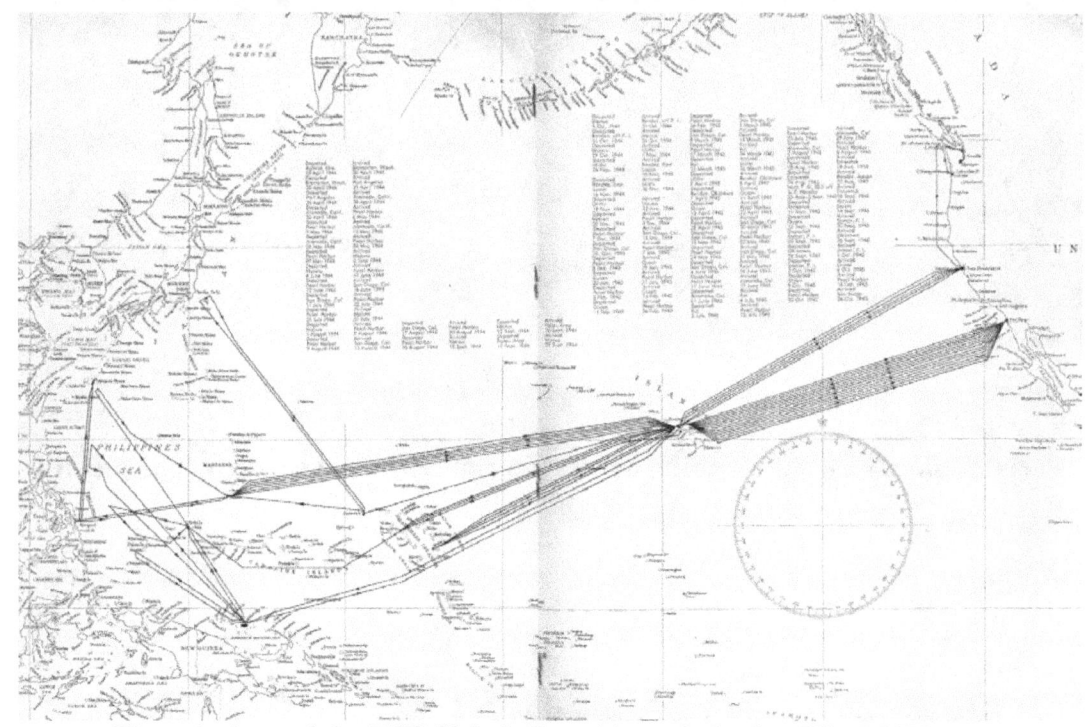

The missions of the USS Sitkoh Bay Aircraft during World War II
Note: California is on the right and Japan is in the Upper Left

History of USS SITKOH BAY:

SITKOH BAY was converted from a Maritime Commission hull (MC hull 1123) by the Kaiser Shipbuilding Co., of Vancouver, Washington. Her keel was laid down on 23 November 1943, and she was launched on 19 February 1944; sponsored by Mrs. Kathryn Mullinnix; and commissioned at Astoria, Oreg., on 28 March 1944, Capt. Robert G. Lockhart, USN, in command.

She spent the month after commissioning completing her fitting out and making short shakedown and trial cruises along the northwestern coast of the United States. On 28 April, the escort carrier entered port at Alameda, Calif., loaded cargo and embarked passengers. She stood out of Alameda on 30 April, bound for Pearl Harbor, and began the first of many routine voyages shuttling planes, pilots, and aircrew men back and forth between the front line and rear areas. The majority of her missions carried her from Pearl Harbor, or via Pearl Harbor from the California coast, to various islands in the southern or central Pacific which served as staging areas for the war being waged farther north or west. In the latter part of 1944, her ports of call were Majuro in the Marshall Islands, and Manus in the Admiralty Islands. From these two points, planes were staged on to the 3d and 7th Fleets, respectively.

In January 1945, the South Pacific was dropped from SITKOH BAY's itinerary, and she concentrated on replenishing the 3rd Fleet in the Central Pacific. Her ports of call included Apra Harbor, Guam, in the Marianas; Roi Harbor, Roi Island, and Eniwetok Atoll in the Marshalls; and Ulithi Atoll in the Western Carolinas. Her missions in early 1945 were in support of the campaigns in the Philippines, the assault on Iwo Jima, and the preparations for the invasion of Okinawa.

SITKOH BAY's only action came on 7 April 1945 while she was delivering Marine Air Group 31 to Okinawa. At 1528, a twin-engine Japanese "Francis" dove at the carrier. SITKOH BAY's antiaircraft gunners combined with a Marine Corsair from BRETON's (CVE 23) combat air patrol to splash the interloper about 100 yards off SITKOH BAY's port beam. The next day, she cleared the area for Guam en route to Pearl Harbor and a return to her replenishment routine.

After the cessation of hostilities with Japan on 15 August 1945, SITKOH BAY joined Task Group 30.8, the replenishment group for the 3d Fleet, and cruised with it off the southeastern coast of Honshu from 25 August until 5 September. On 10 September, she entered Eniwetok and departed the next day for Guam. For the next month, she made voyages between Guam, Samar Island in the Philippines, and Okinawa, returning to Pearl Harbor on 18 October and San Diego on the 26th for an availability period. After further voyages to the Central Pacific, SITKOH BAY returned to the United States and was placed out of commission, in reserve, on 30 November 1946 at Bremerton, Wash.

On 29 July 1950, SITKOH BAY was recommissioned, Capt. C. W. Lord, USN, in command. She was assigned to the Military Sea Transportation Service; and, for the next four years, she sailed between the west coast and Japan, supporting U. N. forces in Korea. Her major ports of call were San Francisco, San Diego, and Pearl Harbor and Yokohama and Yokosuka in Japan. SITKOH BAY departed from this west coast-to-Japan routine three times over those four years. In March of 1951, she delivered a load of Bearcat fighters (F8Fs) to the French forces at Saigon in French Indochina and then visited Manila, P. I., before returning to California-to-Japan runs. In September, she visited Pusan, Korea. SITKOH BAY ventured from her normal sea lanes again in May 1952 when she sailed, via Kodiak and Anchorage, Alaska, on her way back to San Francisco from Yokosuka.

The escort carrier ceased operations again in 1954 and was placed out of commission, in reserve, on 27 July. She joined the Pacific Reserve Fleet and was berthed at San Francisco. On 12 June 1955, the mothballed escort carrier was redesignated a utility aircraft carrier, CVU 86. In mid-March 1958, she changed berthing areas, moving from San Francisco to San Diego. On 1 April 1960, SITKOH BAY, by then reclassified as a cargo ship and aircraft ferry, AKV 30, was struck from the Navy list. Her hulk was sold on 30 August 1960 to Eisenberg & Co., of New York City for scrapping.

SITKOH BAY was awarded three battle stars for World War II service and one battle star for Korean War service.

Uncle Perry Yost served his country in time of war, 1 year, 10 months, 13 days. Upon returning to civilian life, our family almost lost a War Hero as you will read below.

NINE HURT IN CRASH REPORTED IMPROVED

VINITA, Okla., March 23—The conditions of nine persons who were seriously injured Sunday in a two-car crash, five miles south of Afton, were reported to be improving in the General hospital here today.

The patients are Perry Kenneth Yost, 27, Howard Leroy Woolman, 34, Arch Asbury, 38, and Carl Gillebrand, 44, all of Vinita; Richard R. Gray, 27, Langley; Henry Dougherty, 38, his wife, Louise, 33, and their two children, Dennis Ray, 5, and Jeralyn, 11, all of Lakeside, Calif.

Perry Kenneth Yost Accident March 24 1954

Steve Kenney and Sue Yost Perry Yosts first wife Marjorie Sue Fanning

Perry Kenneth Yost and Louise

Perry Yost and Wife Sheila

Perry Kenneth Yost's Grave Stone

Children of Perry Kenneth Yost and Marjorie Sue Fanning are:

Cheryl Sue Yost born December 11, 1947 in Wichita, Kansas. Cheryl married James Jack Forbes born December 20, 1943 in Ardmore Oklahoma. They were married on June 18, 1966 in Tulsa, Oklahoma.

Cheryl Sue Yost then married James A. Clark born April 29, 1941 in Grant, Oklahoma. They were on April 29, 1983 in Ardmore, Oklahoma.

Cheryl Sue Yost and James Jack Forbes had the following children:

Stephanie Suzanne Forbes born July 17, 1969, Mary Elizabeth Ford born March 21, 1973, Jaye Forbes born January 2, 1975.

    Stephanie Suzanne Forbes born July 17, 1969 in Ardmore, Oklahoma. Stephanie married David Bradford Jordan.

Stephanie Suzanne Forbes and David Bradford Jordan had the following children:

    David Bradford Jordan Jr. born March 26, 1998, in Ardmore, Oklahoma.

Mary Elizabeth Forbes born March 21, 1973 in Ardmore, Oklahoma. Mary married Barsoum Eltom in October of 2008 in Ardmore, Oklahoma.

Jaye Forbes born January 2, 1975 in Ardmore, Oklahoma. Jaye married Taylor Foster on October 16, 1999 in Ardmore, Oklahoma.

Jaye Forbes and Taylor Foster had the following children:

    Taylor Brinton Foster II born August 15, 2002 in Muskogee, Oklahoma.
    Ande Grace Foster born June 30, 2006 in Muskogee, Oklahoma.
    As of the writing of this book, Jaye and Taylor are expecting their 3rd child.

Stephen Perry Yost, born February 7, 1953 in Vinita, Oklahoma.
Stephen never decided to marry.

Kenneth Gilbert Yost, born February 21, 1954 in Vinita, Oklahoma. Kenneth married first Rhonda Benedict in 1977. Kenneth married Toni Dixon, born October 8, 1955 in New York.

Kenneth Gilbert Yost 1st wedding

Kenneth Gilbert Yost and Toni Dixon had the following children:

Jesse Kenneth Yost, born October 30, 1990 in AnaHem California.

Roberta "Birdy" Ruth Yost, born October 28, 1928, Spavinaw, Oklahoma. Roberta Ruth Yost married William Herman Haff born October 04, 1926 in Vinita Oklahoma. William Herman Haff passed awayh December 1, 2009 after a relatively short illness in Sand Springs, Okahoma. Birdy was 17 living in Vinita in a rented room at a house about a block from the old High School, she was working at Vinita Hotel as a waitress in the restaurant. Bill's brother, Junior was in a little band. They were playing at the club across near where Wal Mart is and by the rodeo ground. Birdy and her lady friends went to the club to listen to the band. Birdy knew Junior and he introduced Herman to her. Herman took her home that night and proposed to her that night saying, "I am going to take you back to Alabama and make you a Southern Bell." He wanted her to meet him the next morning at the bus stop and leave right then. At the time Herman was in the Army stationed Anastin Alabama and was in town on leave. When Herman came back a year later, Birdy was working for the telephone company. They started dating and eventually got married a year later.

Roberta Ruth Yost age 6

Roberta Ruth Yost William Herman Haff
BOTH PICTURES TAKEN BEFORE BEING MARRIED

Roberta Ruth Yost and William Herman Haff

Roberta Ruth Yost Haff
Retired from Southwestern Bell Telephone Company September 26, 1986 after 37 years as an operator. She served as an operator, service assistant, group chief operator, chief operator (manager) and staff supervisor
She was also the Regent – Tulsa Chapter of National Society of the Daughters of the American Revolution from 1993 - 1995

Roberta Ruth Yost Haff

It should be known to one and all, that I attended many a family gathering at Aunt Birdy's home in Sand Springs Oklahoma. As the descendant of a Yost, we did not have family gatherings at my home, but at Aunt Birdy's everyone was welcome. It felt so good to go to her home when all the relatives were there. Although not everyone could attend because of distance, it was a true Yost gathering. Upon arrival Aunt Birdy would hug one and all when they walked in the door.

> ## A Letter from our Regent...
>
> Dear Daughter's of Tulsa Chapter,
>
> This Regent wishes to commend all of the Daughters in our Chapter who have worked so hard on the various projects of the NSDAR this year. The spirit and cooperation of each of you working together for the good of the Chapter has proved your dedication to the commitments of the NSDAR motto, "God, Home and Country."
>
> The 18 awards you received at the State Conference demonstrated your great and many accomplishments. The Gold Honor Roll Award will be given at Continental Congress.
>
> I want to thank each of you for giving me the opportunity to serve as your Regent for the past two years. It has been a most rewarding experience and I shall always cherish the memories.
>
> Sincerely,
>
> *Roberta*
>
> Mrs. Wm. H. Haff
> Tulsa Chapter Regent

I attended William Herman Haff's funeral in Sand Springs Oklahoma on December 7, 2009. It was a Military Funeral by the United States Army. Roberta Ruth Yost Haff was presented the United States Flag by a perfectly dressed Army Sergeant. William Herman Haff served his country in World War II. It was a very hard funeral to attend, Uncle Bill was always very nice at all the family gatherings at the Haff home at Thanksgiving and Christmas. Uncle Bill was always nice to me and my brother and sister. He was a true American and will be missed.

The thing that will forever stick in my mind is his oldest son Gary Haff carrying the United States Flag so neatly folded by the Active Army Personnel in his arms after the funeral when the church served our family lunch.

William Herman Haff in Ketchum Cemetery, Ketchum Oklahoma

Children of Roberta Ruth Yost and William Herman Haff are:

Peggy Lynn Haff born January 28, 1950, died 1994. Buried beside her father in the Ketchum Cemetery, Ketchum Oklahoma.

Jan Yost holding Peggy Lynn Haff Easter 1951 Yost Farm East of Vinita and GRDA building

Peggy Haff School Picture 1955

Peggy Lynn Haff married Mark Stephen Hale. They had the following children, Lori Anne Hale born December 10, 1970.

Lori Anne Hale born December 10, 1970.

Lori Hale

Peggy and Lori Hale

Lori Anne Hale married Scott Ray Loud.

Lori's children

Peggy Lynn (Haff) Funk in Ketchum Cemetery, Ketchum Oklahoma

Gary Herman Haff born August 01, 1951 in Coffeville, Kansas. He married Debra Anne Lucas born January 27, 1955 in Tulsa, Oklahoma.

Gary Herman Haff

Left: Debra Anne Lucas Grandmother, Debra Anne Lucas, Gary Herman Haff, Nora Jane Paul Yost Gary's Grandmother

Back: Gary Herman Haff, Gary Benjamin Haff
Front: Debra Anne Lucas Haff, Ashley Dawn Haff

Jesse Lee Haff born January 18, 1964, in Tulsa Oklahoma. Jesse Lee Haff married Sonja Schrader born May 30, 1965 in Tulsa, Oklahoma. They were married on August 14, 1987 in Tulsa, Oklahoma.

Jesse Lee Haff

Jesse Lee Haff and Sonja Schrader wedding day

Jesse Lee and Sonja Haff had the following children:

Spencer Lee Haff born April 29, 1993

Joseph Conner Haff born November 24, 1997

Simon Jacob Haff born November 18, 2003

Jesse Brock Haff born April 10, 2006

Joseph Conner Haff, Sonja, Simon Jacob Haff, Lee, Spencer Lee Haff

Jesse Brock Haff, Spencer Lee Haff, Simon Jacob Haff, Joseph Conner Haff

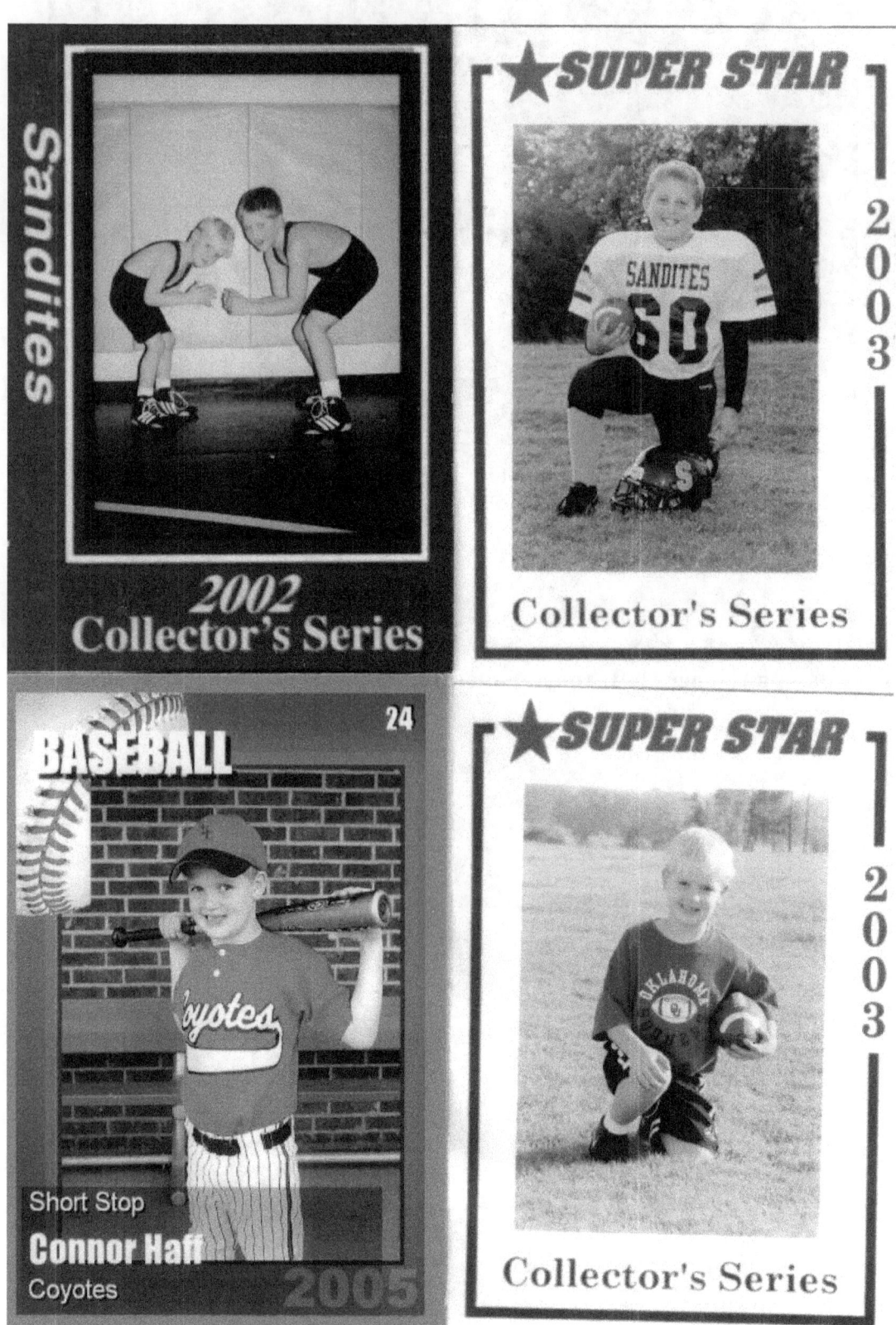

The Haff boys and sports

Sand Springs seventh grade football players Spencer Haff, left, and Luke Owns, right, helped win a national title in November and both are currently wrestling.

Spencer Haff Sand Springs Leader January 3 2007

Gary Herman Peggy Lynn Jesse Lee Haff

James Dillard Yost, born February 20, 1932, Cleora, Oklahoma; died April 01, 2003. In 1952 James married Patricia Kay Shanahan born September 21, 1934 in Vinita Oklahoma.

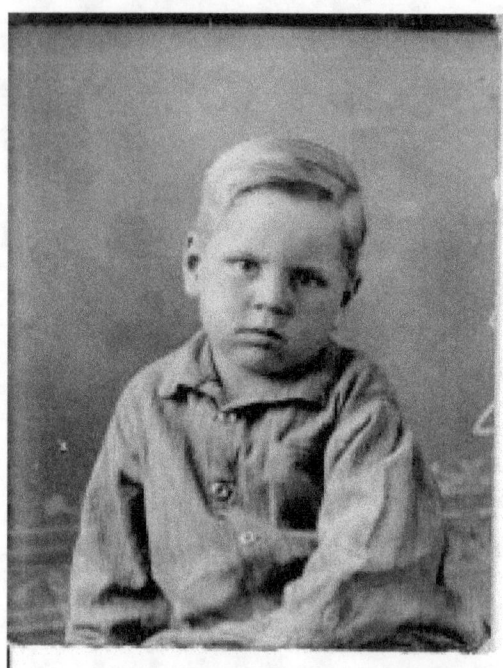

James Dillard Yost Age 3

James Dillard Yost

1947 Vinita Hornets Football Team

1947

Record: 7-2-2. **Coach:** Bob Thomas. **Assistant:** Vernon Muncy. **Points for:** 168. **Points against:** 108. **Accomplishments:** District champion.

Roster: Darrell Baugh, Jerry Zumwalt, Harold Robertson, Roy Shoultz, Joe Glenn, Kenneth Hemphill, Frank Wright, Joe Brooks, Bobby Whitfield, Bill Dail, Bill Meadows, Bill Breedlove, Robert Stephens, Don Casto, W.D. Goins, Bob Jones, Chancy Way, James Robertson, Dee Carrico, Mike Lyne, Bob Wyly, David Sippy, David Corbett, Kenneth Lawson, Jim Ince, Vernon Woolman, James Yost, Willis Jones.

Outlook: The Hornets got a new coach in Bob Thomas, who came to Vinita from Okmulgee and was said to have made a name for himself in high school and college athletics. The team got serious before the season began, voting to go to bed at 10 p.m. on weekdays and slightly later on weekends. Thomas said smoking was out.

Vinita 12, Picher 6 (away) - Don Casto hit Bill Breedlove with a 20-yard TD pass in the final seconds to pull out the win. Breedlove had also scored the Hornets' first TD. An estimated 400 Vinita fans made the trip to Picher.

Vinita 27, Claremore 6 (away) - The Hornets opened their Verdigris Valley schedule with a convincing win.

Vinita 19, Broken Arrow 19 (away) - The Hornets scored twice in the fourth quarter to tie the game. Casto scored on a 1-yard run and then tossed a 4-yard TD pass to David Sippy with less than two minutes remaining. But a conversion pass failed.

Vinita 13, Nowata 6 (home) - Casto saved the game by running down Nowata's Robert Plecker at the Vinita 8 in the final minute. The Hornets then held the Ironmen at the one in the final seconds. Speedy Bobby Jones scored both of Vinita's TDs.

Vinita 21, Miami 6 (home) - Casto scored twice and Kenneth Lawson once. The Hornets dominated the first three quarters, and outgained Miami 258 to 118.

Vinita 6, Pryor 0 (home) - The game against the unbeaten Tigers drew an estimated 3,500 fans, said to be the largest crowd in team history. The first fan arrived at 4:30 p.m., carrying a bottle of milk, a loaf of bread, and a stick of baloney. The game's lone TD came when Jones caught a fumble in midair and returned it 18 yards for a score in the first quarter. Pryor's only threat died at Vinita's 3 with four minutes remaining in the game.

Vinita 13, Pawhuska 13 (away) - A 31-yard pass interference penalty late in the game set up the tying TD by the Huskies. Sippy ran for one TD and caught a pass from Lawson for another.

Vinita 19, Dewey 13 (home) - The Hornets' offense was said to be in high gear as Vinita knocked off a Bulldogger team that would go on to win the Class B state title. Breedlove caught a TD pass from Lawson, who also threw one to Casto and ran for one.

Vinita 18, Sand Springs 6 (away) - The Hornets dominated the Sandites, rolling up 17 first downs to four for Sand Springs, as they earned their first Verdigris Valley championship since the conference was organized in 1925. Vinita got TD runs from Sippy and Breedlove, and David Corbett caught a TD pass from Lawson. With many Vinita fans unable to attend, the game was reported from the sidelines by Francis Goodpaster to approximately 1,000 fans in the high school gym. The fans followed the action on a large board, marked off to look like a football field.

Vinita 14, Bartlesville 20 (away) - Playing in a sea of mud, the Hornets couldn't rally from a 20-0 halftime deficit. Lawson and Breedlove scored in the second half.

Vinita 6, Ponca City 13 (playoff, away) - On Thanksgiving, Dick Powell scored both of Ponca City's TDs in the Hornets' first playoff appearance. Powell scored on a 28-yarder on the Wildcats' first play, after they recovered a lateral. He added a 58-yard TD run in the second quarter, but the Journal reported that Lawson stole the show from the Wildcat star. Lawson threw a 38-yard TD pass to Breedlove in the fourth quarter to cap an 80-yard drive. The Hornets were hampered by a leg injury to Sippy, who played only a few minutes.

Notes: It was mentioned in the Journal that former Hornets Stacey Looney and Alvin Duke were regulars for Arkansas....Coweesta Martin was elected homecoming queen....The Hornets' Verdigris Valley-championship clinching win over Sand Springs earned them dinners courtesy of the Vinita Jewelry Shoppe. There was also some talk of sending them to watch the Cotton Bowl....Breedlove was named to the All-State team....The Hornets' playoff game at Ponca City was broadcast on a statewide radio network with Curt Gowdy as the announcer. Gowdy would go on to become the most well-known TV sportscaster in the country in the 1960s and 70s.

James Dillard Yost's service in the military

James on the left with pilot of the Helicopter on his 8 month cruise on the Ice Breaker below. This is the only time James ever had a beard. He gained his love for all air craft while in the Navy.

James and Patricia Yost

James Dillard Yost over the years

Page 8 - VINITA (Okla.) DAILY JOURNAL, Tuesday, April 17, 1990

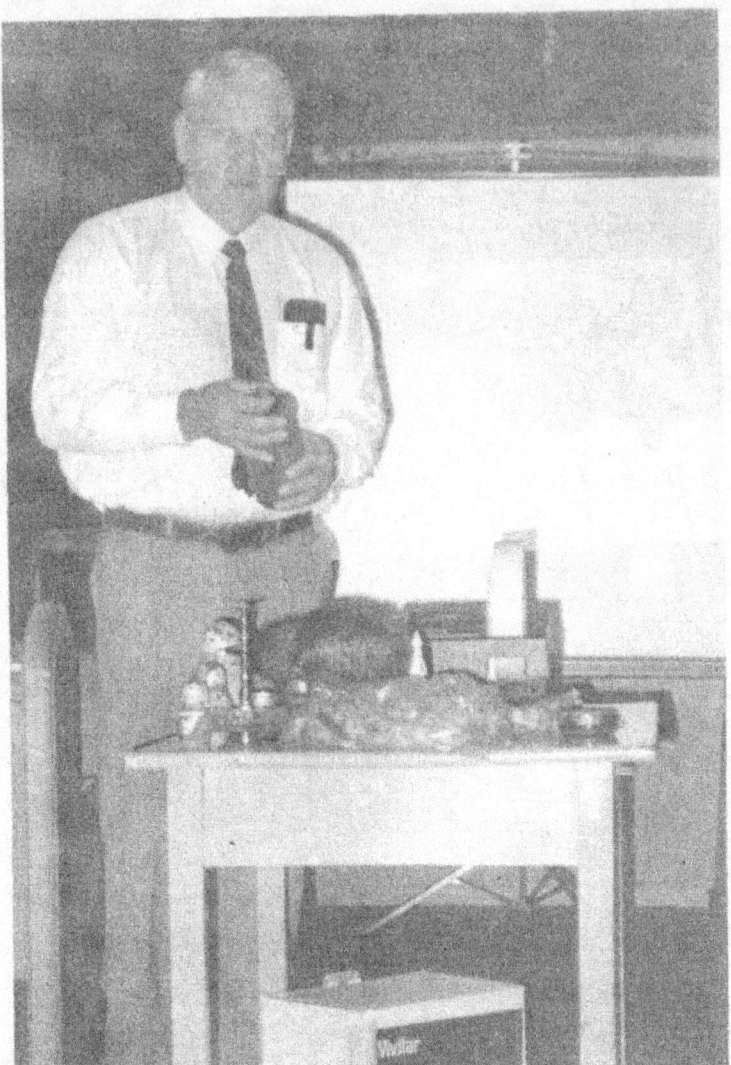

Former Vinitan visits Russia

A former Vinitan, who is now living in Texas, spoke Saturday to members of the First Church of God in Vinita about a business trip he took to Russia.

James Yost, who attended Vinita Schools and is now employed as an aerospace engineer with the U.S. Army ARPRO, Bell Helicopter Textron, Inc., told those gathered that the best food he had while on his trip was on the plane on the way home.

Yost visited the Soviet Union before most of the current changes took place under perestoika and Glasnost. He traveled to Russia with others from the United States, under the Citizen Ambassador program.

He presented slides, showed souveniers and regaled the audience with witicisms of his trip.

He was able to visit many historical sites and four cities.

One of the sites he visited was the Kremlin, he said. He also saw the churches, some built in the 1500s, he said.

Yost was an All-State Football player for Vinita.

James Yost in Russia

Patricia Kay Shanahan Yost and James Dillard Yost

Edward, Ma'Lisa, Patricia, Lynn, James Yost

**Larrie Kay Yost Ciano, Patricia Shanahan Yost (James Yost's widow)
Ma'lisa Kay Yost Mann June 20, 2005**

Page 10 - VINITA (Okla.) DAILY JOURNAL, Thursday, April 3, 2003

Deaths

Yost

James D. Yost, 71, a rancher and retired aeronautical engineer, died Tuesday, April 1, 2003, in Denison, Texas, of complications following heart bypass surgery.

He was born Feb. 20, 1932, in Cleora, the ninth of 13 children of Nora Jane Paul Yost and Raymond John Yost. He grew up in the Vinita area, and was an all-state football player for the Vinita Hornets. He also played for the Navy during four years of military service and served on an icebreaker, which took him to Cuba, Bermuda, Greenland, Newfoundland, and across the Arctic Circle.

James Yost

He developed an interest in helicopters and other aircraft while in the Navy, later enrolling in Oklahoma State University on a football scholarship. After earning his bachelor's degree, he worked as an aeronautical engineer for several aviation companies, including Boeing, LTV, Lockheed, AeroCommander, Rockwell International and General Dynamics. He was a structural specialist and worked on the design of the C-130 and V-22 Osprey aircraft. He ended his engineering career in 1998, retiring from Bell Helicopter Textron in Fort Worth.

Mr. Yost married Patricia Shanahan on Sept. 20, 1952. They celebrated their 50th anniversary last year with a trip to Cheyenne Wells, Colo., to visit old family friends.

Mr. Yost loved travel and because of his professional expertise was often invited to attend and present papers at conferences overseas. He and his wife traveled to England, Scotland, Australia, New Zealand and Mexico together. On his own, he went to Sweden, Russia and China with the People-to-People goodwill program.

Mr. Yost earned his private pilot's license and enjoyed flying for many years as well as writing poetry, reading and watching the History Channel and documentaries. He always looked for a bargain, and purchased his best cowdog, named 'Rat' by his grandchildren, for the price of a biscuit and gravy at Dairy Queen.

Mr. Yost was preceded in death by: his parents; a sister, Irene Rush; and five brothers, Cleve Yost, Harold Yost, Leon Yost, Clyde Yost and Perry Yost.

Survivors include: his wife, Patricia, of Fort Worth; sons, Edward Ray Yost and wife Francie of Dallas, and Lynn Marcus Yost and wife Janene of Garber, Okla.; daughter Ma'lisa Yost Mann and husband Travis of Fort Worth; grandchildren, Katy Anne Yost, James Edward Yost and Thomas Rivers Yost, all of Dallas; a brother, Maurice Yost, of Pryor; and five sisters, Kathryn Gardner of West Point, Texas, Janice Stadler of Tulsa, Roberta Haff of Sand Springs, Beatrice Prine of Bluejacket, and Mildred Andrews of Welch.

The funeral will be held at 2 p.m. Saturday at Luginbuel Funeral Home. Burial will be at Fairview Cemetery.

Visitation will be Friday at Luginbuel's from 6 to 7 p.m.

A memorial service will be held later this month in Fort Worth.

In lieu of flowers, the family requests that memorials be sent to the American Heart Association, Billy Graham Ministries, or the Heart-Menders volunteer group at Texoma Medical Center, P.O. Box 890, Denison, Texas, 75021-0890.

Arrangements are under the direction of Luginbuel Funeral Home.

James Dillard Yost Grave Marker, Fairview Cemetery, Vinita, Oklahoma

Edward Ray Yost born July 1956

Lynn Marcus Yost born March 29, 1961. Lynn married Janene Kay Sheffer.

Lynn Marcus Yost and Janene Kay Sheffer

Ma'Lisa Kay Yost

Ma'Lisa Kay Yost wedding picture

Kathryn Johanna Yost, born November 02, 1933 in Cleora, Oklahoma. Kathryn married James Gardner born September 30, 1929 in Joplin Missouri. Aunt Kathryn was a registered nurse and had a Doctorate Degree in Public Health. She worked 19 years for the City of Houston Health Department.

Kathryn Yost

Kathryn and Jim had the following children, Gregory Allen Gardner born September 16, 1957 in Springfield Missouri, Julie Ann Gardner born December 08, 1958, Kevin Charles "K.C." Gardner, born January 18, 1960 in Corpus Christi, Texas, Kari Joan Gardner born May 17, 1961, Michelle Marie Gardner born May 29, 1964.

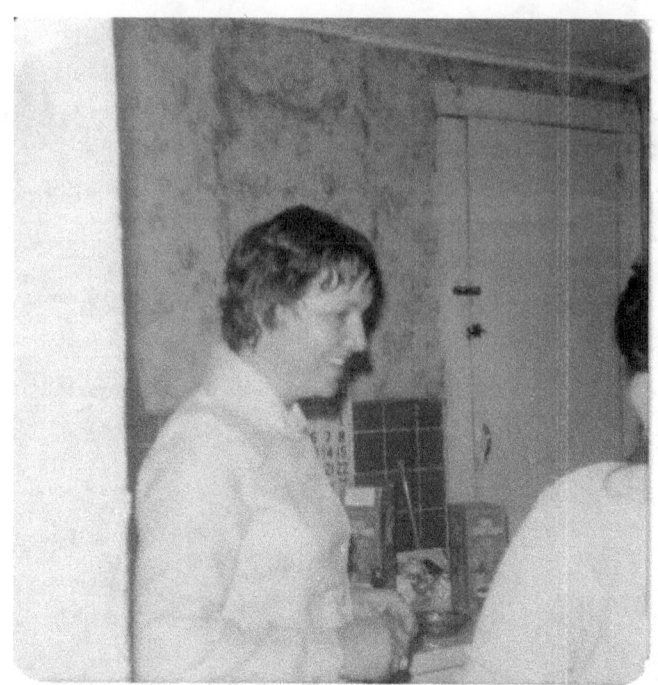

Kathryn Yost Gardner

Greg, Kathy, Kevin, Julie Gardner

Children of Kathryn Johanna Yost and James Gardner are:

Gregory Allen Gardner born September 16, 1957 in Springfield Missouri. He had his College Degree and works in sales.

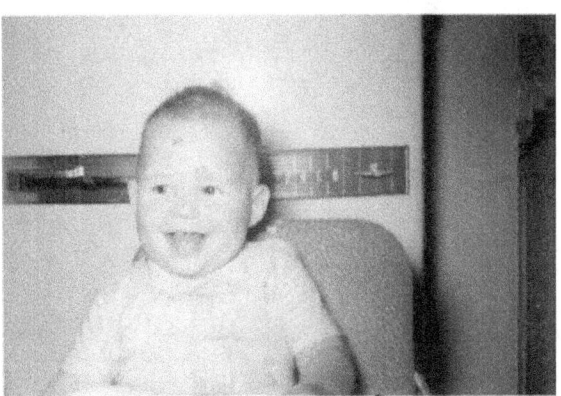

Gregory Allen Gardner as a baby

Greg Julie KC Kari Gardner

Gregory Allen Gardner

Julie Ann Gardner born December 08, 1958. She is a College Graduate from Southwest Texas State University. She teaches High School English.

Julie Ann Gardner

Kevin Charles "K.C." Gardner born January 18, 1960 in Corpus Christi, Texas. K.C. served from 1982 to 1986 as a Navy Medic.

Kevin "K.C." Charles Gardner

Kari Joan Gardner born May 17, 1961. Kari graduated from the University of Houston with a Psychology Degree. Kari then obtained a masters degree in business administration. She married James "Jimmy" Trackwell. Jimmy obtained his CPA and works also for a company that does corporate taxes. Scott is working for the same company as Jimmy and is working with the Republican Party in Harris County and Sara is a civil engineer for a company in Houston. Courtney is a sophomore at Texas Tech and is currently applying to schools of nursing for possible admission.

Back: Scott, Craig, Courtney
From: James and Kari Trackwell

Scott Trackwell and wife Sara Meischen Trackwell

Michelle Marie Gardner born May 29, 1964. Michelle graduated from the University of Houston with a degree in Journalism. She is a Technical Writer for Intermedic. In her spare time she writes Novels.

Michelle Marie Gardner

Clyde Lee Yost, born November 14, 1935, Vinita, Oklahoma; died October 12, 1989, Virden, Illinois. Clyde married Margaret Carol Henson born December 25, 1936 in Springfield Illinois.

School Days
1949 — '50

1952

Record: 0-10. **Coach:** Gene Wolf. **Assistant:** Lou Amaya. **Points for:** 36. **Points against:** 304.

Roster: Tommy Lechlider, Ray Dawson, John Campbell, Steve Griffith, Billy Wayne Smith, Ronnie Ragland, Wayne Rush, Chuck Campbell, Bill Fyffe, Jim Bradshaw, Sam Killion, Robert Phillips, Conaly Reed, John Kapp, Clyde Yost, Jerry Hamilton, Joe Hamilton, Gary Griffin, Gene Johnson, Dale Justus, Elliott Peterson, Tom Montgomery, Louis Harrison, Bob Trickey, Virgil Pryor, Doyle Inman, Harold Waldrop, Bob Patterson, Larry Smith, Dale Erickson, Lawrence Mann, Bobby Monroe, Kay Carver, Arnold Rhinehart.

Outlook: With only four lettermen returning and no starters, the Hornets were picked to finish last in District A-7 in their first season under coach Gene Wolf, who came to Vinita from Afton. It turned out to be all-too-accurate forecast. The Hornets were shut out in their final eight games as they completed only the third winless season in team history.

Vinita 24, Wagoner 33 (home) - The Journal reported that the brilliant running of Wagoner backs Bill Brown and Bob Whitekiller was too much for the "hustling Hornets." It was an offensive explosion for both teams, with Wagoner gaining 507 yards despite losing six fumbles and Vinita gaining 303 yards. Hornet quarterback Virgil Pryor threw three TD passes in the second half, 28- and 30-yarders to Harold Waldrop and a 28-yarder to Larry Smith. The Hornets also got a 60-yard interception return by Bobby Trickey.

Vinita 12, Picher 32 (home) - Picher dominated the inexperienced Hornets, with Earl Shuck scoring four TDs. Pryor and Smith scored what would turn out to be the Hornets' final points of the season.

Vinita 0, Nowata 19 (away) - The Hornets twice stopped Nowata inside Vinita's 5 to keep the game from turning into a rout.

Vinita 0, Broken Arrow 28 (away) - The Tigers got a safety on the opening kickoff when the ball went off a Hornet and Vinita couldn't run it out of the endzone - and the rest of the game went about the same way.

Vinita 0, Claremore 35 (homecoming) - The unbeaten Zebras struck for TDs of 54, 35, 30, and 42 yards. They rolled up 439 yards of offense, while the Hornets managed just 59.

Vinita 0, Miami 60 (away) - Even penalties couldn't slow down the Wardogs, who were flagged for 165 yards. The Hornets lost five fumbles and were without three key players. Miami showed no mercy, leaving its starters in most of the game.

Vinita 0, Pryor 18 (away) - The battle of winless teams determined who would get out of the District A-7 basement. The Tigers' Jerry Trotter threw TD passes of 57 and 66 yards.

1952 Vinita Hornets Football Roster and Season

Clyde Yost Football Vinita High School 1953

ARMED FORCES OF THE UNITED STATES — REPORT OF TRANSFER OR DISCHARGE (DD Form 214)

PERSONAL DATA
- 1. Last Name – First Name – Middle Name: YOST, Clyde Lee
- 2. Service Number: 572 47 49
- 3a. Grade or Rank: IC3
- 3b. Date of Rank: 16 NOV 56
- 4. Department, Component and Branch or Class: NAVY USN
- 5. Place of Birth: Vinita, Craig Co., Okla.
- 6. Date of Birth: 14 NOV 35
- 7a. Race: Caucasian
- 7b. Sex: Male
- 7c. Color Hair: Brown
- 7d. Color Eyes: Brown
- 7e. Height: 72"
- 7f. Weight: 175
- 8. U.S. Citizen: Yes
- 9. Marital Status: Single
- 10a. Highest Civilian Education Level Attained: High School –3
- 10b. Major Course or Field: General

TRANSFER OR DISCHARGE DATA
- 11a. Type of Transfer or Discharge: Release to Reserve
- 11b. Station or Installation at which Effected: USS TARAWA (CVS-40) at New York, New York
- 11c. Reason and Authority: Expiration of Term of Active Obligated Service –203– Article C-10317, BuPers Manual & BuPers Inst. 1910.16
- 11d. Effective Date: 21 JUN 58
- 12. Last Duty Assignment and Major Command: USS TARAWA (CVS-40) COMNAVAIRLANT
- 13a. Character of Service: HONORABLE
- 13b. Type of Certificate Issued: DD217N

SELECTIVE SERVICE DATA
- 14. Selective Service Number: 4 79 35 442
- 15. Selective Service Local Board Number, City, County and State: #79, Bakersfield, Kern Co., Calif.
- 16. Date Inducted: —
- 17. District or Area Command to Which Reservist Transferred: Commandant Naval District
- 18. Terminal Date of Reserve Obligation: 18 JUL 62
- 19a. Source of Entry: Enlisted (First Enlistment)
- 19b. Term of Service: 04
- 19c. Date of Entry: 19 JUL 54
- 20. Prior Regular Enlistments: NONE
- 21. Grade, Rate or Rank at Time of Entry into Current Active Service: SR
- 22. Place of Entry into Current Active Service: Columbus, Ohio
- 23. Home of Record at Time of Entry into Active Service: Rt#1, Piketon, Pike Co., Ohio

24. Statement of Service

	Years	Months	Days
(1) Net Service This Period	03	11	03
(2) Other Service	00	00	00
(3) Total (Line 1 + Line 2)	03	11	03
Total Active Service	03	11	03
Foreign and/or Sea Service	03	03	06

- 25a. Specialty Number and Title: (0000)

26. Decorations, Medals, Badges, Commendations, Citations and Campaign Ribbons Awarded or Authorized
Good Conduct Medal

27. Wounds Received as a Result of Action with Enemy Forces: NONE

29. Other Service Training Courses Successfully Completed
- GTC FOR PO
- NTC FOR IC3
- NTC FOR IC2

VA DATA
- 30a. Government Life Insurance in Force: No

32. Remarks
Entitled to $300.00 Mustering-Out-Pay. $300.00 Paid on DOV 313 Dtd 6/21/58.
"RECOMMENDED FOR REENLISTMENT"

F. J. CURRAN E7020

- 33. Permanent Address for Mailing Purposes After Transfer or Discharge: Rt#2, Vinita, Craig Co., Okla.
- 35a. Typed Name, Grade and Title of Authorizing Officer: W. R. THOMAS, SHIPCLK USN

DD Form 214

Clyde Yost served his County in the United States Navy. He served on the USS Tarawa pictured below. His decorations include the Good Conduct Medal.

Photo # NH 97596 USS Tarawa underway north of the Straits of Messina, Sicily, December 1952

USS Tarawa Aircraft Carrier

Clyde Yost in his Navy Uniform with his little sister Janice Clara Yost

In April of 2007 I came across an old shipmate of Clyde's, Marsolek, Rouch. I asked him to tell me what he remembered of Clyde. Here is our correspondence.

I knew Clyde well, was on the Tarawa for the same time as Yost was. I broke his arm during an arm wrestling match; don't think he ever forgave me for that. Very sorry to hear that he died so young.

Regards, Marsolek IC1 USS Tarawa 54-58

Hi Tim, no pictures to share but a little story.....he was on the Tarawa while we almost got blown up. Being in IC, I disconnected the gyro compass while refueling at sea, that means we were taking aircraft gasoline being pumped to us by a tanker. Anyway, thanks to me, we almost ran into the fueling guys next to us because the compass did not show that we were turning...long story...happy ending for Clyde and Rouch. Good luck with the book.

Clyde Lee Yost and Margaret Carol Henson wedding

Clyde and Margaret Yost

Clyde Yost and Wayne Rush

Clyde Lee Yost

Clyde Lee Yost, my Uncle. I remember when they lived in Tulsa. He was a Great Man, He was a Great Uncle. To this day, I MISS MY UNCLE CLYDE.

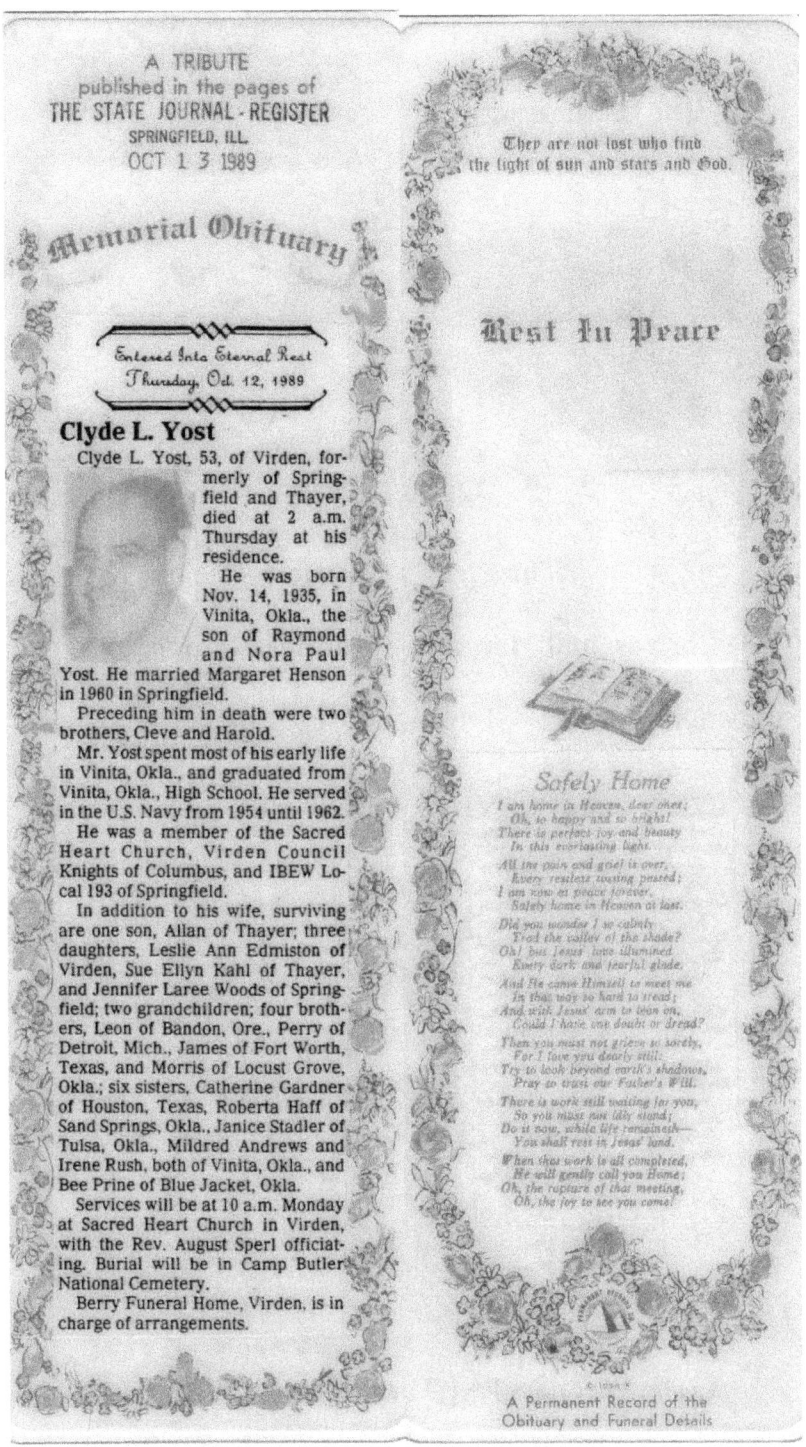

The Clyde Yost Family

Children of Clyde Lee Yost and Margaret Carol Henson are:

Leslie Ann Yost born November 28, 1960

Leslie Yost daughter Theresa   November 1993

Raymond Allan Yost born May 07, 1962

Raymond Allen Yost Baby Picture

Raymond Allen Yost age 6, 1968

Raymond Allan Yost on Boy Scout camp out in Oklahoma

Sue Ellyn Yost born October 13, 1963

Jennifer Laree Yost born January 21, 1969

Jennifer Yost

Margaret, Jennifer, Clyde Yost

Janice Clara Yost, born February 16, 1938, Cleora Oklahoma, died January 24, 2012 in Tulsa, Oklahoma. Janice was buried beside her father at the Yost plot Grand Army of the Republic Cemetery in Miami, Oklahoma. Janice married Edward Purdy Stadler born November 26, 1934 in Claremore Oklahoma. They were married on May 18, 1957 in Tulsa Oklahoma at the 1st United Methodist Church. Janice and Ed met while Ed was in St. Johns Hospital recovering from a car accident in which his father was killed. Janice was working in the hospital as a nurse at the time. The accident occurred in Joplin Missouri.

Longfellow Ms. Rae's Sixth Grade

Janice Clara Yost bottom right

Janice Clara Yost Stadler

Janice Clara James Dillard Clyde Lee Yost at Grand Lake

Janice Clara Yost 11th Grade

Janice Clara Yost Stadler sitting on Truck with Dog

Janice Clara Yost Stadler DAR Awards

Janice Clara Yost Stadler Silver Haired Legislatures Oklahoma 2006

Wedding of Edward Purdy Stadler and Janice Clara Yost

Cobb School 1934
By
Jan Yost Stadler

Cobb School District #53 began the first school day in 1909 and the last class closed in 1968. Early day Cobb School was provided with a water well of good drinking water.

Restroom or toilet facilities were out back. Coal sheds held fuel for the iron pot belly stove centered in the main classroom. Electricity was added in the late thirties. Before that, kerosene or gas lanterns provided light.

Prime time programs for Cobb School was the Pie Supper, Christmas with Cedar Tree, Valentine Day, Easter Egg Hunt, Graduation, and the Last Day of school picnic.

Cobb School contributed to the whole community spirit. The "Pledge of Allegiance" and "Star Spangled Banner", and Prayer was the way morning school began for Cobb kids.

Nativity Scene and Story was the Christmas Program with all the Cobb kids playing the parts of Angels, shepherds, wise men, Mary, Joseph and baby Jesus with animals all about. This peaceful scene was played out before friends, neighbors, relatives, parents and teacher.

The huge cedar tree topped the ceiling and was loaded with ornaments made and hung by the Cobb kids. And then Santa appeared beneath the tree with a bag of goodies and gifts. But, it was the big pie supper and the Cobb kids that usually paid for Christmas gifts and goodies. Extra earned money paid for school improvements.

In 1934, thirty-five students enrolled at Cobb School including Vogels, Wells, Hannas, Weedovers, Hoskins, Watts, Hendricks, to Yost and Hensons and more. The one room school house was full of Cobb kids!

Spelling bees were exciting trials and errors in word knowledge. Prizes were cherished whether in spelling or just attendance in the Bee.

Sports were the top! Whether, it was the broad or high jump. Running the race, or sprint. And basketball games, all drew good crowds.

Speech competition or Dress Revue, the Cobb kids were all in the trials of Craig County. Country Cobb kids knew they had to try hard to win the prize.

Community Spirit was high at Cobb school. World War, depression, or national recognition, Craig County and Cobb school came up first in many Academic and Athletic events!

Walking to and from school was such fun for the Cobb kids. All their friends were together. Just walking the dusty lanes in their bare feet was a pleasure and necessity. Shoes needed to last a whole year of Cobb school.

Hand-me-down shirts, pants, dresses, and coats from older brother and sisters were a real way of life. All coats were very special and treated with care for the time Santa Claus could replace a worn-out coat or deliver new knitted mittens was too good to be true!

Cobb School dog fights were good sport and big claims like, "my dog can beat your dog" was met with laughs and hee haws. Although, there was much depression and soup lines around Cobb school, it was special. Here at Cobb school, there was laughter, jokes, and brags about just who owned the best dog!

Late October, the teacher slumped at his desk in front of the Cobb School students. In a time of big trouble in Dust Bowl Oklahoma, all these school kids were dreaming of Christmas.

With the deep depression and WPA worker all over the place, Beatrice quietly read her book. School was very important to her.

She saw her older brother Leon stuffing a bothersome girl's braid in his inkwell. But she would not say anything; she too was busy getting her lessons.

It was Perry putting black dots on a nosey girl's arm that worried her. And, the Cobb big bully was picking on little Maurice, again.

Sisters Mildred and Roberta were reading their lessons. Although Mildred was grimacing at her scratchy Green Bloomer Basketball suit. Today, they were playing the Sacred Heart Team.

The teacher saw the fooling around and frowned at these boys. But, he could not help smiling at the studious girls.

Roberta sat on the front row. Her eyes were on a book; her mind on the Shetland pony grazing by the window. It was her turn to ride the pony at recess!

The teacher mused on how he could give Cobb Kids a real Christmas with goodies and gifts. The pie supper and turkey raffle might not make enough money to get those gifts and goodies.

Kids reminded the teacher that it was recess time. The big boys with Mildred and some other girls rushed for the Giant Stride. This mass of chains and bars made the Giant Stride a cause of many cuts, scrapes, and bruises. But still, the kids really loved the Giant Stride.

At ten o'clock, the "Up North Boys" made it to school with their jackets jammed with cookies. Following the boys was Asylum Baker. The Cobb kids had stole the Baker's cookies.

As the teacher settled the Cobb Cookie Caper, big boy bully jumped Maurice Yost at the far end of the school ground. Maurice won. When the teacher asked what happened? Leon, the older brother, pointed to "Big Bully" and said, "Ask him, he started it."

But the real excitement at Cobb began with the Pie Supper and Turkey Raffle in October. Girls baked pies beautiful brown while boys scraped up floors for pennies to buy their beau's pie boxes.

Yost's won the turkey raffle and the Cobb kids took turns carrying the bird home. Mom Yost was so happy that she made the bird a pet! That is until the gooney bird hid her nest.

Mildred followed that bird through blackberry bushes, creek and into the big meadow where she found the loaded egg nest! Mildred knew eggs were precious at Christmas time. And she was sure ready for Cobb Christmas tree...after scrambled eggs and ham, the Cobb kids headed for the school's big night.

At the very last minute, the teacher accepted large boxes of Christmas cookies and candy and apples from the Asylum Baker!

There were enough goodies and gifts to fill all the Cobb Christmas socks.

That is the way Cobb Kids had a very old fashion Christmas Tree! And, as Joy danced her tip-tap way across the school stage, Cobb Kids clapped and cheered throughout the Happy New Year!

Children of Edward Purdy Stadler and Janice Clara Yost are:

Back: Edward Purdy Stadler
Front: Anthony Edward Stadler, Alice Gertrude Stadler, Timothy Charles Stadler

Tim, Trudy, Tony, Janice Yost Stadler

Alice "Trudy" Gertrude Stadler born October 08, 1958 in Tulsa Oklahoma. Trudy married Timothy Espinoza born in Ocean Side San Diego, California. Trudy graduated from East Central High School, Tulsa, 1975. She attended Oklahoma State University and there after joined the United States Marine Corps.

Janice Clara "Yost Stadler, Alice Gertrude Stadler, Nora Jane "Paul" Yost

Trudy's life:

Trudy wrote:

Tim and I were married on April 8, 1983 in Jacksonsville, North Carolina by a one-eyed, one-armed justice of the peace. We got married on that date because we were planning the wedding in California for May 28th and Tim had orders to Okinawa. We were stationed at Camp Johnson, Camp Lejuene and both of our commands told us that they would not get us orders together unless we were already married thus the need to go to the local Justice of the peace. We had the "Official Christian" wedding in Whittier California. We have two marriage licenses but they are both packed away along with the children's birth certificates in Northern California and Mom and Dad's place. We shipped off to a year's tour of duty in Okinawa and that was where Barbara was born. I was with 3dFSSG; Supply Battalion and Tim were with Headquarters Battalion. We were at Camp Kinser and lived out in town. Actually the first five months of our marriage, we lived in the barracks. I was in the Women's barracks and Tim was in the men's of course. We got our first car in August and our first home in September. It's been a great life every since we met. Our Father has been good to us.

Alice Gertude "Trudy" Stadler – United States Marine Corps

Timothy John "T.J." Espinoza   Trudy Stadler Espinoza   Gregory Edward Espinoza   Tim Espinoza   Barbara MayLynn Espinoza

1993 Christmas in Phoenix Arizona

Trudy and Tim Espinoza December 2008

Children of Timothy Espinoza and Alice Gertrude Stadler are:

Barbara MayLynn Espinoza born February 04, 1984 in Okinawa Japan

Barbara MayLynn Espinoza December 2008

Barbara MayLynn Espinoza and mother Alice "Trudy" Gertrude Espinoza

Janice Yost Stadler Granddaughter Barbara MayLynn Espinoza Daughter Alice "Trudy" Gertrude Stadler Espinoza

Barbara writing about her 2009 work in China

I have hit the six month mark in my stay in China. The main work I do takes place with the interns in our four story house. These students are part of a three term program which is designed to equip them with knowledge of the Word as well as the ability to study on their own. My dad teaches several different Books and IBS while I teach Apologetics and History of the movement. We have fourteen interns who live with us in the house. Together we participate in different community outreaches which are pictured below. I hope this will give you an idea of what I am doing here in China.

And thus the Yost tradition continues. Barbara does missionary work because she was led into it by her mother and father, and God. The Yost's have always been messengers of the Word of God. My sister's end calling was to spread the word of the Lord. My direction was to follow the Yost's that chose Law Enforcement but always follow God's word.

Timothy John "T.J." Espinoza born August 22, 1985 in Kansas City Missouri

Tim J Espinoza and Grandmother Janice Clara Yost Stadler

Tim J Espinoza 6th grade 11 years of age

Gregory Edward Espinoza born December 09, 1986 in Walnut Creek California

Greg Espinoza 1 year of age

Gregory Edward Espinoza

Children of Edward Purdy Stadler and Janice Clara Yost continued are:

Anthony "Tony" Edward Stadler born March 20, 1960 in Tulsa Oklahoma. Tony graduated from East Central High School, Tulsa, in 1980. Anthony Edward Stadler died July 2, 2009 in Tulsa, Oklahoma. Tony was buried at the Fort Gibson National Military Cemetery. He joined the Oklahoma Air National Guard and served several stints over seas in Sicily, Italy. Tony married Patricia Sue Clark October 1, 1999, in Eureka Springs, Arkansas.

Anthony "Tony" Edward Stadler and Timothy Charles Stadler

Anthony Edward Stadler's service in the military, United States Air Force and Air National Guard, Tulsa Oklahoma.

In military tradition Tony was buried at the Fort Gibson National Cemetery is located in Muskogee County, one mile northeast of Fort Gibson, Okla. It is situated on land that was once part of the military reservation and is within the limits of the Cherokee Nation. Records indicate the area was probably called Ketona prior to 1824.

Anthony Edward Stadler – United States Air Force

Anthony Edward "Tony" and Patricia Sue Stadler

Anthony Edward Stadler
"Tony"

March 20, 1961 – July 2, 2009

God is love. Whoever lives in love
Lives in God and God in him."
1 John 4:16

Anthony Edward Stadler
Ft. Gibson Military Cemetery, Ft. Gibson Oklahoma

Timothy "Tim" Charles Stadler born August 30, 1963 in Tulsa Oklahoma. Tim graduated from East Central High School, Tulsa, in 1981. He attended Oklahoma State

University. He joined the United States Marine Corps Reserves and served from 1981 to 1987. In July 1984 he joined the Tulsa Police Department where he served 25 years attaining the rank of Sergeant. Tim married Kelly Deanne Rainey born December 29, 1966 in Martinsburg West Virginia.

Jean Bottomfield (Edward Purdy Stadler's sister), Timothy Charles Stadler, Alice "Trudy" Gertrude Stadler

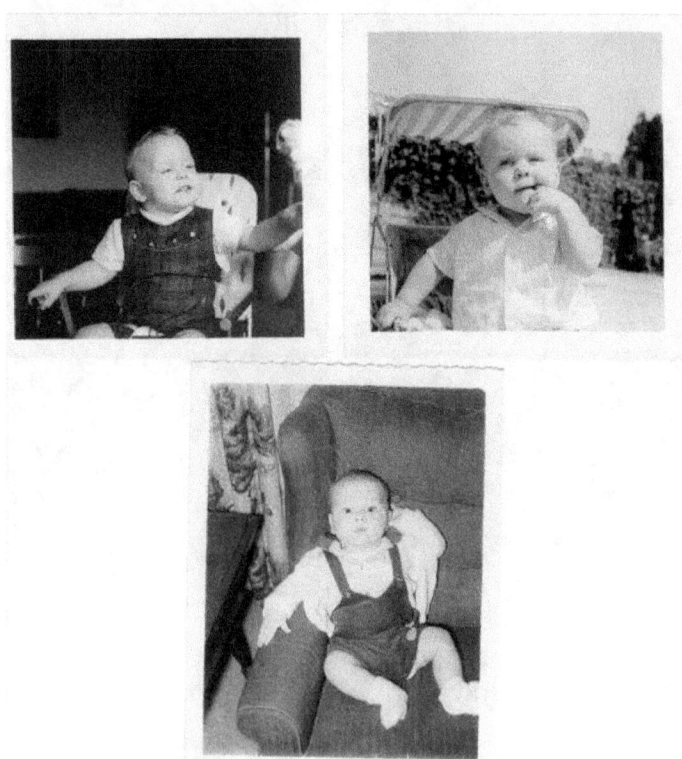

Timothy Charles Stadler

Timothy Charles Stadler's service in the military, United States Marine Corps

Timothy Charles Stadler – United States Marine Corps

**Tim C. Stadler on the left
United States Marine Corps Anti-tank T.O.W. Unit
29 Palms California Marine Corps Base**

**Sgt. Tim C. Stadler, Tulsa Police Department
Service from 1984 to 2009**

Timothy Charles Stadler and Kelly Deanne Rainey Marriage July 3, 1986

Tim Brian Kelly Steven Stadler in Hawaii 1995 after Tim made Sergeant on Tulsa Police Department

Janice Clara Yost Stadler, Lynn Yost, Tim Stadler

Children of Timothy Charles Stadler and Kelly Dianne Rainey are:

Steven Eric Stadler born April 4, 1992 in Tulsa Oklahoma

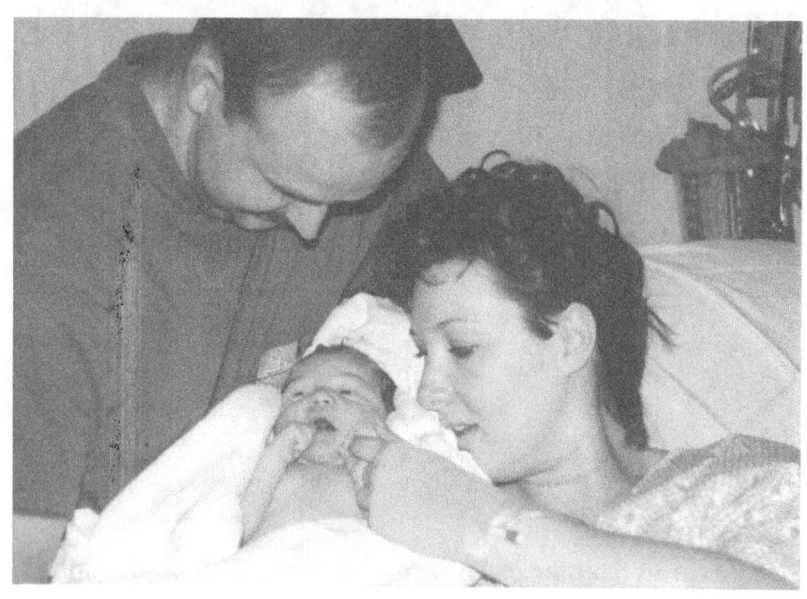

Steven Eric Stadler at St. Francis Hospital, Tulsa Oklahoma with mom and dad

Brian Timothy Stadler at born October 8, 1994, in Tulsa, Oklahoma.

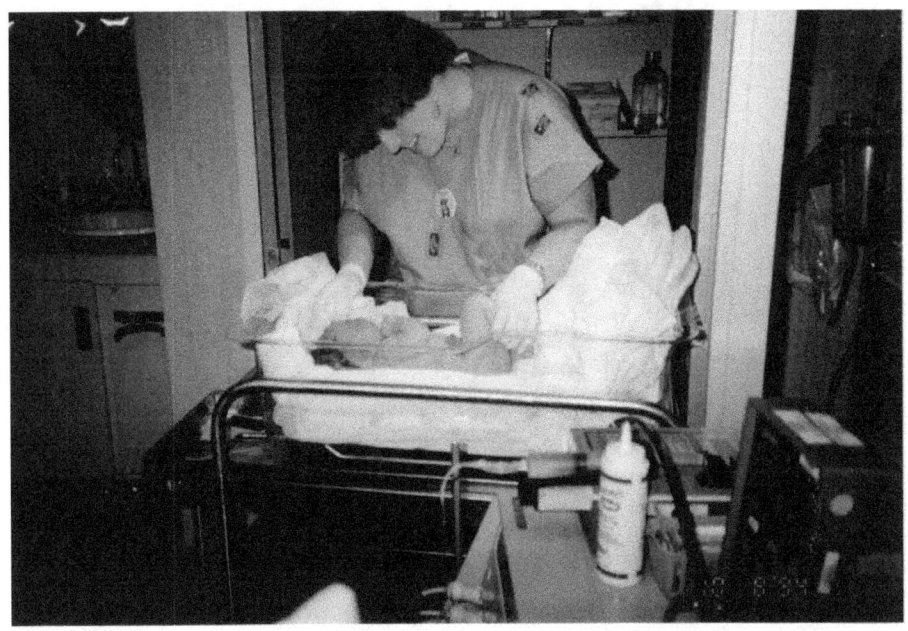

Brian Timothy Stadler born October 8, 1994 in Tulsa Oklahoma

Brian Timothy Stadler May 23, 2001 - Kindergarten

Steven Stadler

Tim, Brian, Steven Stadler

Tim, Steven, Uncle Ed Prine, and Brian

**Lynn and Janene Yost, Janice Yost Stadler, Larrie Kay Yost Ciano, Tim,
Tony Stadler
Brian and Steven Stadler – 2008**

Steven Eric Stadler 2009

Brian Timothy Stadler 2009

www.ingramcontent.com/pod-product-compliance
Lightning Source LLC
Chambersburg PA
CBHW081142290426
44108CB00018B/2416